D0090518

THE ONE PERCENT SOLUTION

THE ONE PERCENT SOLUTION

How Corporations Are Remaking
America One State at a Time

Gordon Lafer

ILR PRESS
AN IMPRINT OF
CORNELL UNIVERSITY PRESS
ITHACA AND LONDON

First published 2017 by Cornell University Press
Printed in the United States of America

Library of Congress Cataloging-in-Publication Data

Names: Lafer, Gordon, author.
Title: The one percent solution : how corporations are remaking America one state
    at a time / Gordon Lafer.
Description: Ithaca : ILR Press, an imprint of Cornell University Press, 2017. |
    Includes bibliographical references and index.
Identifiers: LCCN 2016046219 (print) | LCCN 2016046747 (ebook) |
    ISBN 9781501703065 (cloth : alk. paper) | ISBN 9781501708176 (ret) |
    ISBN 9781501708183 (pdf)
Subjects: LCSH: Corporate power—United States. | Corporations—Political
    aspects—United States. | Business and politics—United States. | Business and
    education—United States. | Labor policy—United States. | Labor unions—United
    States.
Classification: LCC JK467 .L34 2017 (print) | LCC JK467 (ebook) | DDC 330.973—dc23
LC record available at https://lccn.loc.gov/2016046219

Cornell University Press strives to use environmentally responsible suppliers and
materials to the fullest extent possible in the publishing of its books. Such materials
include vegetable-based, low-VOC inks and acid-free papers that are recycled, totally
chlorine-free, or partly composed of nonwood fibers. For further information, visit
our website at www.cornellpress.cornell.edu.

For Merav

And in memory of Talia Ranit Goldenberg ז׳ל

Contents

Acknowledgments

This book is the product of five years of research and writing, preparing legislative testimony, briefing lawmakers, and trying to make sense of the flood of corporate-backed legislation that hit the country starting in early 2011. As long-dormant policies like "right-to-work" were suddenly revived and radical new policies gained currency, economists in a wide range of think tanks and universities scrambled to assess the claims put forth by corporate lobbyists. Every chapter of this book relies, in part, on the expertise that others have brought to bear on these issues. I am particularly indebted to the work of Sylvia Allegretto, Dean Baker, Dale Belman, Donald Cohen, Lee Cokorinos, Laura Dresser, Peter Fisher, Matt Gardner, Amy Hanauer, Ken Jacobs, Jeff Keefe, Mark Levinson, David Madland, Peter Philips, Steven Pitts, and Joel Rogers.

Some of the most important work available to scholars of this period has been done by investigative journalists. Like everyone in this field, I owe a debt to Jane Mayer, Lee Fang, and the Center for Media and Democracy for their pathbreaking work in bringing to light the operations of ALEC and the Koch network.

I hit the academic jackpot when Adolph Reed agreed to be my PhD adviser many years ago, and he has remained a guiding light throughout this project. I have also been fortunate to benefit from the work and wisdom of academic colleagues in Oregon and beyond, including Eve Weinbaum, Janice Fine, Frances Fox Piven, Corey Robin, Michael Yates, John Logan, Stephanie Luce, Ruth Milkman, Gerry Berk, Margaret Hallock, Dan Tichenor, Joe Lowndes, Priscilla Yamin, Marty Wolfson, Glen Perusek, Rosemary Batt, and Tamara Kay.

Alex Molnar, Bob Peterson, and Barbara Miner were particularly generous with their time and helpful in enabling me to understand the extensive scholarship and long history of education reform.

Above all I am indebted to the Economic Policy Institute, whose support made the research for this book possible. I have relied on EPI's work for decades, but during the research and writing of this book, I benefited much more directly from conversation, criticism, and collaboration with the institute's staff. Through EPI, I published a series of reports on topics included in this book, and the book would not have been written without the institute's support for those projects. I'm particularly grateful to Larry Mishel, Ross Eisenbrey, Heidi Shierholz, Elise Gould, Josh Bivens, Doug Hall, Alyssa Davis, Liz Rose, Mary Gable, and Lora Engdahl for their contributions to that work.

I have relied my entire adult life on a set of friends whose comradeship has sustained me through this project as with all that came before, including Hillary Kunins, Michael Berkowitz, Joel Westheimer, Barbara Leckie, Eric Wittstein, Jane Wittstein, Eve Weinbaum, Delia Rickard, Reuven Kleinman, Jonathan Stein, Pete Hallward, Greg Grandin, Derek Spitz, Andy Spitz, Noah Efron, Alisa Klein, Photini Sinnis, George Bourozikas, Rachelle Abrahami, and Artie Farkas.

Two people—both friends and scholars—made particularly important contributions to this project. Janice Fine read early drafts of the manuscript and provided generous and invaluable guidance. Jonathan Stein reviewed the entire manuscript and provided critical editing. Both of them have made the book much better than it otherwise would have been.

The entire book would not have been possible without the work of a superb team of research assistants, including Jennifer Smith, Brian Ott, Camila Alvarez, Martha Camargo, Arthur Phillips, and Simon Davis-Cohen. Above all, I thank Debbie Levy, the most talented researcher I have ever worked with.

At the University of Oregon, I am grateful for the support of a remarkable set of colleagues at the Labor Education and Research Center, including Bob Bussel, Barbara Byrd, Lynn Feekin, Sherman Henry, Leola Jewett, Sarah Laslett, Deb Mailander, Helen Moss, Teri Mellor, Mary Page, Raahi Reddy, Leigh Roberts, Nikki Rudiger, Jennifer Smith, and Marcus Widenor.

At Cornell University Press, Fran Benson's encouragement and guidance were instrumental at every step of the process.

During the course of writing this book, my family suffered several deaths, including those of my father, my mother-in-law, and my niece Talia, to whose memory this book is dedicated. There is nothing good to say about those deaths, but they have heightened my appreciation and gratitude for my mother and sisters and for my extended family here in Oregon.

I am grateful above all for Rachel Kirtner. She is my first and most important intellectual partner, who not only has read and improved on every part of this book but has been my constant companion in making sense of American politics as they've unfolded over the past decade. Her own leadership in the battle for economic justice is a constant source of inspiration: every day that I have spent talking and typing, she has been on the front lines fighting to protect students' right to a decent education and teachers' right to respect on the job. Above all, I'm grateful that at the end of every battle, we get to come back to the home we have built together.

This book is dedicated to my daughter Merav, who lights up my life every day. At ten, she already has a big heart and a keen sense of justice and knows how to stand up for herself and her friends. I can't wait to see the rest of what she does.

THE ONE PERCENT SOLUTION

Introduction

A CORPORATE POLITICAL AGENDA FOR THE TWENTY-FIRST CENTURY

In January 2015, Tennessee's Republican governor, Bill Haslam, unveiled a proposal to expand his state's Medicaid program to provide health insurance to two hundred thousand low-income residents. At the time, Haslam was at the peak of his power: he had just won reelection with 70 percent of the vote and had been named to head the Republican Governors Association. Haslam insisted that his plan was "not Obamacare"; indeed, he had gained concessions from the Obama administration allowing him to write conservative requirements into the program. His Republican colleagues—who controlled both houses of the legislature—supported his proposal, based partly on polling showing widespread voter approval. And yet none of this was enough.

An advocacy group funded by the billionaire Koch brothers, Americans for Prosperity (AFP), sent field organizers into the state, ran weeks of advertising, and staged demonstrations insisting that any Medicaid expansion whatsoever amounted to "a vote for Obamacare." Republican caucus chair Glen Casada termed AFP's campaign "politics of intimidation." But it worked; the governor's bill was defeated. Declaring victory, an AFP spokesman warned that "other governors [should] look at Tennessee as an example."[1]

The Tennessee experience raises important questions about American politics and the forces that shape Americans' economic lives. How could an outside advocacy group overturn the will of elected officials and their constituents? What led a corporate-backed group to undermine its Republican allies? Why would the Koch brothers, whose primary interests are in the oil industry, care enough about

1

Medicaid to bankroll this type of campaign? And finally, if corporate lobbies have the power to do what they did in Tennessee, what else could they do? In what other ways might they be trying to rewrite the rules that govern our economy?

In answering these questions, this book aims to show how America's most powerful corporate lobbies are working to remake the country's economy in ways that will affect all Americans profoundly—and yet are largely invisible to most of us. Understanding these forces' legislative agenda is essential to comprehending America's current political and economic trajectory. Because this agenda has been enacted in state legislatures rather than the U.S. Congress, it is state-level initiatives that form the subject of this book.

The United States is an economy in decline, with an increasing number of Americans unable to support their families at a minimally decent standard of living. In just three years, the post-2008 Great Recession erased two decades of growth in average household income. But the larger concern is a longer-term trend: the dismantling of the New Deal policies that created a booming middle class for several decades in the mid-twentieth century. In the new economy, decline—gradual but relentless—has become the new normal for an increasing share of the country.

This is reflected in rising economic inequality over the past four decades. Income and wealth have become increasingly concentrated, while tens of millions of Americans find themselves unable to attain the standard of living reached by comparable workers a generation or two earlier. The economy has been slowly restructured along lines that steer the bulk of gains into the hands of investors and upper management. For the past fifty years, the share of national income that goes to employees—rather than investors—has been steadily shrinking; by 2010, labor's share had reached the lowest point ever recorded.[2]

The most common explanations for these trends focus on globalization or technology, both of which have indeed contributed to rising inequality. What this book demonstrates, however, is that growing inequality and increased hardship for American workers are also the result of an intentional policy agenda pursued by the largest and most powerful lobbies in the country—those representing the nation's biggest corporations. In fact, that agenda has broadened rapidly, and been pursued with ever shaper ambition, in just the past few years.

The Supreme Court's 2010 *Citizens United* decision ushered in a new legislative era, shaped by the impact of unlimited corporate spending on politics.[3] That fall's elections were the first conducted under the new rules, and they brought dramatic change. Eleven state governments switched from Democratic or divided control to unified Republican control of the governorship and both houses of the legislature. Since these lawmakers took office in early 2011, the United States has seen an unprecedented wave of legislation aimed at lowering labor standards and slashing public services.

The best-known effort came in Wisconsin, where the newly elected Republican governor, Scott Walker, pushed through legislation that effectively eliminated the right to collective bargaining for his state's 175,000 public employees.[4] Yet what happened in Wisconsin was part of a much broader pattern. In the five years following *Citizens United*, bills restricting public employees' collective-bargaining rights were adopted in fifteen states.[5] In the same period, twelve states passed laws restricting the minimum wage, four eased limits on child labor, and nineteen imposed new caps on unemployment benefits.[6]

Many of these bills have been the subject of intensive reporting and debate. For the most part, however, journalists and scholars have focused on one or two specific bills, treating them as the product of local politics or a response to local economic conditions. This book, by contrast, identifies and assesses the corporate economic policy agenda as a whole. It provides the first comprehensive analysis of the goals of America's most powerful lobbies as they have been pursued in the fifty state legislatures in the years following *Citizens United*. The book thus also provides a context for making sense of federal legislative debates under the Trump administration, as the corporate lobbies seek to advance the same agenda in the halls of Congress.

At the heart of this activism are the country's premier business lobbies—the Chamber of Commerce, the National Association of Manufacturers (NAM), and the National Federation of Independent Business (NFIB)—along with the AFP and industry-specific groups such as the National Grocers Association and National Restaurant Association. I have tracked all bills that were enacted with the support of one or more of these organizations, in all fifty states, across a wide range of labor, employment, and economic policy issues. This includes not only restrictions on public- and private-sector unions but also legislation regarding the minimum wage, child labor, wage theft, tipped employees, construction wages, occupational safety, job discrimination, employee misclassification, overtime pay, unemployment insurance, budgetary retrenchment, and privatization of public services. In all, this book provides a comprehensive account of corporate political action on thirty separate but interrelated aspects of policy governing labor, employment, and public services.

When we examine this full range of legislation, certain things come into focus that are impossible to see when analyzing any particular bill. For starters, there is the sheer similarity of the legislation—nearly identical bills introduced in cookie-cutter fashion in states across the country. This highlights the extent to which state politics has become nationalized, with different states' legislation originating from a common source in national advocacy organizations.

Moreover, the corporate vision itself becomes clearer when all its components are brought together. For example, when lobbyists argue in one state against linking the minimum wage to the rate of inflation, the debate may seem to revolve around the pros and cons of indexing. But when one sees the same lobbyists working elsewhere to abolish the minimum wage outright, to lower construction wages, to expand the use of teenage labor, or to force the unemployed to take lower-wage jobs, the local fight about indexing becomes just one feature of a larger tableau.

This book's purpose is to reproduce that tableau. By synthesizing corporate lobbying efforts across diverse issues and all fifty states, it is possible to show the sum, not just the parts, of a cohesive strategic agenda—and thus to see how America's most powerful forces are seeking to reshape its economy, society, and politics.

The Rise of the One Percent Economy

In absolute terms—and certainly relative to much of the world—plenty of America's 320 million people are doing well. However, what was once a widespread and realistic ambition—not to be rich, but to live a good life, free of economic anxiety, and to be able to provide one's children with opportunities for advancement—has become unachievable for most.

What has changed is the diversion of a growing share of income and wealth into the hands of those who already have the most. America's golden age—the three decades following the Second World War—was a time of broadly shared prosperity. The country still cycled through good times and bad, but when the economy grew, most people benefited. In the three decades from 1947 to 1979, every segment of the population gained ground, but income growth was actually faster for the poorest households than for the richest. Although the rich grew richer, the country grew slightly more equal. Since then, exactly the opposite pattern has taken hold. For more than three decades, income has been radically skewed toward the wealthiest, with 40 percent of U.S. households experiencing stagnant or falling earnings (figure I.1).[7]

Underlying the growth in inequality is a breakdown in the relationship between productivity and wages. When workers produce more output per hour—whether through greater effort, better organization, new technology, or higher education—corporate profits grow and real wage increases become possible. For the first three postwar decades, when productivity improved, everyone gained. Indeed, average wage increases tracked productivity almost exactly: from 1948 to 1973, productivity increased by 96.7 percent, and hourly compensation for production and nonsupervisory workers (80 percent of the workforce) rose by 91.3 percent. Over the past forty years, however, productivity has been divorced from wages, as shown in figure I.2. From 1973 to 2013, productivity increased by 74.4 percent, but employee compensation grew by only 9.2 percent.[8] We now inhabit

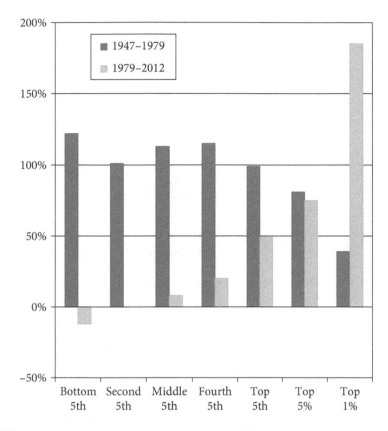

FIGURE I.1. Real family income growth, 1947–2012.

Source: Colin Gordon, "Growing Together, Growing Apart," *Working Economics Blog*, Economic Policy Institute, October 4, 2013, http://www.epi.org/blog/growing-growing.

an economy where, for many millions of Americans, it is possible to work both harder and smarter and still not get ahead.

With employees no longer able to secure their share of productivity gains, Americans' standard of living has slowly deteriorated. Particularly in the two-thirds of the labor market where jobs do not require a college degree, "family-wage" jobs have grown ever scarcer. Nine of the ten occupations projected to add the most jobs in the coming decade are low-wage, with an average salary exactly equal to the poverty threshold for a family of four.[9] The past four decades have been particularly hard on men. From 1979 to 2014, real wages declined for the bottom 60 percent of male workers—meaning that seventy million men in 2014 were working for less than their fathers or grandfathers

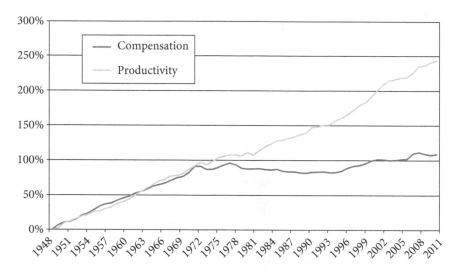

FIGURE I.2. Productivity and hourly compensation of production and non-supervisory workers, 1948–2013.

Source: Analysis of data from U.S. Bureau of Labor Statistics and Bureau of Economic Analysis. Data are for wages and benefits of production/nonsupervisory workers in the private sector and net productivity of the entire economy. Net productivity is the growth of output of goods and services less depreciation per hour. Reproduced from Larry Mishel, Elise Gould, and Josh Bivens, "Wage Stagnation in Nine Charts," Economic Policy Institute, January 6, 2015, http://www.epi.org/files/2013/wage-stagnation-in-nine-charts.pdf.

earned.[10] The total income of American families has done better, increasing slightly over this period.[11] But this was made possible only by a dramatic increase in the number of hours that parents—particularly women—spent at work. As a result, the average middle-class family now works 280 hours per year—the equivalent of seven additional weeks of full-time work—more than they would have in 1979.[12]

The erosion of the labor market has put an increasing number of people at risk of poverty. In any given year, one in seven Americans lives below the official poverty line. But the number living close to the edge is much greater: fully 40 percent of American adults will spend at least one year in poverty during their prime working years.[13] For the first time in fifty years, in 2013 a majority of students in American public schools lived in low-income families.[14] Most disturbing of all, for some of the population, life has been getting shorter. White people still live longer than blacks in America, but because they had greater access to living-wage jobs in midcentury, they also had the most to lose, not only in economic terms but also, it appears, in terms of physical well-being. From 1990 to 2008, life expectancy for white American women without a high school diploma fell by five years and that of men by three years. The exact cause of shrinking life spans is not known, but researchers speculate that it may reflect the growing number of adults without health insurance during this period.[15]

Even for middle-class families with growing incomes, these gains are often insufficient to offset dramatic price increases for the core components—education, health care, and retirement security—that traditionally define a middle-class lifestyle. The average cost of family health insurance, for example, increased by more than 80 percent over the past ten years.[16] Thus, even for those whose earnings have improved modestly, the goals of sending one's children to college and not having to worry about poverty in old age have become increasingly difficult to square.

The economic decline experienced by America's working- and middle-class families is only one side of the story. The other side is skyrocketing wealth for those at the top—even after the 2008 crisis. For the first time ever, in 2012 more than half of all income in America went to the richest 10 percent of the population, a degree of inequality surpassing even that of the late 1920s.[17] While the net worth of the bottom half of households evaporated in 2011–14, that of the richest 1 percent grew by an average of $5 million per family.[18] Indeed, one historian of oligarchy notes that the richest four hundred individuals in the United States now exercise a degree of influence over society comparable to that of the rulers of ancient Rome.[19]

Growing economic inequality has, in turn, created increased political inequality. While business has always enjoyed outsized political influence, its voice has grown even more dominant in recent years. Elections for public office have become dramatically more expensive, rendering politicians all the more dependent on those with the resources to fund their campaigns.[20] The increasing concentration of wealth has produced a growing class of megadonors prepared to spend enormous sums to influence outcomes. And finally, the progressive loosening of campaign finance regulations—culminating in the *Citizens United* decision—has enabled corporations and the wealthy to spend unlimited amounts on elections, and to do so secretly. The intersection of these three factors has dramatically increased the political influence of those at the top of the economy.

At the federal level, the domination of campaigns by a handful of megadonors has been so sudden—more than 60 percent of all personal campaign contributions in 2012 came from less than 0.5 percent of the population—as to render former superstars suddenly obsolete.[21] In his 2000 and 2004 elections, George W. Bush built what was heralded at the time as the most powerful fund-raising machine in American political history, constructed around teams of bundlers dubbed "Pioneers," who each committed to raise $100,000 from his or her circle of friends. This elite fund-raising corps was showered with appreciation, including twenty-four ambassadorships and two cabinet posts. By the time Bush's younger brother began his own presidential campaign, however, the Pioneers had become too small to matter. One businesswoman who had raised $1 million for the 2004 Bush reelection campaign complained in the spring of 2015 that none of the presidential candidates had contacted her. "They are only going to people who are multi-millionaires and billionaires. . . . [T]he people I talk to . . . just don't count anymore."[22]

So, too, political spending was heavily tilted toward corporations long before *Citizens United*; on average, from 2000 to 2010, business typically outspent labor unions by ten to one in federal elections.[23] In theory, *Citizens United* allowed for unlimited spending by both corporations and unions. In reality, however, the resource imbalance between these groups is so extreme as to render the comparison meaningless. The annual revenue of Fortune 500 companies alone is 350 times that of the labor movement.[24] By 2010, unions had already reached their limit of possible spending, with the AFL-CIO forced to cut its political advertising budget and limit itself to "incumbency protection," rather than competing for open seats.[25]

Corporate spending, by contrast, grew dramatically. Advocacy organizations spent just over $140 million on the presidential and congressional elections in 2008. Four years later, advocacy organizations spent $1 billion on federal elections, the great bulk of it from businesspeople and corporate organizations.[26] Both the U.S. Chamber of Commerce and the Club for Growth more than doubled their spending from 2008 to 2012. In addition, a slew of new corporate-funded advocacy organizations appeared during this period. Taken together, spending by the major corporate-funded groups was more than six times higher in 2012 than in 2008.[27]

In addition to the overall increase in spending, the 2010 elections marked the beginning of a fundamental shift in control of electoral politics. As recently as 2008, a team of political scientists at George Washington University, James Madison University and the University of California published *The Party Decides*, a sophisticated account of political parties' controlling role in the selection of presidential nominees.[28] But this analysis has quickly become outdated. In 2016, both the Donald Trump and Bernie Sanders campaigns challenged the role of party elites, with the GOP leadership rendered nearly powerless in the face of Trump's offensive. In down-ballot races, however, the power of party officials has been supplanted not by insurgent candidate campaigns but by private, corporate-funded advocacy groups. For many longtime donors, the ability to contribute secretly to private organizations offers strong incentive to eschew regular campaign contributions. Furthermore, such organizations can do things that parties and candidates cannot. By law, for example, candidates and parties are prohibited from "coordinating" with outside groups, which forces campaigns to operate in the dark regarding the timing, location, and volume of allied activity. In 2010, the GOP found a solution to this problem: the campaign's own advertising plans, previously treated as a closely guarded secret, would now be publicly distributed. Knowing the campaign's planned advertising buys, the outside groups could then freely coordinate a plan to supplement this effort without fear of duplication. The political director for Karl Rove's American Crossroads organization explained that "the [party] committees . . . make their [advertising] buys earlier. . . . That research then helps us on the outside have some sense of where to go."[29] The combination of campaign insiders and outside operatives thus effectively defeated the ban on coordination—but it is now the outside groups, not party officials, who are in position to drive the coordinated strategy.

Beyond advertising, the new private groups have taken on a growing array of responsibilities that had previously been the exclusive preserve of political parties. When Rove launched American Crossroads/Crossroads Grassroots Policy Strategies—just months after the *Citizens United* decision—its declared purpose included much of what had previously constituted core GOP activities. Rove's group would "research, test, educate, and galvanize citizens on high-resonance issues affecting the government and economy . . . shape citizen attitudes with hard-hitting issue advocacy, and . . . build a national grassroots network of center-right supporters who respond to our issue agenda and mobilize them to advocate effectively for policy change . . . [using] list exchanges [and] microtargeting techniques."[30] While Rove's operation worked on list building, messaging, and communications, others were focused closer to the ground. Americans for Prosperity and FreedomWorks built their own field organizations—identifying local community leaders, recruiting and training thousands of volunteers, and running sophisticated voter-contact campaigns. In 2010, the Kochs financed three separate multicity bus tours; the "Spending Revolt" tour alone sponsored nearly 140 rallies, each featuring a GOP candidate and local Tea Party leader.[31] In 2012, Mitt Romney's single largest phone-banking operation was run by AFP.[32] A Koch-funded organization now has joint control over the Republican Party's electronic voter file—the heart of any field campaign. And in preparation for the 2016 elections, the Kochs established their own candidate-recruitment firm, as well as dedicated field organizations aimed at Latino voters, veterans, and millennials.[33]

Thus, it is not simply that politicians have become more dependent on corporate campaign contributions. Rather, the very machinery of elections has increasingly shifted from party to private hands. It is this—the capacity to develop, poll-test, and air advertisements; to recruit, train, and deploy local volunteers; and to tap sophisticated databases to mobilize sympathetic activists on specific issues—that enabled Americans for Prosperity to beat a unified Republican party in Tennessee. The political scientists Theda Skocpol and Alexander Hertel-Fernandez write that "by the mid-1990s, the Chamber of Commerce"—along with NAM and NFIB—was simply "an adjunct of the GOP."[34] If this was true twenty years ago, it is no longer. Corporate efforts to exert greater control over policy decisions have been building for decades. But it has now become impossible to portray the party itself as the prime determinant of electoral and legislative outcomes: in a post–*Citizens United* world, the relationship between parties and "their" outside supporters has been turned on its head.

Corporate Lobbies and the Conservative Base

Since the emergence in 2009 of the Tea Party movement, commentators have routinely portrayed the conservative activist base as the sorcerer's apprentice: an untamed force that has increasingly taken control of the GOP. Following the 2012 elections, the *New York Times* described "Republican-on-Republican warfare," as major donors united to block Tea Party extremists from winning party nominations for federal office.[35] The *Washington Post* spoke of GOP leaders being "in thrall" to the Tea Party, unable to buck conservative activists on critical issues like immigration reform.[36] House Speaker John Boehner's forced resignation in the fall of 2015 was widely seen as a victory of the rank and file over entrenched interests. According to CNN, he and other GOP leaders, such as House Majority Leader Eric Cantor, "succumbed to the storm of conservatives angry at a party leadership they felt was betraying its base."[37] The election of Donald Trump was likewise cast as a revolt by the party's base against its donor class and establishment leaders. Indeed, Trump's candidacy was vigorously opposed by all the major corporate lobbies, and his election marked a setback for them. Nevertheless, they remain the single most influential force shaping Congressional legislation, and, at the state level, the base has never posed a significant obstacle to the corporate legislative agenda. On the contrary, corporate strategists played a decisive role in creating the Tea Party[38] and have been largely successful at channeling its activism in ways that serve their interests.

As the investigative reporter Lee Fang brilliantly recounts, the Tea Party arose from a long process of trial and error, led primarily by the Koch brothers and real estate mogul Howie Rich, who for at least a decade had sought to ignite a grassroots antitax movement branded with the symbols of the Boston Tea Party.[39] This is not to say that the Tea Party is simply a fabrication of corporate power brokers. Participants' convictions are genuine. But it was the corporate money that brought its members together; paid for their buses, stages, listservs, sound equipment, and meeting space; trained and equipped their activists; and broadcast their advertisements. The corporate-backed FreedomWorks even paid Glenn Beck $1 million to read "embedded content" in his newscasts.[40] Without such support, the Tea Party's constituency of disgruntled conservatives would have remained a marginal force in national debates.

From the beginning, the major corporate organizations that helped create the Tea Party—including Dick Armey's FreedomWorks and the Kochs' Americans for Prosperity—sought to harness populist impulses to corporate ends. In 2009, when Georgia legislators considered a dollar-per-pack increase in cigarette taxes to close the state's budget deficit, Philip Morris paid Grover Norquist's Americans for Tax Reform to organize a Tea Party protest in opposition. In 2010, Freedom-Works organized rallies to oppose the federal government's requirement that BP set aside $20 billion to cover damage from the Deepwater Horizon oil spill.[41] Neither issue appears to have been a high priority for many Tea Party activists, but once well-resourced corporate-funded operatives began organizing around them, it was possible to convince the rank and file that both were part of the broader agenda of antigovernment anger.

As Theda Skocpol and Vanessa Williamson note in their landmark study, many genuine and sophisticated activists within the Tea Party were openly skeptical about the agenda of big-money sponsors.[42] Yet for the most part, the initiatives that actually have become law—backed by Tea Party legislators—have been those that serve corporate interests.

From the start, the corporate strategists strove to marginalize Tea Party activists' passion for social conservatism. In 2010, activists worked with Freedomworks head Dick Armey to craft the "Contract from America," presented as a statement of core principles to which Tea Party-backed candidates were required to adhere. And yet every one of the core principles addressed economic concerns, with no mention whatsoever of same-sex marriage, abortion, immigration, or guns.[43] "Social issues may matter to particular individuals, but . . . the movement should be agnostic," argued the attorney who spearheaded this process. "This is a movement that rose [around] . . . economic conservative ideology. To include social issues would be beside the point."[44]

To be sure, the conservative base is not easily controlled, as was made manifest by the Trump campaign. Corporate backers have been forced to tolerate a degree of allegiance to social conservatism and to back off certain proposals in the face of economic populism in order to maintain the right-wing alliance. With the election of President Trump, corporate advocates were forced to relinquish—at least temporarily—their quests for a Pacific Rim free trade treaty and privatizing Social Security. On the whole, however, the legislative record indicates that it is the corporate lobbies, rather than the Tea Party's activists or Trump's grassroots army, that retain the most power to shape state laws. This is true even in Washington, D.C., where Republican senators and congresspeople remain overwhelmingly dependent on corporate largesse; it is truer still in the state legislatures.

Who Are the Corporate Lobbies?

No bill becomes a law without a coalition of political actors behind it. Most of the legislation described in this book—attacks on unions, the minimum wage, and public services—has been advanced by a combination of Republican politicians and conservative advocacy groups. For some parts of this coalition, the primary goal is partisan advantage. Republican strategists such as Grover Norquist have long identified public employees, labor unions, and trial lawyers as three "pillars" of the Democratic Party: unions and lawyers provide campaign funds, and public employees provide the army of volunteers who make phone calls and knock on doors in support of "big government" Democrats.[45] It is no accident that the hardest-fought antiunion campaigns have been waged in so-called battleground states. Cutting off union funds and campaign volunteers in toss-up states such as Michigan, Indiana, Pennsylvania, and Ohio may alter control of the federal government. As Wisconsin's Senate Majority Leader forecast in 2011, "If we win this battle [with public employee unions], and the money is not there under the auspices of the unions, certainly what you're going to find is President Obama is going to have a much . . . more difficult time getting elected and winning the state of Wisconsin."[46]

But behind the Republican operatives, the most important force driving this agenda forward is a network of extremely wealthy individuals and corporations—the key organizations whose agenda this book addresses. All three of the country's largest corporate lobbies—the Chamber of Commerce, National Association of Manufacturers, and the National Federation of Independent Business—are active in state political debates.[47] In recent years, the Koch-funded Americans for Prosperity has joined them as one of the largest and most active forces in state politics. In addition, several industry and employer associations—representing grocers, restaurateurs, and builders, for example—are active in state politics, either directly or through their membership in larger organizations. Above all, the corporate agenda is coordinated through the American Legislative Exchange Council (ALEC).

While these organizations primarily work in tandem with GOP leaders, they should not be understood simply as a component of the Republican Party or even the broader conservative movement. The corporate lobbies have not hesitated to pursue their own interests where these conflict with those of party leaders, even when doing so jeopardizes Republican legislative seats. Likewise, their agenda sometimes confounds party lines—most importantly on education reform, where traditional Democratic supporters in the technology and finance industries work in concert with Republican legislators and conservative corporate groups.

ALEC, the most important national organization advancing the corporate agenda at the state level, brings together two thousand member legislators (one-quarter of all state lawmakers, including many state senate presidents and House Speakers) and the country's largest corporations to formulate and promote business-friendly legislation (see table I.1).[48] According to the group's promotional materials, it convenes bill-drafting committees—often at posh resorts—in which "both corporations and legislators have a voice and a vote in shaping policy." Thus, state legislators with little time, staff, or expertise are able to introduce fully formed and professionally supported bills. The organization claims to introduce eight hundred to one thousand bills each year in the fifty state legislatures, with 20 percent becoming law.[49]

Ultimately, the "exchange" that ALEC facilitates is between corporate donors and state legislators. The corporations pay ALEC's expenses and contribute to legislators' campaigns; in return, legislators carry the corporate agenda into their statehouses.[50] Member corporations also fund the ALEC-affiliated State Policy Network, whose procorporate think tanks produce policy papers in support of model legislation.[51] In the first decade of this century, ALEC's leading corporate backers contributed more than $370 million to state elections, and over one hundred laws each year based on ALEC's model bills were enacted.[52] Through this network, corporate lobbyists have established a well-funded, highly effective operation that combines legislative drafting, electoral politics, lobbying, grassroots activism, and policy promotion.

Both the Chamber of Commerce and ALEC often pursue initiatives that directly benefit the bottom line of particular corporate members. The Chamber advertises itself as the representative of American business generally, but a much smaller circle of very large corporations accounts for most of its budget and dominates its advocacy agenda.[53] In 2009–10, for example, the health insurance industry provided more than $100 million to the Chamber to advocate against health care reform.[54] All three of the world's leading emitters of greenhouse gases—Chevron, ExxonMobil, and BP—are affiliated with the Chamber, which in turn lobbies against regulation of coal mining, fracking, and CO2 emissions.[55] The Chamber has also received significant funding from tobacco companies and is engaged in an international effort to defeat anti-smoking laws.[56]

At the state level, much of ALEC's activity is similarly targeted at issues of direct financial concern to member companies. In one outreach message to potential

TABLE I.1 American Legislative Exchange Council, select current and recent past members

Abbott Laboratories	Darden Restaurants	Microsoft
Aflac	Dell	Mobil
Air Transport Association	Dow Chemical	Monsanto
Alcoa	Dow Corning	Motorola
Allergan	Duke Energy	Nestle
Altria Group	Dupont	News Corporation
Amazon.com	eBay	NFIB
American Association of Health Plans	Eli Lilly	Northrop Grumman
American Bankers Association	Enron	Pacific Gas and Electric
American Cyanamid	Express Scripts	Peabody Energy
Amgen	Exxon Mobil	Pepsico
Amoco	Facebook	Pfizer
Amway	FedEx	PhRMA
Anheuser-Busch	Ford Motor Co.	Procter & Gamble
Archer Daniels Midland	GEICO	Prudential
Arthur Andersen	General Electric	Raytheon
AT&T	General Motors	Sallie Mae
Bank of America	Geo Group	Scantron
Baxter Healthcare	Georgia-Pacific	Schering-Plough
Bayer Corp	GlaxoSmithKline	Seagram & Sons
Bell Atlantic	Google	Shell Oil
Bell Helicopter	Hewlett-Packard	Sony
Blue Cross Blue Shield	Home Depot	Sprint Nextel
Boeing	Honeywell	State Farm
BP	IBM	T-Mobile
Cargill	Inland Steel	Taser International
Caterpillar	International Paper	Time Warner
Chevron	JC Penney	Union Pacific Corp
Chrysler	John Deere & Co.	United Airlines
CIBA-GEIGY	Johnson & Johnson	United Health Group
Coca-Cola	K12 Inc.	UPS
Columbia Healthcare	Koch Industries	U.S. Chamber of Commerce
Connections Academy	Kraft Food	Verizon
Consolidated Edison	Laidlaw	Visa
Coors Brewing Company	Lowe's	Wackenhut
Corrections Corp. of America	Mary Kay Cosmetics	Wal-Mart
Cox Communications	McDonald's	Walgreens
Crown Industries	McKinsey & Co.	Wells Fargo
CVS	Merck	Yahoo!

Source: Adapted from table found in alexexposed.com.

members, ALEC trumpeted its operation as "a good investment" for corporate partners, adding that "nowhere else can you get a return that high."[57] When energy companies invest, ALEC lobbies against state and local environmental controls. When drug companies invest, it supports prohibiting imports of lower-cost drugs from Canada. When Coca-Cola invests, it lobbies against taxes on sugary soft drinks. When private prison operators invest, it advocates for policies that would raise occupancy rates, such as the detention of undocumented immigrants and the restriction of parole eligibility.[58] And when payday loan companies invest, it opposes a law prohibiting such firms from charging more than 36 percent interest.[59]

But both ALEC and the Chamber also promote a broader economic and deregulatory agenda that is not directly tied to the profitability of specific donors. They support cuts to "entitlements" such as Social Security, unemployment insurance, and food stamps; push for more trade agreements on the NAFTA model; seek to shrink public funding for schools; oppose paid sick leave and workplace safety regulations; and work to undermine labor unions and restrict their participation in political debates.[60] Virtually all the initiatives described in this book—including forced privatization, "right-to-work" laws, and abolition of minimum-wage and prevailing-wage laws—reflect model statutes developed by ALEC and promoted through its network. Some of ALEC's most powerful corporate members are also active in the Chamber, and the Chamber itself is an active member of ALEC, as are Koch Industries, NFIB, and Americans for Prosperity. For all of them, this dimension of the legislative agenda is aimed not at immediately enhancing specific companies' revenues but at reshaping the underlying balance of power between workers and employers.

Much of the discussion of campaign finance in recent years has focused on the outsized influence of individual megadonors. Unsurprisingly, the vast majority of the ultrawealthy favor public policies that advance their economic interests. But individuals make poor subjects for political analysis. Some spend money on issues unrelated to their interests—such as Tom Steyer's focus on climate change and Michael Bloomberg's on gun control. Above all, an examination of individual donors leads to a focus on personal convictions, passion, or grudges, which are hard to predict—much less influence.

By contrast, the behavior of corporate lobbies is deliberate, rational, and impersonal. At some point, every major corporate contributor to ALEC convened its government affairs or executive committee to decide to invest resources in the organization. This decision cannot have been the product of personal or ideological conviction unrelated to the company's financial interests; given corporate officers' fiduciary responsibility to shareholders, we must assume that it was based on the belief that it served the company's long-term interests.

In some cases—Coca-Cola's opposition to restrictions on sugary soft drinks, for example—that interest is obvious. In others—restricting eligibility for unemployment insurance or cutting school funding—it is less clear. These cases force us to probe more deeply to understand corporate goals. Likewise, when the country's largest corporations unite to oppose Obamacare, promote guest workers, limit lawsuits for race or sex discrimination, and slash public pensions and library budgets, we must make sense of how these policies fit together into a coherent agenda deemed to serve their self-interest.

For these reasons, this book focuses not on individual donors but on legislation promoted by one or more of the major corporate lobbies. The exception is the Koch brothers' network of advocacy groups, represented at the state level primarily by Americans for Prosperity. While the Kochs may hold deep ideological convictions, they do not act on convictions that are inconsistent with their business interests.[61] Whereas other megadonors may focus on issues unrelated to their business—internet privacy, climate change, or marriage equality, for example— the Kochs focus solely on advancing an ambitious agenda to free corporate owners from the burdens of taxation, regulation, and organized workers. Indeed, the Kochs have a history of employing senior staff who hold positions simultaneously in Koch Industries and in related foundations and advocacy groups in order to ensure that their advocacy funding is aligned with their financial interests. So too, Koch Industries' lobbyists often work in close coordination with the staff of Koch-funded advocacy organizations.[62]

Furthermore, rather than simply contributing to candidates' campaigns, the Kochs have established a uniquely broad network of related organizations—candidate selection and funding vehicles, think tanks, data firms, communications strategists, and grassroots organizers—that together constitute an integrated and formidable political force.[63] In 2014, Americans for Prosperity alone spent $125 million and had five hundred full-time staffers to organize supporters in target states.[64] Finally, the Kochs not only spend their own money on an unparalleled scale; they also serve as organizers and directors of a network of corporate and private donors. In 2016, this network aimed to spend close to $1 billion, significantly more than either the Democratic or Republican parties raised in the 2012 election cycle.[65] The ability to raise such sums, election after election, fundamentally recalibrates the balance of power in electoral politics and must be taken into account in any effort to understand the corporate legislative agenda.

How Does Twenty-First-Century Corporate Politics Differ from What Came Before?

The effort to make sense of the corporate agenda also requires comprehending salient features of the historical context in which it is situated. The struggle between employers and employees—and the outsized influence of business lobbies—is hardly new. Big business lobbies fought against the eight-hour day,[66] Social Security,[67] and the minimum wage.[68] An impressive body of scholarship has shown that the country's big business lobbies have consistently sought to minimize or reverse the accomplishments of the New Deal, starting almost immediately after its inception.[69] Yet the shape of the struggle changes, and we cannot understand corporate lobbies' aims in the twenty-first century simply by examining their behavior in the 1940s or 1970s. Today's corporate agenda is framed, in particular, by rising inequality, a shrunken "economic left," and the impact of globalization and financialization on corporations' strategic plans.

Not all scholars agree that there is such a thing as an overarching "corporate agenda" in politics. The historian Benjamin Waterhouse and the sociologist Mark Mizruchi argue that twenty-first-century corporations are unable to forge a collective policy agenda beyond the particular interests of individual companies.[70] Indeed, there have been some notable disagreements among the corporate lobbies themselves. Americans for Prosperity, for example, opposes the Export-Import Bank and Common Core education standards, both of which the Chamber of Commerce supports. ALEC itself has seen scores of companies drop out in recent years—first in the wake of the Trayvon Martin murder in Florida, a state where ALEC promoted "Stand Your Ground" laws, and then in response to the organization's perceived opposition to climate change legislation. Similar defections have occurred at the Chamber of Commerce.[71]

Yet such disagreements also point to the centrality of the agenda described in this book. ALEC, the Chamber, NAM, NFIB, AFP, and the Club for Growth disagree on various policies, and they have sometimes endorsed opposing candidates in GOP primary elections. But they are fully united on attacking public- and private-sector unions, opposing minimum-wage laws and paid sick leave, restricting unemployment insurance, and supporting large tax cuts and permanent restrictions on public spending. The fact that organizations that may fight over other issues come together around this agenda attests to its centrality: no corporation has ever resigned from ALEC because it disagreed with the organization's position on the minimum wage or paid sick leave.

Many observers have noted that corporate politics have shifted to the right. From the 1960s through the 1990s, the Chamber of Commerce and NAM represented what the sociologist William Domhoff terms the "ultraconservative wing" of the corporate community, while the Business Roundtable comprised more moderately minded CEOs.[72] In the twenty-first century, the Business Roundtable has shrunk almost to insignificance—its 2009–10 lobbying budget was less than one-tenth that of the Chamber.[73] At the same time, the Chamber and NAM have been outflanked on the right by Americans for Prosperity, FreedomWorks, and the Club for Growth. This historical shift, too, must be understood not simply as a product of the Koch brothers' personal ideology or as an expression of a vaguely articulated zeitgeist but as a reflection of structural economic changes.

One of the current economy's distinguishing features is the degree of globalization to which it is subject, relative to earlier periods. It may never have been entirely true that "what's good for General Motors is what's good for the country," as the company's president apocryphally suggested in 1953.[74] But the alignment between corporate and national interests was certainly much closer when companies relied on Americans both to make and to buy their products. Currently, a majority of GM employees and nearly two-thirds of the cars it sells are overseas, with the number of cars sold in China alone surpassing the U.S. total.[75] General Motors remains highly engaged in American politics, as a member of NAM's board of directors, a partner of the U.S. Chamber of Commerce, and an active member of ALEC.[76] But this influence is now exercised on behalf of a company for which American workers' skills and household incomes matter less than ever before.

GM's situation is far from unique. For the first time, many of the country's most powerful political actors are companies whose headquarters may be located in the United States but whose profitability does not primarily depend on the fortunes of American society. Foreign sales now account for 48 percent of the S&P 500's total corporate revenues.[77] Among recent ALEC member corporations, Exxon Mobil, Caterpillar, Procter & Gamble, Pfizer, Dow Chemical, and IBM all earn more than 60 percent of their revenue outside the United States.[78] This marks a new departure in American politics: some of the most influential actors in the legislative process have political interests that are increasingly disconnected from the fate of the country's citizens.

These interests have also been influenced by the dramatic growth of the financial sector relative to the economy as a whole—a process that has fundamentally reshaped corporate priorities. A series of legal and regulatory changes, beginning in the 1970s, gradually allowed pension funds to invest in stocks and higher-risk financial instruments; permitted savings and loans, commercial banks, insurance companies, and investment banks to merge their operations; and created a large market of unregulated investment instruments. Together, these changes triggered a wave of hostile takeovers and leveraged buyouts and led nearly all publicly traded companies to reorient their operations in order to maximize short-term return to shareholders.[79] Whether in response to shareholder demands or to preempt takeover attempts by boosting earnings per share, the country's premier corporations began diverting resources away from investment in plant, labor, or technology in order to free up cash for stock buybacks, increasingly generous dividends, and other investor payouts.[80]

As the economist Eileen Appelbaum and industrial relations scholar Rosemary Batt describe it, corporations have moved from "the 'managerial business model'—in which returns are generated through productive activities overseen by professional managers—...[to] the financial business model in which companies are viewed as assets to be bought and sold for the sole purpose of maximizing profit."[81] In the late 1960s, nearly 60 percent of corporate profits were treated as retained earnings and reinvested in firms' operations.[82] Today that figure is under 10 percent.[83] But this shift toward a financial business model implies a shortening and narrowing in corporate leaders' political horizon as well. To the extent that executives are focused on near-term returns for investors, they are less likely to advocate for social investments like education or transportation—or to support increased taxes to make this spending possible—even if these investments aid their companies' long-term performance.

The combination of globalization and financialization has increasingly led American executives to disengage from the fate of the country's people. Every year since 2011, Harvard Business School has surveyed its alumni—among the elite of U.S. business leaders—on their views of the American economy.[84] The responses suggest, above all, a divorce between corporate and public interests. These executives are simultaneously optimistic about the ability of American firms to compete in global markets and strongly pessimistic about what awaits American workers. The first survey revealed a flood of jobs going overseas—that year, alumni reported fifty-six cases in which their companies moved at least one thousand American jobs overseas, overwhelmingly motivated by cheaper labor abroad. For remaining U.S. employees, a large plurality agreed that their firms would continue to outsource work and reduce wages and benefits in the coming years.[85]

The faculty members who conducted this survey are critical of such practices. "High productivity without jobs—and without jobs at good wages—doesn't build a future," insists the director of Harvard's Advanced Leadership Institute, Rosabeth Moss Kanter.[86] Yet corporate behavior is a product not of executives' moral failings but of the legal and market structures within which they operate. Understanding the political agenda of twenty-first-century corporate leaders means taking seriously that actions that enrich investors while undermining the American job market need not be accidental or mistaken; they may be entirely rational. If companies sacrificed near-term returns for shareholders in favor of long-term social investment, they would soon lose capital and disappear. No amount of moral suasion can change this.

Mizruchi argues that the changing terrain of corporate governance has caused the major business lobbies to become disorganized and dysfunctional.[87] Thus, while corporate leaders of sixty years ago "believed that their own privileges would be secure only to the extent that the society rested on a strong foundation," corporate America in our time has become "fragmented." Its leaders, "while increasingly able to realize their firm-specific interests through lobbying, [are] increasingly less able to provide collective solutions to issues of concern to the business community, and society, as a whole."

The work of the Chamber of Commerce, ALEC, and allied organizations, however, suggests that there is no shortage of coordinated political action, including on broad social issues not tied to the bottom line of particular firms. What has changed is not the ability to act in concert but the underlying interests that shape corporate behavior. Mizruchi complains, for example, that "the corporate community has been unable to provide a solution to the crisis" of education. But what is a crisis for American citizens may simply not be one for many of the most powerful U.S.-based corporations. Rather than assuming corporations have become unable to formulate a coordinated response to shared problems, it is more fruitful to assume that the leading corporate lobbies are acting rationally—and then explore how and why the legislative agenda we are witnessing is deemed to serve their interests. In seeking to make sense of observed corporate behavior, we need to ask the right question, based on a clear-eyed understanding of the present: How might this behavior make sense *under the current conditions* of long-term decline, globalization, financialization, a diminished left, and unrestricted money in politics?

Making Sense of Corporate Motives

The state legislative record provides a richly detailed account of the policy initiatives advanced by the big business lobbies. But how are we to make sense of these? If a state chamber of commerce advocates the expansion of charter schools, for example, is this because member companies are concerned they won't have enough skilled labor to hire and see this as a means of solving that problem? Perhaps it is because charters are cheaper, and companies see them as a way to cut taxes, or because they have financial interests of their own that will benefit from charter industry growth. Or is it simply because companies are concerned about American education and support this cause for the same reasons they donate to parks and hospitals?

More broadly, how should we understand what gives coherence to a state chamber of commerce's disparate legislative priorities, or comprehend the motives behind legislation that has no immediate payoff for a particular member's bottom line? How we answer these questions shapes how we anticipate these actors' initiatives—and thus how others might think about organizing on behalf of an alternative vision of the economy.

Both scholars and journalists have often characterized the most extreme corporate proposals—abolishing the Department of Education, refusing to raise the federal debt limit, privatizing Medicare—as primarily the product of ideology.

The most extensive academic research on the Tea Party and the Koch network has been carried out by a team of political scientists led by Harvard University's Theda Skocpol. Skocpol's book on the Tea Party, coauthored with Vanessa Williamson, distinguishes between "'mainstream' . . . pro-business GOP circles" and organizations such as FreedomWorks and Americans for Prosperity, which are deemed "advocacy groups . . . ideological organizations first and foremost."[88] But "ideological" can have multiple meanings. Clearly, the work of the business lobbies is not ideological in the sense of reflecting a moral commitment that is completely unrelated to financial self-interest, as might be true of a billionaire supporter of marriage equality or opponent of abortion. Too often, the word "ideological" functions as a marker for the point where analysis ends: observers can no longer trace policy positions to obvious material interests, so they label what appears to be irrational or frivolous behavior ideological, turning the term into a catchall category for whatever they can't explain otherwise.

While the convictions that people express may be sincerely held, they tend to be intertwined with our assessment of how they affect our interests. There are of course individuals who advocate passionately for policies that run counter to their financial interests. But they are the exception. And when it comes to deliberate decisions by large corporations, as opposed to personal choices by individual donors, it is even less likely that political advocacy strays far from financial interests.

This does not mean that when corporate executives participate in policy debates, they are merely acting as a mouthpiece for shareholders. The experience of running a company might very well nurture a heartfelt belief that society would be better off if one's firm didn't have to contend with labor negotiations or government regulation. At the same time, those whose personal views coincide with corporate goals are more likely to be promoted to higher levels of authority; to the extent that these views diverge from the company's interests, they are revised or discarded. This is why, in order to understand or anticipate corporate political activity, it is more fruitful to examine business models and profit strategies than to plumb the personal worldviews of senior managers.

This is true even of the Koch brothers, often considered emblematic of the most ideological of corporate interests. Even their behavior expresses no passionate convictions that run counter to or are disembodied from their financial interests.[89] Many observers note that the brothers come from a family of ideologues: their father, Fred Koch, was a founding member of the John Birch Society. Yet his sons, unlike him, do not advocate white supremacy or homophobia; on the contrary, they have launched an initiative to recruit Latino voters into the Republican camp, and David Koch has declared his support for marriage equality. Whatever the Kochs may think privately, their public behavior has almost nothing to do with the social conservatism trumpeted by their father.[90]

Skocpol and Hertel-Fernandez define the Kochs as "individuals who take philosophical and normative ideas as well as material interests very seriously," suggesting that they oppose public employee unions "in part because they see all unions as distortions of the 'free market.'"[91] But the Kochs' actual behavior is rife with contradictions of these supposedly bedrock principles. Koch Industries took maximum advantage of federal subsidies for their oil and pipeline businesses—even engaging lobbyists to ensure these perks stayed in the federal budget.[92] The brothers presumably oppose Iran's form of government but nevertheless employed a foreign subsidiary to sell oil equipment to the country in disregard of U.S. sanctions.[93] According to testimony from one longtime employee, Koch Industries followed a standard practice of cheating customers in measuring quantities of gas bought and sold; the company paid $20 million to settle one lawsuit charging it with stealing oil by this method from a Native American reservation.[94] None of this describes the behavior of a company that is, above all, committed to the principles of a fair and free market. Most telling is the brothers' position on the 2008 Troubled Assets Relief Program (TARP), the bank bailout that served as a prime focus for conservatives' antigovernment rage. Americans for Prosperity initially opposed TARP as an unwarranted government intrusion in the market. But in September 2008, the stock market suffered its largest ever single-day decline, threatening the Kochs' own financial interests. Within forty-eight hours, the Kochs had switched sides, and AFP signed on to a letter urging U.S. senators to support TARP's adoption.[95]

Skocpol and Hertel-Fernandez focus on disagreements between the Kochs and the Chamber of Commerce—which they characterize as a clash between "ideological groups" and "corporate priorities"—as evidence that the GOP's rightward move is driven by principled rather than economic motives.[96] Yet even these conflicts may have less to do with ideology than with competing corporate interests. The authors single out debate over reauthorization of the Export-Import Bank as the leading example of the Kochs' insistence on ideological purity at the expense of economic interests. Koch Industries was determined to block reauthorization, these scholars suggest, because it "views the . . . Bank as antithetical to the free market principles it pursues."[97] But a 2015 report from the Koch-funded Mercatus Center offers an alternative explanation. The bank subsidizes sales of large capital goods produced in the United States—but only if purchased by foreign buyers. Half of the largest sales subsidized by the bank are to foreign energy firms that compete with Koch Industries—which, as an American-based firm, is ineligible for the subsidies. "These foreign concerns," the report concludes, "are collecting subsidies from American taxpayers. . . . The federal government [thus] disadvantages U.S. energy firms."[98] What appears as an ideological difference, then, may simply reflect commercial conflicts of interest between competing business sectors.

The key to understanding the Koch brothers' public-policy priorities and choice of candidates to back is ultimately found on Koch Industries' bottom line. The family firm had good reasons to oppose the Obama administration and Democratic lawmakers. Proposals to reverse the Bush tax cuts for the wealthiest Americans or to regulate the derivatives industry would strike heavily at the Kochs' personal wealth and at a core component of their business.[99] Most important, efforts to regulate greenhouse-gas emissions pose a significant threat to the company's profits.[100] Indeed, as far back as 1993, the Kochs funded Citizens for a Sound Economy (a precursor to FreedomWorks and Americans for Prosperity) to organize rallies against a BTU tax proposed by the Clinton administration. Starting with the first Tea Party Tax Day, AFP worked hard to integrate energy interests into the movement, distributing talking points declaring that "the Obama budget proposes the largest excise tax in history, disguised as a cap-and-trade energy scheme."[101] In 2010, AFP organized a No Climate Tax initiative that called on GOP candidates to pledge never to support climate change legislation; five hundred candidates signed.[102] Legislative responses to climate change are a concern for the Kochs at the state level as well. After AFP helped elect right-wing Republicans to the New Hampshire legislature, for example, one of the victors' first acts in early 2011 was to pull the state out of the New England Regional Greenhouse Gas Initiative, effectively ending a regional effort to control carbon emissions.[103]

Furthermore, even these most extreme of corporate advocates are not so committed to ideological purity that they would rather lose elections than compromise. Again, Skocpol and Williamson's otherwise insightful book gets this point wrong, contrasting Karl Rove's "electability-over-principles" approach with the Kochs' supposed political intransigence.[104] In fact, the Kochs' behavior appears entirely pragmatic; it is simply aimed at different goals. AFP, for example, was so enthusiastic about Paul Ryan's 2010 budget proposal—including gradual privatization of Medicare—that votes on that proposal were used as a political litmus test to determine which members of Congress the organization would support.[105] However, when that proposal proved broadly unpopular (it was blamed for losing the GOP a congressional seat in a May 2011 special election in upstate New York), its backers concluded that Medicare privatization was a bridge too far.[106] None of the organizations that supported it in principle—including the Heritage Foundation and AFP—retained it as a central feature of the 2012 election cycle.[107] Similarly, though Mitt Romney was far from the Kochs' top choice for president, once he secured the GOP nomination, AFP endorsed and campaigned for him.[108]

Whereas getting Republicans elected may be more important to Rove than locking down what they will do once in office, the Kochs and the rest of the "extreme" corporate right are first and foremost committed to corporate-friendly policies. This has created political fissures and competitive primaries. But the Kochs are no less pragmatic than Rove; they simply make different calculations regarding how far right candidates can go and still win. And the electoral record suggests that the two sides may have equal claims to realism. In 2010, for example, half of the Tea Party candidates for the U.S. Senate won, and half lost.[109] The Kochs' aim remains to enact laws and change policies—not to speak truth to power while falling on their sword. What distinguishes the "mainstream" Chamber of Commerce from the "radical" Kochs is not pragmatism but ambition. The Kochs and the Chamber largely share the same economic vision—low taxes, little regulation, few public services, and no unions. What sets the Kochs apart is their belief that it is feasible to realize this vision with bold leaps rather than incremental steps.

A Revolution of Falling Expectations

Rapidly widening economic inequality and long-term uncertainty for a growing number of Americans have produced widespread anxiety, resentment, and rage, which in turn create a politics that is combustible and unpredictable. Anger is voiced in many directions: against banks and insurance companies, against public employees, and against immigrants. The result is a politics rife with contradictions. In 2012, for instance, 75 percent of Montanans voted to do away with corporate personhood, but 55 percent voted for Mitt Romney, who defended it; a majority of New Jersey voters support a significant increase in the state's minimum wage, but a majority also supported Governor Chris Christie, who vetoed the move.[110] Large majorities think both that big government is a problem and that the country's wealth should be much more evenly distributed.[111] At the height of the Occupy Wall Street protests, nearly 20 percent of Republicans—and one-tenth of Tea Partiers—supported the protest movement.[112] And multiple accounts described voters torn between backing Donald Trump or Bernie Sanders in 2016.[113]

For the corporate lobbies, growing inequality poses a central political challenge: how to advance policies that are bound to exacerbate inequality while avoiding a populist backlash. ALEC and Chamber of Commerce lobbyists are aware that much of their agenda is broadly unpopular. This problem was particularly acute in the heat of the 2008 financial crisis and during the onset of the Great Recession. Most of the country blamed the financial crisis on insufficient government regulation.[114] An overwhelming majority—including three-quarters of Republicans—believed the government should ban bonuses in banks that received federal assistance.[115] And nearly 60 percent of the public believed that the government should limit compensation for *all* corporate executives, regardless of whether they had received federal bailout money.[116] Throughout 2007–9, a significant majority of Americans not only supported a "public option" for health insurance but wanted a single-payer system.[117] Finally, for at least a decade, two-thirds of the country has consistently held that corporations pay too little in taxes; in 2015, a majority supported the proposition that "our government should . . . redistribute wealth by heavy taxes on the rich."[118]

The corporate lobbies, understandably nervous about managing these sentiments, have sought to channel economic resentment in benign directions by positioning themselves as the voice of the disenfranchised. The Koch brothers, for example, have created an organization called Generation Opportunity, dedicated to recruiting millennials to the conservative camp. Rather than insisting that the future is bright, the organization's message targets young people's anxiety and anger, which it tries to redirect toward government. "We are the only generation in American history to be left worse off than the last one," the organization's pitch proclaims. "We are paying more for college tuition, for a Social Security system and a Medicare system we won't get to use, $18 trillion in national debt and now an Obamacare system—all that steals from our generation's paychecks."[119] Similarly, a 2015 FreedomWorks fund-raising appeal sought to turn anticorporate sentiment to its advantage, arguing that "while the left is funded by a few rich corporations or billionaires, we're funded by tens of thousands of patriots like you."[120]

In an environment in which populist backlash poses a constant source of concern, it is not enough for the corporate lobbies to draft and advocate for legislation that is narrowly self-interested. They must also anticipate and preempt popular challenges to rising inequality. The record of corporate legislative action suggests that this concern has been embodied in four types of initiatives:

- Laws that constrain or abolish the institutional vehicles through which working people seek to challenge corporate power. This includes not only the elimination of labor unions but also restrictions on citizens' right to sue for corporate malfeasance and limits on government's authority to regulate corporate behavior.
- Privatization of public services, thereby removing focal points around which protest might coalesce. If no public authority is responsible for libraries or bus service, all grievances and demands become customer-service issues rather than policy problems that must be addressed by democratically accountable officials.
- Initiatives to restrict the public's right to vote on redistributive policies, making it illegal for city councils to vote on regulating fracking, policing wage theft, or raising the minimum wage.

- Finally, and most subtly, the corporate lobbies appear to be encouraging a broad cultural shift toward lowered expectations regarding what workers may demand from their employers and what citizens may demand from their government. In this sense, draconian cuts in public services may serve a long-term political strategy, quite apart from their short-term impact on taxes or government regulations: normalizing downward mobility.

Interests, Ideology, and Methodology

In theory, the easiest way to know what drives the corporate lobbies is to ask them. And, wherever possible, I have relied on executives' and lobbyists own explanations for legislative action.[121] However, because politics is so often characterized by dissimulation and misdirection, corporate advocates' policy pronouncements cannot simply be taken at face value. Occasional leaks make clear what we all assume: that spin outweighs candor in political speech. Thus, for instance, a leaked memo recorded pollster Frank Luntz counseling Republicans that to effectively oppose climate change legislation, they should pretend to minimize their economic interests while emphasizing their doubts regarding the underlying science and their commitment to environmental protection.[122] Such leaks are rare, however.

For the most part, we are forced to make the best sense we can of a record filled with contradiction. The Chamber of Commerce, for example, publicly lobbied Congress in support of the Obama administration's stimulus bill in 2009 but the next year campaigned against a Senate candidate on the grounds that he voted for it and thus drove up the national debt.[123] Similarly, in promoting so-called right-to-work laws, the corporate lobbies frequently argue that they are not anti-union but simply support workers' right to choose whether or not to pay dues to a union whose politics they may oppose. In states that already have such laws, however, the same organizations have sought to remove that choice by making it illegal for even those workers who support their union to contribute dues via payroll deductions.

Perhaps the most glaring contradiction is that of Blue Cross Blue Shield (BCBS). At the federal level, the company lobbied hard for the individual mandate to be included in the 2010 Affordable Care Act (Obamacare); at one point, BCBS even threatened to withdraw its support for the Senate legislation because the individual mandate clause was deemed too weak. Simultaneously, however, the company worked with ALEC to craft model legislation calling on states to reject Obamacare on the grounds that the mandate represented an unconstitutional infringement on individual freedom.[124]

In such cases, it is impossible to deduce an organization's political goals simply from its pronouncements. This book's methodology, therefore, is to examine what the corporate lobbies do rather than what they say. It compiles, compares, and contrasts myriad statutes—the totality of laws adopted across the fifty states with the backing of the major corporate lobbies—in order to perceive the unifying goals of an agenda whose components may sometimes appear, at first glance, disjointed or contradictory.

At times, the underlying rationale of corporate policy proposals may be opaque even to some of their supporters. For example, Mizruchi points to the corporate lobbies' virtually unanimous opposition to national health care as a seemingly irrational act. Many of the country's largest corporations bear substantial costs to provide health benefits to their employees; by socializing these costs, companies would be better able to compete with foreign firms whose employees are insured by the public rather than by their employers. Even executives may find the near-unanimous opposition to national health care mystifying. Mizruchi quotes one CEO—who supported a single-payer scheme—explaining his colleagues' motivation by noting that "one [view] inside the business community is a belief that anything the government touches is bad . . . and I share some of that. . . . So there are many who, regardless of any pragmatic benefit to their company, are opposed in any way to government-run programs, government mandate programs. It just doesn't sit well with their philosophy."[125] In fact, opposition to single-payer health insurance may not be simply an irrational manifestation of ideology. The conservative strategist William Kristol famously articulated a logical reason for it in a 1993 memo outlining the dangers of President Bill Clinton's health care proposal. Kristol argued that successful health care reform could fundamentally reshape the way people think about the economy, raising their sense of what the public (through its government) could demand of the private sector. A successful health care initiative, Kristol warned, would mark

> the establishment of the largest federal entitlement program since Social Security. Its success would signal the rebirth of centralized welfare-state policy at the very moment we have begun rolling back that idea in other areas. . . . But the long-term . . . effects will be even worse—much worse. It will relegitimize middle-class dependence for "security" on government spending and regulation. It will revive the reputation of the . . . Democrats, as the generous protector of middle-class interests. And it will . . . strike a punishing blow against Republican claims to defend the middle class by restraining government.[126]

Leaving aside Kristol's partisan concerns, his analysis points to a very concrete business interest. Once Americans discover that they can provide themselves with free health care simply by voting to tax the rich, they may decide to use the same means to provide affordable housing, mass transportation, or small classes for their children. This is the "entitlement culture" that corporate advocates dread— not Social Security, Medicare, or even welfare, but the fear that working- and middle-class families will get the notion to use democracy to create a more equal society. Averting that danger makes it worthwhile for corporations to keep paying the costs of employee health benefits.

While strategists such as Kristol may be able to articulate the threat posed by successful health care reform, not everyone who opposes it—including executives such as the one quoted by Mizruchi—can express their rationale for doing so. "It just doesn't sit well with their philosophy" is not a surprising response. Yet this does not prevent actors from recognizing their interests—even if only instinctively and inarticulately—and behaving in ways that advance them. That is why this book proceeds on the premise that corporations ultimately behave rationally. Rather than assuming that corporate lobbies act against their members' interests, it seeks to identify what those interests are and how they supply the rationale for policy positions—even in cases where businesspeople themselves may be unable to formulate more than an intuitive response.

The Limits of Social Conservatism

For the corporate lobbies, the problem of managing populist anger grew more pronounced as the social causes that long drove the conservative base became politically dysfunctional. In 2010, at the peak of the Tea Party's momentum, Democratic speechwriter Dylan Loewe published a book called *Permanently Blue*, arguing that "the Democratic Party is poised to secure a permanent majority." Loewe's thesis seemed preposterous at the time, and may appear counterintuitive following the election of President Trump, but the book's data are compelling. Latinos constitute the fastest-growing ethnic group in the country, and two-thirds were Obama supporters and Clinton voters. Young voters, eighteen to thirty years old, are significantly more liberal than their parents, and four million more of them join the voter rolls every year. Migration from rural areas to more cosmopolitan suburbs has turned places like Virginia and North Carolina into swing states. And women continue to prefer Democrats by wide margins. "Simply put," Loewe concludes, "everywhere America is growing, it is also liberalizing."[127]

The GOP's traditional strategies for mobilizing its electoral base make this a difficult problem to solve. For several decades, the energy of the GOP base has been largely devoted to campaigns against abortion rights, gay marriage, and undocumented immigrants. The corporate lobbies were largely agnostic on these issues. (David Koch, for example, has publicly stated his support not only for marriage equality but also for abortion rights.)[128] But they were willing to back the GOP's conservative social agenda in exchange for the base's support on taxes, regulation, and antiunionism. Indeed, if the economic agenda were the only reason to vote for candidates, many working-class conservatives might have supported the opponent or stayed home. Conservatives may generally oppose big government and support lower taxes, but many also support higher minimum wages, a right to health care, and higher taxes on the rich.

By 2012—if not 2008—the GOP concluded that the causes that had worked so effectively for so long had become a liability. Opposition to marriage equality, abortion rights, and immigrants was still an effective platform for winning party primaries, but it had become lethal on Election Day. Thus, Republican Governors Association chairman Bob McDonnell warned that "looking at how young voters and minority voters are voting," the GOP faces "an unsustainable trajectory."[129] Karen Hughes, a senior adviser to George W. Bush, likewise bemoaned the alienation of women voters, vowing that "if another Republican man says anything about rape other than it is a horrific, violent crime, I want to personally cut out his tongue."[130]

The politics of marriage equality has shifted particularly quickly. As recently as 2004, Republican strategists, hoping to drive up turnout among conservative voters, helped place antigay referenda on the ballot in eleven states.[131] But by 2010, public opinion had flipped: a majority of voters supported same-sex marriage, and opposition to it was literally a dying phenomenon—the younger voters are, the more likely they are to support marriage equality.[132] In December 2012, the GOP established a blue-ribbon commission headed by party operative Henry Barbour and former Bush spokesman Ari Fleischer, charged with charting a strategic course forward following the party's losses that fall. The resulting blueprint called for a softer stance on social issues, warning that "we need to campaign among Hispanic, black, Asian, and gay Americans and demonstrate we care about them, too."[133]

The GOP thus faced a thorny strategic dilemma in the years following 2010. It needed the social crusades to keep the base energized and avoid the threat of economic populism, but those same crusades risked condemning the party to the political margins. This dilemma stems from a central immutable fact: the GOP's working-class base is at odds with—or at least not sufficiently excited by—the corporate agenda of those who direct and finance the party.

For the Tea Party's corporate backers, the movement represented a bold experiment: an attempt to create a vital, activist base mobilized solely around the principles of small government and low taxes, without the antigay, antiabortion, or anti-immigrant baggage. The corporate organizations that played such a central role in the Tea Party's emergence—Freedomworks and Americans for Prosperity—consistently shunned social issues, despite their popularity among many activists.[134] Instead, corporate-funded groups sought to direct the deep discontent that might manifest itself in anti-immigrant rallies toward purely economic demands. At the height of the movement in 2009–10, the donors succeeded at steering the movement in their chosen direction. While a majority of self-identified Tea Party members opposed both gay marriage and a constitutional right to legal abortions, for example, neither principle was included in the group's manifesto (drafted in partnership with FreedomWorks), the "Contract From America."[135] The slogans on professionally printed signs at early Tea Party rallies included "You are not ENTITLED to What I have EARNED" and "Don't spread my wealth . . . spread my work ethic!" Indeed, even the Bible was invoked on behalf of economic, not social, principles. Numerous Tea Party events featured 2 Thessalonians 3:10: "If any will not work, neither let him eat."

Beyond its single-issue focus, the corporate creators of the Tea Party sought to construct a "movement" that would be entirely under their control. As early as 2006, FreedomWorks head Dick Armey voiced his frustration with the "bully" tactics of Christian conservatives who demanded that the GOP deliver for the religious right. As Lee Fang explains, "Armey had long sought a grassroots base centered on libertarian principles of small government. . . . [He] wanted his own movement independent of preachers and pastors." When the Democratic victory in 2008 forced sharp budget cuts among leading religious right organizations, Armey seized the opportunity to throw off the evangelical yoke.[136] The Tea Party was thus designed to liberate the corporate groups from dependence on base organizations. Instead of a partner, they sought to create a tool. It is instructive that none of the national organizations launched by the Tea Party have defined memberships, elected leadership, or any democratic process whatsoever for setting policies, endorsing candidates, or crafting strategies. While Americans for Prosperity is organized into state "chapters," for instance, none of the chapters have membership meetings, none of their leaders are elected, and none of the positions for which the chapters advocate are decided by popular vote.[137] Instead, the Kochs created AFP as a series of sophisticated contact lists, with voters and activists profiled to identify the issues they are most drawn by. When AFP engages on an issue, the central organization runs advertising campaigns, deploys lobbyists, develops talking points, and makes campaign contributions or issues primary threats, while AFP field organizers contact and activate their list of citizens likely to be supportive on this particular issue. The base thus has no independent voice or decision-making power. It is treated as a resource that can be turned on when needed, left slumbering at other times. This strategy appeared to be largely successful until Donald

Trump used his own mass communications to activate the base in a direction not of the Kochs' choosing.

The donors' dream of creating a conservative base energized solely by anti-governmentalism was uprooted by the Trump campaign. It's impossible to know how the election season might have played out had Trump not entered the race. Every other Republican candidate in 2016 was dependent on the donor class. Thus, from the "conservative" Cruz to the "moderate" Kasich, they all hewed to the corporate line on everything from taxes to trade to Social Security. In Trump's absence, it's possible that base voters would have contented themselves with Scott Walker or Marco Rubio, who voiced sympathetic anger at the "establishment" without actually challenging elite interests. Instead, the Trump campaign exposed and amplified the fault lines that divide the conservative movement's base from its donors.

Trump drove the Republican debate both much further to the right on race, gender, and immigration issues—exactly the passions the GOP elite were hoping to avoid—and, at least rhetorically, challenged the prerogatives of the rich in ways that were unthinkable for any other candidate. He disparaged hedge fund managers as "guys that shift paper around" while "paying nothing" in taxes.[138] He criticized military waste, opposed cuts to Social Security and Medicare, and attacked the NAFTA model of free trade, vowing to reject the Trans Pacific Partnership—a top priority of the corporate lobbies.[139] Trump declared that the health care system was broken because "the insurance companies . . . have total control of the politicians," and he labeled his rivals "puppets" who "traveled to California to beg for money . . . from the Koch Brothers."[140] Calling corporate special interests "bloodsuckers," he insisted that "whether it's the insurance companies, or the drug companies, or the oil companies . . . we're never going to get our country back if we keep doing this."[141] Trump's policies resonated with much of the party's base and simultaneously panicked donors and GOP strategists, who organized sizable war chests devoted to derailing his candidacy.[142] Even here, however, the anti-Trump effort was hampered by the popularity of the candidate's positions. Generally, Trump's Republican critics focused on his business failings, his treatment of women, and his history of prochoice pronouncements. It is telling, however, that none of his opponents' attack ads criticized Trump's position on trade, health care, or taxes; the corporate elite understood that their best interests lay in distracting the base from these issues—not arguing over them.

Numerous commentators have argued that Trump's victory demonstrates that big money can no longer buy elections; the Republican base, they say, finally triumphed over the elites and took over the party. And yet, in key respects, Trump is the exception that proves the rule. His candidacy combined several unique advantages: he is rich enough to be independent of corporate donors;

he is a well-known television personality with a broad and loyal following, and he started his campaign with widespread name recognition; and he is extraordinarily skilled at using both mass and social media to promote himself. Even candidates who matched some of these traits—such as Mike Huckabee, a well-known and pithy Fox News commentator whose politics combine social conservatism and economic populism—proved unable to mount a significant challenge to corporate-backed opponents.

But if it takes someone as exceptional as Trump to offer an alternative to the corporate version of Republican politics, his candidacy cannot be considered the beginning of a new trend. Indeed, his victory had no electoral coattails; he created no movement and he delivered no political support or protection to others. Virtually no members of Congress—much less state legislators—could afford to mimic Trump's platform, regardless of how well he polled. Even politicians who endorsed him, such as New Jersey governor Chris Christie, sought to benefit from Trump's popularity but stopped short of seconding his call to raise taxes on Wall Street or reject the TPP. Still dependent on corporate money themselves, they simply could not afford to follow Trump in policy terms.

Likewise, Trump's election does not imply that the Republicans' pre-2012 emphasis on social issues remains a viable political strategy for the future, or that the demographic shifts projected by Dylan Loewe turned out to be exaggerated. Notwithstanding Trump's victory, large and growing national majorities support marriage equality and legal abortions and oppose the mass deportation of undocumented immigrants. Furthermore, like Obama before her, Hillary Clinton found her strongest support among younger voters, while Trump's support peaked among those age 45 and older.[143] Over time, Trump's constituency will shrink, whereas the Democrats' is growing.

This is not to say that Republicans can no longer win national elections. But they can no longer win with a platform that simply combines corporate interests and social conservatism. A critical component of Trump's support came from working class voters attracted by his promises to tear up NAFTA, tax Wall Street, protect Social Security, and bring well-paying jobs back to depressed communities. The GOP coalition now has at its very heart the contradiction between the corporate agenda and popular pressure—previously channeled outside the Republican party—to combat rising inequality.

Unfortunately, it is likely that most of the economic agenda that emerges from the Republican leadership in the White House, Senate, and House of Representatives will mirror the corporate agenda outlined in this book. Candidate

Trump's senior economic adviser was Stephen Moore, an ALEC scholar and long-time author (together with Arthur Laffer) of ALEC's annual publication ranking state economic policies.[144] Moreover, Trump's legislative partners, House Speaker Paul Ryan and Senate Majority Leader Mitch McConnell, have long been outspoken advocates for the vision promoted by ALEC and allied corporate groups. Even before taking office, Trump indicated support for a dramatic tax cut favoring the rich and for a raft of anti-labor initiatives, including restrictions on the right to overtime pay for those earning between $23,000 and $47,000 per year.[145]

For the corporate lobbies, Republican control of the White House and both houses of Congress presents a rare opportunity to pursue at the national level the agenda they have carried out in the states, including "right to work" laws, school privatization, unemployment insurance reform, repeal of prevailing-wage rules, and drastic cuts to public services. However, if Republicans in Washington follow the same script they have in the states, working Americans will not experience restored prosperity but continued decline. To manage this tension, corporate and GOP strategists will need to devise, by a process of trial and error, some combination of economic provisions and appeals to identity politics. Whether this strategy will succeed—that is, whether enough working-class voters will continue to support the GOP while the party's corporate wing crafts an economy that generates ever-increasing inequality—is now the central question of conservative politics.

For Trump voters no less than for liberal critics, this book aims to make plain the designs behind the corporate activists with whom their elected officials are allied. To the extent that rank-and-file conservatives are following an agenda scripted by ALEC or the Kochs, it is critical that they know where that script truly leads, in all its constituent parts.

Why Study the States, and Why Now?

Most scholarly work on business influence in U.S. politics focuses on the federal government. To understand the current political agenda of the country's biggest corporate lobbies, however, it is much more fruitful to study the states, for several reasons.

For starters, there is simply a much larger volume of legislation to examine. In a given two-year Congress, only a handful of significant policies are enacted. By contrast, ALEC alone estimates that two hundred of its sponsored bills are adopted every year in state legislatures. The ability to examine, compare, and contrast such a large number of bills, across multiple policy areas, makes the states a much richer environment in which to understand the broad transformations that corporate lobbyists are seeking to bring about.

From 2011 through 2016, the federal government was largely deadlocked, impeding enactment even of routine funding bills, much less more controversial policies. Partly for this reason, battles over taxes, labor policy, environmental regulation, immigration, and a host of issues that might otherwise be decided at the federal level played out instead in state legislatures.

The turn to state legislatures also reflects these bodies' increased authority and effectiveness. For three decades, beginning in the Reagan administration, authority over social and economic policy and programs has steadily moved from the federal to state governments. Unemployment insurance, welfare, food stamps, transportation, education, and health care spending rely largely on federal spending, but the states establish the level and conditions of support that federal funding provides. In addition, state legislatures have become more professionalized, with lawmaking increasingly a full-time, paid position, including staff support.[146] Furthermore, in most state legislative bodies, there is no possibility of a minority filibuster; thus, majority control brings much greater lawmaking power in the states than in Congress.[147]

At the same time, many of the factors that strengthen corporate political influence are magnified in the states. First, far fewer people pay attention to state government, implying wider latitude for well-funded organized interests. The political scientist Martin Gilens notes that only when policy debates attract widespread public attention are politicians even modestly responsive to the bottom 90 percent of the population.[148] Yet if such attention is rare at the federal level, it is rarer still in the states. Fewer than one-quarter of adults are able to name their state senator or representative, and fewer than half even know which party is in the majority.[149] Thus, even the crudest form of political accountability—voting against the party in power when the economy turns bad—does not function at the state level.[150]

If most people can't name their legislators, how many are likely to have a well-formed opinion on whether prevailing wages should be required on public construction projects worth more than $25,000? How many can possibly be paying attention to debates about changing the definition of employee "misconduct"—changes that affect eligibility for unemployment insurance benefits? For all practical purposes, these debates take place in a vacuum. Apart from labor unions and a handful of progressive activists, the corporate agenda on such topics encounters little public resistance at the state level because hardly anyone knows about or understands the issues.

So, too, corporate lobbies' financial advantage is magnified in the states (figure I.3). *Citizens United* marked a sea change in state as well as federal politics. As of 2010, twenty-two states maintained bans on independent political expenditures by corporations or labor unions; all were overturned by the Supreme Court's decision. The first major analysis measuring the impact of the legal change on state legislatures found that the net result was to increase the odds of a Republican's being elected by four percentage points, primarily as a result of increased business contributions.[151]

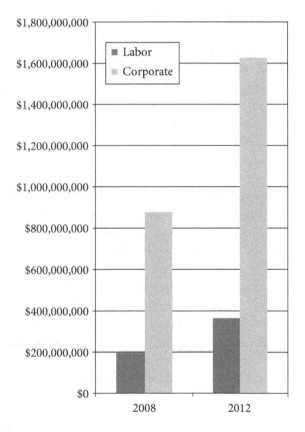

FIGURE I.3. Corporate and union spending on state election campaigns, 2008 and 2012.

Source: National Institute on Money in State Politics, "State Elections Overview," FollowTheMoney, https://www.followthemoney.org.

Because state legislative races are so much cheaper than federal elections, those contributions go much further. Consider North Carolina, where a network of organizations overseen by the supermarket executive and corporate activist Art Pope spent $2.3 million on 27 legislative races in 2010.[152] In 2008, the average North Carolina senate candidate spent a little under $140,000, and the average house candidate spent approximately $60,000.[153] Two years later, Pope's network contributed an average of $134,000 to each of the targeted senate races and $59,000 to each house race—effectively doubling the previous campaign budgets.[154] Republicans won nearly 80 percent of the seats Pope targeted in 2010, and the GOP gained complete control of the state legislature for the first time since Reconstruction.

The corporate lobbies' resource advantage is manifested not only in elections but also in growing influence over the legislative process once lawmakers are seated. Over the past four decades, state legislative districts have been repeatedly redrawn in order to maximize the number of safe seats for each party.[155] As a result, incumbent Republicans have no incentive to govern as centrists but have strong reason to fear a well-funded primary opponent. Such a system in turn maximizes the power of the corporate purse. In competitive districts, the threat to primary an incumbent Republican from the right would be self-defeating—even if effective it would likely result in failure in November. Under current conditions, however, corporate lobbies can wield the threat of a primary challenger to enforce discipline on sitting legislators. In 2013–15, for example, Americans for Prosperity carried out an aggressive, well-funded campaign to attack Republican governors and legislators who sought to take advantage of funds available under the Affordable Care Act to expand Medicaid for their low-income citizens. In Florida, Kansas, Tennessee, and Utah, AFP put scores of staff to work, spent millions of dollars on advertising, conducted intensive phone-bank and canvassing operations in key legislators' districts, and succeeded in reversing plans that initially enjoyed broad Republican support. In Kansas, a national AFP representative publicly warned senators that "we certainly plan to hold accountable every legislator who supports this misguided scheme." The bill's sponsor was shocked, noting that he had never before "heard a [witness] threaten members in testimony."[156]

Such threats—whether implied or explicit—reflect the effective nationalization of state politics in the years since *Citizens United*. The overwhelming majority of legislative initiatives described in this book were crafted with the aid of corporate lobbyists and promoted through ALEC in statehouses across the country. The bills supported by ALEC, the Chamber of Commerce, AFP, NAM, and the NFIB are strikingly similar across a diverse range of states. Goals that were impossible to achieve in Congress proved attainable in the states; thus the corporate lobbies set out to reshape the national economy and labor market by moving a common agenda in fifty venues at once.

For political scientists, the dominant role of national corporate lobbies requires fundamentally rethinking theories of state governance. Chief Justice Brandeis famously suggested that "it is one of the happy incidents of the federal system that a state may, if its citizens choose, serve as a laboratory; and try novel social and economic experiments without risk to the rest of the country."[157] The ideal of state governments as "laboratories of democracy" has infused scholarship ever since. An entire field of study focuses on "policy diffusion"—the question of how new ideas spread from one jurisdiction to another as each state's lawmakers seek to copy the most successful policies that emerge from another's trial and error.[158] But this process has been fundamentally reordered: increasingly, state legislators everywhere start with the same policy goals; the experiments are primarily aimed at determining the extent to which this common agenda is realizable at a given time.

The central themes of this book—increasing economic inequality leading to growing political inequality, the nationalization of state politics by business lobbies seeking to move a fifty-state agenda, and the corporate effort to pass laws that benefit the privileged while undermining workers' market power—are all the product of decades-long developments. None of them sprang up wholly formed in 2010. In particular, the exaggerated influence of moneyed interests has been the subject of public complaints for at least a century. Findings of the political scientists Larry Bartels and Martin Gilens that the views of most of the population are effectively ignored by elected officials are based on data from years before *Citizens United*. Some of the central organizations behind the current corporate agenda—including the American Legislative Exchange Council—were created in the 1970s. Even relatively newer political organizations such as Freedomworks and Americans for Prosperity were in place years before the Court's decision.

Yet a series of events came together in 2009–10 that led to a dramatic upsurge in corporate political activity and created an unprecedented rush of corporate-backed legislation. The economic inequality that had been building since the 1980s produced a new class of billionaire donors willing to spend previously unthinkable sums on politics.[159] In 1982, the top one-tenth of 1 percent of the population accounted for approximately 10 percent of all political donations. This figure grew gradually over the next three decades, reaching just under 30 percent in 2010 before shooting up to 40 percent in 2012.[160] The 2008 election—which put Democrats in control of both houses of Congress as well as the White House—struck fear into the hearts of energy executives worried about climate change legislation, financial titans anticipating new regulations, and insurance companies facing the demand for affordable health care. These fears in turn drove scores of new donors to join the Chamber of Commerce or the Koch network. As one Koch insider describes, "Obama's election sparked such vitriol on the right that [the Kochs] were almost overwhelmed by the number of wealthy donors eager to join them. Suddenly they were raising big money!"[161] The first Koch donor summit, in 2003, drew only 15 participants.[162] As late as June 2009, the event raised just $13 million. By 2015, however, the network had attracted 450 donors and solicited nearly $900 million for the upcoming election season.[163] Longtime campaign finance watchdog Fred Wertheimer commented that "we've had money in the past, but this is so far beyond what anyone has thought of it's mind-boggling."[164] The *Citizens United* decision was critical to the growth of the Kochs' and similar corporate advocacy groups—particularly those who wanted to shield donors' identity.[165]

Alongside this corporate political resurgence, 2010 was also marked by dramatic developments in both the fiscal condition and partisan control of state governments. Dramatic budget shortfalls in almost every state in 2009 and 2010—a follow-on effect of the worst financial crisis since the Great Depression—created a political climate in which ideas that in better times might have been deemed too radical (such as abolition of collective bargaining rights) became politically feasible. At the same time, just months after the *Citizens United* decision, GOP strategists turned to newly unrestricted corporate coffers in order to launch the Redistricting Majority Project—"RedMap" for short—aimed at winning control of legislatures that would be charged with redrawing congressional districts following the 2010 census. This effort—funded by the U.S. Chamber of Commerce, American Crossroads, and ALEC member corporations—helped turn eleven new states all red, with Republicans controlling the governor's office and both legislative chambers.[166] Critically, this sweep included a belt of states running across the upper Midwest, from Pennsylvania to Wisconsin. Newly empowered in traditionally prounion states that are battlegrounds in national politics, corporate lobbies and their legislative allies moved quickly to enact sweeping reforms intended to advance their economic agenda and cement their political advantage. The goals of the corporate lobbies were not new, but their ability to achieve legislative goals was greatly accelerated under the new conditions. Thus, for example, as of 2010 only four states had placed restrictions on project labor agreements in the construction industry; from 2011 to 2015 nineteen more states passed such laws.[167]

For all these reasons, studying state legislation in the years following *Citizens United* provides by far the most comprehensive picture of the corporate lobbies' policy priorities, and the best road map for the type of initiatives that should be expected from a federal government under unified Republican control. During this period, America's most powerful lobbies have been pursuing an ambitious agenda that aims to fundamentally reshape the balance of power between employers and employees. To the extent that they succeed, this agenda is likely to increase inequality, make life materially harder for millions of families, and undermine the political and legal rights of American workers.

This book is built on a fifty-state, thirty-issue, five-year database of corporate-backed legislation. But it is not a statistical analysis of when, where, and how corporate elites get their way. Ideally, the book would include statistical evidence identifying the conditions under which corporate-backed bills are most likely to be adopted. But this is simply not possible given data constraints. *Citizens United* has led to a proliferation of vehicles for untraceable political spending, making it frequently impossible to connect the dots between corporate actors and legislative outcomes. Furthermore, the corporate agenda is carried out through an integrated network that operates on multiple channels at once: funding ALEC to write bills, craft legislative talking points, and provide a meeting place for legislators and lobbyists to build relationships; supporting local think tanks in the ALEC-affiliated State Policy Network to produce white papers, legislative testimony, opinion columns, and media experts; contributing to candidate campaigns and party committees; making independent expenditures on behalf of lawmakers or issues; and deploying field organizers to key legislative districts. But there are no data with which to measure the relative impact of these disparate activities, and some of the most potent—such as threats to support a primary opponent—are understandably kept secret.

The statistical analyses of the political scientists Martin Gilens and Alexander Hertel-Fernandez both make important contributions to understanding corporate political power, but both also point to the limits of such research. Gilens uses public opinion surveys from the 1980s and 1990s to show that federal policymaking predominantly follows the views of the richest 10 percent of the country rather than the less affluent majority. This is an important finding, but it says nothing about how elite opinion translates into legislation. Furthermore, Gilens looks only at issues that were sufficiently salient that the broad public had an opinion about them; the majority of issues taken up by state legislators do not meet this threshold, and thus the data tell us nothing about them. Similarly, Hertel-Fernandez compared ALEC model bills with actual state legislation in order to examine which legislators were most likely to replicate ALEC's templates.[168] He concludes that ALEC language is most used by those who agree with ALEC's position but lack the staff capacity to research and write their own legislation. This is a useful finding but also a modest one. Although a small question (staff capacity) is answered, the bigger question goes unanswered—how do so many legislators come to support ALEC's agenda? And even to make his modest claim, Hertel-Fernandez was forced to go back to 1995 in order to find usable data. The limitations in these works are not the authors' fault; they are inherent in the data.

Thus this book does not present a statistical model calculating the factors that make corporate lobbies succeed or fail. Instead, its focus is on understanding the underlying rationale and ultimate goals of these most powerful organizations.

Each of the book's chapters addresses a particular policy area, but each is structured to follow a similar methodology. Each chapter begins with general background descriptions of the legislative initiatives that the corporate lobbies are proposing in this policy area. I then outline the arguments that corporate advocates voice on behalf of these initiatives, in their own words. Next I examine these claims against the economic evidence. In every case, the claims of corporate advocates are found to have no basis in scientific evidence. Furthermore, in many cases the claims made for one policy are contradicted by rationales voiced for another—suggesting that lobbyists themselves may not believe their own arguments. Finally, I step away from the arguments lobbyists offer the public and look at the most likely actual impacts of these proposals. I assume that staff members at the Chamber of Commerce and allied business lobbies are aware of what the economic evidence points to as a policy's most likely impact and that they promote these policies not because they believe their own spin but because they believe *those impacts* serve the long-term interest of their member corporations. This raises the most important question: Why would these companies view outcomes such as lower wages, a less effective education system, or a less healthy population as meeting their interests? This is the heart of the book's work: looking not at what the corporate lobbies say but at what they do, assuming that these actions embody rational corporate interests, and then weighing what those interests might be. Each chapter works to answer this question for a particular policy area. In this sense, each chapter also brings the overarching corporate agenda into more complete focus. The book begins by plumbing the corporate rationale for dismantling public employee unions and defunding public services; it then proceeds to make sense of the agenda for undermining private-sector unions and lowering labor standards for nonunion workers. I then examine why the corporate lobbies might see an interest in dismantling the public education system, and finally I seek to understand corporate antiunionism not as an ideological impulse but as a component of this broader agenda for rewriting the rules of our economy.

Chapter 1 examines attacks on the public sector—both eliminating employee union rights and slashing public services. Beginning in early 2011, these policies were promoted as a response to the record-level budget deficits that nearly all states then faced. But there is no economic evidence to suggest that overpaid unions caused the deficits or that abolishing union rights would resolve them. There is no statistical correlation between states' budget deficits and the presence or strength of public-sector unions. Indeed, in Texas, a state with one of the largest deficits, no public employees have a right to collective bargaining. More tellingly, the states that enacted the largest public-sector layoffs and compensation cuts do not correspond to those that faced the biggest deficits. Retrenchment was done not as an economic necessity but as a political choice.

Beyond the attacks on public-sector unions, the fiscal crisis of 2010–11 also served as an occasion to enact dramatic cutbacks in funding for schools, health care, libraries, transportation, and other essential public services. Once again, the location and size of cutbacks were not based on areas where budget deficits were most severe. Furthermore, rather than treating service reductions as a temporary tragedy, to be reversed when revenues were restored, legislators in many states sought to lock in retrenchment through new tax cuts for the wealthy or by enacting constitutional restrictions on future spending.

This chapter seeks to answer a central question that runs through much of recent state politics: Why would large, private corporations spend significant time, money, and energy fighting public employee unions in Wisconsin or Ohio? And why would corporate lobbies seek to shrink essential services—independent of any budgetary need—and then lock in a skeletal level of services as the new norm? For Republicans, the attack on public employee unions entailed clear partisan goals. This chapter seeks to look beyond those goals, to understand the strategic aims that underlie the corporate lobbies' efforts to dismantle the public sector.

In several states, those promoting restrictions on public-sector unions initially insisted that they had no objection to private-sector unions. Ultimately, however, the same lobbies that played a leading role in undermining public-sector unions have also championed right-to-work laws and restrictions on construction industry wage standards—both of which target private-sector unions. Beginning in 2011, right to work became a top priority of corporate lobbies nationwide; the chambers of commerce of Indiana, Wisconsin, and New Mexico, for example, all named right to work their top legislative priority.[169] Proposals were introduced in nearly twenty states and were adopted in Indiana and Michigan in 2012 and in Wisconsin in 2015. Chapter 2 examines the arguments around right to work and assesses corporate motives for deunionizing the private sector.

Those leading the attacks on public employee unions in Wisconsin and elsewhere have often portrayed themselves as champions of hard-working nonunion taxpayers in the private sector. But what are the corporate lobbies actually doing for such workers? Chapter 3 presents a comprehensive account of how corporate lobbies and their legislative allies have sought to undermine labor standards and workplace rights in the nonunion economy. The chapter details the record of corporate-backed state legislation governing the minimum wage, tip credit, child labor, overtime, employee misclassification, wage theft, sick leave, occupational licensing, workplace safety, meal breaks, workplace discrimination, and job-based safety-net programs such as unemployment insurance. On every one of these topics, corporate lobbies and their legislative allies have sought to reduce nonunion wages and benefits and abolish, weaken, or undermine the procedural rights of nonunion workers.

Chapter 4 explores how a combination of interests—partisan politics, anti-unionism, the drive to eliminate social entitlements, and unprecedented financial interests in privatization—come together around the issue of education reform. In the years since 2011, more legislation has been adopted on education than in any other area of labor relations or public services. Furthermore, while most of the issues discussed in the book play out along partisan lines, the attack on public education has brought corporate Democrats into an alliance with their conservative counterparts. The chapter examines corporate-backed legislation addressing a number of related issues: teacher evaluation and tenure, teacher collective bargaining, class size, certification requirements, charter schools, voucher programs, breadth of curriculum, school funding, teacher recruitment and training, high-stakes testing, and the promotion of digital and online instruction. It assesses both the pedagogical evidence underlying this legislative agenda and the political and economic interests driving it. In particular, the active engagement of many firms that have no direct financial interest in education reform highlights the broader corporate interest in reshaping public services and public expectations.

Chapter 5 returns to an examination of antiunionism, this time viewing it in the context of the broader corporate agenda. Fewer than 7 percent of private-sector employees in the United States now have unions, and many of the most active companies in ALEC face little near-term threat of unionization. What, then, explains the high priority corporate lobbies have placed on undermining unions? I believe the answer to this question lies primarily in understanding the ways in which unions affect the lives of *nonunion* workers—both in the labor market and through political action. The centrality of the legislative attack on unions makes sense only when understood as an attempt to remove a political obstacle to a broader economic agenda that is primarily aimed at the 88 percent of the labor force that is nonunion. This logic becomes clear in the examination of "paycheck protection" laws that restrict the ability of unions to spend money on political action. Antiunion legislation is thus shown to be a critical piece of a much broader agenda to reshape the U.S. labor market as a whole.

To be clear, the focus on corporate antiunionism is not meant to obscure the legitimate criticisms that may be made of labor unions. In recent decades, too many unions have become overly bureaucratic and disconnected from their members. Faced with existential threats, too many have become defensive and uncreative. Too many have become overly focused on legal contract obligations and lost sight of broader social visions. Some unions lack a robust democratic process or are not sufficiently inclusive of diverse membership. These are serious issues, and union members who complain about these dynamics do so with justice. Indeed, there is a long history of such debates and a substantial critical literature on these topics, produced primarily by dissidents and reformers within the labor movement itself.[170] But these are not the reasons for which unions are under attack by the corporate lobbies. On the contrary—if unions were stronger, more visionary, more democratic, more inclusive, with more members engaged in more creative tactics, this would make the labor movement a much more formidable opponent for ALEC and the Chamber of Commerce and would heighten, not lessen, the corporate drive to eliminate unions from the economy. These complaints are all reasonable subjects of discussion for scholars, commentators, and especially union members themselves. But they are not reasonable explanations for corporate political activity.

The book's conclusion addresses the political dynamics that position growing populist sentiment against increasing corporate dominance, particularly in state governments. For all their impressive victories, the corporate lobbies remain largely unpopular. Bipartisan majorities support raising the minimum wage, establishing a right to paid sick leave, limiting class size in public schools, and increasing taxes on the rich. Progressive legislation on these issues has been adopted in scores of cities and states. Nor is this limited to liberal jurisdictions. In Arizona, for instance, the same electorate that chose Trump over Clinton also voted to raise the state's minimum wage and establish a right to paid sick leave.[171] The depth of support for both the Trump and Sanders campaigns in 2016 underscores the widespread anger with growing inequality. Some may hope that working-class conservatives become so engrossed in identity politics that progressive economic demands are forgotten, but this is unlikely. For the elite—promoting legislation that will make life materially harder for the majority of Americans—further pursuit of their agenda inevitably requires a shrinking of democracy. In part, this shrinking has taken the form of restrictions on voting rights. In addition, the corporate lobbies have mounted an ambitious campaign to prohibit cities within a given state from raising employment standards in the local economy and are using their influence in state governments to promote a balanced budget amendment to the U.S. Constitution, in order to block future generations of voters from reversing corporate-friendly austerity policies.[172] The conclusion thus points to what is at stake not only in terms of economic gains but also in the very nature of our democracy.

We live in an unstable time, and the politics of economic policy remain full of contingency. Regardless of which side of the argument one prefers, this book hopes to enable readers to enter that debate with eyes wide open.

WISCONSIN AND BEYOND

Dismantling the Government

In January 2011, legislatures across the country took office under a unique set of circumstances. In many states, new majorities rode to power on the energy of the Tea Party "wave" election and the corporate-backed RedMap campaign. Critically, this new territory included a string of states, running across the upper Midwest from Pennsylvania to Wisconsin, that had traditionally constituted labor strongholds (figure 1.1). In addition, this was the first class of legislators elected under post–*Citizens United* campaign finance rules, and the sudden influence of unlimited money in politics was felt across the country. Finally, the 2011 legislative sessions opened in the midst of record budget deficits, creating an atmosphere of fiscal crisis that made it politically feasible to undertake more dramatic legislation than might otherwise have been possible. Any one of these things—a dramatic swing in partisan control, the suddenly heightened influence of moneyed interests, or a nationwide fiscal crisis—would be enough to change the shape of legislation. Having all three come together in one moment produced something akin to a political perfect storm.

For the corporate lobbies and their legislative allies, the 2010 elections created a strategic opportunity to restructure labor relations, political power, and the size of government. With no guarantee that their dominance would last into the future, the 2011–12 legislatures were animated by an urgency to lock in ambitious reforms while it was politically feasible. In this chapter, I will both describe the breadth of this legislative offensive and seek to make sense of its underlying motives and ultimate objectives.

FIGURE 1.1.   November 2010: Eleven states newly put GOP in control of the governor's office and both legislative chambers.

Starting in 2011, the country has witnessed an unprecedented wave of legislation aimed at eliminating public employee unions or, where they remain, strictly limiting their right to bargain. At the same time, the overall size of government has been significantly reduced in both union and nonunion jurisdictions. The number of public jobs eliminated in 2011 was the highest ever recorded, and budgets for essential public services were dramatically scaled back in dozens of states. All of this—deunionization, sharp cuts in public employee compensation, and the dramatic rollback of public services—was forcefully championed by the corporate lobbies, who made shrinking the public sector a top policy priority in state after state.

The rationale most commonly offered for this retrenchment was that budget deficits were the result of overspending bureaucrats and overly generous union contracts. Both public employee compensation and public service budgets, advocates proclaimed, needed to be radically restructured in order to restore the country to fiscal health.

Upon close examination, however, this argument simply does not fit the economic facts. There is no statistical correlation between the size of budget deficits and the presence or strength of labor unions. The deficits were not caused by overspending but, overwhelmingly, by the recession itself. Furthermore, the harshest antiunion laws, the most draconian cuts in pension benefits, and the steepest layoffs of public employees did not occur in the states facing the largest deficits. Examining the fiscal and legislative landscape of the country as a whole, it is clear that these measures were enacted not where they were economically necessary but where they were politically possible.

Furthermore, cuts in public services were not made reluctantly—as a temporary calamity to be mitigated wherever possible—but were embraced by legislators as an affirmative policy choice. Many of the states that enforced the most draconian cuts simultaneously adopted new tax breaks for corporations and the wealthy. So too, when legislators were faced with the opportunity to restore services after the economy improved and tax revenues rebounded in 2013–14, many chose instead to enact yet further rounds of corporate tax cuts. Finally, corporate advocates and their legislative allies have sought to lock in cuts made in the depths of recession by adopting constitutional amendments that would make it difficult or impossible to ever restore public services.

All of this challenges us to understand the following: If wage cuts and union restrictions were not a response to fiscal emergency, what was their purpose? And why would lobbyists and lawmakers choose to lock in cuts to school, transportation, and health funding even after the recession passed and services could be restored? This chapter aims to answer these questions.

A "Showdown" with Public Employee Unions

In early 2011, business-backed governors across the country proclaimed that government unions were to blame for the budget deficits then afflicting nearly every state. Corporate advocates argued that taxpayers were being held hostage by a cycle of corruption in which public employee unions helped elect officials who then negotiated unaffordable sweetheart contracts, from which unions siphoned off dues money to feed back into the campaign coffers of favored politicians.

The ALEC scholar Bob Williams took pains to distinguish this critique of public-sector unions from a professed respect for their private-sector counterparts. Industrial unions are compelled to honor their employer's bottom line, he explained; by contrast, public employees' only bottom line is whatever they can squeeze out of taxpayers. Furthermore, public officials are afraid to offend the union for fear of risking reelection. In this way, Williams reasoned, "collective bargaining [makes] government employees . . . 'super citizens' . . . [while] the rest of the taxpayers are relegated to second-class status."[1] It's no wonder that Williams provides no data to substantiate his theory; in reality, many unions negotiate with officials they campaigned against or help elect governors only to see them cut pension benefits after winning office. But the images Williams conjures up—lazy government employees living high off the hard-earned tax dollars of private-sector workers—were ubiquitous in 2011–12 and no doubt compelling to many.

This argument came at a propitious moment for corporate interests. In the aftermath of the Wall Street mortgage scandal and the ensuing economic crash, public sentiment turned sharply against those perceived as responsible for both the recession and the longer-term trends of growing inequality. In 2008, three-quarters of Americans believed that president George W. Bush's economic policies had made the country worse off; the following January, Bush left office as the least popular president in recorded history.[2] When gas prices rose sharply that summer, the public pointed to the oil industry, the Bush administration, and commodities traders as those responsible for the hardship.[3] A majority of the country blamed insufficient government regulation for contributing to the financial crisis, and an overwhelming number—including three-quarters of Republicans—wanted to ban executive bonuses at banks that received federal assistance.[4] In the fall of 2011, this brewing discontent was ignited by the Occupy Wall Street movement, which gave voice to widespread resentment against the finance industry and the country's economic elite.

Against this backdrop, corporate lobbies and their allied lawmakers promoted a new definition of inequality, tapping into the same anxiety and resentments that fueled support for Occupy but channeling that anger in a direction that was benign for the donor class. Rather than naming investment banks or corporate executives as the villains, this narrative pointed at public employees.[5] Thus, New Jersey governor Chris Christie explained that society had become divided between "two classes of people . . . public employees who receive rich benefits and those who pay for them."[6]

Based on this argument, Wisconsin's "Budget Repair Bill" largely eliminated collective bargaining rights for the state's 175,000 public employees. While not expressly outlawing unions, the bill's effect is similar. Public employees are prohibited from negotiating about anything other than wages; wage increases for local government employees are limited to the rate of inflation and must be approved by referendum of local voters; unions can no longer require those who benefit from contracts to pay their fair share of the costs of administering them, and even those who volunteer to pay union dues can't do so through the state payroll system; all unions must hold an annual referendum and win support from a majority of all eligible employees in order to remain in existence; and participation in any type of job action is grounds for immediate dismissal. The bill also completely stripped union rights from faculty and graduate student employees in the state university system.[7]

FIGURE 1.2.   Legislation restricting public employees' collective bargaining rights, 2011–15.

Wisconsin's was the most notorious legislation adopted during this period. But during the course of the next four years, fifteen states passed laws mandating statutory restrictions on public employees' collective bargaining rights (figure 1.2).[8] Beyond Wisconsin, for instance, collective bargaining rights were eliminated for Tennessee schoolteachers, Oklahoma municipal employees, graduate student research assistants in Michigan, and farm workers and child care providers in Maine.[9] Michigan and Pennsylvania both created "emergency financial managers" authorized to void municipal union contracts. New Jersey's and Minnesota's legislatures both restricted public employees' right to bargain over health care.[10] Ohio adopted a law—later overturned by citizen referendum—that largely mirrored Wisconsin's, outlawing strikes and prohibiting employees from bargaining over anything but wages. In Indiana, where Governor Mitch Daniels had issued an executive order abolishing state employee collective bargaining rights on his first day in office in 2005, lawmakers codified this ban into statute in order to prevent its possible overturn by future governors.[11]

None of the lawmakers carrying out this agenda had campaigned on a platform of abolishing union rights. When such measures were announced, they took the public everywhere by surprise. In Wisconsin, the state's leading newspaper identified sixty different campaign pledges that Walker had offered during the course of the 2010 election season; not one entailed eliminating collective bargaining rights.[12] Indeed, the governor himself described the introduction of his "Budget Repair Bill" as having "dropped the bomb."[13] The same was true for other states that passed similar laws. Thus these laws were not crafted in response to public opinion or as an outgrowth of public debate. They originated instead in the long-standing plans of corporate lobbyists who suddenly saw an opportunity to take down the opposition.

Former Speaker of the House Tip O'Neill once famously quipped that "all politics is local"—suggesting that even members of Congress are ultimately elected on the basis of their reputation for solving local problems.[14] The past few years, however, have stood this axiom on its head. Local politics have become nationalized, with state legislation written by lobbyists representing national and multinational corporations. In each state, residents understandably focused on local legislators as the architects of the antiunion edicts. In fact, lawmakers were enacting the agenda of national corporate interests that had spent years preparing for just such a moment.

In Wisconsin, even before the new governor was sworn in, the president of the Koch-funded Americans for Prosperity traveled to Madison to urge Walker to provoke a "showdown" with public employee unions, explaining that AFP was promoting this same strategy in Indiana, Ohio, and Pennsylvania.[15] It's not clear if the impetus for Walker's bill lay in this visit or elsewhere. But with the Kochs serving as one of the largest contributors to his campaign, there is no doubt that their word carried significant weight in the governor's office.

Wisconsin's Budget Repair Bill (Act 10) marked a singular triumph for the ALEC network. Not only did the bill embrace principles laid out in ALEC model legislation, but its passage was made possible by an extensive corporate investment in local politics. Walker himself is an alumnus of ALEC, and from 2008 to 2012 he received over $400,000 in campaign contributions from ALEC-member companies. In addition, forty-nine members of the 2011 Wisconsin legislature were ALEC members, including both the speaker of the house and the senate president; the latter was ALEC's state chair, a position that carries with it an affirmative obligation to promote the organization's model bills.[16]

When it was unveiled, the Wisconsin law received enthusiastic support from both state and national business lobbies. The U.S. Chamber of Commerce lauded Walker for showing that "collective bargaining is not a right but a costly entitlement."[17] Wisconsin Manufacturers and Commerce (WMC)—the state's premier corporate group—hailed Act 10 as a "landmark achievement" that "diminish[ed] the strength and power of public employee unions."[18] The corporate lobbies continued to invest in this offensive throughout Walker's battle with senate Democrats and union protesters. At the height of protests, AFP launched a $400,000 advertising campaign supporting Walker's initiative.[19] And when the governor was challenged in a recall election the following year, WMC contributed $3 million toward keeping him in power.[20]

Are Public Employees to Blame for State Deficits?

In state after state, debates over antiunion measures were cast as a response to fiscal concerns. Facing dramatic budget shortfalls, it was necessary to make hard choices. One might disagree about exactly where cuts should be made, advocates argued, but the need to somehow rein in labor costs was beyond question.

It turns out, however, that this storyline does not fit the facts of economic reality. Rather than extorting above-market wages, an apples-to-apples comparison shows that public employees generally make slightly *less* than similarly skilled private-sector employees.[21] Furthermore, the timing of the budget crises that swept the nation in 2010–11 makes clear that these crises could not have been caused by excessively generous employee compensation.

The budget shortfalls came on suddenly, as shown in figure 1.3. As recently as 2007, forty of the fifty states enjoyed budget surpluses.[22] Three years later, the states faced a combined shortfall of almost $190 billion, by far the largest on record.[23] Whatever caused the crisis, then, must have occurred in 2008–9. There was certainly no dramatic increase in employee compensation in these years. On the contrary, both the number of public employees per capita and the proportion of state budgets devoted to employee compensation were flat for the preceding decade.[24]

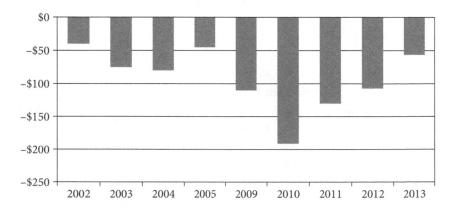

FIGURE 1.3. Aggregate state budget gaps, 2000–2011. Adapted from figure 2 in Phil Oliff, Chris Mai, and Vincent Palacios, "States Continue to Feel Recession's Impact," Center on Budget and Policy Priorities, June 27, 2012, http://www.cbpp.org/sites/default/files/atoms/files/2-8-08sfp.pdf.

What occurred in that short time span was not any increase in state spending but rather, a dramatic falloff in revenues, caused by the collapse of the housing market and the onset of the Great Recession.[25] Budget deficits struck nearly every state, regardless of their public employees' union status.[26] Indeed, the state of Texas—which prohibits collective bargaining for nearly all public employees— faced a massive, two-year budget shortfall of $18 billion, or 20 percent of state expenditures.[27]

Because unions did not cause the deficits, it should be clear that ending unions' bargaining power was not undertaken as a strategy for solving states' fiscal problems. There may be times when employee concessions are needed to help close budget gaps, but such concessions in no way require curtailing bargaining rights. Nowhere was this clearer than in Wisconsin itself. At the start of 2011, Wisconsin was one of the few states not facing a budget crisis; on the eve of Governor Walker's inauguration, the state's nonpartisan legislative research office announced that Wisconsin would begin the year with a $121 million surplus. The budget went into the red only after the governor, as one of his first acts in office, enacted large new tax cuts for the business community.[28] The disconnect between union busting and fiscal necessity became painfully clear during debates over the governor's budget proposal. When Wisconsin unions announced they had agreed to all of Governor Walker's economic proposals— including significant benefit reductions—Walker declared that, despite having been granted everything he claimed was needed to close the budget gap, no deal would be acceptable as long as workers retained the legal right to negotiate. Under questioning by members of the U.S. Congress two months later, Walker conceded that some of the most draconian provisions in his legislation wouldn't save the state money.[29] So too, Ohio governor John Kasich—who championed a law similar to Wisconsin's, only to see it overturned by a subsequent voter referendum—conceded his proposed law "does not affect our budget."[30] In short, the attack on collective bargaining rights was not a fiscal strategy but primarily a political agenda unrelated to budget requirements.

Political and Economic Impacts of Antiunionism

Politics is always complex, and legislation is almost always the result of a coalition of forces with overlapping interests rather than the backroom plot of a single, coherent organization. The attack on public employee unions brought together antiunion ideologues, Republican Party strategists, and antitax conservatives, along with the corporate lobbies, with each group pursuing its own interest in curtailing unions.

There is no doubt that the attacks on public employee unions were driven in part by Republican hopes of defunding their political opposition. GOP strategists have long identified labor unions as one of the central foundations of the Democratic Party.[31] After decades of assault on private-sector unions, in 2009 the number of union members in the public sector outnumbered those in the private for the first time in American history.[32] This made public employee unions a particularly enticing target for those looking to shift the balance of political power. "Every worker who doesn't join the union," reasoned the conservative strategist Grover Norquist, "is another worker who doesn't pay $500 a year to organized labor's political machine."[33] So too, the American Enterprise Institute hailed Wisconsin's antiunion law as "defunding of the Democratic party shock troops."[34]

The impact of Act 10 on the Wisconsin labor movement has indeed been calamitous. Within three years, the number of Wisconsin public employees who were union members fell by almost one hundred thousand.[35] The Wisconsin State Employee Union saw its budget cut by two-thirds during that period, with one conservative group estimating that the law cut off $2 million per year in union political spending.[36] Thus those who hoped Act 10 would change Wisconsin's political landscape saw their wish come true.

The loss of collective bargaining also led to a marked decline in public employees' standard of living. By mandating increased employee payments for health insurance and pensions, Act 10 imposed an effective 12 percent pay cut, followed by a two-year wage freeze. Under these conditions, one employee explained, "We live paycheck to paycheck."[37] Wisconsin was the first state in the country where public employees won the right to organize, and Madison is home to the American Federation of State, County and Municipal Employees' (AFSCME's) first local union. By 2014, the president of AFSCME Local 1, an information technology specialist and mother of three, had been forced to take a second job at a local restaurant and was supporting her family with food stamps.[38]

In Wisconsin and elsewhere, attacks on state and local government had particularly damaging effects on African American workers. Historical discrimination in the private sector, combined with a series of equal employment initiatives in the public sector, long ago made government employment the backbone of the black middle class.[39] By 2010, 21.2 percent of all black workers were public employees, with African Americans 30 percent more likely than others to be employed by the government.[40] The public sector is important to black communities not only for the number of jobs it provides but also for the quality of those jobs. The median wage earned by black employees is significantly higher in the public sector than in other industries, and the gap between black and white wages is smaller.[41] Public service has been particularly important for black professionals. When the Great Recession hit, over 26 percent of black college graduates, significantly more than their white counterparts, were employed in state or local government.[42] Thus any cutback in public employment—in addition to its impacts on the broader economy—is also an attack on the black middle class. "When people think about racial discrimination, they think about someone in a Klan sheet," explains the University of California economist Steven Pitts. "It's important to understand that even if someone like Scott Walker does not express an overt prejudice toward blacks, their policies still can have racial impacts."[43] By slashing public-sector jobs, Walker and like-minded governors effectively pushed many black workers out of the middle class.

Who Benefited from Cutting Public Employee Paychecks?

In state after state, the attack on public employee unions was cast as a defense of hard-working nonunion taxpayers in the private sector. Private-sector workers were encouraged to believe that if public employees' compensation were cut, the savings would end up in their own pockets. But what actually happened?

It is difficult to answer this question for the country as a whole. In many states there are no data with which to quantify the total value of public employee cutbacks, much less to trace how those savings were allocated. It is clear, however, that many states enacted new tax cuts for the wealthy at the same time that they cut compensation for public employees, thus transferring income from working- and middle-class families to those more privileged.

Because Wisconsin's Act 10 was the subject of such intense debate, more data are available regarding its impacts. Governor Walker projects that in the four years from 2011 to 2014, cuts to public employee pensions and health insurance made possible by Act 10 have "saved the taxpayers some $3 billion."[44] Assuming this figure is roughly accurate, where did this money go? Some of the cuts in teacher pay and benefits likely went to make up for the Walker administration's $900 million reduction in aid to local school districts.[45] The majority almost certainly went, as the governor claimed, to "the taxpayers"—though not necessarily the same taxpayers the public was led to imagine. In the years from 2011 to 2014, Wisconsin legislators enacted a series of tax cuts whose value over that period totaled approximately $2 billion.[46] An analysis of these cuts shows that the poorest 20 percent of households received a benefit of just $48 per year, and the average benefit for the entire bottom 60 percent of families was $118. But the richest 20 percent of households received an average of $681 per year, and the top 1 percent received over $2,500 per year.[47] In total, fully half of the tax cuts went to the richest 20 percent of the state's population, with another quarter going to the next 20 percent. The bottom 60 percent of the state's population was provided just over one-quarter of the funds to split among themselves (figure 1.4).[48] Cutting public employee benefits to fund tax cuts was not, then, a transfer from the "haves" to the "have-nots" but just the opposite—$2 billion taken from working and middle-class families and given predominantly to the privileged and elite.[49]

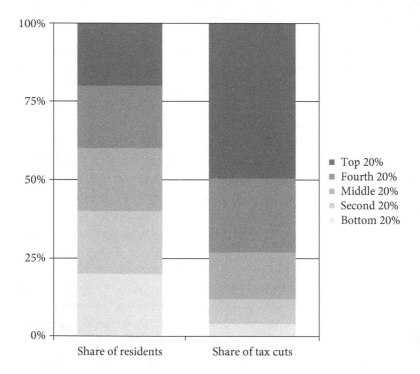

FIGURE 1.4.   Distribution of Wisconsin tax cuts by income group, 2011–14.

Source: Wisconsin Budget Project, "Missing Out: Recent Tax Cuts Deliver Little to People Who Earn the Least," June 3, 2014, http://www.wisconsinbudgetproject.org/wp-content/uploads/2014/05/Missing-out.pdf.

The Attack on Public Pensions

Together with restrictions on collective bargaining, many legislatures have mandated direct cuts in public employee compensation. From 2011 to 2014, thirty states passed laws that froze wages or cut health or pension benefits. While it is difficult to calculate with great accuracy, the total number of employees affected by these cuts appears to exceed nine million.[50]

By far the most common such initiative has been aimed at public employee pensions. Virtually all of the pension reforms adopted follow ALEC proposals—increasing employee contributions, raising the age of retirement and the number of years' service required for vesting, and above all, moving from defined-benefit to defined-contribution plans.[51] Particularly in jurisdictions without unions, making retirees pay to fill budget gaps was a politically easy way to address recession-induced deficits.

These cuts have taken a dramatic toll on the lives of public employees. While public rhetoric portrayed government retirees as a privileged class living a life of ease on Cadillac pensions, the truth was far more stark for most employees. For many, pension cuts came after decades of carefully holding together a monthly budget. A Detroit librarian, for example, explained that "for more than three decades . . . I lived frugally. . . . My pension has to . . . pay for groceries, gas in my car, and a health care plan since the City no longer provides one. . . . For me [the cutback] has meant delaying important medical procedures until I can afford the co-pay."[52] For many, pensions represented a modest security scraped together over decades of lean living. "For my first 15 years," a science teacher explains, "I worked a second job, and my wife worked part-time, simply to get by. Between the two of us, we barely made enough money to cover the mortgage, pay off student loans and raise our two children, thanks to wage freezes and benefit cuts. Through it all, I paid 7.5 percent of every paycheck toward my retirement. I knew my modest pension would be the bedrock for my family's long-term financial security."[53] Far from representing a privileged class forced to scale back to normal lives, these were hard-working families whose modest measure of security was pulled out from under them.

Conservative politicians and corporate-funded think tanks have maintained an unrelenting drumbeat claiming that pension plans are bankrupt and unaffordable, imposing unbearable burdens on the backs of taxpayers. The ALEC-affiliated Heartland Institute warned in 2010 that "taxpayers in almost every U.S. state owe large and possibly unpayable retirement pensions to the men and women who work for the government."[54] "The problem we face is simple," Chris Christie declared in his 2011 state-of-the-state address. "Benefits are too rich, and contributions are too small, and the system is on a path to bankruptcy."[55]

Corporate advocates pointed to unaffordably generous union pensions as one of the key drivers of budget deficits. But there is no evidence to support this claim. The gap in pension funding is a relatively new phenomenon. In the year 2000, public employee pensions, on aggregate, were funded at just over 100 percent of liabilities; during the ensuing decade, a combination of recession and cutbacks in employer contributions reduced that rate, but it never fell below 84 percent—a level considered healthy by accounting standards—until 2009.[56] Second, many states with weak or nonexistent unions faced pension deficits similar to the national average. South Carolina's pension fund, for example, faced a deficit significantly greater than those of California, Michigan, Massachusetts, or New York.[57] No public employee in South Carolina has the right to collective bargaining; furthermore, the GOP has controlled both houses of the legislature for the past fifteen years and the governor's mansion for twenty-six of the past thirty years.[58] Are we to believe that this state's pension shortfall results from Governors Sanford's and Haley's kowtowing to labor leaders?

In fact, like fiscal problems generally, pension shortfalls were overwhelmingly a product of the recession. Nearly 90 percent of the funding gap faced by state and local governments was due to the stock market collapse in 2007–9, followed by the collapse of the housing market, which had a severe impact on local government revenues.[59] The deficits were caused not by public pensions but by the Wall Street mortgage scandal that triggered a financial meltdown. The notion that the country faced a pension "crisis" was based on extreme assumptions regarding what constitutes prudent investment—embraced by conservative commentators but not by actual pension managers—whose effect was to artificially triple or quadruple the estimate of unfunded liabilities.[60] In reality, most states' liabilities were quite modest even in the immediate postrecession years and could have been closed by a variety of moderate measures.[61]

Instead, corporate lobbies both in 2010 and today advocate dramatic cutbacks in pension benefits and, above all, an end to defined-benefit plans. ALEC's "Statement of Principles on State and Local Government Pensions," for instance, focuses on one overriding goal: "that defined benefit plans be replaced by defined contribution plans."[62] This long-standing conviction predates both the recession and any crisis of underfunding. At least as far back as the year 2000—when the nation's public employee pension funds were funded at just over 100 percent—ALEC legislation called for moving public employees into privately managed defined-contribution systems.[63]

Again, the pattern of pension cutbacks cannot be explained by fiscal exigency. Florida, North Carolina and Wisconsin, for example, are among the states that enacted the harshest cutbacks in pension benefits. Yet just prior to the recession, these states boasted funded ratios of 105.6 percent, 106.1 percent, and 99.5 percent, respectively.[64] As Scott Walker prepared to take office, Wisconsin had one of the healthiest pension funds in the country, funded at 99.7 percent of liabilities.[65] Most tellingly, the switch from defined benefit (DB) to defined contribution (DC) plans does not actually save money, but the opposite. Providing any given level of benefits for retirees costs almost twice as much through a typical DC plan.[66]

What, then, leads corporate lobbies to put such a high premium on abolishing secure retirement plans? Much has been written about the finance industry's interest in privatizing pensions, and there is no doubt that this has been one of the driving forces behind the call for dismantling publicly run funds.[67] But what about the nonfinancial corporations that make up the bulk of ALEC and Chamber of Commerce membership? In 2011, for instance, the ALEC task force that oversaw pension reform issues was chaired by Kraft Food, Inc.[68] Why would Kraft and other nonfinancial firms devote significant time, money, and effort to privatizing public employee pensions? Answering this question will shed light on the broader puzzle of why large private corporations would expend resources on dismantling public employee unions.

Beyond Wall Street, it seems that corporate employers generally share an interest in eliminating public employees' ability to retire with a secure, guaranteed income. This cannot be explained simply as a means of lowering corporate tax bills in the states. The more compelling interest appears to lie in the concern that higher compensation for unionized public employees creates pressure on nonunion employers to compete for the most skilled labor. As shown in figure 1.5, over the last several decades, private-sector employers have been steadily eroding pension benefits. By 2011, only 18 percent of private employees enjoyed defined pension plans.[69] Unsurprisingly, these are overwhelmingly concentrated in unionized workplaces.[70]

While defined-benefit plans were disappearing from private industry, in 2011 nearly 80 percent of state and local government employees still retained such benefits.[71] This did not make their total compensation higher than otherwise similar private-sector workers, but the security offered by defined benefit pensions is highly prized and serves as a significant factor in recruitment and retention of employees.[72] In this sense, public pension plans may exert market pressure for private firms to improve their own terms of employment—particularly in labor markets where the government is a dominant employer.

Beyond the economic value of public employee pensions, the mere existence of defined-benefit plans raises a challenge for corporate employers.

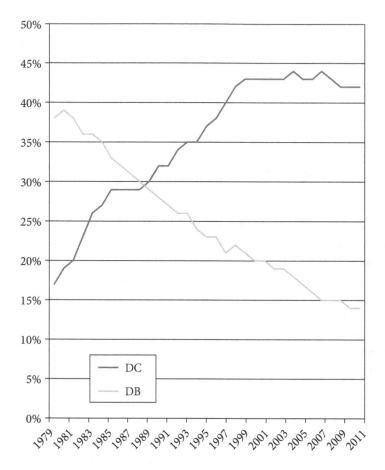

FIGURE 1.5. Private sector workers with defined benefit or defined contribution plans, 1979– 2011.

Source: U.S. Department of Labor Form 5550 summaries through 1998. EBRI estimates 1999–2010 using PBGC, CPS, and U.S. DOL data published in "FAQs about Benefits—Retirement Issues: What Are the Trends in U.S. Retirement Plans?," Employment Benefits Research Institute, 2015, http://www.ebri.org/publications/benfaq/index.cfm?fa=retfaq14.

Such plans—regardless of the specific terms they offer—hold up the *idea* of being able to retire in security: that after a lifetime of work one shouldn't have to worry about ending life in poverty. The existence of defined-benefit plans in the public sector stokes a potential sense of *entitlement* among other workers—the notion that if they give all their working lives to private employers, perhaps they too should have earned the right to retire on a secure income.

Corporate commentators echo these concerns—not a worry about fiscal conservation per se but tempering the level of expectations created by public employee benefits. Thus, FreedomWorks published a 2013 brief criticizing public pensions as contributing to the problem of "American entitlements."[73] Likewise, a senior *Forbes* columnist argued that public employees should not be allowed to expect higher standards than their private-sector counterparts. "In private-sector America your job, assuming you still have one, hangs on the fate of the economy. If your employer ever offered a pension for life . . . odds are it has stopped doing so, or soon will. Those retirement accounts you scrimped and saved to assemble? . . . They aren't doing so well. In private-sector America the math leads to the grim prospect of working longer and living poorer. . . . [But] in public-sector America things just get better and better."[74]

But this professed empathy for private-sector workers does not lead to a call for improving standards for those workers. Indeed, progressive legislators in a number of states have recently proposed creating retirement savings accounts, in funds managed by public pension advisers, for private-sector employees whose firms offer no such benefit. (Such proposals have often been supported by public employee unions looking to bring up the floor of retirement benefits in the labor market as a whole.)[75] In their most modest version, such proposals require nothing of employers but to allow an additional line on electronic payroll deductions. Yet when Illinois became one of the first states to adopt such a statute, it was vigorously opposed by the state's business lobbies. The Chamber lashed out at the bill for imposing an "unnecessary mandate" and creating "competition with plans readily available in the private sector."[76] The favored solution of corporate advocates, then, is not to rescue private-sector retirees from "living poorer" but to cut public employees down to this level.

To this end, ALEC specifically calls for public employee compensation – above all pensions—to be scaled back to the level provided by private employers. In 2011, ALEC issued a model bill titled "Resolution to Align Pay and Benefits of Public Sector Workers with Private Sector Workers," proclaiming that "the legislature of . . . {insert state}: will oppose any tax increase at the state level, until all levels of state government have evaluated their current compensation . . . practices to align them with those in the private sector." The law specifically mandates that "retirement benefit obligations to all state and municipal workers shall be immediately adjusted to a level comparable to that of private sector workers."[77] This call to action was taken up in 2012 by the Florida Chamber of Commerce, which named pension reform one of its legislative priorities for that year. Florida's state pension was among the nation's most solvent, yet the chamber nevertheless called on lawmakers to "make public employee benefits . . . consistent with those offered by the private-sector," including eliminating defined-benefit plans for all new hires.[78] It appears, then, that the intense corporate focus on abolishing defined-benefit plans is driven by the desire both to avoid market competition and to eliminate from popular imagination the notion that we might have a right to a secure retirement.

Private-sector workers have been encouraged to believe that they will benefit from the deunionization of public employees. In reality, it is likely that many will see their own compensation suffer as their employers face decreased pressure to compete with a government union standard. On average, if one compares union and nonunion employees in the same occupation and industry, of similar age and education backgrounds, those with a union earn 15 percent higher wages and have a 20–25 percent better chance of getting health insurance or pensions through their employers.[79] In places where unions are strong, union standards have a positive spillover effect for unorganized workers, as their employers are forced to improve their own compensation or risk losing the best employees to a unionized workplace. As the economists Larry Mishel and Matthew Walters have shown, this effect is most pronounced where unionized employers represent a significant share of area jobs.[80]

A similar dynamic holds for public employers. Where public employment plays a leading role in local labor markets, it influences wage and benefit standards in the broader private economy. In my hometown of Eugene, Oregon, for instance, the largest employer is the University of Oregon. If administrative employees at the university get health insurance through their union—which they do—this increases pressure on private employers to approach this standard, if not match it, if they hope to attract the most talented employees. Conversely, cutting public employee compensation reduces competitive pressures on private-sector employers. Thus, at least in those areas where government is a leading employer, the degradation of public-sector labor standards can be expected to undermine the bargaining leverage of private-sector workers across the labor market as a whole.

As shown in Table 1.1, there are a surprising number of cities in which state or local government constitutes the single largest employer. In these communities, cuts to public employees are likely to have negative spillover effects for private-sector workers in any occupation that competes with the government. Few employees are likely to connect the dots between public-sector cutbacks and private-sector stagnation. For the country's corporate leaders, however, the connection is easy to see.

TABLE 1.1   Select cities with largest employers (excluding U.S. government)

CITY	LARGEST EMPLOYER
Albuquerque, NM	University of New Mexico
Ann Arbor, MI	University of Michigan
Austin, TX	Austin Independent School District
Baton Rouge, LA	State of Louisiana
Birmingham, AL	University of Alabama
Bismarck, ND	State of North Dakota
Boise, ID	State of Idaho, including Boise State University
Casper, WY	Natrona County School District
Cheyenne, WY	State of Wyoming
Chicago, IL	Chicago Public Schools
Cobb County, GA	Cobb County School District
Columbus, OH	State of Ohio, Ohio State University
Detroit, MI	Detroit Public Schools
El Paso, TX	El Paso School District
Greensboro, NC	Guilford County Public Schools
Honolulu, HI	City and County of Honolulu
Jackson, MS	State of Mississippi, University of Mississippi Medical Center
Jersey City, NJ	Hudson County
Kansas City, KS	University of Kansas Hospital and Medical Center
Las Vegas, NV	Clark County School District
Lincoln, NE	State of Nebraska, Lincoln Public Schools
Little Rock, AR	State of Arkansas
Los Angeles, CA	Los Angeles County, LA County Unified School District
Miami, FL	Miami-Dade County Public Schools
Minneapolis, MN	State of Minnesota
Missoula, MT	University of Montana
New York, NY	City of New York, NYC Public Schools
Oklahoma City, OK	State of Oklahoma
Philadelphia, PA	City of Philadelphia
Phoenix, AZ	State of Arizona
Raleigh, NC	State of North Carolina
Richmond, VA	Virginia Commonwealth University and Health System
Salt Lake City, UT	State of Utah
Santa Fe, NM	State of New Mexico
Tacoma, WA	State of Washington
Tampa, FL	Hillsborough County School District
Topeka, KS	State of Kansas
Trenton, NJ	State of New Jersey
Tucson, AZ	University of Arizona

Source: www.city-data.com.

Beyond Unions: Shrinking the Government

To many, the attacks on public employees in Wisconsin, Ohio, and elsewhere appeared simply to be a manifestation of antiunionism. However, the track record of the corporate lobbies makes it clear that anti-unionism is only one part of a broader agenda that aims to shrink the size of government as a whole. Corporate advocates have pursued this objective in both union and nonunion jurisdictions, and in places like Wisconsin public service cuts have continued long past the point where unions were decimated and compensation costs slashed. The sweeping cuts made to education, transportation, health care, and other vital services point to a drive to pare back the scope of government as an end in itself, separate from anything to do with wage standards or unions.

In the years following the Great Recession, business-backed legislators have eliminated hundreds of thousands of government jobs and sharply curtailed public services. While these steps, like deunionization, were typically justified as a response to budget deficits, the evidence suggests something else must be at work. Deep, permanent cuts in the scope of public services have been advocated by ALEC and the Chamber of Commerce for all states, and at all times, no matter what fiscal conditions they faced. Perhaps most strikingly, the largest cutbacks in public services and layoffs of public employees did not take place in the states with the largest budget deficits. In 2011, state employment fell more sharply than in any year since the government began keeping track in 1955.[81] Yet these cuts do not correlate with the states that faced the largest fiscal challenges. From January through December 2011, 230,000 jobs were eliminated in state and local government.[82] Texas alone cut 68,000 jobs, accounting for 31 percent of the total. An additional 88,000 positions—41 percent of the total—were eliminated in the eleven states that in November 2010 had just put Republicans in control of all branches of state government. These eleven newly "all-red" states laid off an average of 2.5 percent of their government employees in a single year; by comparison, the other thirty-nine states together averaged cutbacks only one-fifth as large. As depicted in figure 1.6, these eleven states plus Texas accounted for nearly 72 percent of the public jobs eliminated in 2011,[83] yet in that same year, these twelve states accounted for just 12.5 percent of the aggregate state budget shortfall.[84] Thus the relationship is exactly the opposite of what one would expect if decisions were based on economics: more than two-thirds of total job cuts came from states that accounted for just one-eighth of the total state budget shortfall.

In what follows, I first examine the large-scale layoffs and budget cuts that helped define the postrecession period and then consider what economic motives might lead corporate advocates to pursue such a radical course.

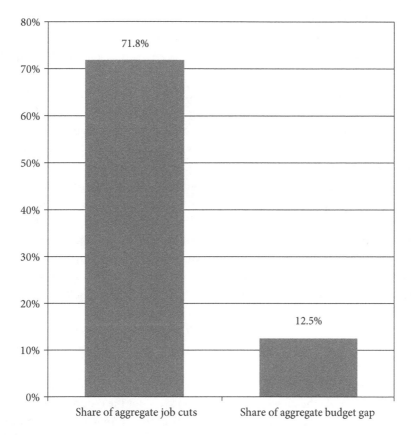

FIGURE 1.6.   Share of aggregate state budget gap and public employee job counts accounted for by newly "all-red" states plus Texas, 2011. Author's calculations based on Bryce Covert and Mike Konczal, "The GOP's State Project of Slashing the Public Workforce," Roosevelt Institute, March 27, 2012, www.rooseveltinstitute. org/sites/all/files/GOPProjectSlashingPublicWorkforce.pdf; and Elizabeth McNichol, Phil Oliff, and Nicholas Johnson, "States Continue to Feel Recession's Impact," Center on Budget and Policy Priorities, January 9, 2012, www.cbpp.org/cms/index. cfm?fa=view&id=711.

In the absence of legislative action, economists would normally expect public-sector employment to rise and fall in step with the private sector. When the private economy contracts, tax revenues fall and layoffs ensue; when the private economy rebounds, revenues are replenished and the government starts rehiring. In recent years, however, the cuts in public employment far exceeded the level of job losses in the private sector. The Great Recession began in December 2007, and by June 2009 the country was officially in recovery.[85] Private-sector employment began to rebound early in 2010 and grew steadily from that point, adding more than four million jobs over the next two years. During the same period, however, the public sector kept shrinking. By the summer of 2014—five years after the recovery began—public employment remained far below its 2008 level.[86]

The widespread layoffs are even more dramatic given that, in the past, public employment typically increased even during recessions as a simple result of population growth.[87] As the population increases, communities need more schools, bus routes, health clinics, police, garbage service, and libraries simply to provide the same level of services to a growing citizenry. Furthermore, demand for public services rises in times of recession, and elected officials have traditionally looked to government employment as a countercyclical stimulant to offset the impact of the downturn. "Why is the recovery from this recession different from . . . past recessions?" asked the chair of the Yale economics department in June 2012. "In the past," he answered, "local government employment has been almost recession-proof."[88] The combination of failing to add jobs to serve the growing population while actively eliminating many existing jobs made for a much more dramatic gap between the normally expected size of government and its actual numbers. By July 2014, state and local government would have needed to add 1.8 million employees in order to restore the level of public services they had provided in 2008.[89]

Taken together, the cuts to public employment were of such a magnitude as to impact not only the directly affected individuals but the economy as a whole. By the spring of 2012, the chief economist at Moody's Analytics declared that "job losses at state and local government [constitute] the most serious weight on the job market."[90] That same month, the Wall Street Journal calculated that the national unemployment rate would have been a full percentage point lower had state and local governments kept employment at its prerecession levels.[91] "If the government had done what it normally does and employed more people during the recovery," one financial analyst explained in 2013, "the unemployment rate would be a lot lower . . . and there'd be a lot less talk about food stamps and how miserable the recovery has been."[92]

The Nobel Prize–winning economist Joseph Stiglitz, among others, called for an increase in federal aid to state and local governments in order to mitigate the layoffs.[93] But conservative politicians and corporate-funded think tanks argued just the opposite: that cutting public employment was exactly what was needed to stimulate the recovery. Mitt Romney, the 2012 Republican presidential candidate, criticized President Obama precisely on this score, charging that "[the president] says we need more firemen, more policemen, more teachers," when in fact "it's time for us to cut back on

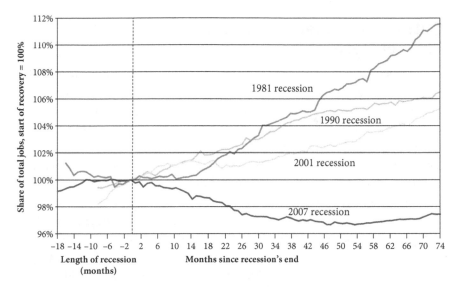

FIGURE 1.7. Job change for public-sector workers since the start of each of the last four recoveries. Public data exclude temporary census workers. The line for each recession begins at the official start of the recession, so the length of the line to the left of zero indicates the length of each recession.

Source: Economic Policy Institute analysis of Bureau of Labor Statistics' Current Employment Statistics public data series.

government and help the American people."[94] "The best way to stimulate the economy," insisted a senior fellow at the Koch-funded Cato Institute, is "to shrink government . . . lower marginal tax rates, and streamline regulations."[95] The corporate right's exhortations for an unprecedented policy of cutting taxes and services in the midst of recession was not an evidence-based policy and indeed did not yield the economic growth its proponents forecast.[96] In every other downturn—under both Democratic and Republican administrations—significant increases in state and local governments were a key element in the country's emergence from recession. There was no reason to believe that tax cuts were the key to economic recovery. However, continuing tax cuts achieved something else: they dramatically—and perhaps permanently—shrank the size of government.

Thus, the failure to restore public employment—indeed, the ongoing cuts during the period of recovery—set this period apart as qualitatively different from what came before. The extremes of unemployment and retrenchment were the product not of a particularly severe recession but of a political commitment to shrinking the size of government, regardless of its economic impact.

Cutting Essential Services at a Time of Need

Legislators faced truly stark budget shortfalls in 2011, leading them to consider drastic cuts to essential services. In Arizona, the governor proposed cutting off health insurance for nearly three hundred thousand people—including some in the middle of chemotherapy or dialysis treatments.[97] Texas eliminated more than ten thousand teaching jobs, cut funding that supported full-day prekindergarten programs for one hundred thousand at-risk kids, and announced plans to consider closing 850 of the state's 1,000 nursing homes, potentially forcing frail, low-income elderly residents into the streets.[98]

State governments managed the fiscal crisis, in part, by cutting aid to cities and counties, resulting in stark cutbacks at the local level. The city of Camden, New Jersey—one of the most dangerous in the country—laid off half its police force.[99] Muncie, Indiana, eliminated so many firefighter positions that the area of the city that fire trucks can reach within eight minutes was cut in half.[100] Cleveland announced plans to lay off five hundred teachers in the fall of 2012, projecting that class size might increase to as many as forty students as a result.[101] In Palm Beach County, four years of successive budget cuts resulted in eliminating 20 percent of the workforce by 2012; further cuts in 2012–13 raised the prospect that the government might be unable to meet its legal obligations. "Here is the dilemma," explained the county clerk. "I take an oath as a constitutional officer to provide services to the public," including keeping vital records and running a court system. "Do I get sued by the public because I . . . have to close one day a week? Or do I lay people off, and end up in the same scenario?"[102]

As described earlier, conventional wisdom is for government spending to increase during a recession. Demand for public services increases in hard times, including direct services such as health care and transportation as well as food stamps, unemployment insurance, and other social benefits that are designed to expand during economic downturns. This time, however, the corporate lobbies pushed forcefully—and unanimously—in a different direction. ALEC's assessment of state economic policies, for example, completely dismisses any benefit that may be derived from public services, treating taxes as simply removing money from the public without providing any measurable value in return. ALEC ranks the economic vitality of the fifty states on the basis of their support for "pro-growth" policies; of the fifteen measures used to define state rankings, two-thirds relate to limiting taxes.[103] Among other proposals, ALEC calls for replacing graduated taxes with a flat tax and eliminating the inheritance tax,[104] abolishing capital gains taxes,[105] locking in the Bush tax cuts,[106] and adopting constitutional amendments to limit future spending.[107] From this point of view, the fiscal crises brought on by the Great Recession were not a tragedy to be overcome but an opportunity to be exploited, in order to correct what these lobbies saw as a long history of overfunded government.

Dramatic Cuts in Public Services

In state after state, budget cuts in line with corporate principles were enacted by Republican leadership and ALEC-affiliated legislators and adopted with the vocal support of business organizations. For poor and working-class families, one of the critical losses was the closure of public libraries. Two-thirds of public libraries report that they are the only source of free access to computers and the internet in their communities. In addition, 80 percent help patrons conduct job searches, learn basic computer skills, find and fill out forms for public assistance, and access free online homework and SAT practice tests.[108] Unsurprisingly, as the recession hit, the demand for library services increased.[109] Despite this growing need, however, library services are being shrunk rather than expanded. In 2011–12, twenty-three states cut funding for public libraries,[110] with Texas eliminating nearly two-thirds of its library funding. Michigan reported twenty libraries shuttered that year, four of them in Detroit.[111] In New Jersey, dramatic budget cuts by Governor Christie led the city of Camden to close all three of its public libraries.[112] And the Charlotte, North Carolina, library system laid off three hundred employees, closing four of its twenty-four branches and cutting its hours by more than half.[113]

Local health departments similarly found their staffs drastically reduced at the height of the recession, just when record numbers of unemployed and uninsured Americans turned to them for help (figure 1.8). By January 2010, twenty-three thousand jobs had been eliminated from the country's public health infrastructure. As a result, 13 percent of local health departments cut back on immunization programs, and one-quarter cut programs for neonatal and child health care. Programs to identify and treat vision and hearing problems in school-aged children and to inspect food safety standards in local restaurants were among the functions eliminated by health departments under budgetary siege.[114] One department reported having to cut a cervical cancer screening program that had previously provided early detection for local residents; as a result, the agency reported that "we expect . . . [a] decrease in the survivability of cancer."[115] Officials further reported that if the nation faced an outbreak similar to the H1N1 flu epidemic, many localities would be unable to vaccinate their communities.[116] Even as the economy recovered and tax revenues rebounded, however, these cuts

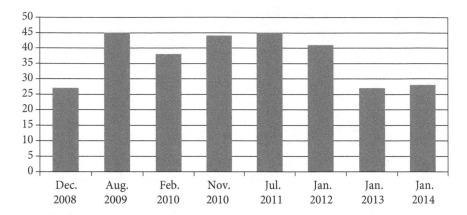

FIGURE 1.8.   Share of local health departments with budget cuts, 2008–14.

Source: "Local Health Department Budget Cuts and Job Losses: Findings from the 2014 Forces of Change Survey," National Association of City and County Health Officials (NACCHO), April 2014, http://www.naccho.org/topics/research/forcesofchange/upload/Budget-Cuts.pdf.

were not restored. Instead, public health funding continued to be cut rather than replenished. In the 2013–14 fiscal year, 28 percent of local health departments saw their budgets cut, marking the eighth consecutive year of cuts and bringing the total number of public health jobs eliminated from local governments since the start of the recession to over forty-eight thousand.

Local transit services likewise fell victim to multiple rounds of budget cuts. Public transit systems are particularly critical for enabling low-income residents to get to school or work and for transporting senior citizens who can't afford or aren't able to operate a car. In North Carolina, for instance, researchers reported that two-thirds of public transit riders in 2011 had incomes of $25,000 or less. Lack of transportation was reported as one of the most important barriers to employment for those out of work, yet the typical resident was unable to reach 70 percent of metro area jobs within ninety minutes by public transit.[117] In 2011, three-quarters of the nation's large urban transit systems cut staffing; 70 percent reduced services, and half increased fares.[118] By 2012, total funding for all state and local highway and mass transit systems was 15 percent lower than it had been a decade earlier.[119]

Transit cutbacks have been particularly devastating for elderly and disabled riders. In Milwaukee, the paratransit system stopped delivering disabled riders to their doors and pared back service to the minimum required by federal law—delivering people to within three-quarters of a mile of a regular bus route.[120] In Ohio, more than one in seven public transit passengers are senior citizens or people with disabilities, who often rely on this service to access dialysis and other medical treatments. Yet multiple transit systems were forced to reduce service or raise fares. In Indiana, the American Association for Retired Persons (AARP) joined a coalition of mayors and community organizations supporting a Republican-authored proposal to allow cities within the state to establish mass-transit districts.[121] Yet Americans for Prosperity fought bitterly against this initiative, along with similar transit expansion plans in Tennessee, Virginia, and Florida. The organization was successful in shrinking rapid-transit plans for Nashville and in completely scrapping plans for a high-speed rail system in Florida.[122] AFP's position was seconded by the Heritage Foundation, which is opposed in principle to public transportation funding, arguing that there is no need for a tax-funded "centralized transportation system" when the "private sector has demonstrated its prowess" in solving such problems.[123]

Finally, budget cuts were particularly widespread—and particularly devastating—in the country's school systems. In 2010–11, 70 percent of all U.S. school districts made cuts to essential services.[124] Despite widespread evidence of the academic and economic value of preschool education, twelve states cut pre-K funding that year, including Arizona, which eliminated it completely.[125] Ohio repealed full-day kindergarten and cut its preschool program to the point that it served 75 percent fewer four-year-olds than it had a decade earlier.[126] Pennsylvania also cut back from full-day to half-day kindergarten in many districts— including Philadelphia, which also eliminated 40 percent of its teaching staff, cut its English-as-a-second-language program in half, and increased elementary school class sizes from twenty-one to thirty.[127] More than half the nation's school districts changed their thermostat settings—making classrooms hotter in summer and colder in winter—to reduce energy costs.[128] In Florida, the Seminole County school board proposed raising thermostats to seventy-eight degrees, the maximum allowed by law.[129] The Tucson, Arizona, school district eliminated geometry, art, drama, and photography classes; increased class sizes to up to forty students; and was still fined for failing to provide the minimum required instruction hours for seventh and eighth graders.[130] North Carolina cut its textbook budget by 80 percent.[131] Research shows that the availability of trained librarians makes a significant improvement in student reading and writing skills, yet by 2014 one-third of public schools in the country lacked a full-time certified librarian.[132]

The cuts to schools, libraries, transit and health care not only eliminated essential services, but also imposed new costs on working and middle-class families. The economic elite may be able to afford to send their children to private school, buy premium health insurance, purchase their own books and internet service, swim in private pools rather than public parks, and drive where they want rather than wait for public transit. But for the millions of working- and middle-class families that rely on such services in their daily lives, the net result of public service cuts was to make life both harder and more expensive.

What is most striking about these cuts is that lawmakers often treated retrenchment not as an undesirable, temporary necessity but rather as an opportunity to make what they perceived as long-overdue adjustments. It would have been easy, for instance, to structure cutbacks as temporary measures, with services set to be restored when economic growth reached a given level or state coffers were replenished. But no legislature took this route.

Indeed, if elected officials were simply concerned with closing budget gaps, they had many alternative methods for achieving this end.[133] For instance, in 2011 the deficits in all fifty states could have been erased entirely through two simple policy changes: undoing the Bush tax cuts for the top 2 percent of income earners and taxing capital gains at the same rate as ordinary income.[134] Both of these policies are within the power of states to enact, without waiting for Congress to act, and both ideas enjoyed popular support. Yet no state ever seriously explored this road to fiscal balance.

On the contrary, many legislatures enacted new tax giveaways to corporations and the wealthy even at the same time that they were slashing funding for schools, libraries, and health care. In total, twelve different states that enacted dramatic service cuts in 2011 also provided large new tax cuts.[135] Michigan, for example, adopted a bill, authored by an ALEC member, that eliminated the state's primary business tax and substituted a flat 6 percent corporate tax—costing the state $1 billion per year in lost revenue—even while drastically cutting k–12 funding.[136] Despite the dire impact on education, the corporate tax cut was vigorously supported by the Chamber of Commerce, National Federation of Independent Business, and Michigan Restaurant Association.[137] And in the same year that Ohio ended full-day kindergarten, Republican legislators phased out the state's inheritance tax—which had only ever affected the wealthiest 7 percent of estates—forgoing almost $300 million a year in funds that had been primarily dedicated to local government services.[138] This bill, too, received the avid support of the Chamber of Commerce (which hailed it as "the culmination of a decade-long advocacy effort"), National Federation of Independent Business (listing it among its "key victories"), and Americans for Prosperity, which applauded legislators' "political courage" in abolishing inheritance taxes.[139]

These new tax cuts came despite the fact that states were still suffering from cuts to essential services that have never been restored. As shown below (figure 1.9), for instance, in 2014–15 at least thirty states were still spending significantly less on k–12 education than they had in 2008.[140]

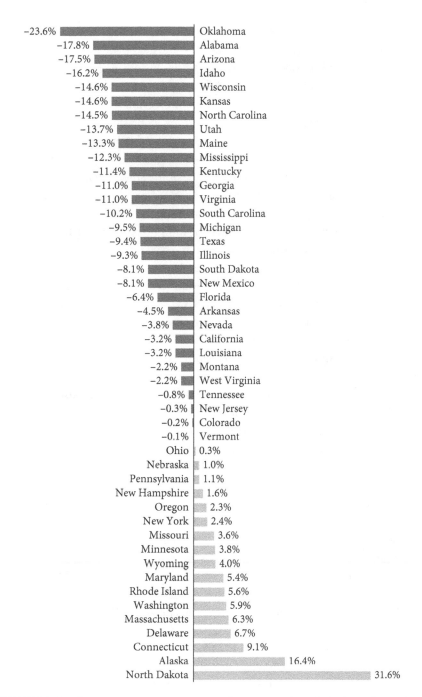

FIGURE 1.9. Percentage change in spending per student, inflation-adjusted, FY08 to FY15. Hawaii, Indiana, and Iowa are excluded because the necessary data to make a valid comparison are not available.

Sources: Center on Budget and Policy Priorities analysis and Center for Education Statistics enrollment estimates.

Rather than seeking paths to restore essential services as revenues recovered, corporate lobbyists sought to lock in these cuts and guarantee that services would never be expanded beyond their fiscal crisis level. Both ALEC and Americans for Prosperity have long urged legislators to adopt a so-called taxpayer bill of rights (TABOR)—a constitutional amendment that limits future spending. The TABOR formula typically prohibits states from increasing annual budgets by more than the combined rate of inflation plus population growth.[141] At minimum, this means that public services per person can never be improved or expanded beyond the level in place at the time of the amendment. Such laws also prevent states from effectively aiding those in need or adopting countercyclical measures during economic downturns. Furthermore, because the cost of core public services such as health care and education increases faster than the general rate of inflation, spending limits tied to the consumer price index force real (inflation-adjusted) *reductions* in service levels over time. Colorado is the only state to have implemented a TABOR provision to date, and its impacts were so troubling that the state's citizens voted in 2005 to suspend the TABOR formula.[142] But to enact such measures in the depths of recession would entail even greater sacrifices. TABOR-style proposals would take cuts made in response to record budget deficits caused by the worst economic downturn in seventy years and lock these in as the new high-water mark of public services that could never be exceeded, even after economic recovery. This is exactly what the corporate lobbies advocated and what several states pursued.

In Michigan, legislators adopted a ballot referral asking voters to amend their state's constitution to require a two-thirds supermajority approval for any future tax increases. The National Federation of Independent Business hailed this measure as a means to "lock down . . . substantive tax reforms" that had recently been enacted. "We're concerned that things will change," NFIB state director Charles Owens explained, "We'll have a new makeup in the legislature and . . . some of the progress that we've made on tax policy here [could] be eroded."[143]

Florida's constitution already caps tax increases, with maximum increases set by a moving five-year average of personal income growth. Yet legislators asked voters to approve an even stricter standard, limiting revenue growth to the TABOR formula of population growth plus inflation. The Chamber of Commerce strongly promoted this proposal, and the bill's prime sponsor—ALEC member and Florida Senate president Mike Haridopolos—championed TABOR as a route to "less government, less taxes and more freedom."[144]

Perhaps the most dramatic example of corporate priorities comes from Arizona, a state often touted as a model for conservative policy. As described previously, Arizona lawmakers called for drastic cuts to both education and health services in 2011, including eliminating all funding for preschool. Rather than conserving revenue in order to minimize these impacts, however, legislators enacted significant new cuts to both the state's commercial property tax and its corporate income tax, at an annual cost set to reach $538 million within five years.[145] This measure—cosponsored by twenty-three ALEC members including the speaker of the house—was strongly championed by the National Federation of Independent Business and the Chamber of Commerce, which celebrated it as "historic legislation."[146] Nationally, the cost of prekindergarten averaged just over $4,100 in 2011.[147] Thus, for $538 million, Arizona could have kept nearly 130,000 low-income four-year-olds in school. There is simply no way to avoid the conclusion that legislators preferred to kick poor children out of school in order to give the money to business owners. Finally, the same legislature voted to enact a TABOR statute—later vetoed by the governor—that would have made it nearly impossible to ever restore preschool funding in the future, no matter how the economy might improve.[148]

The Arizona votes to eliminate prekindergarten, cut corporate taxes, and lock in cuts through a TABOR amendment were all made by the same legislators, with the same leadership, in the same session, and with the backing of the same corporate lobbies. For these actors, cuts to public services were not a temporary and regrettable necessity but a desirable end in themselves.

As the economic recovery slowly gained momentum, state deficits shrank or disappeared. In the 2012–13 fiscal year, average state tax revenues were nearly 6 percent higher than in the year before.[149] By January 2014, a number of states enjoyed significant surpluses. Yet rather than restore cut services, many acted quickly to get rid of surpluses through additional tax cuts, keeping both the size of the public workforce and the scope of public services at recession levels despite the fiscal opportunity to restore them. "What do you do with a surplus?" asked Wisconsin Governor Walker. "You give it back to the people who earned it."[150]

Indeed, Governor Walker has twice chosen to create budget deficits where none previously existed by instituting new tax cuts devoted primarily to corporations and the wealthy. As the economy improved, Wisconsin ended the fiscal year on June 30, 2013, with a surplus of over $750 million.[151] Rather than restoring badly needed services, Walker initiated a new round of tax cuts; eight months later, the state was facing a $2 billion shortfall for the 2015–17 budget cycle.[152] Throughout this period, critical public services remained severely underfunded. By 2014, the state was providing $1,014 less per student than it had in 2008—the second-steepest education funding cut in the country.[153] Its spending on higher education had been cut by 22 percent over the same period, and in early 2015 Walker announced plans for a 13 percent reduction in funding for the University of Wisconsin system—the largest cut in the state's history, which Dean Rebecca Blank predicted would result in "layoffs in all of my schools and colleges."[154] As the Fitch ratings agency noted, each time Wisconsin's books bounce back into the black, "the state continues to adjust its tax code, offsetting revenue growth."[155] Walker's behavior, then, is not that of an official looking to preserve public services in the wake of fiscal distress, but the reverse: a leader creating fiscal shortfalls in order to slash public services.

North Carolina's business-backed legislators similarly chose to enact dramatic new tax cuts rather than restore badly needed public services. In the 2012–13 school year, the state eliminated 5,200 teaching positions and 4,100 other school professionals such as career counselors and school psychologists.[156] Yet rather than restoring services as the economy recovered, the legislature in 2013 adopted what ALEC hailed as "monumental tax reform," cutting the top income tax rate by 25 percent and corporate income taxes by more than half and abolishing the state's inheritance tax.[157] When the new cuts are fully phased in, they will cost over $700 million per year, with almost 90 percent of this amount going to the wealthiest 5 percent of the state's population.[158] As in Wisconsin, the law created a new fiscal crisis for the state, just when the economic recovery might have enabled lawmakers to restore essential services. As a result, in 2014, the state's per-pupil funding for k–12 education remained 14.5 percent below its 2008 level, while spending on higher education was down by almost 25 percent.[159] The 2014–15 budget cut an additional $76 million from the University of North Carolina and raised community college tuition to offset state funding cuts.[160] Nevertheless, the Chamber of Commerce hailed the bill—whose sponsors include two powerful ALEC-affiliated committee chairs—as "historic reform," crowing that employers could expect to save $2.1 billion over the next five years.[161]

The desire to lock in budget cuts rather than restore services as revenues rebound was similarly evident in Texas, another state frequently touted as a national model by both the U.S. Chamber of Commerce and ALEC. As described earlier, Texas enacted draconian cuts in 2010–12. But by January 2013, the economy had rebounded, state revenues were up 12.4 percent, and budget officials projected an $8.8 billion surplus. Rather than restoring services, however, Governor Rick Perry insisted the state had "[brought] in more than we need" and called for a constitutional amendment allowing "excess tax receipts" to be rebated to taxpayers.[162] In 2013, Texas legislators adopted a series of new tax cuts aimed primarily at corporations, including a $1 billion cut in business income taxes, celebrated by ALEC as "a rededication to the pro-growth tax and fiscal policies that have made Texas the economic powerhouse it is today."[163] The state additionally cut the tax rate for franchise businesses, which the Texas Association of Business and Chambers of Commerce proclaimed "means at least $700 million in business tax relief."[164] Finally, at a time that per-pupil funding remained nearly 10 percent below its 2000 level, the legislature cut property taxes earmarked for local school districts, reducing education funding by approximately $4 billion over an eight-year period.[165] This bill, championed by four ALEC-affiliated committee chairs, came at a time when six hundred school districts—representing three-quarters of the state's student population—had filed suit against the state for inadequate funding. In the 2013–14 school year, an estimated 130,000 students were taught in classes that exceeded the state class-size cap.[166] In August 2014, a district court judge ruled that the previous years' cuts to school funding were in violation of the state constitution.[167] Nonetheless, the new cuts in school funding were celebrated by the Texas Association of Business and Chambers of Commerce as "help[ing] business expand by extending school property tax breaks."[168]

Thus, for the corporate lobbies, the budget crises of recent years were greeted as an opportunity to advance an agenda that had long lingered on right-wing wish lists and suddenly became politically possible. Seizing on the moment of fiscal crisis and partisan advantage, they sought to force the deepest cuts possible and then to lock in measures that would prevent a future return to a more robust public sector.

What's It All About?

The corporate lobbies have pursued an agenda that steadily shrinks public services, including education, health care, libraries, recreation, parks, and transportation. This agenda serves to lower corporate tax bills and creates new markets for those hoping to profit from the privatization of public services. But there are deeper rationales underlying the erosion of public services. As described earlier, shrinking the public sector has long been championed as a means of both undermining the Democratic Party and weakening the capacity of public agencies to regulate private business. So too, cutting public spending clearly makes corporate tax cuts more feasible. Beyond these calculations, however, the insistence on permanently shrinking the size of government—even in times of trouble—shifts the balance of economic power toward corporate employers in two broader, if less obvious, manners. First, to the extent that essential services are supplied as a universal right of citizenship, the public becomes that much less dependent on private employers. This, indeed, is part of the right's historic opposition to unemployment or welfare benefits—to the extent the employees can meet economic needs through government programs, they are able to be that much more selective in determining what job, at what wage, they are willing to accept. By contrast, to the extent that public health clinics, bus service, and internet access are no longer available, the population is made more reliant on private wages to meet their needs. Every reduction in public services serves, at least to some slight degree, to undercut the bargaining leverage of employees in the labor market and shift the balance of power toward employers.

At a deeper level, the elimination of basic services serves, over time, to lower popular expectations regarding the standard of living to which one is entitled. For the economic elite—the few seeking to extend their rule over the many—the central political question of this time is how to accelerate economic inequality without provoking a political backlash. A key component of the answer to this question appears to be an attempt to engineer what might be termed a revolution of falling expectations among the public. When people no longer feel that they have a right to a decent education, a right to low-cost transportation to and from work, a right to affordable tuition for college-aged kids and affordable health care for aging parents, or a right to retire after a lifetime of work with some modicum of security, everyone becomes more insecure, considers oneself lucky to hold on to increasingly meager benefits, and is less likely to complain about what is lacking and more appreciative of what one still has. In this manner, the shrinking of public services over time lowers the popular sense of entitlement and in turn helps ease the acceptance of corporate privilege.

Just how ambitious the public's sense of entitlement might get is within the memory of many corporate executives. In the 1970s, the expectations of government –of what citizens had a right to expect simply by dint of being members of society—reached a level now hard to imagine. The original language of the 1978 Humphrey-Hawkins Full Employment Act, for instance, required the federal government to provide all Americans with "equal opportunities for useful and rewarding employment" and created a "Job Guarantee Office," responsible for creating "such policies and programs as may be needed to attain and maintain genuine full employment." These clauses were stripped from the bill before its adoption, but their inclusion in the original version of a serious, high-priority bill is testament to then-reigning common sense regarding what Americans could demand of government.[169]

In the long economic decline that has followed, corporate leaders regularly remind us—both as workers and as citizens—that we need to recalibrate our expectations downward. Thus one legislative sponsor of Ohio's Senate Bill 5— which would have abolished most public employee bargaining rights—insisted that public employees "shouldn't be concerned about their level of pay. They should be concerned about the fact that they have a job. We've got 10 percent of people without jobs. Be glad you have a job. Would you rather have no job or a pay cut?"[170] In an era of long-term economic decline, such dampening of expectations may become more important than ever for those seeking to advance an agenda of ever-increasing inequality. As large class sizes; the absence of well-tended parks, pools, or libraries; and longer and less reliable commutes gradually become the new normal, life expectations are ratcheted downward. For corporate elites presiding over an economy in decline and seeking to advance policies that are likely to make life harder for the majority, this lowering of expectations serves an important function—regardless of whether it is the result of an intentional strategy or something accidentally stumbled into that turned out to prove useful. Such considerations may seem too vague or ideological to be part of a corporate political strategy. Yet in seeking to make sense of an agenda that includes an intensive, multipronged campaign to shrink or eliminate public services—beyond any consideration of unions, politics, or budget gaps—it is impossible to make all the pieces add up without accounting for these motives.

The attack on public services thus dovetails with antiunionism but is independent of it. The raft of legislation advanced against public employee unions and public services was everywhere justified as a necessary response to fiscal crisis. It is clear, however, that legislators were driven less by a heartfelt urgency to close budget gaps than by the opportunity to advance long-held goals of restricting union rights, lowering wage standards, shrinking public services, and depressing popular expectations for what Americans have a right to demand of either private employers or public officials. Politicians often engineered the very budget crises they then decried and then used these crises to advance this long-standing agenda. The record of corporate-backed legislation indicates that it is this goal—limiting the expectations and bargaining power of working people—that animates the unprecedented retrenchment of these years, rather than any overriding fealty to fiscal conservatism or antiunion ideology.

DEUNIONIZING THE PRIVATE SECTOR

In 2006, Indiana governor Mitch Daniels was the guest of honor at a dinner hosted by the Teamsters union. The year before, on his first day in office, Daniels had issued an executive order abolishing collective bargaining for state employees. Now he had come to reassure the Teamsters that nothing similar was coming their way. "I'm a supporter of the labor laws we have in the state of Indiana," the governor promised. "I'm not interested in changing any of it. Not the prevailing wage laws, and certainly not the right to work law."[1] Just one year after the *Citizens United* decision, however, Daniels reversed course and signed right to work into law. And in 2015, Indiana repealed its prevailing wage law.

Daniels's comments singled out the two types of laws most feared by private-sector unions: so-called right-to-work laws (RTW) designed to undermine private-sector unions, and prevailing wage laws, specifically targeting unions in the construction industry. RTW does not, as the uninitiated might suppose, entail any guarantee of employment for those ready and willing to work. Rather, it makes it illegal to negotiate a union contract that requires all employees who benefit from the terms of the agreement to pay their fair share of the costs of negotiating and administering it. RTW laws thus put unions in the unique position of being required by federal law to provide all their benefits and services for free, without being able to charge for those services. Their most direct impact is to erode unions' budgets and, ultimately, to make them financially unviable. Thus private-sector unions regard RTW as an existential threat akin to that posed by the restriction of bargaining in the public sector.

While RTW laws affect all private-sector unions, their impact is lessened in the construction industry. Because construction unions provide highly specialized training for their members, skilled tradespeople generally remain dues-paying members even under RTW laws. Instead, what strikes at the viability of building trades unions is the abolition of prevailing wage—a New Deal-era principle that publicly funded construction should not undercut the going wage in a local area. Undoing such laws allows low-wage contractors to flood into an area, underbid better-paying union contractors, and slowly drive them out of this critical part of the industry.

When the national legislative offensive against public-sector unionism got under way in 2011, its champions insisted—like Daniels—that their concern was strictly limited to government employees. Elected officials went out of their way to distinguish the dismantling of public-sector bargaining from their support for private-sector unions. In Wisconsin, for instance, Governor Walker proclaimed private-sector unions "my partner in economic development" and pledged that he would do "everything in my power" to guarantee that RTW legislation "is not going to get to my desk."[2] Similarly, when Rick Snyder campaigned for the office of governor of Michigan in 2010, he insisted that RTW would "create a divisive atmosphere that would prevent too many good things from happening."[3] In 2011, Snyder supported legislation curtailing collective bargaining rights for public employees but repeatedly stressed that he had no interest in RTW.

However, after successfully passing laws to weaken public-sector unions, Indiana, Michigan, and Wisconsin all did exactly what their governors had forsworn. Indiana was the first to abolish public-sector union rights, and it became the first to adopt RTW, with Governor Daniels signing the law in early 2012. Elsewhere, the strategy was first to cripple public employee unions and only afterward to focus on the private sector. Shortly after being sworn into office, Wisconsin governor Walker was approached by an important donor who asked if there was "any chance we'll ever get to be . . . right-to-work?" "Well," Walker answered, "the first step is we're going to deal with collective bargaining for all public employee unions, because you use divide and conquer. . . . That opens the door once we do that."[4] That, indeed, appears to be the strategy that Walker and others followed. At the end of 2012, Michigan governor Snyder reversed his earlier position and signed a RTW law that was sprung on the public in a lame-duck session and rushed from introduction to signing—with no committee hearings or public comment—in less than a week.[5] In Wisconsin, Walker continued to pronounce RTW a "distraction" through the end of 2014 but apparently decided the timing was right shortly thereafter, and in February 2015 signed RTW into law.[6] Finally, after enacting RTW, all three states turned their focus to the construction industry. In 2015, Wisconsin sharply restricted its prevailing wage law, and Indiana abolished its altogether; in 2016, corporate donors launched a campaign for Michigan to follow Indiana's example.[7] Thus, the repeated disclaimers that attacks on public employees had no bearing on the private sector turned out to be false. The same lawmakers, backed by the same corporate interests, showed an equal commitment to combating unions wherever they might exist.

This chapter examines the corporate lobbies' efforts to deunionize the private sector. RTW has been promoted as both an economic strategy for boosting job growth and a moral principle for safeguarding workers' freedom of association. I explore both these claims in detail. Not only is neither sustained by the facts, but the arguments articulated by RTW boosters are so slipshod, constructed with what appears to be such casual disregard for methodological rigor, that they beg for an alternative explanation of what motivates their supporters. There is no question, however, that deunionizing both the private sector generally and the construction industry in particular represents a top priority for the corporate lobbies. Indeed, passing these laws was accomplished only with heavy-handed pressure that often threatened the cohesion of the Republican legislative caucus itself. In this sense, this part of the legislative record also provides a window into the shifting balance of power that has seen corporate lobbies exercise increased control over the legislative and party leaders who ostensibly run the state. In what follows, I first describe the politics of RTW, noting how firmly the corporate lobbies insisted on pursuing this goal even in the face of bruising political infighting. I then examine the proponents' arguments on their own merits. Finally, since the rationales offered for these laws appear to be more calculating than genuine, I seek to understand what it is that actually makes this agenda such a high priority for corporate lobbyists. In doing so, this chapter represents a first step toward assembling a broader understanding of the corporate agenda, encompassing the private sector as well as the government.

Winning Ugly: The Road to RTW

Passing RTW laws was neither easy nor pretty. This was not an issue that lawmakers had campaigned on, and public opinion was mixed at best.[8] Perhaps with this in mind, legislators took extraordinary steps to limit public debate on the issue. In the week leading up to the first hearing on the 2012 Indiana bill, access to the capitol was restricted for the first time in the state's history. While the capitol had earlier accommodated as many as 12,000 antiabortion protesters, the state now announced that safety dictated that no more than 1,300 protesters would be allowed inside the building.[9] Michigan likewise took the unprecedented step of locking citizens out of the capitol until forced by court order to open its doors.[10] In Wisconsin, a majority of voters opposed RTW from the moment it was introduced to the day the bill was signed.[11] As hearings were getting under way, a coalition of over four hundred construction contractors began airing TV ads in opposition to RTW; legislative leaders scrambled to rush the bill through for fear the ads might sway public opinion.[12] For the Wisconsin Senate hearing, 1,750 people registered to speak in opposition to the bill, with only 25 in favor; in response, lawmakers prematurely cut off public comment, with the committee chair invoking a "credible threat of disruption"—later revealed to be a plan by several union activists to stand up during the hearing—and calling on state police to escort lawmakers out and evacuate the building.[13] In Indiana, Democrats proposed letting the voters decide the issue by referendum—a suggestion supported by 70 percent of Indiana voters, but rejected by GOP leadership.[14] In Michigan, concern that voters might use the referendum process to repeal RTW led legislators to add a token budget appropriation to the bill that, under state rules, makes citizen repeal significantly more difficult.[15]

RTW also created significant ruptures within the Republican Party itself. In every state that passed RTW laws, Republicans enjoyed large majorities and did not need any Democratic votes. Nonetheless, enough moderate Republicans opposed RTW that leadership was forced to resort to harsh tactics that at times threatened to tear the fabric of party cohesion. In New Hampshire, RTW was passed in early 2011 but vetoed by the state's Democratic governor. Republican majorities in both houses were easily large enough to override a veto, but a significant number of these had reservations about the bill. House Speaker (and ALEC member) Bill O'Brien spent seven months seeking to schedule a vote at a time when enough opponents would be absent that supporters could constitute a two-thirds vote to override the veto. Along the way, O'Brien suspended mileage expense reimbursement to discourage rural representatives from making the trek to the capitol;[16] a Republican opposed to RTW who had been granted an aisle seat because of disability found his spot moved to the middle of a row;[17] and three party leaders, along with a committee chair, were removed from their posts for refusing to support the bill.[18] Tensions grew so high that one Republican legislator introduced an "anti-bullying" bill aimed at Speaker O'Brien, which would have protected lawmakers from behavior that "physically harms," "causes emotional distress," or "creates a hostile work environment" for legislators.[19]

For the corporate lobbies, RTW was a sufficiently urgent priority that they were committed to winning at almost any political cost—including substantial political damage to the Republican legislative caucus. At the federal level, Skocpol and Hertel-Fernandez pose a central question: Why aren't politicians behaving the way political science models predict—moving to the center in order to capture as much of the electorate's support as possible? On issues as diverse as the minimum wage, infrastructure spending, Social Security, and climate change, the GOP has moved to an increasingly extreme position—further to the right not only of the national center but also of its own registered voters.[20] Both they and Mayer conclude that the power of moneyed backers has increasingly led congresspeople to pursue the corporate agenda even at the cost of making the party's electoral prospects more daunting.[21] In the states as well, the legislative battles over RTW point to a triumph of corporate interests over purely partisan motives. From a strictly political viewpoint, legislative leadership should be concerned above all with maintaining its majority, making party leaders loath to force members of their caucus into votes that might undermine their popularity with the public. If the GOP were simply driven by protecting or expanding its partisan power, it would have avoided issues that cause schisms within the party or weaken the reelection chances of sitting members. In the RTW fights, the interests of the party's corporate backers trumped such partisan calculations, forcing action on a controversial issue that many Republicans might have preferred to avoid.

In Michigan, the strategy for enacting RTW came from corporate organizations outside the legislature, led by Amway CEO Dick DeVos. DeVos, whose family has given well over $40 million to Michigan GOP campaigns and is a major supporter of the ALEC-affiliated Mackinac Center, brought together a circle of business supporters from across the state and beyond, including the casino tycoon Sheldon Adelson and the Texas investor Harold Simmons. Together, they hired ad firms and bought airtime to blanket the state with pro-RTW messages, developed talking points, and brought in outsiders such as the veteran GOP pollster Frank Luntz to rally jittery lawmakers on the opportunity to "make history." They even paid to reserve the lawns surrounding the capitol for the entire month of December, in order to forestall any possibility of Wisconsin-style protests.[22]

The 2012 elections produced contradictory results in Michigan. A union-backed ballot initiative that would have enshrined collective bargaining rights in the state constitution was soundly defeated—with opposition organized by a DeVos-led clique of corporate funders. However, while voters returned Republicans to power in both chambers, their majority was both slimmer and less conservative. DeVos and allies determined that rather than wait till the newly elected lawmakers took office in January 2013, it was preferable to push through RTW during a December lame-duck session.[23] Quietly in the weeks after the 2012 election, they pressured Republican lawmakers to advance RTW legislation despite their fear of triggering widespread protests. The senate majority leader, Randy Richardville, who had previously pledged his opposition to RTW, was pulled into a private room with DeVos and a dozen other big-money donors and told to "grow a set and move this legislation." Undecided GOP lawmakers were warned they would face well-funded primary opponents if they did not support the bill and were promised financial backing if they faced a recall election as a result of supporting RTW.[24] While these conversations were ongoing, the public, largely because of Governor Snyder's repeated disclaimers, was unaware that dramatic legislation might be in the offing. As late as December 4, 2012, Snyder stated that he had not yet made up his mind on the issue.[25] Two days later, he suddenly announced that he had determined to support RTW.[26] That same day, both houses of the legislature introduced bills—largely drawing on ALEC model language—sent them straight to the floor with no committee hearing or public comment, and voted their approval.[27] On December 11—less than one week after it was introduced—Governor Snyder signed the bill into law.[28] One week after that, polls showed a majority of Michiganders opposed to the new RTW law and Snyder's popularity had plummeted.[29] Yet for RTW's corporate backers, this political cost may have been well worth the price of victory.

Thus in multiple states, RTW was adopted because it was an urgent priority of corporate lobbies even when it was not supported by the public, and this urgency was sufficient to convince legislative leaders to push the bill through even at significant cost to their own caucus.

The Argument for "Right to Work"

While Republicans may have been conflicted over RTW, the corporate lobbies had no such doubts. Both ALEC and the U.S. Chamber of Commerce uphold RTW as one of the essential keys to economic growth. Similarly, the national Americans for Prosperity organization declared Indiana's adoption of RTW the single most important legislative victory of 2012.[30] Wherever RTW has been adopted or seriously considered, the text hews closely to ALEC model language, and the bill has been sponsored by ALEC members—often in senior leadership positions.[31] The Indiana Chamber of Commerce, Wisconsin Manufacturers and Commerce, and New Mexico Association of Commerce and Industry—the leading business organizations of each state—all named RTW their number one legislative priority.[32]

As the country struggled with near-record unemployment followed by anemic recovery, RTW was promoted as a quick, dramatic, and tax-free strategy for putting people back to work. In Indiana, the Chamber of Commerce dubbed RTW "the single most important step Indiana lawmakers could take in putting more Hoosiers back to work," projecting that RTW would raise family income by nearly $12,000 per year—a far greater impact than policy analysts claim for any other economic development strategy.[33] The business-backed Michigan Freedom to Work coalition likewise forecast that, with RTW, "new businesses, manufacturing plants, and ... jobs will flow" into the state.[34] In Illinois, the local SPN affiliate declared that RTW would "save Illinois' middle class."[35]

Unfortunately, none of these claims are supported by economic data. The best economic evidence shows that, all else being equal, the impact of RTW laws is to lower wages by approximately 3 percent—for both union and nonunion employees—and to decrease the odds of getting health insurance or a pension through one's job. Despite cutting compensation, however, RTW has no impact whatsoever on job growth. Because the economic argument used to support these laws—that weakening unions makes for a more prosperous economy—also underlies a wide range of related policies, I will examine the claims of RTW proponents in some detail.

The Real-World Impact of RTW

Before showing what RTW statutes accomplish, it's important to clarify what they are. RTW has nothing to do with anyone's being forced to be a member of a union or to contribute to social or political causes one may oppose. Both those things are already illegal. What the law does allow is that if employer and employees agree, they may negotiate an agreement requiring all employees who benefit from the terms of a union contract to share in the costs of negotiating and administering it. RTW makes such clauses illegal. Because federal law requires unions to extend contract benefits to all employees in a workplace, RTW creates an incentive for employees to enjoy these benefits without contributing to the costs of achieving them.

When RTW laws are adopted, some number of employees stop paying dues—possibly out of antiunion animus but more likely simply because they can do so with no loss of benefits. It is common for a full-time union staff representative to be responsible for 1,000–1,500 employees—negotiating contracts, representing employees in grievance proceedings, filing OSHA complaints, organizing workers to protest or picket in support of contract demands, and building effective coalitions with community organizations around shared interests. If 20 percent of employees stop paying dues, the same staff person becomes responsible for representing that many more employees. This makes it harder to represent them effectively in contract negotiations or grievance hearings; as a result, even more employees may see reason to stop paying dues. In this way, RTW is less a cliff than a snowball—an ongoing downward trend toward poorer contracts, lower wages and weaker unions. Furthermore, if a labor organization is asked to help a group of employees organize a new union in their workplace, staff must weigh the likelihood that the new unit will someday contribute sufficient dues to repay the cost of the organizing effort. This is not an issue of profiting from organizing but simply of any organization's ability to continue operations over the long term. Labor unions overwhelmingly rely on employee dues for their operating income.[36] If the costs of organizing new workplaces are never recouped, a union will eventually be forced to shut its doors. Because RTW makes this a more difficult calculation, it also makes unions less likely to organize new workplaces in RTW states and this, over time, restricts the unionized share of the workforce. The most recent statistical study estimates that even in low-unionization states, the impact of RTW is to cut the share of workers who have unions by one-fifth.[37]

The premier research on the impact of RTW was conducted in 2011 by economists Elise Gould and Heidi Shierholz—who has since been appointed chief economist for the U.S. Department of Labor.[38] Gould and Shierholz controlled for forty-two separate factors, including the educational level and demographic makeup of a state's workforce, its relative concentration in major industry sectors and occupational groups, the degree of urbanization, and the relative cost of living across the states. Their analysis found that, other things being equal, the impact of RTW is to decrease wages by 3.2 percent—for both union and nonunion workers—while worsening the odds of getting health insurance through one's job by 3 percent and the chance of receiving employer-supported pension benefits by 5 percent.[39] It is noteworthy that these findings apply to nonunion as well as union employees. As discussed earlier, where unions are strong, they create competitive pressures that raise the pay of nonunion workers in the local labor market.[40] When unions are weakened, the process functions in reverse.

The fact that RTW lowers wages and benefits should not be surprising. On the contrary, this is its *purpose*. As the ALEC scholar Richard Vedder—author of multiple studies promoting RTW—explains, "unionization increases labor costs . . . [and thus] makes a given location a less attractive place to invest."[41] RTW is intended to solve this problem by weakening unions, lowering labor costs, and thereby attracting outside manufacturers into a state. This is how RTW is *supposed* to work; if it didn't lower wages, it wouldn't serve as an attraction for employers.[42] Thus, RTW entails a conscious strategy of lowering wages and benefits for both union and nonunion employees, pitched as a means of bringing more jobs into the state.

Unfortunately, however, while RTW succeeds at lowering wages and benefits, it has no impact whatsoever on job growth. The single most influential claim made by RTW proponents is the insistence that fair-share states are being "redlined" by companies that will locate only in states with RTW laws.[43] When Oklahoma debated RTW in 2001, the most important piece of testimony came from a site location consultant who reported that "when companies start looking for a relocation site, the second most important [criterion] they list is whether a state is a 'right-to-work' state. . . . If the answer is 'no,' then they won't even consider that state. This means that you are cut off from 90 percent of the relocating companies."[44] Likewise, Wisconsin Manufacturers and Commerce president Kurt Bauer claimed that "it is well known that site selectors who decide where businesses expand or relocate shun [fair share] states like Wisconsin."[45] Similar claims have been repeated in every state where RTW has been debated. None of the claimants, however, has ever provided data to support those assertions. Furthermore, while the thesis is everywhere voiced with great conviction, the actual claim of how many firms are influenced by RTW has varied wildly from one legislative debate to another. The share of companies who won't move to a fair-share state—supposedly based on feedback from a nationally representative sample of employers—was announced as 30 percent in New Mexico,[46] 30–40 percent in Indiana,[47] 50 percent in New Hampshire,[48] 60 percent in Missouri,[49] and 90 percent in Oklahoma.

The truth is that there are no data underlying any of these statements: all the numbers provided are the product of ideological conviction rather than empirical observation. When Indiana RTW sponsor Senator Jim Buck was asked, "Do you know of companies that have said 'no, thanks' to Indiana because we are not a Right to Work state?" Buck promised, "I can get you a list"—but no such list was ever produced by Buck or anyone else.[50]

In fact, the actual record of state economic development activity belies these claims. In 2012, the Indiana Economic Development Corporation (IEDC) compiled an analysis of all companies that state officials courted but did not succeed in recruiting over the preceding three years. Since nearly all of these decisions predated RTW, it is instructive to examine whether companies were avoiding Indiana because of its fair-share law. According to IEDC records, however, the vast majority of these companies either chose not to build anywhere or preferred another state's cash incentives or site infrastructure. Only 3 percent said their decision was related to labor availability or cost; there is no number at all reported for companies saying they stayed away because of fair share.[51]

The argument for RTW is further undermined by the very logic of market competition. RTW is typically promoted as a means for one state to gain a competitive advantage over its neighbors. Clearly, however, the more states adopt RTW, the less any of them enjoy an advantage. Thus, Indiana was urged to adopt RTW because, as the only RTW state in the upper Midwest, it would become a "magnet for job creation."[52] Shortly after Indiana enacted its law, however, corporate lobbyists set out to erase this advantage. Legislators in neighboring states were warned that if they remained fair share they risked watching their industrial base slip across the border. That is, the same supposed market advantage that was promoted to Hoosiers as the reason to adopt RTW was presented to neighboring states as a grave danger to be eliminated. In this way, corporate lobbyists played each state off against the other, urging the first to lower wages in order to lure jobs away from its neighbors and then insisting next-door states must cut their own wages to counteract this threat—resulting in lower wages and weaker unions on both sides of the border and no change in the relative draw of either locale. Ultimately, the same corporate lobbies that champion RTW in the states are simultaneously promoting a *federal* RTW law. If this effort succeeds, unions will be weaker and wages lower in every state, and no state will enjoy a competitive advantage.

In fact, the actual economic evidence regarding RTW is quite clear: the policy succeeds at weakening unions and lowering wages but has no impact on job growth.[53] The history of studies measuring RTW's impact on job growth entails successive efforts to separate out the impact of RTW laws from other factors that influence employment growth. Over time, as scholars have developed more exact statistical techniques, the measured impact of right-to-work laws has shrunk even smaller, with recent research finding they have no impact whatsoever.

One of the studies most commonly cited by corporate-funded think tanks is that of Thomas Holmes, who compared manufacturing employment on the borders of RTW and fair-share states over the period from 1947 through the mid-1990s. Using county-level data, Holmes found that when crossing into a right-to-work state from a fair-share state, one was likely to find both an increased share of employment concentrated in manufacturing and a higher growth rate for manufacturing employment. There are several shortcomings to Holmes's study, however.[54] Most important, he made no claim that RTW itself accounted for the differences he noted. Instead, he used right-to-work laws as a proxy for a wide array of other policies. "Right-to-Work states," Holmes explained, "historically have pursued a number of other smokestack-chasing policies, such as low taxes, aggressive subsidies, and even, in some cases, lax environmental regulations. Thus, my results do not say that it is right-to-work laws that matter, but rather that the 'pro-business package' offered by right-to-work states seems to matter."[55]

The history of successive RTW scholarship is a progression of using ever-more exact measures in order to accomplish what Holmes did not: distinguishing the impact of this one policy from other factors that shape state economies. Over the past decade, a series of academic studies have deployed increasingly sophisticated means of measuring RTW's impact on job growth. The more scholars are able to control for other factors, the clearer it becomes that these laws have little or no impact on job growth.[56]

In 2015, two of the nation's preeminent labor economists—Harvard's Richard Freeman and Rutgers University's Paula Voos—issued a policy brief that, while not advocating for or against RTW per se, provided a series of methodological guidelines for researchers studying the issue. Among other recommendations, they urged analysts to "consult the major, rigorous studies" done to date and take care that new studies "compare with what we know." Freeman and Voos identify five "recent RTW studies using sensible statistics and methodology" that they suggest taking as a framework of established knowledge against which new studies should situate their findings. These studies were undertaken by different authors working independently of each other and using different statistical methods, yet they all reached similar conclusions: other things being equal, the impact of RTW is to lower wages and benefits while having no effect on job growth.[57]

RTW in a Globalized Economy: Learning from Oklahoma

It's not clear that right-to-work laws, in themselves, have ever had a significant impact on employment growth. To the extent that they may have, however, that time is past. Globalization sets our economy fundamentally apart from what came before. Thus it may have been true in the 1970s or 1980s that companies were leaving the North or Midwest for the South and Southwest in search of cheaper labor. But the 1994 North American Free Trade Agreement (NAFTA) and the normalization of U.S.-China trade relations, coupled with China's entry into the World Trade Organization (WTO) in 2000–2001, marked a fundamental shift in the landscape of manufacturing location choices. When firms can relocate to countries where wages are 90 percent below U.S. levels, the fact that RTW lowers wages by 3 percent is simply not a significant draw. In the current economy, employers whose location decisions are determined by low wages are overwhelmingly moving to China or Mexico—not to RTW states within the United States.

For this reason, Oklahoma—the only state to have enacted an RTW law in the era of globalization and for which we have sufficient data to assess impacts—provides the most instructive case study for gauging the likely impacts of RTW in the current economy.[58] When Oklahoma adopted RTW in 2001, corporate lobbyists and allied officials made dramatic claims regarding the necessity of adopting RTW in order to safeguard the state's economic future. "Right to work is one of the single most important reforms our state can make," asserted the house Republican leader, Representative Fred Morgan. "Right to work will bring prosperity and promise to our state."[59] In fact, every prediction made about RTW in Oklahoma proved false. The law was promoted as a strategy for boosting manufacturing employment. Yet not only did manufacturing employment not grow dramatically, but, after increasing steadily over the previous ten years, it fell in every year during the decade after adoption of RTW.[60]

To provide the most sophisticated analysis of Oklahoma's experience, University of California economist Sylvia Allegretto constructed a statistical model based on Holmes's concept of comparing job growth in neighboring counties, one of which is RTW and the other fair share. From 1996 to 2006—five years before and after the adoption of RTW—Allegretto measured Oklahoma employment trends in manufacturing and in the economy as a whole, using an extensive data set that closely parallels the U.S. census.[61] Allegretto tested for this impact in nearly every way imaginable. She compared all the counties in Oklahoma with all counties in neighboring states and with all counties in the United States. She compared Oklahoma border counties, paired with adjacent counties in neighboring states. She tracked the shift in Oklahoma's relative performance for each individual year leading up to and following the adoption of RTW. No matter how the data were analyzed, the result was always the same: the adoption of RTW in Oklahoma had no positive impact whatsoever on employment. In every instance, the effect of the law was either statistically insignificant or, more often, significant and negative.[62]

As described above, the central claim of RTW proponents in Oklahoma was that the law would bring an increase of "eight to ten times" in the number of new companies coming into the state. As shown in figure 2.1, however, data from the state's Department of Commerce do not bear this prediction out.[63] Not only was there no dramatic increase in the number of new firms moving into the state, but the rate of new arrivals actually *decreased* following the adoption of right to work. In the decade preceding RTW, Oklahoma welcomed an average of forty-eight new firms per year, creating an annual total of nearly 6,500 new jobs. In the ten years following the state's adoption of RTW, however, the average number of jobs brought into the state was one-third lower (averaging 4,244 from 2001 to 2010) than when Oklahoma was a fair-share state.

The failure of RTW to attract employers to Oklahoma fits with what employers themselves say regarding location decisions. *Area Development* is the premier magazine of the site location consultant industry and is a thoroughly apolitical publication that takes no position on RTW or other policy issues. Each year, the magazine surveys small manufacturers, asking them to rank the factors that most influence their location decisions. Not only is RTW not the controlling factor in their decisions; it's not even close. In 2013 it was ranked twelfth in importance; indeed, in the preceding ten years of surveys, RTW never ranked among the top ten most important factors shaping location decisions.[64]

	Manufacturers		Service Industries		Total, Mfg & Services	
Year	Plants	Jobs	Facilities	Jobs	Facilities	Jobs
1990	62	2,461	15	795	77	3,256
1991	45	2,424	17	2,563	62	4,987
1992	50	3,066	11	1,717	61	4,783
1993	38	1,899	8	1,160	46	3,059
1994	45	4,211	21	4,917	66	9,128
1995	20	2,353	12	5,940	32	8,293
1996	37	1,926	23	5,612	60	7,538
1997	23	2,207	15	3,233	38	5,440
1998	24	1,399	19	3,797	43	5,196
1999	30	3,347	15	5,267	45	8,614
2000	13	1,806	18	6,055	31	7,861
2001	19	1,612	9	1,200	28	2,812
2002	23	1,865	8	1,510	31	3,375
2003	32	2,506	7	1,454	39	3,960
2004	24	2,629	12	3,841	36	6,470
2005	26	2,722	15	3,641	41	6,363
2006	30	5,106	12	2,251	42	7,357
2007	21	2,253	14	2,665	35	4,918
2008	9	388	7	1,855	16	2,243
2009	10	861	6	640	16	1,501
2010	16	1,657	19	1,780	35	3,437
Annual Average, Various Periods						
1991–2000	33	2,464	16	4,026	48	6,490
2001–2010	21	2,160	11	2,084	32	4,244
2001–2005	25	2,267	10	2,329	35	4,596
2006–2010	17	2,053	12	1,838	29	3,891

Source: Oklahoma Department of Commerce

Announced New and Expanded Manufacturers and Services, 2010 Annual Report, January 2011.

FIGURE 2.1.   Announced openings of new manufacturing and service facilities in Oklahoma, 1990–2010.

Following this accumulation of evidence, RTW advocates have, at long last, begun to hedge their claims. As Wisconsin's RTW debate got under way in 2015, the National Right to Work Committee spokesman, Stan Greer, conceded that "we're not purporting to prove that right-to-work produces superior economic performance."[65] Greer's is a dramatic admission after years of strenuous declarations to the contrary. Yet rather than signaling a retreat from RTW, concessions such as Greer's have simply served as an opportunity for supporters to pivot from economic to moral arguments.

Is "Right to Work" about Strengthening Workers' Rights?

When confronted with the facts of RTW's economic failure, proponents often fall back on an insistence that, economics aside, this is about freeing workers from the coercion of mandatory dues. "It's not just about . . . job growth," insisted Representative Eric Burlison, a Missouri RTW sponsor. "It's about giving individuals freedom."[66] But the suggestion that RTW boosters are driven by a concern for workers' rights flies in the face of the broader pattern of corporate behavior and advocacy. First, it is instructive that the requirement to pay union dues appears to be the only form of coercion from which corporate lobbies seek to liberate workers. When Oregon adopted a law protecting employees from being forced to attend political, religious, or antiunion meetings, for instance, the U.S. Chamber of Commerce joined the state's premier business lobby in suing to block the law from taking effect.[67] RTW backers, it seems, do not believe in a right to work free of forced political indoctrination; the only right they're committed to protecting is the right to withdraw support from independent workers' organizations.

Furthermore, unions are hardly unique in requiring membership dues. In most states, for instance, any attorney who wants to appear in court must be a dues-paying member of the bar association. One may dislike the bar association, disagree with its policies, or even oppose the very concept of a bar association—but must still pay dues if he or she wants to appear in court. Condominium or homeowners associations similarly require dues of their members. Home buyers can't choose to live in a condominium development but protest that their personal ethics prevent them from paying association fees. Yet the corporate lobbies pushing RTW are nowhere championing a "right to practice law" or "right to live" where one likes without forced dues. Even for libertarian-leaning organizations such as Americans for Prosperity or the Club for Growth, RTW is not part of a broader principle that individuals should not be required to pay fees in return for professional or personal benefits. There is no broader principle; the only organizations these lobbies seek to undermine are labor unions.

Indeed, unions in RTW states are the only organizations in the country that are required to provide all benefits for free and prohibited from requiring those who enjoy the benefit to pay their share of the costs of obtaining them. Non-dues-paying employees receive the same wages and benefits as union members. Furthermore, if a non-dues-paying employee has a problem at work, the union is required to represent her—including providing an attorney at no charge if one is needed—exactly as it would a dues-paying member.

Upon signing RTW into law, Rick Snyder, the governor of Michigan, described the statute in Orwellian terms. "It's really giving workers choice," he insisted. "This is just making it clear that unions need to show a value proposition to workers. And if they show that proposition, workers should be excited to join a union. . . . [I]f they don't see value, that could be a message to a union that they need to do new and innovative things to reinvent themselves to be more successful. All of us can win through this process."[68] But choosing whether to pay dues has nothing to do with whether one sees value in a union if the value is guaranteed and the dues optional. Indeed, if Snyder was genuine, he might seek the same success in state government that he offers unions—provide a good "value proposition" to citizens and see if they choose to voluntarily pay taxes in return for public services; if not—take that as constructive feedback than can help hone the state's services, ultimately making it a better state for everyone!

Most tellingly, employer associations and corporate lobbies themselves refuse to live by the same rules they seek to impose on workers. In Owensboro, Kentucky, the Building Trades Council resigned its membership in the local Chamber of Commerce but asked if it could continue to receive full member benefits despite no longer paying member dues. Absolutely not, answered the Chamber. "It would be against Chamber by-laws and policy to consider any organization or business a member without dues being paid. The vast majority of the Chamber's annual revenues come from member dues, and it would be unfair to the other 850+ members to allow an organization not paying dues to be included in member benefits."[69] The Chamber's logic is simple: if it had to provide all its services for free, with dues strictly optional, it would go out of business. This, then, is the true goal of RTW and the reason why economic evidence seems to have no impact on the conviction with which supporters promote this policy. It's neither about jobs nor about freedom. It's about stopping workers from having an effective voice in negotiating with their employers.

The Union Difference and the Rationale for RTW

To some, it may seem odd that RTW could represent such a critical priority for the corporate lobbies—even given their antiunion animus. After all, with only 7 percent of private-sector workers organized, it would seem that tax laws, trade treaties, tort reform, or even highway construction would have a greater impact on the private economy than state labor laws. Why, then, have corporate advocates prioritized RTW over these more traditional economic development policies?

In part, the answer to this question is political. The labor movement serves as the primary political counterweight to the corporate agenda on a long list of issues that are not per se labor-related. To the extent that unions can be removed as a politically meaningful force, the rest of the agenda becomes much easier to execute.

Beyond this, however, there is nothing more primary for employers' economic interests than maintaining control over the labor force. For more than a century, labor relations have stood at the absolute center of corporate political mobilization. The 1935 National Labor Relations Act, creating the federal right to collective bargaining, marked what the sociologist William Domhoff terms "the most consequential loss for the corporate community since it came of age in the 1870s and 1880s."[70] Forty years later, this view still held resonance. In the 1970s, it was the fight against labor law reform and a right to full employment that galvanized business political mobilization and led to the creation of the modern corporate lobbies.[71] In the decades since, the fights against striker replacement legislation under President Clinton and against labor law reform at the start of the first Obama administration each elicited the broadest and most aggressive political mobilization of corporations in their times.

The rise and decline of unions over the past century has had a profound impact on the country's distribution of income. Recent data suggest that deunionization is the single most important factor accounting for wage stagnation among the broad middle class (defined as the middle 60% of wage earners) (see figure 2.2).[72] One study calculates that if workers' share of national income had not declined after 1980, the average employee would have earned an additional $5,000 per year in 2007, before the onset of the recession. Furthermore, this massive transfer of income from workers to employers is correlated not with the rise of new technologies but with the decline of unions. "What we have," the sociologist Tali Kristal explains, "is a large decrease in labor's share of income and a significant increase in capitalists' share in industries where unionization declined, and hardly any change in industries where unions never had much of a presence. This suggests that waning unionization, which led to the erosion of rank-and-file workers' bargaining power, was the main force behind the decline in labor's share of national income."[73]

In the absence of unions, labor standards are being ratcheted downward, with degraded conditions becoming the norm in many industries. A growing number of national chain companies now compensate branch managers with bonuses that are dependent on keeping labor costs low.[74] As a result, poverty has become a condition not only of the jobless but increasingly also of low-wage workers. In 2014, 52 percent of all fast-food workers lived in families

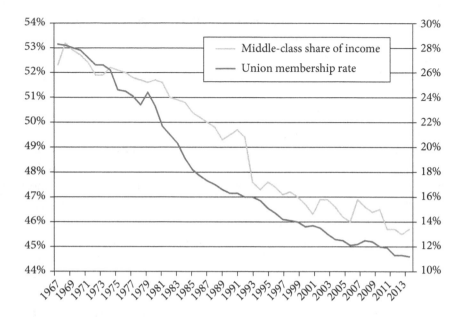

FIGURE 2.2. Middle-class share of income declines along with unionization, 1967–2013.

Source: Alex Rowell and David Madland, "New Census Data Highlight Why the Middle Class Needs Strong Unions," Center for American Progress, September 18, 2015, https://www.americanprogressaction.org/issues/labor/news/2015/09/18/121549/new-census-data-highlight-why-the-middle-class-needs-strong-unions.

that relied on some form of public assistance; the same is true for 48 percent of home-care workers.[75] The absence of paid sick leave has become so standard in low-wage industries that more than half of all food service workers now go to work when they're sick, for fear of losing income or losing their jobs.[76] Even professional employees have suffered setbacks in compensation standards. The percentage of recent college graduates who are provided health insurance through their jobs, for instance, has been cut in half over the past twenty-five years.[77]

In the aftermath of the Great Recession, the weakness of the labor market has emboldened employers to further downgrade job standards. In 2015, the National Federation of Independent Business posted an article for its member companies titled "Kissing Employee Raises Goodbye," reporting that coming out of the recession, "many businesses [are] forego[ing] the once-commonplace annual raise in favor of offering more bottom line-friendly benefits."[78] A leading human resources firm explains that "there is a quiet revolution in compensation," with the share of total payroll devoted to salary increases at an all-time low and a proliferation of free meals, gift cards, and birthdays off offered in lieu of raises.[79]

At the same time, employers responded to the recession by intensifying work quotas—and then retained these requirements as the new normal following the recovery. In 2013, the *Los Angeles Times* reported that

> in their zeal to make sure that not a minute of time is wasted, companies are imposing rigorous performance quotas, forcing many people to put in extra hours, paid or not. Video cameras and software keep tabs on worker performance, tracking their computer keystrokes and the time spent on each customer service call. Employers once wanted long-term relationships with their workers. At many companies, that's no longer the case. Businesses are asking employees to work harder without providing the kinds of rewards ... that were once routine. Employers figure that if some people quit, there are plenty of others looking for jobs. ... The Great Recession ... [has] enabled companies to offer less and demand more.[80]

Unions pose a fundamental challenge to all of this—not merely to the distribution of wages but also to the speedup of work expectations, the increased surveillance, the absence of internal ladders of promotion, and the substitution of token gestures for real rewards. By empowering employees at each work site to negotiate with management over the full range of policies that govern their working lives, unionization offers a unique vehicle for challenging the full complement of practices that have come to define the new norm of degraded labor standards. For the corporate lobbies, the prospect of such a challenge supersedes all other legislative concerns.

It is important to remember that while unions currently represent fewer than 7 percent of private-sector workers, the possibility of renewed organizing is ever present. Preventing a resurgence of union organizing is not a one-time act but, rather, requires ongoing vigilance on the part of employer organizations. In this regard, the current period of economic decline and increasing hardship is a double-edged sword. On one hand, increased insecurity makes employees more pliable and less likely to put themselves at risk by leading organizing drives in their own workplaces. At the same time, economic anxiety also increases the desire for the improved security that unions bring. Depending on which poll one believes, there are approximately thirty-five million nonunion workers who wish they had a union at their workplace.[81] For the corporate lobbies, the weakness of the labor movement can never be taken for granted but must be constantly reasserted. The gap between unionization rates in the public and private sectors illustrates the impact of systemic and continuous union repression in the private workplace.

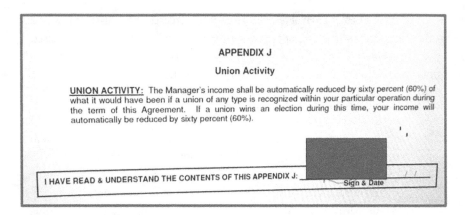

APPENDIX J

Union Activity

UNION ACTIVITY: The Manager's income shall be automatically reduced by sixty percent (60%) of what it would have been if a union of any type is recognized within your particular operation during the term of this Agreement. If a union wins an election during this time, your income will automatically be reduced by sixty percent (60%).

I HAVE READ & UNDERSTAND THE CONTENTS OF THIS APPENDIX J: _____
Sign & Date

FIGURE 2.3. Menards.

Employers are estimated to spend hundreds of millions of dollars per year on a network of attorneys and consultants who specialize in preventing private-sector employees from exercising their right to collective bargaining.[82] The decline of private-sector unions has been made possible only by continued devotion to this craft. Many of the most prominent corporations active in ALEC and similar organizations have been engaged in ongoing efforts to prevent their own employees from organizing.[83] Although the details of such efforts are typically hidden from public view, occasional leaks reveal the intensity of employers' dedication to keeping their firms "union free." In 2015, for instance, Menards—a major Midwest hardware retailer whose owners are prominent supporters of Governor Walker, participants in the Koch network of donors, and funders of the ALEC-affiliated Mackinac Center—required that all new managers, as part of their employee orientation, sign a document stating that their pay would be cut by 60 percent if employees organized a union (figure 2.3).[84] For these firms, RTW holds the prospect not just of winning one round of union avoidance but of permanently crippling the labor movement and dramatically reducing the risk of ever having to negotiate with organized employees. This—together with the imperative to remove unions as political opponents—is what makes RTW such a high priority.

Lowering Labor Standards in the Construction Industry

In addition to the right-to-work assaults on private-sector unions as a whole, the years following *Citizens United* brought a series of attacks aimed specifically at lowering labor standards in the construction industry. Construction plays a critical role in the U.S. labor market as one of the most important sources of skilled, decently paying jobs that do not require a college degree and that cannot be shipped abroad. In addition, construction is projected to be one of the fastest-growing industries during the coming decade, second only to health care.[85] Efforts to lower wages, benefits, and working conditions in this industry are likely to have far-ranging impacts for working- and middle-class communities across the country. The organizations representing antiunion construction owners and investors—including the Chamber of Commerce, Business Roundtable, and Associated Builders and Contractors—have sought for decades to lower wages and diminish workers' bargaining power in this industry.[86] The elections and fiscal crisis of 2010 provided a political opening to pursue these goals by outlawing or restricting the use of both project labor agreements and prevailing wage laws.

Project Labor Agreements

A project labor agreement (PLA) is a labor-management accord established at the start of large, complex construction projects involving multiple types of contractors, which sets the terms of employment for all contractors on the job. PLAs were first developed on the big public works projects of the 1930s. At Grand Coulee and Hoover Dams, project managers sought to avoid a potentially endless series of labor negotiations as one contract after another came up for renewal, causing expensive delays and generating a steady threat of strikes. The elegantly simple solution was to put all workers under a single, umbrella contract that was tailor-made for that specific project. Any contractor—union or nonunion—can work on projects under a typical PLA, as long as it abides by the established terms of employment. In recent years, agencies often negotiate concessions, such as no-strike clauses or reduced premium pay, as part of the terms of a PLA. The past two decades have also seen more than one hundred PLAs that include requirements for local hiring, establishment of local apprenticeship programs, and preferential job access for women and people of color.[87] PLAs are not limited to the public sector; a significant number of private corporations—including Boeing, Disney, Inland Steel, Toyota, ARCO, and Pfizer—have chosen to use PLAs because they see them guaranteeing high-quality craftsmanship and timely, safe, and cost-efficient construction.

Despite these advantages, the corporate lobbies are united in seeking to prohibit the use of PLAs in order to force down the level of compensation on publicly funded projects. Nineteen states passed laws outlawing or restricting the use of project labor agreements in 2011–15 (figure 2.4). PLAs have never been required by statute; rather, they are an available option that state agencies may

FIGURE 2.4.   Restrictions on prevailing wage and project labor agreements, 2011–15 (light, PLAs; dark, prevailing wage; striped, both).

choose to use if they deem it beneficial. Each of the bills passed, then, does not overturn a government mandate but, on the contrary, imposes one—prohibiting public agencies from using PLAs even where those responsible for the project might think it useful.

The Attack on Prevailing Wage Laws

Prevailing wage laws were first adopted by state legislatures in the late nineteenth and early twentieth centuries as a means of guaranteeing that publicly funded construction did not serve to undermine wage standards in local communities. Thirty-one states plus the District of Columbia now uphold some form of prevailing wage law. Such laws require states to survey construction employers, determining the wages and benefits provided for various skilled occupations. The typical rate for each occupation is deemed the "prevailing" wage for that local area. Publicly funded construction projects are then required to pay this wage to all workers employed on the project, union or not. Such laws thus create a level economic playing field between union and nonunion contractors, in which firms may compete based on project design, craft skill, or managerial acumen, but not by cutting wages.

Perhaps unsurprisingly, nonunion contractors whose primary competitive advantage lies in low wages have long advocated the repeal of such laws. Following the urging of corporate lobbyists, in 2011–15 nine states passed laws that significantly scaled back prevailing wage standards, ranging from complete repeal to restricting the law's coverage or revising the method of calculating mandated wage rates. In Louisiana, Arizona, Iowa, and Idaho—all states that have no prevailing wage laws—legislators adopted statutes proactively prohibiting cities, counties, or school districts within the states from adopting their own construction wage standards.[88]

The campaign to dismantle prevailing wages doubtless reflects nonunion contractors' desire to drive higher-wage competitors out of business. In addition, however, prevailing wages threaten to raise the economic expectations of the nonunion workforce. One conservative think tank explains that "many contractors who are paying market wages to their employees are reluctant to bid on public works construction projects. It is difficult to explain to an employee why he or she is making more money one day working on a public works project than the next day, doing exactly the same work on a private job."[89] The difficulty is doubtless increased by employees' realization that union workers get paid the higher wage every day of the year, while they—as soon as the public works project is over—are back to earning much less. By eliminating prevailing wage laws, nonunion employers may hope to muffle their own employees' demand for improved treatment.

The attacks on PLAs and prevailing wage are components in a broader effort to dismantle labor market protections for both union and nonunion employees in the construction industry—beginning with eliminating licensing requirements for electricians and plumbers. Licensing requirements limit the supply of skilled labor and enable licensed tradespeople to command higher wages. Thus, ALEC promotes the Professional Licensure and Certification Reform Act, which bans occupational licenses that "protect a particular interest group from economic competition."[90] The organization's Economic Civil Rights Act likewise argues that occupational licensing violates "the fundamental civil right" of "individuals to pursue a chosen business or profession" and prohibits all occupational licenses unless they are "demonstrably necessary . . . to fulfill legitimate public health, safety, or welfare objectives."[91]

Finally, the Associated Builders and Contractors and Associated General Contractors are both members of the U.S. Chamber of Commerce-sponsored Essential Worker Immigration Coalition (EWIC), which advocates for the right of construction contractors to import large numbers of temporary "guest workers" to serve as a low-wage construction workforce. In testimony before Congress, the EWIC specifically identified construction as one of the key industries in which, contractors claim, they cannot find enough American workers.[92] The danger of this proposal is not the presence of immigrant workers in the construction industry but the fact that immigrants would be forced to work under conditions of intimidation and without the job protections afforded citizens. The proposal favored by EWIC would import temporary workers with a visa not to the United States but to a specific employer—who could deport employees at will. Under such conditions, wages in the construction industry would be driven down by locking low-wage immigrants into a legal status under which they would be afraid to ever complain, write a letter to the editor, speak to a politician, organize a protest, or join a union; thus they would be more likely to accept wages and working conditions that citizens would not tolerate and in this way would serve to drive down labor standards across the industry.

Thus, as with RTW, it appears that the assault on union standards in the construction industry is not part of an agenda to improve life for nonunion workers but is rather the leading edge of an agenda that, if fully realized, would drive down labor standards for millions of both union and nonunion employees across this industry. What was portrayed in Wisconsin as a limited offensive against the overreach of unionized public employees turns out to be a much broader agenda that aims to remake the labor market for nearly all Americans.

REMAKING THE NONUNION ECONOMY

Across the country, the attack on public employee unions has been framed as an effort to help hard-working nonunion taxpayers in the private sector. Wisconsin governor Scott Walker famously justified his elimination of union rights by insisting that "we can no longer live in a society where the public employees are the haves and taxpayers who foot the bills are the have-nots."[1] Indeed, even the attacks on private-sector unions are often couched as a strategy for reining in union bosses who drive investment out of state, protect bad workers at the expense of good, and extort dues money from unwilling employees. The corporate lobbies argue that even in the private sector, unionized workers live undeservedly better than others by coercing employers into paying unjustifiably high wages, whose cost is borne by consumers in higher prices.[2] Cutting unions down to size would somehow—though the mechanism is not entirely clear—benefit the vast majority of Americans who have no union.

But what does the legislative record reveal about this argument? What are the corporate lobbies actually doing for hard-working nonunion taxpayers in the private sector? It appears that they are, in fact, doing everything possible to undercut wages, benefits, bargaining power and legal protections for nonunion workers, the same as for unionized employees.

For the 93 percent of private-sector employees who have no union contract, laws on matters such as wages and sick time define employment standards and rights on the job. The record of the past five years indicates that the national corporate lobbies have been engaged in a broad, ambitious, and relentless assault on the rights that govern the nonunion workplace. In 2011–15, twelve states passed laws restricting the minimum wage; four lifted restrictions on child labor; and nineteen imposed new limits on benefits for the unemployed. Following the lead of the corporate lobbies, states also passed laws stripping workers of overtime rights, repealing or restricting rights to sick leave, and making it harder to sue one's employer for race or sex discrimination and easier to deny employees' rights by classifying them as "independent contractors." This chapter provides an overview of the corporate assault on the laws that define labor standards for all those who work without the protection of a union contract.

Minimum Wage

There are few institutions that impact the lives of low-income workers more directly than the minimum wage. Because the federal minimum wage is not indexed to inflation, American workers endure wages significantly below those of their counterparts in past decades. In real terms, the federal minimum wage peaked in 1968; if that wage had kept pace with inflation, it would now be set at $10.93—50 percent above its actual level.[3] By 2011, more than one in four private-sector workers in America were working for less than the 1968 minimum wage.[4] Raising the minimum wage to $12.00 by 2020, as was proposed by congressional Democrats, would benefit nearly 38 million American workers—including nearly one-third of all women workers and almost 40 percent of all black and Latino workers—providing a total wage increase of over $100 billion per year.[5] The success of corporate lobbies, year after year, in defeating efforts to adjust the federal minimum wage for inflation, means that tens of billions of dollars per year that would have gone into workers' paychecks have instead gone into the pockets of business owners.

While the minimum wage has fallen behind the inflation rate, the costs of critical needs such as education and health care have increased even more steeply than overall inflation. As a result, the number of hours low-wage workers must toil in order to meet their basic needs has expanded to an untenable point. In 1979, for example, a college student would have to work 254 hours at minimum wage in order to pay one year's tuition at a public university; by 2010, an equivalent student would have had to work more than three times as long—923 hours—in order to achieve that same goal. A single parent earning minimum wage in 1979 needed to work 329 hours to pay for his or her family's health insurance policy; by 2010 the equivalent parent needed to work 2,079 hours—40 hours a week, 52 weeks a year—to pay for family health insurance, with not a dime left over for any other need.[6]

The inadequacy of current minimum wages is even more stark when compared with increases in worker productivity. Over the past five decades, productivity has steadily increased, and according to standard economic theory, wages should increase roughly on par with productivity. But in recent decades, wages have largely remained flat even while productivity and profits increased, as workers were increasingly unable to secure raises through either collective bargaining in the workplace or progressive measures in state legislatures. If the federal minimum wage had kept pace with productivity increases since 1968, it would now be triple its current value.[7]

Multiple academic studies show that states can increase minimum wages without risking job loss.[8] Furthermore, while a significant minority of low-wage workers are employed by small businesses that may be unable to afford improved compensation, nearly two-thirds work at corporations with more than one hundred employees.[9] At the fifty largest low-wage employers, profits rebounded quickly after the recession: executive compensation averaged $9.4 million in 2011, and firms returned nearly $175 billion to shareholders in dividends and share buybacks. Wal-Mart—the country's largest low-wage employer and a long-term participant in ALEC—remained profitable throughout the Great Recession, paying its CEO $18.1 million and spending $11.3 billion on dividends and share buybacks in 2011.[10]

Unsurprisingly, the minimum wage is one of the few areas of bipartisan consensus in the country. In 2015, 71 percent of voters—including 50 percent of Republicans and 76 percent of independents—supported increasing the minimum wage to $10.10.[11] Nonetheless, the corporate lobbies have fiercely opposed any increase in the minimum wage, and indeed, have sought every possible opportunity to lower existing minimum wages or to create loopholes that exempt employers from the requirements of the law.

ALEC promotes model legislation that calls for complete abolition of the minimum wage, arguing that such laws "represent an unfunded mandate on business by the government, and . . . make it difficult for small business . . . to hire new employees due to artificially high wage rates." The "forces of supply and demand," the bill's preamble insists, "are more capable than the government" of determining fair wages.[12]

For states that may not be ready to repeal the minimum wage, ALEC offers a model bill to block any increase in the wage rate, as well as a separate resolution opposing any attempt to link minimum wages to the CPI.[13] The resolution opposing inflation adjustment argues that "minimum wage is . . . an opportunity to learn valuable on the job training skills" that would be lost if the wage were adjusted upward for any reason and reasserts that "the best government policies to aid low wage workers . . . leave employers free to make wage decisions based on market conditions."[14]

Finally, ALEC calls on states to actively ban localities from adopting their own minimum wage standards. In many states, big cities are more progressive than the state as a whole. As a result, as of 2010, 123 cities or counties across the country had adopted ordinances mandating minimum wage, living wage, or prevailing wages higher than the state standard.[15] To combat such initiatives, ALEC's Minimum Wage Repeal bill abolishes any existing local minimum wage laws and forbids localities from enacting wage laws in the future.[16]

The U.S. Chamber of Commerce similarly opposes even the federal minimum wage, arguing that the law is "is counterproductive to job growth" and asserting that, as a matter of principle, "we don't think the government ought to be in the business of setting wages."[17] The Chamber likewise opposes any increase to the minimum wage[18] or any efforts by states or localities to set minimum wage rates higher than the federal.[19] Indeed, the Chamber's ranking of state employment policies marks down any state that doesn't actively prohibit localities from adopting living wage laws.[20]

Beginning in early 2011, a series of laws was adopted advancing this agenda. New Hampshire legislators repealed their state's minimum wage, overriding a gubernatorial veto.[21] Although the state already had the lowest minimum wage in New England, House Speaker (and ALEC member) Bill O'Brien argued that enforcing a minimum wage of any kind sent "exactly the wrong message to employers."[22]

Other states stopped short of outright repeal but took steps in that direction by enacting new exemptions or creating subminimum wages for new categories of workers. In a 2011 bill sponsored by Shantel Krebs, an ALEC member and the former house majority whip, and heavily promoted by the restaurant association, South Dakota repealed the minimum wage for much of its summer tourism industry, exempting any "amusement or recreational establishment" that operates for less than seven months out of the year.[23] After South Dakota citizens voted to raise the state's minimum wage in a 2014 referendum, the Retailers Association came back and, in 2015, successfully lobbied for new legislation—again, introduced by an ALEC member—that created a subminimum wage for youth employees.[24] In communication with its members, the association expressed particular pleasure that—unlike the state's regular minimum wage, which is indexed to inflation—this new subminimum rate "will NOT go up automatically every year."[25]

Maine made it easier for employers to classify workers as disabled and thus pay them a subminimum wage. Previously, disabled persons could apply for a state certificate permitting them to work for less than minimum wage for a period of one year. The new law allows employers, rather than employees, to apply for the certificate, provides certificates for multiple employees, and doubles the length of time employees can be paid subminimum wages. Further, rather than the state setting the subminimum wage, the new statute allows employers themselves to determine how disabled employees are and therefore how low a wage each deserves.[26]

In other states, the business lobbies tried but failed to advance legislation repealing or restricting state minimum wage laws—but these attempts serve as guideposts for an ongoing campaign that we should expect to see resurrected in coming years. Most tellingly, in Nevada, Missouri, and Arizona, corporate lobbyists sought to use their influence in the state legislature in order to undo the will of voters who, in previous ballot initiatives, had approved indexing their state minimum wage to the rate of inflation. In Nevada, the Retail Association joined the Las Vegas and Reno Chambers of Commerce in promoting a bill that would have removed minimum wage standards—previously established by popular referendum—from the state constitution.[27] In Missouri, the Chamber of Commerce and allied business organizations presented Republican leaders with a six-point plan that included capping minimum wage increases, overruling a 2006 referendum that linked minimum wage to the CPI.[28] In Arizona, 71 percent of voters supported a 2004 proposal indexing their state minimum wage, but in 2012 corporate advocates urged lawmakers to abolish this requirement. This time, despite the vocal support of the Restaurant Association, legislators were forced to relent when the move generated broad popular criticism.[29]

In other cases, corporate-backed lawmakers have simply refused to enforce laws already on the books. Wisconsin's minimum wage is set at the federal level, and Governor Walker has argued that increasing that level is a "job-killing agenda."[30] Yet the state's constitution includes a commitment—dating back over a century—that requires employers to pay a "living wage," defined as sufficient for an employee to "maintain himself or herself" in "reasonable comfort, reasonable physical well-being, decency, and moral well-being."[31] In the fall of 2014, one hundred Wisconsin employees filed complaints with the state Department of Workforce Development charging that their wages—for many, the minimum of $7.25 per hour—did not meet this standard. One waitress complained that she "often put off paying for my diabetes test strips because I can't afford them."[32] A hotel housekeeper likewise reported that she "couldn't buy both bread and hot dogs for my kids."[33] After the state rejected these claims, a coalition of labor and community organizations filed suit against the Walker administration for failure to enforce the law.[34] In response, Walker submitted a July 2015 budget bill—backed by Republican legislators and signed into law by the governor—that stripped the living-wage requirement from the state's constitution.[35]

Increasingly, the corporate lobbies have focused on exercising their influence in state legislatures to prohibit more progressive cities within the state from improving labor standards in their own jurisdiction. Indiana was the first to heed

ALEC's call and adopt legislation—strongly supported by the state Chamber of Commerce—that prohibits local governments from adopting a minimum wage higher than the state's.[36] In recent years, eight more states have followed suit, all banning local officials from the right to consider the types of policies already in place in more than one hundred localities.

Minimum Wage for Tipped Employees

The failure of minimum wages to keep pace with inflation has had particularly stark consequences for the 3.3 million Americans who work as waiters, waitresses, bartenders, and bussers. In 1966 the federal government established a subminimum wage for tipped employees, on the theory that tips would bring them up to the level of the standard minimum wage. At the time, the tipped wage was set at a level equal to 50 percent of the regular minimum. However, the tipped wage has been frozen—at $2.13 per hour—for twenty-five years, and is now equal to just 29.4 percent of the minimum wage.

Two-thirds of the country's tipped employees are female, and more than half are twenty-five years old or older.[37] How these employees are treated varies by state. In eighteen states, tipped workers are entitled only to the federal subminimum wage of $2.13 per hour. Twenty-five states have established a tipped wage that is below the regular wage but higher than the federal rate. Only seven states mandate that tipped employees be paid the regular minimum wage.

The economic impact of subminimum wages is dramatic for these employees and their families. The poverty rate for waiters and waitresses—who comprise the bulk of all tipped employees—is more than twice that of the workforce as a whole. Furthermore, the share of waitstaff in poverty rises in direct proportion to state wage laws. In states where waitstaff receive the full minimum wage, 10.2 percent are poor; in states with a tipped wage set somewhere between $2.13 and the federal minimum, waitstaff poverty is 14.4 percent; and in states that apply the federal subminimum wage of $2.13, waitstaff poverty stands at 18 percent.[38]

There is broad popular support for eliminating the subminimum wage for tipped employees; one 2015 poll found that 71 percent of Americans believe waiters and waitresses should be paid the normal minimum wage.[39] Yet corporate lobbies resist every attempt to move in this direction. On the contrary, two states have recently sought to *lower* the tipped minimum wage, while two others worked to redefine "tips" in ways that weaken employees' right to keep what they earn.

Legislators in both Arizona and Florida sought to lower their states' tipped minimum wage. Both states enforce tipped wages that are below the regular minimum wage but higher than the federal tipped rate; the object of legislators in both cases was to push tipped wages closer to the federal rate. Neither state presented evidence suggesting that the current wage levels create economic harm. On the contrary, the National Restaurant Association identified Arizona and Florida as two of the fastest-growing restaurant industries in the country.[40] In Florida, the Restaurant and Lodging Association worked with legislative allies to introduce a bill that would effectively cut the state's tipped minimum wage from $4.65 to $2.13.[41] The Restaurant Association protested that the state's $4.65 tipped wage was "just . . . very unfair," insisting that "it's just going to be a matter of time before the back of this industry breaks. Minimum wage is killing them."[42] Thus, with the avid support of both the Florida Chamber of Commerce and Associated Industries of Florida, the Restaurant Association set out to overturn both the voters' will and the state constitution.[43] While neither this bill nor Arizona's was ultimately enacted into law, they both provide a measure of how far employer associations may go to cut employee wages.

A different strategy was attempted in Wyoming and Maine, where legislators sought to revise the legal definition of wages in order to divert tip income away from employees and into the hands of their employers. In Wyoming, a bill cosponsored by a group of ALEC-affiliated legislators and backed by the Restaurant Association would have given employers the right to force employees to pool their tips.[44] While employees may have previously chosen to pool tips, this was done voluntarily on their own initiative. In many restaurants, bussers who are legally considered tipped employees in fact receive little if any tip income.[45] As a result, employers are required to pay them the regular minimum wage. By forcing more highly tipped waitstaff to pool earnings, employers may avoid this obligation—essentially cutting the take-home pay of waitstaff by making them pay the bussers' wages, with employers pocketing the difference as increased profits.

In 2011, Maine legislators adopted a new law declaring that "service charges" do not legally constitute tips and therefore that they are not the property of waitstaff but may be taken by the employer.[46] The statute—sponsored by an ALEC member and supported by the Restaurant Association—does not require restaurants to notify customers that servers do not receive the service charge; many patrons likely believe this charge constitutes the gratuity and therefore provide little if any additional tip.[47] As in Wyoming, then, the Maine law constitutes a direct transfer of income from employees to owners, accomplished through simple political power.

Finally, Montana's legislature passed a law that—while maintaining a subminimum wage for tipped employees—nevertheless mandated that tips could *not* be counted as wages for purposes of workers' compensation claims. This law—strongly supported by the Restaurant Association and the Montana Chamber of Commerce but ultimately vetoed by the state's Democratic governor—would thus have allowed employers to pay subminimum wages on the grounds that tips constitute wages and then, if employees were injured, insist that tips not be counted when calculating workers' lost wages.[48]

Wage Theft

While low wages pose a critical problem, millions of Americans face an even more elemental challenge: the inability to obtain even those wages they have legally earned. The country is suffering an epidemic of wage theft, as large numbers of employers violate minimum wage, overtime, and other wage and hour laws with virtual impunity.

A landmark multicity study in 2009 revealed alarming patterns of illegally withheld earnings. Fully 64 percent of low-wage workers have some amount of pay stolen out of their paychecks every week, including 26 percent who are effectively paid less than minimum wage. Fully three-quarters of workers who are due overtime have part or all of their earned overtime wages stolen by their employer. In total, as of 2009 the average low-wage worker lost a stunning $2,634 per year in unpaid wages, representing 15 percent of their earned income.[49] Indeed, the amount of money stolen out of employees' paychecks every year is greater than the combined total of all the bank robberies, home robberies, gas station robberies, and convenience store robberies in the country (figure 3.1).[50] It is hard to imagine a more fundamental need of hard-working, low-wage Americans than simply rigorously enforcing the wage laws that are already on the books.

Enforcement of wage and hour laws has long been strikingly lax. When the federal minimum wage law was first established in 1941, there was one federal workplace inspector for every 11,000 workers. By the end of the Bush administration in 2008, the number of laws inspectors were responsible for enforcing had multiplied significantly, but the ratio of inspectors to workers was more than ten times worse, with 141,000 workers for every federal enforcement agent.[51] By 2012—even after the Obama administration added nearly three hundred new enforcement staff members—the number of federal workplace investigators was such that the chance of an average employer's being investigated in a given year was just one one-thousandth of 1 percent.[52]

Budget cuts have exacerbated this crisis even further at the state level. A majority of states have reduced the number of staff dedicated to wage and hour enforcement.[53] In most, this has been a consequence of across-the-board budget cuts, but in some cases enforcement of workplace laws has been singled out for

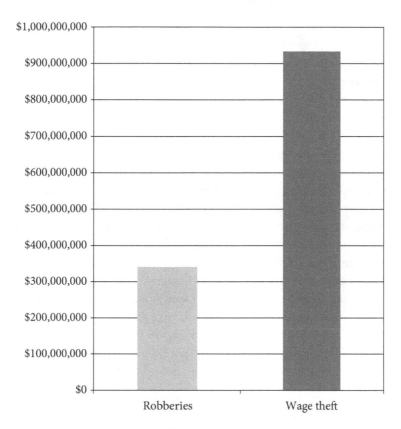

FIGURE 3.1. Wage theft compared with combined total of bank, home, street, gas station, and convenience store robberies, 2012.

Source: Brad Meixell and Ross Eisenbrey, "An Epidemic of Wage Theft Is Costing Workers Hundreds of Millions of Dollars A Year" (Economic Policy Institute Issue Brief No. 385, September 11, 2014), http://www.epi. org/publication/epidemic-wage-theft-costing-workers-hundreds. Wage theft value is from EPI survey of federal and state departments of labor. Robberies value is from Federal Bureau of Investigation, *Crime in the United States 2012,* Table 23: "Offense Analysis," http://www.fbi.gov/about-us/cjis/ ucr/crime-in-the-u.s/2012/ crime-in-the-u.s.-2012/tables/23tabledatadecoverviewpdfs/table_23_offense_analysis_number_and_ percent_ change_2011-2012.xls.

defunding. The U.S. Chamber of Commerce opposes the very notion of state-level labor enforcement as "duplicative . . . requirements . . . [that] complicate an employer's human resources functions," and judges states with no labor enforcement staff to embody a superior business climate.[54] In this vein, Ohio's General Assembly voted to completely eliminate funding for labor inspectors in 2011, leaving no staff to enforce state minimum wage, overtime, child labor, or prevailing wage laws. Funding was partially restored by the state's Controlling Board, but even so, the state was left with only six inspectors for the entire workforce.

A seventh inspector was slated to begin work later in 2011, at which point each agent would have responsibility for enforcing the rights of 616,000 private-sector workers. Yet in that same year, the Ohio House adopted a budget that would cut the workplace enforcement budget by a further 25 percent.[55]

The Missouri house speaker and ALEC member Steven Tilley likewise called for the complete elimination of funding for his state's nine labor investigators.[56] In 2010, Missouri's Department of Labor collected $500,000 in restitution for prevailing-wage violations and issued 1,714 citations for child-labor violations.[57] Tilley charged that investigators were being "overzealous," particularly in prosecuting complaints of employers cheating on prevailing wages.[58] Ultimately, Tilley compromised with the state's Democratic governor, and the adopted budget eliminated only two of the nine investigators rather than the entire staff.[59] In either case, meager enforcement staff means that there is little meaningful protection for employees' rights under law.

Indeed, because the enforcement mechanisms are so paltry and the penalties for stealing wages are generally so modest, even employers who have been found guilty and forced to pay penalties for wage theft often choose to continue the practice. One U.S. Department of Labor investigation found that more than two-thirds of employers who had previously been found to have broken wage and hour laws continued to operate in violation of the law.[60]

The Battle over Wage Theft Ordinances

The Progressive States Network—a national organization of state legislators—has identified the key elements of effective policy for combating wage theft. These include requirements that employers keep detailed pay records and allow employees to receive an itemized explanation of how each paycheck is calculated; the right of state authorities to inspect employers' records; workers' private right of action to sue for unpaid wages as individuals or in class actions; protection of complainants against retaliation by their employers; and the provision of attorney fees, damages, and penalties as part of the enforcement process.[61] The corporate lobbies, in turn, have been working hard to prohibit just such enforcement mechanisms. In 2011–12, these efforts came to a head in Florida.

A recent study from Florida International University estimates that $60–$90 million per year is stolen out of Florida workers' paychecks.[62] Yet since Florida's legislature abolished the state's Department of Labor in 2002, there are no state enforcement personnel to combat this problem.[63] Further, the state attorney general has failed to bring a single case of wage theft in recent years. Thus the only means for seeking enforcement under current law is for employees to turn to the Legal Aid Society, which relies entirely on volunteer attorneys.[64]

In 2010, Miami-Dade County responded to this crisis by instituting the nation's first broad municipal wage theft law. Enforcement is carried out by the Department of Small Business Administration through a streamlined process similar to small claims courts; employers pay the costs of county hearings—making enforcement costless to taxpayers—and employees are entitled to recover up to double damages. In its first year, the county prosecuted over six hundred claims of stolen wages and recovered over $1.7 million in illegally withheld pay.[65] On the basis of this success, Broward County adopted a similar statute, and the model seemed poised to spread across the state.

Almost immediately following the adoption of the Miami-Dade ordinance, however, business lobbies began pushing legislators to overturn the ordinance and prohibit other localities from adopting similar laws. The Florida Retail Federation filed a lawsuit—ultimately rejected by the court—arguing that the wage theft ordinance was unconstitutional.[66] At the same time, business lobbyists set out to prevent new counties from taking action.

In 2011, Palm Beach County debated establishing a system similar to that of Miami-Dade. It took up this proposal in response to the evident failure of its existing employer enforcement system: in one five-month period in 2011, Miami-Dade had recovered 46 percent of the disputed wages brought to its attention; by comparison, Palm Beach County, relying on legal aid volunteers, had recovered only 2.5 percent.[67] Yet business lobbyists fought vigorously against the adoption of the Miami-Dade model, with Florida Retail Federation spokeswoman Samantha Padgett arguing that "in these economic times it doesn't encourage business development to add additional regulations."[68] At the end of 2012, county commissioners sided with business lobbyists and rejected the proposed ordinance in favor of an alternative scheme, promoted by the Business Forum and Associated Builders and Contractors, that simply provides legal aid $125,000 per year to respond to wage theft using volunteer attorneys.[69]

The years since have seen a series of battles at the county and municipal level, with two counties and the city of St. Petersburg adopting wage theft regulations and the business lobbies in every case seeking to limit or weaken regulations. To a large extent, local debates have come to revolve around the relative merits of the Miami-Dade versus Palm Beach models. When Hillsborough County (Tampa) debated the issue in 2015, the business community pushed hard for a Palm Beach model of simply subsidizing legal aid to handle complaints. It is instructive that as of that debate, Miami-Dade had spent just $55,000 per year and had resolved 12 percent of its complaints, restoring $800,000 in stolen wages, in the previous year, while Palm Beach spent more than twice as much and had resolved fewer than 1 percent of its cases, recovering just $100,000 in stolen wages.[70] Thus corporate advocates lobbied for a more expensive system that accomplished less rather than a cheaper one that made it easier for workers to hold their employers accountable to the law.

While local employer associations fought the Palm Beach ordinance, their statewide organizations pursued legislation that would repeal existing wage theft ordinances and prohibit similar measures in the future. A 2012 bill—avidly supported by the Chamber of Commerce, Retail Federation, and other business lobbies—stipulated that "a county, municipality, or political subdivision of the state may not adopt or maintain in effect any law, ordinance, or rule that creates requirements, regulations, or processes for the purpose of addressing wage theft."[71] The legislation passed in the house of representatives but was not ultimately adopted into law, and corporate lobbies received widespread criticism for the effort.[72] Nevertheless, this remains a priority of the state's business organizations; in 2014, the Chamber of Commerce again lobbied for a bill banning local wage theft ordinances.[73]

As the problem of wage theft has gained increased national attention, efforts to address the problem have been launched by local activists—and opposed by corporate lobbyists—in a growing number of states. In January 2013, the city of Memphis debated adopting its own wage theft ordinance—opposed by the local Chamber of Commerce as "a shakedown operation for attorneys."[74] Two months later, state legislators preempted Memphis by adopting a Chamber-backed bill that replicated the exact language rejected in Florida, prohibiting all local laws regulating wage theft.[75] The bill—celebrated by the NFIB as a "victory"[76]—was sponsored by two ALEC members.[77] Another legislator explained that "we need to not only protect the wage earner, we need to protect the wage supplier—the employer."[78] In 2015, Michigan followed Tennessee's lead and became the second state to prohibit local governments from regulating wage theft, in a bill avidly supported by the state Chamber of Commerce, Association of Manufacturers, and NFIB.[79]

In opposing local ordinances, business organizations often argue that county-by-county laws create regulatory havoc for statewide businesses. But these same organizations are no less assiduous in opposing statewide solutions to the problem. In Iowa, the National Federation of Independent Business celebrated the defeat of a statewide wage theft bill as one of the year's "biggest wins," explaining that increased enforcement against "non-payment and underpayment of wages, violation of tipping laws, unauthorized or illegal paycheck deductions, and incorrect classification of employees to avoid paying minimum wage and overtime . . . would have burdened small business owners with mounting regulations and paperwork."[80] So too in California, after a study found that only 17 percent of wage theft claims were ever paid, lawmakers proposed new legislation in 2014 that would allow liens to be placed against the property of a business accused of wage theft until the claim was resolved. The Chamber of Commerce denounced the bill as a "jobs killer" and issued a declaration of opposition signed by dozens of business organizations, including the NFIB, Grocers Association, Hospital Association, Hotel and Lodging Association, Landscape Contractors Association, Restaurant Association, Retailers Association, and Construction Employers' Association.[81] With this full-court corporate press, the bill failed.[82]

Thus, corporate lobbies are working strenuously to deny employees any easy mechanism—whether at the local or state level—for ensuring they receive even those wages they have legally earned. ALEC's Economic Civil Rights Act insists that all Americans have a fundamental "right to earn an honest living," and it invokes this right as an argument against licensing requirements for plumbers and electricians.[83] But if the right to earn an honest living means anything, it must include the right to be paid what you earn. Faced with evidence of widespread threat to this most fundamental right, however, ALEC is silent.

Child Labor

In the 2012 presidential debates, candidate Newt Gingrich famously criticized child labor laws as "stupid" and specifically called for schools to replace unionized custodians with lower-wage student employees.[84]

Idaho was the first state to make Gingrich's vision reality when it adopted a law allowing kids as young as twelve to be employed for up to ten hours per week doing cleaning and other manual labor around their schools. In the Meridian district—which championed the new law—spokesman Eric Exline touted the program as a means of saving money by avoiding having to hire adults, and of teaching middle school students the valuable "job skills" that "you have to be on time [and] you have to do what you're asked, what your supervisor is telling you."[85]

Wisconsin focused on older students—aged sixteen and older—but enacted much more sweeping legislation, abolishing all restrictions on the number of hours minors are permitted to work during the school year. Previously, sixteen- and seventeen-year-olds could not work more than five hours a day on school days, and not more than six days in a row. Despite substantial evidence that increased workloads make it more difficult for students to concentrate in school, the new law frees sixteen- and seventeen-year-olds to work an unlimited number of hours per week, seven days a week, throughout the school year.[86] The bill's passage was celebrated by the Wisconsin Grocers Association, which explained that grocers are not "trying to overwork these kids or create a sweatshop," but "just want to give kids that great first opportunity you get in a grocery store."[87]

Maine followed in Wisconsin's footsteps, if not going quite so far. Legislators adopted a law that—with the strong support of the Maine Restaurant Association— expands the number of hours high school students can work from four to six per school day and from twenty to twenty-four per school week.[88] One of the bill's sponsors explained that students "could get home from school at 3:00 and could work from 4:00–9:00. They'd still have plenty of time for homework. Most of these kids are generally up well past 10:00. They could work a 3:00–9:00 shift."[89] Indeed, this legislator suggested that the very concept of child labor codes might be objectionable. "Kids have parents," insisted Representative Bruce Bickford. "It's not up to the government to regulate everybody's life and lifestyle. Take the government away. Let the parents take care of their kids."[90]

Michigan likewise increased, from fifteen to twenty-four, the number of hours students may work during a school week.[91] The bill, sponsored by the house majority leader, was championed by a wide range of corporate lobbies and low-wage employers' associations, including the Chamber of Commerce, Small Business Association, NFIB, Grocers Association, Lodging and Tourism Association, Licensed Beverage Association, and Association of Home Builders.[92] Perhaps most outspoken was the Michigan Restaurant Association, which, despite a statewide unemployment rate of 10.6 percent, told legislators that "many restaurants cannot find enough adult labor to fill available positions" and need the teenagers to stay afloat.[93]

While Idaho, Wisconsin, Michigan, and Maine are the only states to have actually passed legislation rolling back child labor protections, similar proposals were advanced in a variety of other states, including Missouri, where the state senator and ALEC board member Jane Cunningham proposed allowing children of any age to work unlimited hours and removing the state's authority to inspect children's working conditions.[94] Thus the corporate lobbies are actively working to promote longer work hours for youth, and to use this labor force to undermine wage standards for adult employees. Unsurprisingly, like the construction industry, many of those advocating for expanded youth work hours—including the Restaurant Association, Hotel and Lodging Association, and Association of Home Builders—are also urging the federal government to allow them to import increased numbers of low-wage guest workers.[95]

Overtime

While expanding the use of low-wage teenaged labor, employers have also sought to limit the provision of overtime wages for adult staff. In several states, corporate lobbies sought to undo legal requirements to pay overtime rates for employees working more than forty hours per week.[96]

Maine stripped away truck drivers' right to overtime pay, as long as companies pay them on a nonhourly basis.[97] For drivers, overtime pay is not only a critical source of income but also an important brake on the incentive to operate extreme shifts. By contrast, the new law—sponsored by an ALEC legislator who also opposed the minimum wage—provides an incentive to pay drivers per load delivered or mile driven, which in turn may encourage them to push themselves to unsafe limits of endurance.[98]

In Nevada, one of the few states that still require overtime pay for employees who work more than eight hours per day, business lobbyists sought to repeal this right.[99] The bill, cosponsored by four ALEC-affiliated senators, did not ultimately become law.[100] It did, however, receive vocal support from Chamber of Commerce officials, who noted that the U.S. Chamber of Commerce had graded Nevada's employment law "very poorly," in part because it required overtime after eight hours' work. Abolishing the right to daily overtime, the Las Vegas Chamber argued, "would significantly aid both employers and employees in achieving efficient and flexible scheduling."[101] Though this initiative was not adopted into law, it helps identify the goals that corporate lobbies continue to pursue. So too at the federal level, when the Obama Labor Department announced plans to reverse Bush administration rules that denied overtime rights to millions of white-collar workers, the U.S. Chamber of Commerce fought strenuously against the proposal, ridiculing the notion that government "knows best . . . how much employees should be paid."[102]

Misclassification of Employees as "Independent Contractors"

One of the most common means by which employment standards are lowered or evaded is the reclassification of employees as "independent contractors"— often leaving employees ineligible for unemployment insurance or workers' compensation, and removing them from minimum wage, overtime, and labor law protections. It is common for employers to inaccurately and illegally declare employees to be contractors. A 2000 study by the U.S. Department of Labor, for instance, found that between 10 and 30 percent of audited employers misclassified workers.[103] In many states, there is no mechanism for workers to challenge their boss's designation except for filing unemployment or workers' compensation claims—meaning one must be fired or injured before there is any legal avenue for contesting one's status.[104] In some industries, misclassification has become so commonplace that well-meaning employers are under pressure to wrongly classify their own employees in order to not be undercut by less ethical competitors.[105]

States vary in their legal tests for distinguishing between employees and independent contractors, but the most common standard is known as the "ABC test." By this definition, a person must satisfy three tests to be deemed an independent contractor:[106]

- No outside party controls or directs one's work, either on paper or in fact;
- The service one provides is either outside the normal type of work that the client performs or outside the normal geographic area where the client performs services; and
- The individual is genuinely engaged in an independent business, often measured by the fact that the contractor works for more than one client.

National corporate lobbies are dedicated to dismantling this definition in order to make it easier to classify employees as contractors. ALEC's Independent Contractor Definition Act, for example, eliminates two of the three traditional criteria: it allows independent contractors to do work that is a standard part of the employer's work and allows them to work for one employer only.[107]

The U.S. Chamber of Commerce likewise urges states to give employers wide leeway in determining employment status. The Chamber's national ranking of state employment policy grades states on "the strength of acceptance of the independent-contractor relationship," with the highest scores reserved for states that allow employers free rein in classifying the workforce as they see fit.[108] Colorado, by contrast, was graded poorly for its "presumption of employee status" and for having "created a complaint process for workers who believe they have been misclassified as independent contractors."

Both Maine and New Hampshire have taken steps to put the ALEC and Chamber of Commerce philosophy into law. Until 2010, the Maine statute had maintained the traditional "ABC" test. In 2012, however, the state adopted a new test, which eliminates the requirements that a contractor work for more than one client and perform work outside the core functions of the firm.[109] The new law was championed by both the Maine Chamber of Commerce and the National Federation of Independent Business.[110] New Hampshire likewise adopted a law weakening the standards required before one can be classified an independent contractor. Under previous law, one had to set one's own price, provide the primary tools of the job, pay for work-related expenses, and derive one's income from the difference between the price charged and the expenses incurred. In a 2012 law praised by the National Federation of Independent Business and deemed "one of the year's most important" measures by the *New Hampshire Business Review*, all these requirements were abolished.[111]

Sick Leave

Apart from wages, one of the most fundamental labor standards shaping work life is the ability to stay home in the event of illness without fear of termination. Nearly forty million workers—almost 40 percent of the country's private-sector workforce—currently have no right to even a single day of paid sick leave.[112] These employees commonly go to work sick, or leave sick children home alone, out of fear of dismissal. Even if they are not terminated, the loss of pay they suffer takes a dramatic toll—particularly since jobs without sick pay are concentrated among low-wage workers. Thus, a typical family of four with two working parents who have no paid sick leave will have wiped out its entire health care budget for the year after just three days of missed work.[113]

In the absence of federal action to address this problem, states and cities have begun to fashion their own solutions. San Francisco established the first local right to paid sick leave in a 2006 referendum. Five years later, the law appears to have been an enormous success in allowing workers to care for themselves and their families—and contrary to the predictions of business lobbyists, there is no evidence of employees having misused their newfound rights.[114] In the years since, multiple evaluations have reached similarly positive conclusions.[115] By 2015, four states and nineteen cities had established a right to some minimal level of paid sick leave.[116]

Yet corporate lobbies remain adamantly opposed to such legislation, with the U.S. Chamber of Commerce arguing that a legal right to paid sick leave would "interfere with an employer's ability to maintain a reliable, stable workforce, and . . . exacerbate well-documented employee misuse of [medical leave laws]."[117] Corporate lobbyists have conducted vigorous battles at the city level.[118] Their primary strategy, however, has been to deny city councils—or residents—the right to even vote on this question. In 2011, the Wisconsin legislature preemptively banned any locality from establishing sick leave policies that are more generous than the state's (which provides no right to paid sick leave whatsoever) and, in an effort supported by Wisconsin Manufacturers and Commerce, retroactively abolished the right to sick leave that had been established in the city of Milwaukee, approved by 68 percent of voters in a 2008 referendum.[119] Shortly after its passage, this law was touted by ALEC activists and soon became a model promoted in other states. As with minimum wage laws, the battle over the right to paid sick leave has become a contest between the power of public opinion in large cities and that of corporate lobbies in state legislatures. In Michigan, the Chamber of Commerce warned its membership that "mandatory paid leave initiatives are sweeping the country. . . . We need to get ahead of this issue."[120] Following

Wisconsin, twelve additional states have adopted statutes that make it illegal for cities or counties within their borders to create a right to paid sick leave—whether by council vote or citizen referendum.[121] This series of bills, often introduced by ALEC members, were promoted by a broad range of corporate lobbies, including Chambers of Commerce, the NFIB, Associations of Manufacturers, Americans for Prosperity, Associated Builders and Contractors, and many state restaurant associations. Voicing a common refrain, the Arizona NFIB framed the problem as "Big Labor and their allied pressure groups [seeking] to impose . . . benefits . . . in municipalities controlled by the Left," arguing that such "job killing" laws "create a serious drag on economic development."[122]

Thus employer associations and corporate lobbyists have sought not only to lower the wages of nonunion employees but also to forestall the possibility of improving job standards through local democratic action.

Workplace Safety Standards

Just as Republicans used their newfound majorities to roll back union rights, so too they worked to scale back regulations governing workplace safety and health. In Michigan, the legislature adopted a package of bills—supported by the Chamber of Commerce, NFIB, and Michigan Manufacturers Association—that make it nearly impossible for state authorities to issue any workplace safety regulation that is more strict than existing federal OSHA rules.[123] Michigan specifically prohibited state authorities from issuing any regulation protecting workers from repetitive motion injuries—a position strongly supported by the Chamber of Commerce, Restaurant Association, and NFIB.[124] In recent years, the dangers of repetitive motion injuries—which had not been understood at the time the initial OSHA regulations were adopted forty years ago—have been widely documented. It is estimated that twenty-eight thousand Americans a year suffer repetitive motion injuries on the job, with a majority losing more than twenty days of work as a result.[125] The business lobbies, however, have fought to restrict job protections to those dangers that were known at the time of OSHA's creation in the 1970s.

Michigan's bill follows ALEC model legislation, which argues that "state ergonomic regulations would place businesses . . . at a competitive disadvantage to businesses in other states."[126] This, of course, is a problem that could easily be solved by adopting ergonomic safety standards at the federal level. However, ALEC is also on record opposing federal OSHA ergonomic standards—on the grounds that federal OSHA should leave such issues to "the purview of the state legislative and administrative bodies."[127] Thus, at any level of government, the corporations funding ALEC are hard at work seeking to block any expansion of workplace safety protections despite the widely documented costs of such injuries.

Meal Breaks and Weekends

The assault on labor standards has extended even to the right to meal breaks on the job and rest on the weekend. In its ranking of state "pro-growth" employment policies, the U.S. Chamber of Commerce gives demerits for states that maintain legally required meal or rest breaks.[128] In 2012, the New Hampshire House of Representatives voted to repeal the requirement that employees be granted a thirty-minute (unpaid) meal break after five consecutive hours of work.[129] The bill's advocates suggested that the requirement constituted unnecessary over-regulation. In reality, even in states that do require meal breaks, it is not unusual for employers to violate this right. In 2005, for example, Wal-Mart was found to have illegally denied lunch breaks to 116,000 current and former employees and was forced to pay restitution totaling $57 million in unpaid wages.[130] A 2008 survey found that 69 percent of low-wage workers who were entitled to meal breaks were denied part or all of their break time.[131] Nevertheless, the Chamber of Commerce spoke approvingly of the New Hampshire legislation.[132]

In 2013, Arizona became the first state to prohibit local governments from establishing a right to meal or rest breaks, as part of a broader bill preempting local minimum wage or sick leave standards.[133] The bill—introduced by an ALEC member—was strongly supported by both the NFIB and the Restaurant Association, whose lobbyist argued that such "mandates ... do not consider the unique scheduling conflicts of the restaurant industry."[134]

In 2015, Wisconsin legislators and Governor Walker adopted a proposal—which legislators reported was originally brought to them by the state's premier business lobby—to do away with the statutory right to one day's rest per week.[135] Under previous law, employees could not work seven days in a row without a day off. Rather than a right guaranteed under law, the corporate lobbyists argued that rest days "should be a decision exclusively between the employer and employee."[136] The new law—whose sponsors included four ALEC members—states that employees may "voluntarily" waive this right.[137] "We're excited about this new freedom for workers," exclaimed a representative of Wisconsin Manufacturers and Commerce, which joined the Grocers Association in promoting the law.[138] In a nonunion workplace, however, the notion of "voluntarily" waiving one's rights has little meaning. For instance, employers may decree that extra hours, preferred shifts, or even promotions to higher pay will go first to those who volunteer to forgo a day of rest. Since the law provides no protections against this type of coercion, employees who gave up their rest day under threat of economic penalty would still be considered to have volunteered.

Employment Discrimination

Alongside efforts to undermine wage and benefit standards, employer lobbies have also launched a policy offensive aimed at limiting the ability of employees to protect themselves against race, sex, and other forms of illegal discrimination on the job. While such discrimination remains illegal in every state, corporate representatives have sought to erect a series of barriers making it increasingly difficult to prove charges of discrimination and restricting potential penalties for those employers found guilty of discrimination.

The U.S. Chamber of Commerce has long opposed legislation that would allow employees to prove discrimination based on an employer's track record of hiring and promotion, rather than requiring proof of individual supervisors' specific intent to discriminate. Indeed, the Chamber's state rankings give superior scores to states with the most restricted rights to sue and the most modest penalties for employers found guilty of discrimination.[139] Both the Chamber and the NAM opposed federal pay equity laws for women, with the NAM arguing that such rights would "open the floodgates to unwarranted litigation against employers."[140] In a similar vein, ALEC promotes model legislation opposing comparable-worth laws—which require that female-dominated occupations be paid the same as similarly skilled but traditionally male jobs. "A government mandate such as Comparable Worth," ALEC insists, "artificially drives up the costs of engaging in economic activity [and] invariably constricts job creation."[141]

Both organizations vigorously oppose statutes that allow victims of discrimination to sue for compensatory and punitive damages rather than solely to recover back wages. When employees are dismissed for discriminatory reasons, they often experience related economic calamities such as losing their car or home or incurring increased medical expenses due to personal and financial stress. Nevertheless, the U.S. Chamber of Commerce insists that recognizing a right to such damages "further increas[es] the opportunity for frivolous litigation,"[142] while ALEC's model legislation declares such rights "a serious economic threat to all employees and employers whose welfare depends on the prosperity that our free enterprise system affords."[143]

Since 2011, both Wisconsin and Missouri have passed laws reflecting these views. In Wisconsin, legislation introduced by seven senators—all ALEC members—repealed the right of victims of employment discrimination to sue for compensatory and punitive damages.[144] This bill—signed by Governor Walker in 2012—was passed with the vocal support of employer associations. The state's primary corporate lobby, Wisconsin Manufacturers and Commerce (WMC), warned that the right to damages for discrimination victims "has had a negative influence on the Wisconsin business climate."[145] WMC was joined by a wide array of employer groups—including the NFIB, the Wisconsin Builders Association, the Grocers Association, Hospital Association, Hotel and Lodging Association, Insurers Alliance, and Restaurant Association.[146] With their newfound legislative allies, these organizations triumphed, leaving workers unable to recover damages and significantly decreasing the penalty for employers found guilty of discrimination.

In Missouri too, business organizations lobbied both to make discrimination harder to prove and to limit employer liability. This effort followed a meeting in early 2011 at which the Chamber of Commerce and allied corporate lobbyists presented Republican leaders with a six-point plan for legislative priorities, including raising new barriers to proving a charge of discrimination.[147] In addition, the bill strictly limited employees' right to collect damages even after companies were found guilty of discrimination.[148] Although this legislation was vetoed by Missouri's Democratic governor, it remains a key goal of the state's Chamber of Commerce. In 2015, a Chamber–award-winning state senator introduced a bill that not only revived the 2012 proposal but also capped back-wage claims; the chamber testified in support of the bill—which died in committee—noting that it represented "a Chamber priority for a number of years."[149] Restricting employees' right to sue is not the top priority of business lobbies, but it is universal. Thus for instance, the New Hampshire Business and Industry Association and the Texas Association of Business both fought against legislative proposals to extend the statute of limitations for filing employment discrimination suits, one successfully and one not.[150] While fighting state antidiscrimination statutes, these same organizations have been promoting a growing corporate practice of requiring new hires to waive their constitutional right to sue over job discrimination and instead refer all complaints to an internal, company-run arbitration process. This practice was pioneered, in part, by ALEC-member companies Walgreens and Novartis, both found guilty in large class-action suits for race and sex discrimination, with the legal argument for barring such suits championed by the U.S. Chamber of Commerce.[151]

Unemployment Insurance

Unemployment insurance (UI) was established in response to the Great Depression, as a means of helping hard-working Americans survive periods of joblessness. In addition to providing much-needed relief to the families of those out of work, UI also plays an important role in shaping informal negotiations between workers and employers. In the absence of UI, the unemployed would be desperate to take any job they could find, as quickly as possible. This desperation would not only lead to harmful results for the families of such employees; by flooding the labor market with desperate job seekers, it would also lower wage standards throughout the local economy. By providing a modicum of support, UI takes the edge off this desperation and thus shifts the balance of power between employers and would-be employees in a subtle but significant manner. Those out of work still face daunting conditions and stiff pressure to find work as quickly as possible. But UI makes it conceivable to turn down the lowest-paying and most dangerous jobs in order to search for a position with better pay and conditions that builds on one's established skills.

Over the past two decades, corporate lobbies have worked continuously to tighten eligibility requirements for UI, making it harder for those out of work to access benefits. As a result, in 2014 the share of all unemployed workers who actually received UI fell to 27 percent, an all-time low.[152] More recently, the corporate lobbies have aimed at cutting benefits even for those who do qualify.

In 2011–15, nineteen states passed legislation placing new restrictions on UI benefits.[153] Most of the new laws reduced the level of benefits provided, the number of weeks one can receive benefits, or some combination of these. Indiana, for example, reduced the average benefit by 25 percent.[154] Wisconsin instituted a one-week waiting period before unemployed workers can start collecting benefits; across the state, this change was expected to take over $40 million away from those recently unemployed.[155] In North Carolina, the Chamber of Commerce lobbied successfully for a bill that cut the maximum benefit by one-third and limited benefits to as little as twelve weeks, the shortest duration in the country.[156]

This wave of UI "reforms" reflects the priorities of the corporate lobbies. The U.S. Chamber of Commerce ranks each state's UI policy, reserving the highest grades for states that provide the most meager benefits.[157] ALEC's ultimate goal is showcased in its Full Employment Act, which completely eliminates welfare, UI, and food stamps, instead requiring that jobless Americans work at minimum wage—for public or private employers—in order to earn any such benefits. Anyone who turns down any minimum-wage job offer is immediately cut off from unemployment benefits.[158] Thus ALEC's vision is not simply to save tax dollars by reducing public expenditures on UI but to force workers into low-wage work rather than allowing them to hold out for better jobs, and to drive down wage standards across the economy through the presence of a perpetual stream of workers forced to choose between minimum wage and hunger.

In addition to simple benefit cuts, states have adopted two other types of UI reform that are noteworthy. First, legislators imposed new requirements on the types of jobs unemployed workers must accept. Three states (Arkansas, Maine, and Tennessee) forced people to get back to work sooner, and at lower pay, or be disqualified from UI. Maine reduced from twelve to ten weeks the period during which unemployed workers may seek a job in their previous line of work and geographic area, after which they must expand their job search to other occupations and parts of the country.[159] Tennessee adopted a statute put forth by a group of ALEC-affiliated senators, which mandates that laid-off employees may search for jobs that pay the same as their previous position for only thirteen weeks.[160] After that point, they must accept any job that pays at least 75 percent of their previous wage rate, or be cut off from unemployment benefits; the required wage level drops to 70 percent of their previous job after twenty-five weeks; and 65 percent after thirty-eight weeks. Thus, in a future recession similar to that of 2011, when 113,000 people in Tennessee were out of work for at least twenty-seven weeks, this full complement of workers would be forced back into the labor market at jobs paying two-thirds or less of their previous wages.[161]

To ensure that these rules are strictly enforced, Tennessee's statute requires that all UI recipients submit detailed weekly reports proving that they applied for at least three jobs per week—and further requires that the state Department of Labor audit at least one thousand unemployed workers each week in order to ensure that these procedures are enforced. It is striking that, while business lobbies everywhere seek to defund and restrict the enforcement capacity of government agencies in general and labor departments in particular, the Tennessee statute (strongly supported by both NFIB and the Chamber of Commerce) suggests that the business lobbies are not against public spending or regulatory capacity per se. They are against regulatory capacity that serves to strengthen the hand of workers and citizens vis-à-vis large corporations. But when the state functions to enforce discipline on employees to the benefit of employers, these same lobbies are happy to expand public budgets and state bureaucracy.

The centrality of discipline to corporate-backed unemployment reform is even more apparent in recent laws that use UI to extend control over *current* employees. Nine states have amended their UI statutes in ways that increase employers' control over those who remain on the job, by radically rewriting UI eligibility requirements.[162]

Traditionally, unemployment benefits are provided to anyone laid off unless that person was fired for reason of "misconduct." Misconduct does not include incompetence or failure to meet production quotas—this would simply demonstrate that one was not good at the job and was therefore fired and eligible for benefits. Rather, statutes traditionally defined misconduct only as "willful and wanton" refusal to meet performance standards. Under the new generation of laws supported by business lobbyists, employees who are fired for any violation of a workplace policy *other than* production quotas can be deemed guilty of "misconduct" and declared ineligible for UI benefits. In Arkansas, for instance, the Society of Human Resource Managers (SHRM) lobbied successfully for a bill that significantly expanded the definition of misconduct. SHRM explains the impact of the state's new law, noting that "under [preexisting] law, an employee discharged for poor performance is entitled to benefits unless the employer can prove the employee's poor performance was intentional"; but under the new law, "violations of behavioral policies (as opposed to violations of performance standards) are misconduct for which an employee is disqualified" from UI.[163]

The new statute specifically identifies absenteeism as a policy area that may disqualify employees from receiving unemployment benefits. Under the state's previous law one could not be disqualified based on absenteeism as long as the reasons for absence were meritorious; the statute mandated that "in all cases of discharge for absenteeism, . . . reasons for the absenteeism shall be taken into consideration for purposes of determining whether the absenteeism constitutes misconduct." The new law, however, mandates that "the individual will be disqualified if the discharge was pursuant to the terms of a bona fide written attendance policy . . . regardless of whether the policy is a fault or no-fault policy."[164] Thus, as long as employees received a written policy on absenteeism, any violation of that policy may not only lead to termination but also disqualify one from unemployment benefits. For the nearly forty million Americans who don't have a single day's sick leave, for instance, this means that the decision to stay home when sick, or when caring for a sick child, may not only result in losing one's job, but also in being declared guilty of misconduct and cut off from unemployment benefits.

Tennessee followed the same principle, with a bill the *Nashville Business Journal* described as enjoying the "full-throated support" of the Chamber of Commerce and NFIB.[165] The authors of the new law—almost all ALEC members—redefine misconduct as any "violation of an employer's rule [that is] . . . reasonably related to the job environment and performance."[166] The statute specifically cites "deliberate disregard of a written attendance policy" as grounds for deeming a worker ineligible for unemployment benefits.[167] The NFIB was quick to seize on this language, urging member employers to "make sure you have a written attendance policy that each employee has reviewed and signed," so that any unexcused absences may be used to terminate employees without recourse to UI.[168]

So too, Florida legislators redefined misconduct to mean any violation of "reasonable standards of behavior which the employer expects."[169] In the summer of 2012, a Florida lifeguard was famously fired for running to rescue a drowning man who was located outside the zone his employer was contracted to patrol in Hallandale Beach. "We have liability issues and can't go out of the protected area," explained his supervisor. "He knew the company rules."[170] Under the new law, such heroism may not only get Florida lifeguards terminated, but will also be deemed misconduct that renders the hero ineligible for unemployment insurance.

But the Florida statute—authored by an ALEC member and supported by the Chamber of Commerce—goes even further, specifying that employees may be deemed ineligible for UI "irrespective of whether the misconduct occurs at the workplace or during work hours."[171] Thus, if one's company has a policy against employees dating one another or posting work-related comments on a personal Facebook account, ignoring these rules may leave one cut off from UI.[172] In this way, the corporate lobbies are using UI reform not only to limit the prerogatives of unemployed workers but also to dramatically increase control over those currently on the job.

Throughout the past five years, those leading the call to scale back public-sector union rights have often presented themselves as the champions of nonunion private-sector workers weighed down by the tax burden of supporting overcompensated public employees. In his 2016 presidential bid, Scott Walker touted his record as a governor who "took on the unions and won," thus proving his capacity to "fight and win for the hardworking taxpayers."[173] Yet at every turn, the corporate lobbies and allied lawmakers such as Walker have sought to erode or abolish the wage standards, benefits, and workplace rights of nonunion, private-sector workers. So too, antiunion spokespeople have sometimes argued that employees no longer need unions because federal and state laws now take care of any problems unions might once have been needed to address. Americans for Prosperity's Michigan director, for instance, promoted a right-to-work law in part by explaining that while "early unions fought for better pay, safer working conditions and shorter work hours," these "protections [are] now mostly granted by federal and state law."[174] The track record of recent years shows, however, that the same organizations seeking to erode union rights are simultaneously working to undermine exactly those laws that protect pay, ensure workplace safety, and regulate hours of work. The vast majority of American employees go to work every day for a private company, with no union protections. For these workers, it is not a union contract but state and local laws that shape working conditions and frame the balance of power between employers and employees. Corporate rhetoric around these laws sounds different from that aimed at public servants— rather than attacking overpaid employees, they stress the need for flexibility, the danger of government mandates, and the power of unrestrained entrepreneurialism to lift all boats. But the aim of these arguments is ultimately the same: to restrict, weaken, or abolish laws governing wages, benefits, or working conditions; to preempt, defund, or dismantle every legal or organizational mechanism through which workers may challenge employer prerogatives; and to block, wherever possible, citizens' ability to exercise democratic control over corporate behavior.

THE DESTRUCTION OF PUBLIC SCHOOLING

> Elementary and secondary schooling in the U.S. is the country's last remaining socialist enterprise. . . . The way to privatize schooling is to give parents . . . vouchers, with which to pay tuition at the K–12 schools of their choice. . . . Pilot voucher programs for the urban poor will lead the way to statewide universal voucher plans. Soon, most government schools will be converted into private schools or simply close their doors. Eventually, middle- and upper-income families will no longer expect or need tax-financed assistance to pay for the education of their children, leading to further steps toward complete privatization. . . . This is a battle we should win. . . . But in the short term, there will be many defeats caused by teacher union opposition.

—Joseph Bast, president, Heartland Institute (ALEC affiliate)

In 2014, New Orleans's Recovery School District became the first all-charter district in the United States.[1] The teachers' union, which boasted seven thousand members on the eve of Hurricane Katrina, has been completely wiped out: the recovery district is entirely nonunion. Following the hurricane, every one of New Orleans' teachers was summarily fired. The new teachers are younger, whiter, and less experienced; two-thirds of them lack traditional certification.[2] More than one-quarter of the teaching staff leaves every year, but the system relies on Teach for America to supply a steady stream of fresh recruits.[3] The schools are now operated by private corporations, including some of the country's largest charter chains, which often boast of maintaining a strict regime of "no-excuses" discipline for poor city kids.[4] While these schools are publicly funded, the local community has no control over their methods, curriculum, or quality, because they are not overseen by any democratically elected school board.

There is no evidence that this sweeping transformation has improved education for the city's students: declarations of success have repeatedly been undermined by evidence of data manipulation, including the expulsion or "counseling out" of low-scoring students. After ten years, the most rigorous and impartial research concludes that it is simply impossible to tell whether the reforms helped or hurt New Orleans schoolchildren—partly because the data have not been made publicly available.[5] It is clear, however, that New Orleans offers no model for success. Louisiana has one of the lowest-performing school systems in the country—with reading and math scores ranked forty-seventh out of the fifty states—and New Orleans is close to the bottom of this low-performing state. Of seventy school districts in the state, New Orleans ranks sixty-sixth in achievement tests, with the result that most of the city's high school students can't qualify for one of the state's four-year colleges. And even this disappointing result is overstated, because New Orleans has the highest dropout rate in Louisiana, with many low-scoring students leaving school as early as the seventh grade. Finally, across the state, public schools outperform charters by a wide margin.[6]

Despite this questionable track record, virtually every aspect of the New Orleans model is being vigorously promoted across the country. The privatization of the city's school system began following Katrina, when the Bush administration refused to pay for reopening public schools, instead providing $45 million for charter schools to take their place.[7] But in the years since, the transformation has been championed by both Democrats and Republicans, with Obama administration Secretary of Education Arne Duncan among those holding that Katrina was "the best thing that happened to the education system in New Orleans."[8] The Netflix CEO and education entrepreneur Reed Hastings has called on others to follow the New Orleans all-charter model, specifically lauding the fact that "they don't have elected school boards."[9] Both Tennessee and Michigan have adopted laws creating special authorities to convert big-city public schools to privately run charters, with many other states considering similar proposals. And in 2015, the Broad foundation recruited the former Louisiana superintendent of schools to lead a privately funded $400 million campaign to replace half the schools in Los Angeles with charter schools.[10]

At first glance, it may seem odd that corporate lobbies such as the Chamber of Commerce, NFIB, or Americans for Prosperity would care to get involved in an issue as far removed from commercial activity as school reform. In fact, they have each made this a top legislative priority. As a result, in recent years there has been more legislation adopted related to education than to any other area of social or economic policy. From 2011 to 2015, at least eight states passed laws limiting the union rights of schoolteachers; nine states increased the use of student test scores for teacher evaluation; seventeen expanded online instruction; and twenty-nine passed laws encouraging the privatization of education through vouchers or charter schools. This unprecedented rush of legislation is not a response to sudden educational crisis: American students' reading and math scores have remained largely unchanged for forty years.[11] Rather, it represents long-held ambitions that became politically possible following *Citizens United*, project RedMap, and the Great Recession–induced fiscal crisis.

The campaign to transform public education brings together multiple strands of the agenda described in earlier chapters of this book. The teachers' union is the single biggest labor organization in most states—thus for both antiunion ideologues and Republican strategists, undermining teachers' unions is of central importance. Education is one of the largest components of public budgets, and in many communities the school system is the single largest employer—thus the goals of cutting budgets, enabling new tax cuts for the wealthy, shrinking the government, and lowering wage and benefit standards in the public sector all naturally coalesce around the school system. Furthermore, there is an enormous amount of money to be made from the privatization of education—so much so that every major investment bank has established special funds devoted exclusively to this sector. There are always firms that aim to profit from the privatization of public services, but the sums involved in k–12 education are an order of magnitude larger than any other service, and have generated an intensity of corporate legislative engagement unmatched by any other branch of government. Finally, the notion that one's kids have a right to a decent education represents the most substantive right to which Americans believe we are entitled, simply by dint of residence. In this sense, the epigraph that introduces this chapter is correct—for those interested in lowering citizens' expectations of what we have a right to demand from government, there is no more central fight than that around public education.[12] In all these ways, then, school reform presents something like the perfect crystallization of the corporate legislative agenda, uniting in one issue the goals of antiunionism, partisan politics, restructuring labor markets, redefining citizens' expectations of government, and the transfer of enormous sums from public to private hands.

Education policy is also the grounds on which corporate interests come together across partisan lines. The unparalleled sums of money at stake in the privatization of schooling have brought traditionally Democratic donors in the finance and technology industries into the school reform debate. The oil money behind Americans for Prosperity and the hedge fund managers that lead Democrats for Education Reform rarely support the same candidates for public office, but they are united in their advocacy for school reform legislation. Thus education reform also illuminates the extent to which, when required, corporate interests trump those of party politics.

Unlike narrowly defined issues such as raising the minimum wage, the corporate agenda for education reform is composed of a wide array of related initiatives. In any given state, corporate lobbyists may be advocating just one of these—eliminating tenure, for instance, or introducing online courses. But these strands come together to form a coherent vision. In states across the country, corporate lobbyists have supported a comprehensive package of reforms that includes weakening or abolishing teachers' unions, cutting school budgets and increasing class sizes, requiring high-stakes testing that determines teacher tenure and school closings, replacing public schools with privately run charter schools, diverting public funding into vouchers that may be used for private school tuition, lowering training and licensing requirements for new teachers, replacing in-person education with digital applications, and dismantling publicly elected school boards. Almost all of these initiatives reflect ALEC model legislation, and have been championed by the Chamber of Commerce, Americans for Prosperity, and a wide range of allied corporate lobbies.

Despite prolific claims to the contrary, corporate-led education reform does not represent an agenda to improve American education or expand the life chances of poor urban youth. As will be shown below, the corporate agenda would lead to a divided country, where the children of the wealthy will be taught a broad curriculum in small classes led by experienced teachers, while the rest of the nation will be consigned to a narrow curriculum delivered in large classes by inexperienced staff—or by digital applications with no teachers at all. These reforms run counter to the types of schools that privileged parents demand for their own children and that are generally recognized as the best schools in the country or the world.

Political science traditionally views policy initiatives as emerging from either reasoned evaluation of what has worked to address a given social problem, or a strategic response to public opinion. But the corporate agenda for education reform is neither. Its initiatives are not the product of education scholars and often have little or no evidentiary basis to support them. They are also often broadly unpopular. For example, a majority of the country opposes using tax dollars to pay for students to attend private schools.[13] Sixty percent of the public says entrance requirements for teacher-training programs should be made more rigorous, and three-quarters believe teachers should spend at least one year practice teaching under the guidance of a more experienced mentor before being given responsibility for a class of their own.[14] What parents want most of all are smaller class sizes.[15] And while legislators debate what percentage of teacher evaluations should be based on student test scores, nearly 70 percent of parents—including a majority of voters in both parties—oppose test scores playing any role at all in teacher evaluations.[16] In this sense, education policy also provides an instructive window into the ability of corporate lobbies to move an extremely broad and ambitious agenda that is supported neither by social scientific evidence nor by the popular will.

Budget Cuts and Crowded Classrooms

Scholars have spent more than a century studying, measuring, and debating the elements that define a good education, and there is no simple formula that captures the lessons of that work. However, there are several aspects of what makes for good schools that are worth highlighting both because they are supported by particularly strong evidence and because they stand in sharp contrast to the model of education being encouraged by corporate reformers. One of the most fundamental factors affecting the quality of education is the number of students in a class. The largest-scale study of class-size impacts was Tennessee's Student/ Teacher Achievement Ratio (STAR) program, which concluded that students in smaller classes performed significantly better in both reading and math.[17] In the twenty years following STAR, a host of studies examined this question, reaching similar conclusions: Holding class size to eighteen or fewer students in grades k–3 produces significant benefits in both reading and math, with the greatest impacts on African American, Latino, and low-income students.[18] As the education scholar Alex Molnar explains, in small classes

- Children receive more individualized instruction.
- Teachers can focus more on direct instruction and less on classroom management.
- Teachers identify learning disabilities sooner, but fewer children end up going into special education classes because teachers can support them within small classes.
- Teachers are more able to give children from low-income families and communities a critical, supportive adult influence.
- Teachers are better able to engage family members and to work with parents to further a child's education.
- Teachers burn out less.[19]

In addition to the measurable impact on student performance, teacher surveys show that smaller class sizes produce a fundamental shift in how teachers conduct their classes. A three-year study of teacher practice concluded that "much less time is spent in dealing with misbehavior in a small class. . . . Teachers [also] develop a greater knowledge and understanding of each child. . . . Because there is more time to interact with each child, teachers come to know the total child—his or her interests, habits, perspectives, strengths, weaknesses, and other characteristics."[20] Thus, education scholars have long held that the single most effective means of improving education is to significantly decrease class sizes.

Yet as discussed in chapter 2, recent years have seen unprecedented cuts in school funding, which reversed a thirty-year trend of state governments' working actively to shrink class sizes.[21] In 2010, the national student-teacher ratio increased for the first time since the Great Depression.[22] For the most part, increased class size occurred as a byproduct of budget cuts. However, legislators in several states intentionally acted to enlarge class sizes. In Texas, legislators voted to lift the state's cap of twenty-two students per class in kindergarten through fourth grade.[23] Ohio likewise voted to relax its class size limits.[24] In Florida—a state often held up as a model of education reform—legislators in 2010 proposed lifting the state's constitutional cap on the size of core classes, but voters refused. In response, the legislature in 2011 redefined two-thirds of the classes previously deemed part of the "core" curriculum as noncore.[25] Within weeks of the change, Miami Beach High's ninth-grade world history class required twenty minutes simply to take attendance because it contained fifty-four kids and forty desks— more than double its size the year before.[26]

While inflated class size was justified as a necessary result of budget shortfalls, legislators in these states had many alternatives for coping with the recession's temporary deficits. Instead, they often chose not only to cut education spending but to exacerbate those deficits with new tax cuts. In Florida, both the Chamber of Commerce and the Restaurant Association had long called for "reforming" the class-size caps, which they decried as a "financial burden on . . . taxpayers."[27] When lawmakers acceded to this request in 2011—redefining the core curriculum and cutting per student spending by $500—they simultaneously adopted a bill cosponsored by a quartet of ALEC legislators that abolished corporate income taxes for nearly half the state's businesses—a move hailed by the Chamber of Commerce as a first step toward a complete phase-out of corporate income taxes.[28] Likewise, Ohio's loosening of class-size standards came in the same session that lawmakers voted to phase out the state's inheritance tax. The defunding of education, then, has been a conscious policy choice. There is simply no escaping the fact that elected officials—and their business backers—actively legislated classroom crowding in order to divert funds to corporations and the wealthy and, I believe, as part of a broader agenda aimed at dismantling the public education system.

Vouchers

The agenda of defunding the school system is further evident in the push to adopt voucher programs, in which parents are given a prorated share of the education budget that they are then free to spend on the school of their choice, including private schools. From 2011 to 2015, eighteen states established some form of voucher program. Vouchers are typically introduced as a limited, targeted intervention aimed at helping the neediest families but then expanded gradually to cover the general population. The country's oldest voucher program was established in Milwaukee in 1990 and was restricted to poor children in failing schools and capped at a limited number of participants.[29] In 2011, Governor Walker removed the cap, raised the income eligibility threshold, and expanded the program to include students in suburban counties.[30] In 2013 the program was expanded yet again, this time to cover the entire state.[31] Indiana and Ohio were the first two states to establish voucher programs that are available statewide and not limited to failing or underperforming schools. While both programs have income eligibility requirements, they are quite generous; in Indiana, nearly two-thirds of the state's students qualify.[32]

Voucher supporters have used a wide variety of rationales to promote continual, incremental program expansions. In Arizona, for instance, a team of ALEC-member legislators including both the senate president and the speaker of the house passed three separate bills in 2014 expanding the voucher program, first for special-needs children, then for siblings of students already receiving vouchers, and finally for the children of military personnel killed in the line of duty.[33] While special justifications were offered for each of these initiatives, the proponents' ultimate goal was made clear in a fourth bill, sponsored by the speaker of the house and the house majority whip (who is also ALEC state chair) and enthusiastically endorsed by Americans for Prosperity. This legislation would have opened the voucher program to all low-income students in the state and then raised the qualifying income threshold by 15 percent per year until every student in the state was eligible.[34] Although this bill did not become law, it points to the overriding goal of complete privatization of education. Tim Jones—the former Missouri house speaker and ALEC chair and current (in 2017) head of that state's Club for Growth chapter—explained in 2015 that "education is the only thing protected from the free market," and vouchers are a means to remedy that.[35]

If the true goal of vouchers were what its proponents originally suggested—helping poor families send their kids to better schools—legislators would be careful to marshal resources toward this end. At a minimum, we would expect states to enact "maintenance of effort" requirements that stop private schools from simply increasing tuition by the amount of state vouchers—resulting in no change in educational access but a net transfer of public dollars to private hands. Yet not a single state has mandated such rules. As voucher legislation has evolved, it has become an increasingly open door through which public school budgets are siphoned away. One of the most expansive programs was adopted in Georgia—modeled on ALEC legislation—where tuition tax credits are available to rich students as well as poor, to those who spend their whole lives in private school as well as those who have transferred from a failing public school, and can be claimed by corporations donating to private schools as well as by tuition-paying parents. When this legislation was adopted in 2013, it received the enthusiastic backing of both the state Chamber of Commerce and Americans for Prosperity, which crowed that "anytime you can successfully privatize a vital government service and … [give] a tax credit … it's a win-win."[36] The increasing looseness of voucher regimes—the fact that vouchers function in large part not to expand school choice but to subsidize families who always have and always would have sent their children to private school—suggests that part of the agenda behind such legislation is simply to drain resources away from public school systems, hastening the moment of their collapse. More than a decade ago, a conservative manifesto was issued by a coalition of religious and corporate-funded advocates, including the president of the Koch-funded Cato Institute, declaring that "I proclaim publicly that I favor ending government involvement in education."[37] Vouchers are clearly part of the strategy for realizing this ambition.

High-Stakes Testing

The linchpin of corporate education reform is the demand that standardized tests be used to determine the pay, promotion, and termination of teachers and the funding or closing of schools. Like much of the corporate agenda, the impetus for this policy does not derive from scientific evidence. Research shows, for instance that the "subjective" grades given by high school teachers are a better predictor of college success than the "objective" SAT or ACT exams—presumably because teachers' evaluations are based on a broader understanding of students' capacities, progress, and personalities.[38] In Finland, regularly ranked one of the world's best school systems, there are no standardized tests whatsoever.[39] Nevertheless, corporate advocates incessantly proclaim that high-stakes testing is necessary to ensure school "accountability." In 2009, only fifteen states included any measure of student progress in teacher evaluations. By 2012, thirty-two states required that standardized tests serve as a component of teacher evaluations, and nine states insisted they be a "central" criterion.[40]

As an example of how such policies work in practice, Louisiana adopted new requirements in 2012, mirroring ALEC legislation, which require that a teacher be rated "highly effective" for five out of six years in order to earn tenure. Effectiveness is based half on supervisor evaluations and half on student test scores. For the latter, the state takes the last three years of test scores for all of a teacher's students; adds factors for disability, attendance, discipline, and poverty; and then computes a statistical projection of what such students would normally be expected to score in the current year. To be rated highly effective, a teacher must beat the projection. To the extent teachers are successful under this system, improving test scores will cause a continual upward adjustment of statistical expectations; eventually, no matter how high the quality of teaching, most teachers will be unable to meet the "highly effective" definition.

One of the impacts of making teacher tenure and school funding dependent on student test scores is that schools come to shrink their curricula to a narrow focus on math and literacy—the only subjects tested. Music, art, physical education, laboratory science, social studies, and foreign languages have been scaled back or eliminated in school districts across the country.[41] Further, even in those subjects that are tested, pressures to teach to the test threaten to make education a more shallow and less meaningful endeavor. Teachers are under pressure not only to restrict their teaching to what's on the tests but also to spend considerable time teaching test-taking strategies rather than any content at all. One teacher illustrates the shortcomings of a test-centered curriculum by recalling that

> in the . . . social studies field tests, one question asked which Constitutional Amendment gave women the right to vote. Students could know virtually nothing about the long struggle for women's rights and answer this question correctly. On the other hand, they could know much about the feminist movement and not recall that it was the 19th and not the 16th, 17th or 18th Amendment that gave women the right to vote. . . . My students [engaged in] . . . roleplaying . . . [and] exercised their multicultural social imaginations—listening for the voices that are often silenced in the traditional U.S. history narrative, and becoming more alert to the importance of issues of race and class. However, this kind of teaching and learning takes time—time that could be ill-afforded in the fact-packing pedagogy required by multiple-choice tests.[42]

Rather than encouraging a focus on reaching the neediest students, test-based evaluation creates pressure for a more instrumental approach to classroom management. For a teacher being judged by students' test score average and who has a low-scoring student in the class, the incentive is either to concentrate on drilling that individual to bring up her score or to ignore her altogether in favor of devoting effort to more improvable students who will contribute to raising the class's average.

Finally, test-based curricula differentiate students only along one dimension. Children differ not only in how *much* they learn but also in *how* they learn. When kindergartners and first-graders are first grappling with basic math concepts, some do well by practicing equations, others by making and crossing off marks on paper, others through stories about quantities of things gained or lost, others by physically manipulating sticks or blocks. This is part of what makes it impossible for teachers to assign even the best-conceived lesson plan to all students. Part of the task of any teacher is to determine which mode of learning is best suited to which children. For several decades educators have sought to identify the specific different ways that children learn, in order to help teachers provide appropriate pathways for each child. One recent study suggests that the range of preferred student learning strategies might include the following:

- Verbal/linguistic (embodied in "preparing a report" or "writing a play or an essay")
- Bodily/kinesthetic ("develop a mime" or "work through a simulation")
- Musical/rhythmic ("compose a rap song or rhyme")
- Naturalist ("discover or experiment" or "look for ideas from nature")
- Visual/spatial ("draw a picture" or "design a graphic")
- Interpersonal ("work with a partner or group")
- Logical/mathematical "(create a pattern" or "timeline") or
- Intrapersonal ("review or visualize a way to do something" or "write in a journal")[43]

There is no precise dividing line between various ways of learning, and it is impossible to run controlled experiments with young children; thus there is no conclusive statistical proof identifying a specific set of "learning styles" that teachers should build curricula around. Nevertheless, there is broad agreement among both parents and teachers that different children learn in different ways.

The 2012 National Teacher of the Year explains how central this diversity of learning strategies is to the work of teaching:

> I think what the best teachers are, are seekers. We are given a family's . . . most precious resource, their child. And our job is to send them out better than when they walk through the door. And better doesn't necessarily mean that they can ace a standardized test. Better means that I have seen deep within each child what his or her unique potential is. And so great teachers give assignments that . . . [require] debating skills one day. And the next day, it will be a research skill, and the next day it will be artistic or musical because we're looking for what each child's native talent and capacity is, so that we can provide the education that that child needs and help him or her find her best path to success.[44]

All parents hope to have a teacher who sees the individual strengths and needs of their child. But under the pressure of high-stakes testing, the type of pedagogy described by the Teacher of the Year is something teachers engage in at their own risk; the far safer course is to forget about drama or debating and focus on mastering the material that's on the test.

Charter Schools

One of the primary uses of standardized tests has been to document the low performance of schools in poor urban areas and demand that they be replaced with privately run charter schools. From 2011 to 2015, twenty states passed laws expanding the authorization of charter schools. The charter industry doubled in size in five years and now educates over 2.5 million students in 6,500 schools.[45] Again, however, there is no evidentiary basis for this policy: the record shows charter schools are no better—and often worse—than traditional public schools.

The original image of a charter school revolves around a lone dedicated educator, or a local community of parents, who decide to take over a school and make it into something better. In reality, rather than a proliferation of small experiments, the last few years have witnessed a pattern of corporate consolidation. By 2011 fewer than 17 percent of charter students were in schools run by companies that operated three or fewer schools. The majority were overseen by corporations operating ten or more schools.[46]

As charter schools have grown over the past two decades, multiple studies have compared their performance with that of traditional public schools. The conclusion of the most rigorous and impartial research is that there is no evidence to believe that charter schools improve the quality of education—either among their own students or by increasing competitive pressure on publicly run schools. One recent meta-analysis reviewed the results of eighty-three studies conducted over twelve years, concluding that "on the whole, charters perform similarly to traditional public schools."[47]

The largest national studies have been conducted by the Stanford University–based Center for Research on Education Outcomes (CREDO), an organization generally supportive of charter schools. Comparing math scores of charter and public school students, CREDO's 2009 study found that 17 percent of charter schools had superior growth in math scores, 37 percent were inferior, and 46 percent were "statistically indistinguishable" from public schools. Averaged across all schools, the impact of attending a charter school was a slight—but statistically significant—negative impact for both math and reading gains.[48]

When CREDO updated its research in 2013, it found that 29 percent of charter schools had achieved math gains that were superior to those of their public school counterparts, 31 percent were inferior, and 40 percent were statistically indistinguishable (figure 4.1).[49] However, this improvement does not necessarily mean that charter schools got better at teaching math; the improved numbers are largely a reflection of the fact that a significant number of poor-performing schools were closed between the two studies and therefore not included in the 2013 sample.[50] Across all groups, researchers reported that the impact of poverty

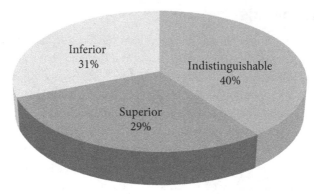

FIGURE 4.1. How charter schools compare with public schools, math test score gains, 2013.

Source: "National Charter School Study, 2013," Center for Research on Education Outcomes, Stanford University, 2013, http://credo.stanford.edu/documents/NCSS%202013%20Final%20Draft.pdf.

was significantly greater than any impact produced by the choice of charter or public school.[51]

In many cases, charter schools do worse than public schools. In Indiana, nearly half the state's charter schools received grades of D or F in 2012; more than half of those had scored this low for at least two years.[52] In Ohio, which has authorized charter schools in the state's eight biggest cities for nearly twenty years, nearly 90 percent of the state's charter students were in schools ranked D or F in 2012–13.[53] Online charter schools are by far the fastest-growing segment of the industry, now operating in seventeen states, and also by far the worst. In 2015, CREDO found that compared with traditional public school students, students at online high schools lost the equivalent of 72 school days in reading skills and 180 days in math. As one commentator observed, "It's as if the students did not attend school at all when it comes to math."[54]

Even the highest-ranked charter schools appear to have succeeded at improving students' test scores without necessarily improving their longer-term career readiness or life chances. A 2016 Texas study found that even the best of that state's charter schools failed to increase students' employability or earning potential after graduation from high school.[55] This suggests that the apparent accomplishments of even "high-performing" charter schools may simply reflect a focus on drilling students to score higher on standardized tests without meeting their broader educational needs.

The track record of charter schools is yet more troubling when one takes into account measures other than standardized tests. For instance, teacher turnover is twice as high at charters as at traditional public schools.[56] This is particularly true for those schools that rely on Teach for America, more than half of whose recruits leave their low-income school placements as soon as their two-year commitment is up.[57] One of the central challenges of low-performing schools is precisely that they fail to retain experienced teachers. The National Commission on Teaching and America's Future reports that "staff churn . . . is concentrated . . . in chronically underperforming schools serving low-income children. These schools rarely close the student achievement gap because they never close the teaching quality gap. . . . [T]heir students struggle year after year with a passing parade of inexperienced beginners, while students in high performing schools enjoy the support of teams of accomplished veterans."[58] Particularly for the neediest students, who may be facing personal and family stress in addition to academic challenges, the presence of a mature stable adult who knows the student's community is often critical; yet it is most lacking precisely in the charter networks that are being promoted across the nation's poor cities.

Education Reform: An Evidence-Free Zone of Public Policy

Over the past two decades, privatization advocates have vacillated between charter schools and vouchers as the desired strategy for breaking up the public school system. But the evidentiary basis for voucher programs is as weak as that for charters. A comprehensive review of the nation's longest-standing voucher programs—in Milwaukee, Cleveland, and Washington, D.C.—concludes that "achievement gains for voucher students are similar to those of their public school peers."[59] In Cleveland, reports show that public students often outperform voucher students on state proficiency tests.[60] In Wisconsin, state test results published in March 2011, providing the first direct comparison of student achievement in Milwaukee's public and private-voucher schools, showed not only that the two groups of students had largely similar experiences but that those participating in the voucher program actually had slightly worse achievement levels.[61]

One of the most striking features of education policy debates is that repeated reports of charter or voucher failure seem to have no impact on the policy's promotion. One of the earliest and best-known charter companies, for example, is the White Hat chain of schools launched by Ohio businessman and Republican donor David Brennan with backing from the Walton Family Foundation. One branch of Brennan's business consisted of a chain of highly profitable "Life Skills Centers" for high school students, which often operated out of strip malls, with three shifts of students per day and no music, art, sports, extracurricular activities, or even cafeterias, in a physical space too small to accommodate full enrollment because the school operated on the assumption of high absenteeism.[62] In

2010–11, when 52 percent of all schools in the country achieved "adequate yearly progress" (AYP) under the federal No Child Left Behind standards, only 7 percent of White Hat schools reached this mark—the worst record of any large charter company in the nation.[63] Yet none of this prevented the company's expansion. By 2011 it was operating forty-five charter schools in six states.[64]

When Wisconsin's voucher schools were shown to perform more poorly than their public counterparts, the Walker administration's response was to exempt voucher schools from future testing requirements. Vouchers are valuable because they create choice, the governor's spokesman insisted, regardless of their performance.[65] The education policy director at the corporate-funded American Enterprise Institute likewise explains that "20 years in, it's hard to argue that the nation's biggest and most established voucher experiment has 'worked' if the measure is whether vouchers lead to higher reading and math scores. Happily, that's never been my preferred metric for structural reforms. . . . Choice-based reform shouldn't be understood as that kind of intervention. Rather, choice-based reform should be embraced as an opportunity for educators to create more focused and effective schools and for reformers to solve problems in smarter ways."[66] Thus, where advocates insist on strict, measurable accountability for public schools, privatization is declared valuable by ideological fiat, impervious to educational outcomes.

In most states, private schools are not required to participate in state-mandated standardized tests or to report student performance metrics to any public authority. Thus voucher programs have often expanded in an accountability-free zone. For charter schools too, corporate lobbyists have pushed for broad exemptions from the types of accountability standards imposed on public schools. ALEC's Next Generation Charter Schools Act, for instance, mandates that "a charter school shall receive funding . . . that is equal to the amount that a traditional public school would receive," but that "a charter school is exempt from all statutes and rules applicable to a school, a board, or a district."[67] Charter schools operate on multiyear contracts with their charter authorizer, and only that authorizer—not the state or local school board—can revoke the charter or close the school. So too, charter schools are exempt from most teacher evaluation laws. The Louisiana statute demanding highly effective teaching standards, for example, does not apply to charter school teachers. Thus even if the same tests are administered in charter and public schools, they are not put to the same use. What are high-stakes tests for public schools are effectively no-stakes tests for voucher or charter schools.

This raises an obvious question about the purpose of standardized tests and the agenda of those promoting them. If the best way to identify effective models of schools is to make funding dependent on test scores, why isn't that also good for charters and vouchers? And if teacher evaluation is really about weeding out bad apples, why isn't it required for charter and voucher school teachers? The contrast between these two regimes calls for an alternative explanation. It appears that the goal of testing teachers is not primarily to distinguish between more and less talented staff, but to undermine the collective voice of teachers as a group, and that the primary purpose of school testing is not to identify the most promising models of education but simply to close public and expand privately run schools.

Indeed, corporate advocates not only have promoted policies without evidentiary backing but have often promoted exactly those policies the evidence warns most strongly against. Averaged across all schools in the nation, there is little measurable difference between charter and public schools. Researchers have, however, pointed to several policies that would improve the performance of charter schools. First, charter performance is best in states that strictly limit the number of charter authorizers, making it harder for unscrupulous operators to cultivate a willing sponsor. Second, charter schools do better in states that have relatively fewer of them. Finally, the single worst-performing schools are for-profit online charters.[68] Unfortunately, ALEC and allied corporate lobbies advocate policies that run exactly counter to these findings: they call for expanding the number of both charter schools and authorizers, and vigorously promote the growth of online education.[69]

Education Technology and the Replacement of In-Person with Digital Instruction

Despite their poor performance, virtual schools have constituted the fastest-growing— and by far the most profitable—sector of the charter industry.[70] Indeed, the potential for profit in education technology—whether through entirely online schools or digital products used in traditional classrooms—has generated a vast new industry and has brought some of the country's wealthiest and most powerful corporations into the education policy debate. ALEC, Americans for Prosperity, the Chamber of Commerce, and a host of corporate-funded think tanks are all advocates for replacing human instruction with digital applications, and seventeen states have adopted legislation promoting these methods.

Research suggests that any number of school models might be more beneficial than online instruction. Why, then, is this what's being promoted by the country's most powerful lobbies? Because, in the words of legendary bank robber Willie Sutton, "that's where the money is." As education technology investor Reed

Hastings explains, the great financial advantage of digital education is that "you can produce once and consume many times."[71] Critically, ALEC model legislation—now adopted in five states—requires that even entirely virtual schools be paid the same dollars per student as traditional schools. As a result, profit margins for digital products are enormous. It is no wonder that investment banks, hedge funds, and venture capitalists have all flocked to this market.

In 2010, the investment banker Michael Moe launched the first annual conference bringing education policymakers together with technology firms and investors. By 2014, nearly three hundred companies presented new education-technology products to potential customers and investors at a similar gathering.[72] Applications are now being sold for almost everything—an app for student behavior management, an app for English language learners, an app for ninth-grade reading, an app to replace guidance counselors. Almost none of these have been tested by any education authority, and almost none are the products of teachers or education scholars. Their promotion and adoption are driven not by a need identified in the classroom but by a combination of venture capital and technology firms eager to tap an emerging market with unrivaled potential. "Education is a $3.8 trillion industry globally," the organizers of Moe's Education Innovation Summit explained, but "the industry is significantly undercapitalized."[73] In Rupert Murdoch's words, American education is "a $500 billion sector . . . waiting desperately to be transformed."[74]

Wall Street looks at education the same way it regards Social Security—a huge flow of publicly guaranteed funding that is waiting to be privatized, if only the politics can be worked out. The 2010 elections marked a major step forward for this effort. Within months, Florida's new governor signed a bill requiring that high school students take at least one online course as a condition of graduation.[75] At a meeting of New York investors later that year, one adviser gushed that "you start to see entire ecosystems of investment opportunity lining up" in k–12 education.[76] Indeed, over the past ten years, venture capital investments in education have grown nearly tenfold, from $13 million to $1.25 billion.[77] At the heart of these opportunities, *Princeton Review* founder and education entrepreneur John Katzman explains, is the question of "how do we use technology so that we require fewer highly qualified teachers?"[78]

This is the essential education policy goal of the financial sector: to replace costly and idiosyncratic human teachers with mass-produced and highly profitable digital products and to eliminate the legal and political structures that inhibit a free flow of public tax dollars to these private products. In 2013, the average annual return to venture capital funds was 15 percent.[79] There are any number of educational innovations that might hold more promise than technology. One recent study, for instance, found that intensive small-group tutoring allowed low-income black high school students to learn the equivalent of three years of mathematics in one academic year. At least one school successfully recruited a corps of retirees to provide such tutoring at modest cost, thus making the program financially viable.[80] Another program created summer school classes of twenty students with two teachers each and saw enormous progress made by low-income Baltimore students who had previously been failing.[81] But such programs have no place in the portfolio of reforms called for by corporate advocates because there is no way to turn a profit from them. To the extent that investors influence education policy, then, we are witnessing elementary and high school pedagogy being redesigned around a financial bottom line: teach whatever you want, however you want, as long as it generates at least a 15 percent rate of return.

The colonization of education by technology relies on standardized testing to create its market. Test scores are the metric by which applications aspire to prove their worth and the currency in which they are advertised to new customers. Even more important, standardized testing is what turns thousands of individual school districts—each potentially with its own needs, values, and educational philosophy—into a national market. The Obama administration's deputy secretary of education—a longtime education investor and cofounder of a charter school chain—explained that Common Core standards are valuable because they let education firms create products that can "scale across many markets," solving the problem of the "fragmented procurement market" that previously stymied investors.[82]

The education technology industry is explicit about the fact that its market expansion depends on political engagement. Michael Moe—now head of an education-focused venture capital fund—has issued a corporate manifesto calling for sweeping legislative and policy changes to convert education from a public service to a private market; the declaration includes a diagram depicting business interests and "change agents" fighting unions and "status quo" defenders for the future of public schooling.[83] In 2011, K-12, Inc.—the nation's largest for-profit online school—chaired ALEC's education task force. That year, Florida became the first state in the country to adopt a law—sponsored by the state's ALEC chair and backed by the Chamber of Commerce—requiring online education as a condition of graduation. Idaho quickly followed suit—again with a bill sponsored by an ALEC legislator and supported by the state Chamber of Commerce; by 2015 five states had adopted such laws.[84] Despite the dismal results of online education reported above, the industry has been growing by leaps and bounds. In 2014, when an investment firm issued an optimistic projection for K-12, Inc., it specifically cited the company's "competency in lobbying" and "success in working closely with state policymakers . . . to enable the expansion of virtual schools" as keys to continued growth.[85] As one venture capitalist explains, market growth depends on overcoming opposition from "unions, public school bureaucracies and parents." By 2014, this investor was confident that "the education market is ripe for disruption."[86]

The extent to which investment banks, hedge funds, and venture capitalists have come to drive education policy can be seen in local as well as state politics. Traditionally, a rule of thumb in urban political science is that money in city politics comes primarily from the real estate industry. Zoning decisions are the biggest item of economic value under the control of most city governments; thus developers have the greatest financial stake in who occupies city hall. Recently however, bigger money has come to play. In 2007, Democrats for Education Reform—headed by New York hedge fund managers—were instrumental in electing Corey Booker and a slate of allied council candidates to run the city of Newark, New Jersey.[87] In 2011, the Louisiana Association of Business and Industry contributed $250,000 to elect reform-minded candidates to the state board of education. In Denver, the president of the school board was elected in 2009 with just $310 in campaign contributions; two years later, as part of a reform slate, this candidate and two others received over $200,000 apiece, primarily from corporate donors.[88] The Denver money came, in part, from an advocacy group named Stand for Children, which in turn had received nearly $2 million from investment firms. Wall Street firms are investing in municipal elections because cities now have something to sell beyond zoning decisions: their school systems.

Deprofessionalization—The Deskilling of Teachers

The emphasis on technology also helps explain the corporate lobbies' otherwise counterintuitive advocacy for lower teacher training and certification requirements. Whether in virtual or real classes, the charter school model often entails a curriculum narrowly focused on test preparation, delivered by a largely inexperienced, inexpensive staff designed to be replaceable after two or three years. In addition, as for-profit corporations come to represent a larger share of the charter industry, and as even nominally nonprofit schools develop partnerships with for-profit content providers, the new education industry is looking to deliver its product in a less costly and more controlled manner. From the point of view of charter corporations, it is irrational to think that each individual teacher should develop his or her own idiosyncratic means of teaching the laws of physics or the history of the American Revolution.

For the same reason, corporate lobbyists put little stock in the value of retaining long-term teachers. In fact, research shows that experienced teachers make for better education. Of course, individual teachers may be good or bad at any stage in their career. But other things being equal, teachers—like most professionals—get better with practice. On average, teachers are at their peak performance when they have twenty years' experience on the job. One study that examined the impact of teacher experience specifically in low-performing schools found that for the first twenty years, every additional year of teachers' experience translates into statistically significant improvements in students' educational achievement. After twenty years on the job, the impact of additional teacher experience becomes, on average, negative. However, this decline is sufficiently modest that a teacher with thirty years on the job still performs better than one with only ten years' experience.[89]

The school system in Finland—one of the world's best—seems to embody what most parents would hope for in their children's teachers. All teachers must be certified with a university degree in education, with no alternative routes to certification; middle and high school teachers generally cannot be employed without a master's degree.[90] Because the profession pays well and is treated with respect, it also attracts a high caliber of applicants. Fully 100 percent of Finland's schoolteachers come from the top third of their college graduating classes; the comparable figure in in the United States is only 23 percent, and in high-poverty schools only 14 percent.[91] As one of Finland's top education officials explains it, teachers are not simply knowledgeable in their subject area but are getting degrees in the pedagogy of *how to teach* it. For instance,

> The education of mathematics teachers . . . is based on subject didactics.
> . . . This guarantees that newly trained teachers with master's degrees
> have a systemic knowledge and understanding of how mathematics is
> learned and taught. . . . [Science teachers' training is] focused on build-
> ing pedagogical content knowledge. . . . Thus the science curriculum . . .
> has been transformed from traditional academic knowledge-based to
> experiment- and problem-oriented curriculum.[92]

Further, Finnish teachers are expected to continue honing their craft over the course of an extended career. The director general of the country's Ministry of Education explains that the school system follows a practice of "trust-based educational leadership" that endows teachers with "the full range of professional autonomy to practice what they have been educated to do: to plan, teach, diagnose, execute, and evaluate."[93] Rather than a routine that one learns once and repeats annually, teaching is treated as an endeavor of constant reflection and refinement in which the skills teachers bring to a classroom evolve and improve over time.

At home, however, state policies have been moving in the opposite direction. As long ago as 2001, the ALEC-affiliated Mackinac Center called for "privatizing or even loosening teacher certification."[94] In recent years, five states have adopted legislation doing just that. Many more, however, have either largely or completely exempted charter schools from certification requirements, and have allowed Teach for America staff to take sole responsibility for a class after no more than six weeks' training. The preamble to ALEC's Alternative Certification Act complains that "to obtain an education degree, students must often complete requirements in educational methods, theory and style rather than in-depth study in a chosen subject area," and calls for "alternative teacher certification programs to prepare persons with subject area expertise and life experience to become teachers." In 2013, Wisconsin adopted ALEC standards for charter school teachers, requiring that the state certify teachers as long as they have a BA and demonstrated proficiency in their subject matter, thus granting licenses to people who may have studied English or biology but have not spent a day mastering the pedagogy of how to teach these subjects.[95]

This stripping out of pedagogical training runs counter to common experience. When adults are asked to name their best English or math teacher, what makes their choices stand out is not that the person knew how to count or spell better than others, but how they taught the material. Yet this nearly universal recognition is ignored by corporate advocates. In Texas, the Chamber of Commerce in 2015 called for "alternative certification programs that provide school districts flexibility in hiring people holding bachelors' degrees or higher who pass certification exams."[96] For charter schools, ALEC goes further; its 2014 model Public Charter Schools Act states simply that "teachers in public charter schools shall be exempt from state teacher certification requirements."[97] And given the choice, charter schools increasingly choose to avoid certification. At one celebrated charter chain, executives openly disdain the value of teacher education programs, preferring to rely on a system of pay incentives to reward teachers for achieving math and reading test score goals.[98]

So too, the combination of pay cuts, deunionization, crowded classrooms, and teaching to the test has created a crisis in teacher recruitment and retention, leading to a less experienced, higher-turnover teaching staff. Teachers complain not only of financial stress and crowded classrooms but of the increasing difficulty of doing the work they entered the profession to carry out. One longtime history teacher, for instance, voiced his dismay in a public resignation letter that describes a system nearly diametrically opposite to the Finns':

> I have always [believed in] teaching "heavy," working hard, spending time, researching, attending to details, and never feeling satisfied that I knew enough on any topic. I now find that this approach to my profession is not only devalued, but denigrated and in some quarters despised. ... "Data driven" education seeks only conformity, standardization, testing and a zombie-like adherence to the shallow and generic Common Core. ... Creativity, academic freedom, teacher autonomy, experimentation and innovation are being stifled. ... Teachers [are] not permitted to develop and administer their own quizzes and tests ... or grade their own students' examinations. The development of plans, choice of lessons and the materials to be employed are increasingly expected to be common to all teachers in a given subject. This ... smothers the development of critical thinking in our students and assumes a one-size-fits-all mentality more appropriate to the assembly line than to the classroom. ... There is little time for us to carefully critique student work, engage in informal intellectual discussions with our students and colleagues, or conduct research and seek personal improvement through independent study. We have become increasingly evaluation and not knowledge driven. ... My profession ... no longer exists.[99]

Indiana is often hailed as one of the models of corporate-backed education reform. Between 2011 and 2015 legislators in the Hoosier state adopted new statutes restricting teachers' right to collective bargaining, expanding both charter schools and vouchers, authorizing online education, lowering certification standards, requiring that teacher evaluations be based on student test scores, and replacing across-the-board pay increases with merit pay that is reserved for those with the highest test scores and often comes in the form of a onetime bonus rather than a permanent raise. As a result, by 2015 the state faced an unprecedented teacher shortage. Over the preceding five years, both the number of newly licensed teachers and the number of students enrolling in teacher education programs fell by one-third.[100] Similarly, Kansas lawmakers over the same period enacted dramatic budget cuts, established a voucher program, lowered licensing requirements, restricted collective bargaining, and eliminated teachers' right to due process in challenging tenure decisions—and produced what one superintendent declared the worst teacher shortage on record. The number of nonretiring teachers who either left the state or quit the profession in the 2013–14 school year was more than 50 percent higher than it had been just three years earlier. In the summer of 2015, hundreds of teaching positions stood vacant just weeks before the start of the school year, leading some schools to hire less qualified staff and others to combine two classes into one overcrowded room in order not to abandon students to a teacherless classroom.[101]

Yet the response of the corporate lobbies and conservative legislators has been not to raise teacher salaries or improve working conditions in hopes of recruiting and retaining more highly qualified teachers, but the opposite: to repeatedly lower certification standards in order to access a larger pool of applicants who are willing to work under these degraded conditions. In Kansas, legislators solved the shortage of licensed teachers by entirely waiving licensing requirements for six school districts, including two of the state's largest.[102] In Wisconsin, Governor Walker kept licensing in place but continued to water down its meaning, proposing that anyone with "real life experience" and a bachelor's degree be eligible for certification—an innovation heartily endorsed by the Heritage Foundation.[103]

When Wisconsin lowered its licensing standards, one education scholar noted the "interesting juxtaposition" of legislators' simultaneously raising performance standards for public schoolteachers while lowering the requirements for new teacher certification.[104] This may be exactly the type of contradiction that leads observers like Mark Mizruchi to conclude that the corporate lobbies are unable to formulate a coherent strategy for addressing the nation's education crisis. In fact, however, ALEC, the Chamber of Commerce, and AFP have all championed both test-based "accountability" and "alternative" certification standards.[105] Thus, we must look for an underlying rationale that makes sense of these not as contradictory but as complementary policies. High-stakes tests are designed to undo tenure and close public schools. As that is accomplished, a new education system will emerge, which runs on cheaper, high-turnover instructors who follow canned curricula geared around test preparation and thus have no need for the levels of professionalism aspired to by previous generations of teachers.

What Does It All Mean, and Where Does It All Lead?

Putting together all the pieces of corporate education reform paints a troubling picture for the future of schooling. Over the past decade, the corporate agenda has advanced by fits and starts and through trial and error, experimenting with a variety of means for achieving reform, uncertain whether charters or vouchers represent the best model for remaking education, and with sometimes significant disagreements between competing corporate groups—AFP differs from the Chamber of Commerce, for instance, as to whether the Common Core or some other standard represents the best vehicle for measuring school performance. Yet running through this extensive and varied history is a clear and consistent focus on a few key priorities broadly shared by all the corporate lobbies. Through one route or another, they aim to replace public oversight with privately run schools, to downgrade the standards of teaching as a profession, to narrow curricula for most students, and to use for-profit digital products for a significant portion of the school day. In addition to all this, they aim to dissolve both the institution of education as a public good and the very idea of education as an entitlement of citizens that the government is responsible for providing.

In short, what was accomplished by hurricane in New Orleans is being pursued elsewhere by legislation. The path to privatization is increasingly straightforward: use standardized tests to declare poor schools "persistently failing"; put these under the control of a special, unelected authority; and then have that authority replace the public schools with charters. In its most ambitious version, this takeover strategy is being forced on tens of schools at a time. In 2011, both Tennessee and Michigan created special districts to take over low-scoring schools; in both cases, the superintendent was specifically authorized to replace public schools with charters.[106] In 2014–15, corporate lobbyists and Wisconsin legislators promoted bills to bypass the middle step and simply require that low-performing public schools be replaced by privately run charters.[107] Since test scores are primarily a function of poverty, it's no surprise that 80 percent of Tennessee's schools targeted for privatization are in Memphis, nor that the Michigan and Wisconsin bills focus, respectively, on Detroit and Milwaukee.[108]

Recently, corporate-backed advocates have begun insisting that no public authority whatsoever should be responsible for running schools. Neerav Kingsland, CEO of New Schools for New Orleans, warns that superintendents "must not succumb to the temptation to improve schools through better direct operation. Rather, [they] . . . must humbly acknowledge that a marketplace of school operators will . . . out-perform even the best direct-run system."[109] Reed Hastings similarly suggests that the role of elected school boards be limited to "bringing to town more and more charter school networks. Sort of like a Chamber of Commerce would to develop business."[110]

Thus, what "slum clearance" did for the real estate industry in the 1960s and 1970s, high-stakes testing will do for the charter industry: wipe away large swaths of public schools, enabling private operators to grow not school by school, but twenty or thirty schools at a time.

As noted, the fastest-growing sector of the for-profit charter industry is online.[111] However, the market for entirely virtual schools is limited, particularly in poor cities, where fewer parents can serve as the stay-at-home tutors required to supplement online modules. Investors thus face a contradiction: the greatest opportunity for charter school growth is in poor cities, but this is also where wholly online schools are least likely to flourish. The solution has appeared in the emergence of "blended learning" schools, where students attend physical schools but spend a portion of their day online. One of the exemplars of this model is the Rocketship Company, based in Silicon Valley with additional schools in Milwaukee, Nashville, and Washington, D.C.; the president of the Metropolitan Milwaukee Association of Commerce (MMAC) sits on Rocketship's board, and the company's model was upheld both in Milwaukee and by ALEC affiliates nationally as a model for what should replace troubled public schools.[112]

Rocketship's model is based on four principles. First, the company cuts costs by replacing teachers with technology. Starting in kindergarten, students spend one-quarter of their class time in teacherless computer labs, using video game–based math and reading applications. The company has voiced hopes of increasing digital instruction to as much as 50 percent of student learning time. Second, Rocketship relies on a corps of young, inexperienced, and low-cost teachers.[113] Teacher turnover is dramatic—approaching 30 percent in 2012–13—but the company contracts with Teach for America to supply a continuous stream of replacements. Third, the school has narrowed its curriculum to a near-exclusive focus on math and reading. Since both Rocketship's marketing strategy and teachers' salaries are based on reading and math scores, other topics are treated as inessential. There are no dedicated social studies or science classes, and the schools have no music classes, no foreign languages, no guidance counselors, and no libraries. Finally, Rocketship maintains a relentless focus on teaching to the test. Students take standardized tests every eight weeks; following each, the staff spends a full day revising lesson plans with an eye to improving scores. Rocketship boasts of its "backwards mapping" pedagogy—starting with test standards and then developing lesson plans to meet them. Rocketship is, as near as possible, all-test-prep all-the-time.[114]

The Rocketship model points to a critical distinction in the role of technology. Students in privileged schools often make extensive use of technology. But while these students are encouraged to be *active* users of technology—writing code, editing films, recording music, and designing graphics—Rocketship's students are *passive* users of technology, essentially plugged into video game–based applications designed to drill them for upcoming tests.

Rocketship itself is nonprofit, but its operation blurs the line between profit and nonprofit. For instance, Rocketship has received generous funding from both Reed Hastings and a fund headed by the venture capital executive John Doerr. In turn, Doerr and Hastings are among the primary investors in DreamBox—a for-profit math application that Rocketship uses in its computer labs.[115] The U.S. Department of Education reviewed DreamBox in December 2013, concluding that it has "no discernible effects on mathematics achievement." After

Rocketship-commissioned consultants offered further data, the DOE upgraded its assessment of DreamBox to "potentially positive" impacts based on "small evidence." Normally, if superintendents were presented with a curriculum rated somewhere between "no discernible effect" and "potentially positive" based on "small evidence," they might choose to look elsewhere. But if Rocketship rejects DreamBox, it may endanger funding critical for corporate growth. Thus, pedagogical choices are made not on the basis of what's best for students, but at least partially based on the financial interests of private investors.

The DreamBox story points to a second explanation for corporate animosity toward elected school boards. With charter schools, tech companies can cut a deal with a single executive, covering hundreds of schools, and product choice may reflect financial rather than pedagogical criteria. By contrast, public school curricula are set by officials who are accountable to a locally elected board and are prohibited from any financial relationship with vendors. As Hastings explains, "School districts . . . [are hard] to sell to because . . . [they] are really reacting to voter forces more than to market forces."[116] For investors, then, elected school boards are viewed primarily as obstacles to market growth.

The most extreme school makeover plan—and the most radical vision for eliminating public oversight of k-12 schooling—comes from Michigan. In 2012, a secret clique of gubernatorial aides and technology industry representatives cooked up a proposal to issue Detroit students "EduCards"—modeled on food stamp debit cards—loaded with each student's education funding. Students would be encouraged to enroll in a combination of courses from different schools—including for-profit online vendors—with each class receiving an equal share of student tax dollars. The state's commitment was limited to a narrow curriculum of basics. Beyond that, the Detroit News explained, "students could use leftover money on the 'EduCard' for . . . Advanced Placement courses, music lessons, sport team fees, [or] remedial education."[117] When the Michigan plan was leaked, public outcry forced the plotters to back off. But its outlines offer a troubling vision of where the industry may be headed.

At its most ambitious, the education reform movement has already begun to challenge the fundamental notion of education as a public right. When Michigan took control of a Detroit-area school district in 2012 and hired a private charter company to run the entire district, the American Civil Liberties Union filed a class-action suit alleging that the state was abandoning its responsibility to provide a decent education to Michigan children. In response, the Snyder administration argued that once it contracted with the private operator, the government no longer bore responsibility for guaranteeing any particular quality of education.[118] Ultimately, the state appeals court went even further than the governor, ruling that—regardless of privatization—the state has no constitutional obligation to provide students any particular standard of education.[119] The full ramifications of this decision are not yet clear, but it opens a legal door to the final unraveling of public schooling.

It is clear what venture capitalists and hedge fund investors hope to get out of education reform; so too for Republican strategists looking to defund unions. More broadly, and for those corporate organizations that have no direct financial stake in the industry, the dismantling of education may—whether consciously or not—play a central function in lowering expectations and accustoming the public to make do with conditions of increased inequality. Education is the one remaining public good to which most Americans still believe we are entitled by right of citizenship; destroying it through privatization may have far-reaching ramifications in erasing the commonsense consensus for using progressive taxation to provide universal services. There is nothing more personal to most adults than their children, and the experience of gradually coming to accept larger and still larger classes; further cutbacks in art, language, and science; with spottier instruction from more poorly trained teachers, has a deeply personal effect. In addition, education itself is intrinsically linked to expectations. Apart from conveying knowledge, school also conveys powerful messages of what is expected of students and what they should expect of themselves. Traditionally, part of the role of teachers is to encourage students to raise their sights, to aim higher, to gain a greater sense of their own capacities, and to be bolder in what they hope to accomplish in life. If the role of teachers is scaled back to test preparation, delivering lessons based on nationally marketed curricular products, and limited to a few narrowly defined subjects, instructors come to convey the opposite: don't think too much of yourselves; we don't think it's worth investing too much in you.

In this sense, it may be meaningful that some of the states most often held up as exemplars of corporate reform have also been leaders in the political censorship of school materials that might encourage populist mobilization against the economic elite. ALEC's Founding Philosophy and Principles Act calls on all states to institute mandatory civics courses stressing core principles including small government, "freedom of individual enterprise," and "limitations on government power to tax."[120] Florida embodied this spirit in a 2006 law requiring that only "factual" history be taught in school, defined to include "the nature and importance of free enterprise."[121] Arizona in 2012 shut down the teaching of Mexican American Studies in Tucson high schools, banning any courses that "promote resentment of a particular race or class of people"; the law's author complained that ethnic studies was teaching students resentment toward "the white power structure."[122] Finally, in Indiana, Governor Mitch Daniels instituted a systemwide overhaul of the state's teacher-training standards with the sole motive of removing Howard Zinn's *A People's History of the United States* from the curriculum.[123]

Long ago, an adviser to Presidents Nixon and Reagan noted the pitfalls that could come from educating working-class students in a time of economic scarcity. "We are in danger of producing an educated proletariat," he warned. "We have to be selective about who we allow to go through higher education. If not, we will have a large number of highly trained and unemployed people."[124] No one since has spoken this logic out loud. Yet, whether consciously or not, for those at the top of the economy it may still be true that, in periods of long-term decline, the last thing you want is a lot of well-educated poor people. Thus for reasons of social strategy as well as financial interest, the dismantling of public education may serve the broader corporate aim of accelerating inequality while forestalling populist backlash.

What Defines Good Schools?

While there are decades of scholarly research pointing to the importance of small classes and broad curricula, there is a much simpler way to judge the value of these things: by observing which schools the country's elite select for their own children. While these schools include technology, it is not used to substitute for teachers. On the contrary, *Forbes*'s review of the country's top schools stresses that it is "tiny classes" and "individualized attention" that "help students earn their way into the best colleges."[125]

Even those insisting on a stripped-down version of education as public policy choose something different for their own children. Thus, Chicago's mayor, Rahm Emanuel—who famously fought with teachers over class size and test-based evaluations—sent his own children to the University of Chicago Lab School. The school has seven full-time art teachers and three libraries, and the school's director, David Magill, writes that "world languages, libraries and the arts are not frills. They are an essential piece of a well-rounded education." Further, Magill explains that his school does not evaluate teachers on the basis of standardized tests: "Measuring outcomes through standardized testing and referring to those results as the evidence of learning and the bottom line is misguided," he explains.[126]

So too, in Wisconsin Rocketship's most important backer is the Metropolitan Milwaukee Association of Commerce. In 2013, the MMAC testified in support of a bill that would make it easier for companies like Rocketship to expand, dubbing such schools "the best of the best."[127] Yet the suburban hometown schools of both MMAC's president and its chairman, which are ranked among the state's best, look very different. Both have approximately fifteen students for every licensed teacher, or half the Rocketship ratio. Both provide music, art, and libraries with professional librarians. And both boast veteran teaching staffs, with 90 percent of teachers at one school holding graduate degrees.[128] Thus while the Rocketship model may be rhetorically touted as the gold standard for poor neighborhoods, it appears that corporate leaders implicitly recognize the value of a broader education.

Manufactured Failure: Understanding the Corporate Agenda

Decades of studies confirm that the single most important factor affecting educational achievement is inequality of wealth and poverty. Since the inception of testing under No Child Left Behind, students from economically disadvantaged families have *never* scored higher than their better-off peers—at any age, in any state.[129] The impact of poverty similarly outweighs any difference between charter and public schools for students of any ethnicity, income level, or disability.[130] This is partially because students from poor families start school with less exposure to reading, writing, and vocabulary. But poverty's impact on education is often much simpler and cruder than underexposure to vocabulary. As one scholar notes,

> First, health matters. Children who can't see well can't read as well as those who can, and lower-class children, on average, have poorer vision than middle-class children. Lower-income children have a higher incidence of lead poisoning, poorer nutrition, and higher rates of iron-deficiency anemia, which result in impaired cognitive ability. They have greater exposure to environmental toxins, air pollution, and smoke, and therefore greater incidence of asthma. Lower-class children have less adequate pediatric care, resulting in more frequent absences from school.... The lack of affordable housing for low-income families [also] has a demonstrable effect on average achievement. Children whose families have difficulty finding adequate housing move frequently, and student mobility is an important cause of low achievement. Teachers cannot work as effectively with children who are in their classrooms for a short time as with those who stay longer.[131]

The single most important step policymakers could take to improve the education of disadvantaged students would be to make it easier for their parents to earn a living wage—or to ensure a sufficiently strong safety net to enable jobless families to live decently. Instead, many of the same corporate organizations advancing education reform also support economic policies that make it more difficult for families to pull themselves out of poverty. It is simply impossible to declare oneself against the minimum wage, against food stamps, against public housing, against mass transit, against unemployment insurance, and against wage theft enforcement and simultaneously proclaim one's commitment to closing the education gap.

The corporate lobbies' proposals to replace public schools with privately run charters are presented as a needed response to "failure." Yet by supporting reduced school funding and opposing economic policies that make it easier for families to work their way out of poverty, these organizations are helping create the conditions most likely to ensure failure. Indeed, the business lobbies appear to be in the position of first helping to *create* educational failure and then proposing to sweep in and solve the problem through privatization.

Understanding the corporate agenda also helps make sense of the myriad attacks on teachers' unions seen in states across the country. It is telling that while teachers have been attacked as overpaid, restrictions on collective bargaining have not aimed at their ability to negotiate wages or benefits. Instead, they have overwhelmingly focused on the right of teachers to voice proposals regarding standards of educational quality. In both Indiana and Idaho, for instance, lawmakers prohibited teachers from bargaining over class size, technology, professional development, performance evaluations, or curriculum—anything but wages and benefits. Michigan's law adds the privatization of school services to the list of topics forbidden from negotiations.

At the heart of the offensive against teachers' unions is the idea that teachers are selfish, placing their own interests ahead of their students'. But the legislative record suggests just the opposite. In the fall of 2010, the Florida education advisor and charter champion Patricia Levesque advised reformers that they needed to "spread" the teachers' union thin by introducing a plethora of antiunion bills. It didn't matter so much whether those items passed or failed; by occupying the attention and energy of union leaders, they would enable more important items such as charter expansion to fly through the legislature "under the radar."[132] In 2015, the chairman of the Oklahoma Republican Party likewise argued that teachers should be banned from paying union dues through their employers' electronic payroll system not because union economic demands were too high but because they were "block[ing] some of the most important education reforms . . . such as school choice."[133] If only unions restricted their concern to their own wages and benefits, they might be less subject to attack. The primary cause for antiunion animus from the corporate lobbies, it appears, is not that teachers' wages are unaffordable but that they represent the primary political obstacle standing in the way of the unbridled triumph of corporate education reform.

SILENCING LABOR'S VOICE

The Campaign to Remove Unions from Politics

One of the central political puzzles of recent legislative history is why large private corporations devote such substantial efforts to dismantling public employee unions.

Earlier chapters of this book described the labor market effects that make unions a larger concern than their numbers might otherwise suggest: strong unions create competitive pressure for other employers to raise wages, and keep alive the possibility of new waves of organizing in response to widespread hardship. But the legislative record makes clear that in addition to these economic concerns, the corporate lobbies seek to erase unions as a political force. Across the country, ALEC, the Chamber, AFP, and others have promoted laws that restrict the ability of unions to collect dues from their members—particularly those dues used for political purposes. These laws are independent of initiatives to restrict collective bargaining, impose wage cuts, or outlaw fair-share agreements. Instead, these laws are targeted at those employees who choose to be union members, prohibiting their paying dues through the public payroll system and, in the private sector, creating cumbersome and costly bureaucratic procedures aimed at discouraging union political activity. From 2011 to 2015, legislatures in ten states adopted such laws, with proposals under active consideration in many more.

For Republican strategists, the impetus for getting unions out of politics is obvious. But the corporations that dominate ALEC or the U.S. Chamber of Commerce are less interested in partisanship per se than in enacting a particular policy agenda. Further, while such laws have been adopted in the political battleground states of Michigan and Wisconsin, they have also been enacted in locales such as Georgia and Oklahoma, where Republicans have little cause for worry about legislative control. Thus this offensive cannot be explained simply as a means of gaining partisan advantage. Why, then, are they motivated to devote such resources to this effort?

This chapter examines the recent history and legislative debates surrounding union dues and political spending. Examining this set of laws and the vigorous advocacy efforts mounted on their behalf fills in a crucial piece of the puzzle in understanding the corporate agenda, further explaining why unions remain such a central target of the corporate lobbies, and foreshadowing what the country might look like if ALEC succeeds in its mission.

Those who call for restricting the use of union dues for politics describe their goal as safeguarding workers' rights by ensuring their dues aren't used for political causes they oppose. In fact, these laws create one-sided rules that strictly limit unions while giving free rein to corporate political activity. The intensity that advocates bring to this issue points to its central importance. Bringing together the broad agenda described in earlier chapters with corporate lobbyists' own rationale for restricting union politics leads to a new understanding of business antiunionism. The corporate lobbies seek to eradicate unions because, even in its weakened and shrunken state, the labor movement poses the one significant political obstacle that prevents ALEC and the Chamber from remaking laws with a completely free hand. Overwhelmingly, this is not a contest over union rights themselves; the vast majority of the issues on which labor and business battle primarily affect the 88 percent of American workers who are not protected by a union contract. A close analysis of this issue, then, turns on its head one of the central themes of antiunion politics. Union political activity is under the gun not because it serves to enrich members at the expense of the public, but the opposite: it is primarily because of what they do for nonunion workers— advocating for minimum wage, sick leave, and similar rights—that unions have come under such sustained assault. This, finally, explains why defunding union political operations remains such a high priority even for corporations whose own employees are nonunion.

The Role of Unions in Politics

In 2012, the Princeton political scientist Martin Gillens published groundbreaking research on how economic inequality affects elected officials' responsiveness to the policy preferences of their constituents. Gillens's results are bracing: elected officials respond almost exclusively to the views of the wealthiest 10 percent of the population. Average citizens have no independent sway over elected officials, and even when the bottom 70 percent of the population disagrees with the wealthiest 10 percent, it is the elites' view that most often wins out. "The preferences of the vast majority of Americans," Gillens concludes, "appear to have essentially no impact on which policies the government does or doesn't adopt."[1]

The one force that even modestly counteracts the influence of the rich is public awareness; thus Gillens reports that politicians are relatively more responsive to low-income voters during presidential election years, when the public as a whole is paying greater attention to politics.[2] But public engagement on policy issues is hard to come by. Furthermore, political knowledge is greatest among the affluent and weakest among the working class and poor.[3] Thus, in order to pass progressive economic legislation that runs counter to the interests of the affluent, one must build political awareness and excitement precisely among that part of the population that is least likely to be engaged.

Unions play a unique role in this equation. By aggregating the financial contributions of what are still nearly fifteen million members, unions provide by far the largest source of financial support for progressive economic policies. Beyond money and volunteers, unions serve several additional functions that are less visible but equally critical in American politics. First, internal political organizing means that union members—and their families—are more likely to vote than otherwise similar voters.[4] Unions also organize workers across race and gender lines that otherwise typically separate communities, creating the possibility for effective action on broad economic interests. Moreover, political conversations among union members change how people understand politics and how they vote. Voters often hold contradictory beliefs that can lead either right or left. When unions set out to educate members on a political issue, with thousands of employees volunteering to educate their coworkers, the impact can be very powerful. Thus one analysis found that union members were dramatically more likely to vote for Barak Obama in 2008 than otherwise similar but unorganized voters.[5] Finally, unions often make it possible for working-class Americans to voice political demands they might otherwise find uncomfortable or even shameful. Part of the deep experience of class is the widespread propensity to blame oneself for economic hardships.[6] The sociologist William Domhoff argues that "it is only when people are part of collective efforts that they overcome their tendency to blame themselves."[7] For a lone individual, demanding a right to paid sick leave, affordable health care, or accessible public transportation may seem selfish, pitiful, whiny, or simply futile. As part of a mass organization that voices collective demands for society as a whole, what may be shameful as an individual becomes

FIGURE 5.1.   Legislation restricting union dues collection or political activity, 2011–15. Arizona, Missouri, and Ohio laws were vetoed or overturned.

much more palatable. In all these ways, then, labor unions serve an irreplaceable role in facilitating the political voice of the nonrich. Unions' political strength has been radically degraded over the past few decades, and the labor movement has mostly been losing. Nevertheless, to imagine the American polity without the labor movement is to imagine the elite of Gillens's analysis with completely unchecked power.

Unfortunately, this is exactly the policy direction that the nation's most powerful corporate lobbies have been promoting in state legislatures across the country. The past five years have seen the corporate lobbies engaged in a relentless effort to cut off union dues in order to silence labor's voice in policy debates. From January 2011 through the end of 2015, ten states passed some version of such laws, with numerous other legislatures still considering their own proposals (figure 5.1).[8]

The Origins of "Paycheck Protection"

For twenty years, a coalition of conservative activists, Republican lawmakers, and corporate lobbyists have championed legislation requiring unions to obtain annual written authorization from each member before spending any of that member's dues on political activities. Dubbed "paycheck protection" by its supporters, such legislation has an obvious logical appeal: workers should not be forced to contribute to political causes they do not support. As will be shown below, the actual function of these laws is to stifle the political voice of workers—a goal made ever clearer as the policy has evolved to take increasingly ambitious forms.

The first "paycheck protection" proposal—California's Proposition 226 in 1998—was initiated by a religious organization that had previously championed a law allowing public funds to be diverted to religious schools. When voters rejected this idea, backers concluded that their failure was due to the opposition of the teachers' union; they launched paycheck protection not in order to safeguard the rights of teachers but to remove teachers' collective voice from state politics.[9] Then–House Speaker Newt Gingrich was among those who campaigned for the bill, along with the Chamber of Commerce, NAM, NFIB, Grover Norquist's Americans for Tax Reform, and the Koch-funded Citizens for a Sound Economy, a precursor to today's Americans for Prosperity.[10]

Despite its defeat by California voters, corporate lobbies trumpeted Proposition 226 as a model for other states. In the same year that Proposition 226 was put on the ballot, ALEC adopted a model Paycheck Protection Act, distributed to legislators across the country.[11] The following year, it unveiled the yet more ambitious Public Employee Freedom Act and Public Employer Payroll Deduction Policy Act, both of which prohibit public employees from contributing any type of dues through the payroll system—even if the contribution is voluntary and even if the dues are not used for political purposes.[12]

Proponents of so-called paycheck protection alternately claim that these bills will save taxpayers money, remove the government from the role of collecting funds used for political purposes, and increase workers' control over how their wages are spent. The actual record of such legislation, however, suggests that their true aim lies elsewhere.

Assessing Claims: "Paycheck Protection" Creates No New Rights for Workers

Even in its most limited form—simply requiring that each union member provide annual written authorization before his or her dues can be spent on political activities—paycheck protection serves to hamstring workers' political voice and tilt the political playing field toward corporate power. To begin, it is critical to note that such bills do not provide employees with any rights they don't already possess under law. By law, unions may contribute to political campaigns only through a political action committee (PAC), which cannot be funded from regular dues money but only through separate, voluntary contributions by individual union members. Further, even more general political activities such as issue advocacy, voter registration drives, and independent expenditures in support of endorsed candidates cannot be funded by dues money from any individual who objects to these priorities. Under both federal and state law, no employee—whether in the private sector or the public—can be forced to pay even one cent to support a politician or political cause that he or she opposes. Even in the strongest union states, all employees have the right to withhold any portion of their dues that might be used to fund political activities.

In championing Missouri's 2012 paycheck protection bill, that state's Chamber of Commerce argued that "employees who pay union dues have no say whether campaign contributions are taken out of their dues, or where those contributions are directed."[13] This is false: employees have complete say over whether campaign contributions may be taken out of their dues.

Indeed, workers have multiple channels through which to control union political priorities. As stated above, every employee has the right to refuse to contribute dues to political causes. In addition, of course, every union member has the right to vote out current union leadership and elect leaders whose political preferences reflect their own—or who pledge to avoid politics altogether. Finally, all union members can vote to get rid of their union entirely. Thus, at least three legal channels exist for employees who disagree with their union's political activities—they may withhold their dues money as individuals, they may elect new leadership, or they may disband the union. All these things are legally straightforward, and all of them occur every year. But they happen in exceedingly small numbers, suggesting that it is corporate lobbyists—rather than a silent majority of employees—who are most opposed to unions' political activism.

Muffling Workers' Collective Voice under Cumbersome New Bureaucracies

While paycheck protection laws do not give employees new rights, they do raise significant barriers to the ability of organized workers to participate as full partners in political debates. By requiring annual written notice from each individual employee, such laws impose an extensive new bureaucratic obligation on unions. Even considering only those employees who wholly support their union's political activity, a union would need to devote considerable time, energy, and staff resources to meeting with each individual member each year and to distributing, collecting, filing, and forwarding to state officials tens of thousands of forms annually. The resources devoted to this operation must be deducted from those needed to negotiate contracts and represent employees in disputes with management. In other contexts, corporate lobbies vociferously oppose even milder procedural hurdles to political participation. For example, ALEC staunchly opposes proposals that would require political advertisements to simply list their top contributors, arguing that this represents "an onerous burden on the organization, which has the effect of chilling speech."[14] Yet ALEC and other corporate lobbies seek to impose much more onerous burdens on unions. Ultimately, the requirement of collecting thousands of individual authorization forms each year effectively mandates either that dues be raised in order to pay for the activity of keeping authorization forms current or that employees receive poorer representation, as staff time is diverted from representational to bureaucratic activities, hence undermining the union's effectiveness.

Furthermore, it is likely that a significant number of those who support their union's political activity would nevertheless miss their annual filing deadline, at least for some months. This is not a special feature of labor unions; if we were all required to reapply every year for car insurance, garbage pickup, or newspaper subscriptions, it is likely that some of us would miss the deadline—particularly if it were impossible to renew by phone, e-mail, or any means other than signed hard-copy statement. Even if it took only a couple of months to correct this omission, union dues would go unpaid for that time. Spread over tens of thousands of members, such natural pitfalls are likely to result in significant lost revenue.

It is instructive that no paycheck protection law provides an option for employees who support their union's political program, have supported it for years, and don't want to fill out annual forms. An employee is not permitted, for instance, to sign a document committing to pay dues until such time as he notifies the union otherwise. It is hard not to view this as taking away such employees' right to contract.

One Rule for Unions, Another Rule for Corporations

Business lobbies claim that their support for paycheck protection legislation is based on a commitment to individuals' right to control what type of politics their money supports. But they vigorously oppose the same principle when it is applied to corporations.

In 2011, in response to the *Citizens United* ruling, ten states considered bills that would have required corporations to obtain shareholder approval for political donations. With ALEC lobbying against them, all ten were defeated.[15] In September 2010, ALEC adopted a resolution arguing that "shareholder approval schemes, in which a corporation's shareholders . . . are required to give approval of a corporation's political expenditures, place an onerous burden on these organizations, which serves as a barrier to free speech."[16]

This issue came to a head in 2011, when the New York legislature considered a bill that would have required corporations to obtain annual written authorization from a majority of shareholders before spending treasury funds on politics. In response, ALEC published an "issue alert" arguing that such requirements would "deter . . . [corporations] from participating in political debate" and asserting that the bill "stifles . . . public debate and undermines the very purpose of the First Amendment." Furthermore, ALEC insisted that shareholder approval of political donations is unnecessary because "shareholders always have the option of voting out board members and removing management who engage in independent expenditures contrary to the interests of the company and its owners."[17] This exact same logic applies to unions as well, of course. Yet what ALEC characterizes as an intolerable impediment to First Amendment rights for corporations, it vigorously promotes for labor unions.

Even in the treatment of payroll deductions themselves, corporate-backed legislation establishes a stark double standard. In Missouri, the house majority leader and ALEC state chairman, Tim Jones, explained his support for that state's 2013 bill by arguing that "no one should be forced to make compulsory contributions to an organization which will use the funds to support candidates that the worker may not support."[18] This sentiment was repeated by Americans for Prosperity, which trumpeted the legislation as guaranteeing workers the "freedom to decide whether or not their earnings are put toward political activity to which they may object."[19] So too, the Missouri Chamber of Commerce declared it supported the law because "people have a right to designate which candidate gets support with their money."[20] But all these principles apply only to money contributed to workers' organizations—not that contributed to corporations.

At the time this bill was being debated, the state of Missouri offered public employees more than 450 options for electronic payroll deductions. Many of these are payments to corporations that use their revenue, in part, to fund political lobbying and campaign contributions. Among the most noteworthy are the following:[21]

- Health insurance payments for the Missouri Consolidated Health Care Plan, which is operated by United Medical Resources, a division of the (ALEC member) United Health Group. United Health Group used treasury funds to support an ambitious political program, including $3.4 million in lobbying activities in 2012.

- Insurance premium payments to Coventry Health Care, which spent over $1 million on lobbying activities in 2008–9 during the height of congressional debate over health care reform.
- Insurance premiums used to pay the (ALEC member) Express Scripts Company, which administers the state's prescription drug benefit; Express Scripts spent nearly $1.9 million to lobby Congress in 2012 and $340,000 to lobby Missouri lawmakers.
- Hospital gap insurance purchased from the (ALEC member) AFLAC Corporation, which made campaign contributions totaling $2.5 million in 2012 and spent $21 million on lobbying over the preceding five years.
- Purchasing tax-sheltered annuities through the Aetna Insurance Company. Aetna spent $17.6 million on lobbying in the five years leading up to 2012, including $4.1 million that year. The company also contributed more than $2.2 million to state and federal candidate campaigns in 2012.

In regulating dues deductions for labor unions, paycheck protection laws assume that, unless it is held in a separate segregated account, all money is fungible. Unions are required to treat all expenses as if they are paid in equal shares by each member's dues; thus members who object to supporting political activities must have their dues reduced by that amount—not simply told that *their* dues won't go to politics and others will pay more in their place. This is made clear, for instance, in the Missouri bill's requirement that "individuals who do not authorize [political] contributions . . . shall not have their dues . . . increased in lieu of contribution."[22]

If the same logic applies to all deductions, insurance companies can't plausibly declare that no part of *Missouri* employees' premiums are used for lobbying activities. Rather, some portion of every dollar employees pay to banks and insurance companies must be assumed to support corporate political activities. ALEC's Paycheck Protection Act declares that "taking political contributions from workers without their fully informed consent violates these workers' rights."[23] It appears, however, that this principle applies only to organizations that are politically opposed to ALEC. In every state where paycheck protection has been advanced, contributions to investment banks and insurance companies— including ALEC member firms—are untouched by the law, leaving corporations completely free to deduct moneys out of employee paychecks and use them for political purposes without employees' knowledge or consent.

This double standard lies at the heart of the corporate legislative agenda, and occasionally is expressed in particularly naked terms. In Tennessee, for instance, both the Chamber of Commerce and the NFIB urged legislators to approve a pair of bills embodying this contradictory logic.[24] One bill gave corporations the right, for the first time ever, to make direct contributions to candidate campaigns—extending corporate rights even beyond those established in *Citizens United*. The second bill would have made it a class C misdemeanor for a labor organization to contribute to a candidate for public office. Both bills were sponsored in the house by a former Republican caucus chair and in the senate by an ALEC member, and both received the enthusiastic backing of business lobbies.

Paycheck Protection 2.0: No-Win Reporting Requirements and an Expanding Scope of Prohibited Activities

As the corporate lobbies have won more victories in state legislatures, they have been emboldened by success and have become yet more ambitious. Both Arizona and Missouri have moved beyond traditional paycheck protection legislation to create added reporting requirements that pose significant new financial threats to unions engaged in political activity. Under current state and federal law, unions must file annual reports showing what percentage of their expenses was devoted to political activities. Each year's report determines the percentage rebate that must be awarded in the following year to those who opt out of supporting their union's political agenda. By contrast, the new Arizona and Missouri laws require unions to determine *in advance*, and announce at the start of each year, how much they will spend on political activities in the coming year. This declaration in turn determines what share of dues is waived for that year's nonsupporters. It is illegal for a union to spend more than its predicted political budget, with Arizona imposing a fine of $10,000 per employee on a union whose political spending exceeds projections.[25] Yet it is easy to imagine how political events unforeseen at the start of a year might end up requiring greater than anticipated resources, leaving unions facing untenable financial choices. For example, Ohio's legislature adopted S.B. 5 in March 2011, largely eliminating bargaining rights for the state's four hundred thousand public employees. Opponents of the bill gathered 1.2 million signatures in order to force a citizen referendum, and in November 2011, Ohioans voted to overturn the law. The response to S.B. 5 entailed intensive activities by thousands of union members. But since neither legislators nor the governor had campaigned on such antiunion proposals, this fight could not possibly have been anticipated at the start of the year. The law thus puts unions in a no-win bind. If a union underestimates its political needs, it risks being unable to respond to potentially existential legislative threats Yet to the extent a union cautiously overestimates its anticipated political budget, it forgoes that much greater a share of dues revenue.

Together with such high-risk reporting requirements, labor opponents have also sought to broaden the definition of "political" activities subject to funding restrictions. Where the first generation of such bills aimed at a traditional understanding of union political activity—financial, advertising, and field support for candidate or initiative campaigns—recent laws passed in Alabama, Arizona, Kansas, and Missouri all aim at a broader scope of activity. Alabama's Act 761, for example, defines "political activity" to include "public opinion polling," "any form of political communication," "any type of political advertising," "phone calling for any political purpose," or "distributing political literature of any type."[26] For Alabama union members to make voluntary dues contributions through the payroll system, their unions would have to disavow any of these activities, conducted with any part of the organization's budget. Kansas's law similarly makes it illegal—even for employees who voluntarily choose to pay dues—to use electronic payroll deductions to process dues payments earmarked for "political purposes," broadly defined to include any "act done . . . in a way to influence or tend to influence, directly, or indirectly, any person . . . to vote for or against any candidate for public office."[27] The state Chamber of Commerce testified in support of the bill, with its director of legislative affairs explaining to lawmakers that "I need this bill passed so we can get rid of public sector unions."[28] Paul Kersey, longtime "labor expert" for the Heritage Foundation, ALEC, and multiple states' corporate-funded think tanks, declared the 2013 Kansas law a "good step" but rued that "it could have been stronger."[29]

Finally, Arizona's 2011 law—designated a "priority bill" by the state Chamber of Commerce—requires that both public- and private-sector unions get annual written authorization from each member before spending any amount of dues money for "political purposes," defined as "supporting or opposing any candidate . . . political party, referendum, initiative, [or] political issue advocacy." Thus at the same time that corporations are being freed to engage in ever more extensive political activity, unions are being restricted from engaging in activities that were legal even before *Citizens United*.

Silencing Workers' Voice: The Increasingly Ambitious Aims of "Paycheck Protection" Legislation

As ALEC, the Chamber of Commerce and allied corporate lobbies have refined their paycheck protection strategies, it is increasingly clear that the goal of such legislation is simply to silence workers' voice in politics. Over the past five years, a majority of the states adopting paycheck protection laws were right-to-work states.[30] In such states, it is already law that no employee can pay any amount of union dues unless he or she actively chooses to sign up as a union member. Thus, every individual paying dues is—by definition—doing so by personal, voluntary choice.

What, then, is the purpose of paycheck protection laws in states that already have right-to-work laws? For employees who have not affirmatively chosen to be dues-paying union members, paycheck protection laws will have no effect whatsoever; employees will not be asked each year whether they would like to contribute to union political activities. The *only* impact of such a law, then, is to impose a vast and costly bureaucratic machinery on those employees who have specifically chosen to be dues-paying members. Rather than enhancing employee choice, paycheck protection bills in these states serve primarily to frustrate the choice that has already been made by those who voluntarily contribute union dues.

The paycheck protection measure adopted in the right-to-work state of Alabama stands in direct contradiction to ALEC's 1998 insistence that "workers have a right to control their own political contributions."[31] Act 761—authored by the majority leader and ALEC member Senator James Waggoner—prohibits payroll deduction of dues for any "membership organization which uses any portion of the dues for political activity."[32] Thus rather than insisting on workers' right to control where their money goes, the bill removes their ability to choose to contribute to political causes. California's Proposition 32—a failed 2012 ballot initiative backed with tens of millions of dollars from corporate and antiunion advocates—similarly aimed to completely ban the use of payroll deductions to pay dues that might be used for political activities, even if employees submitted annual written authorization indicating their desire to make such voluntary contributions.[33] In all these cases, it appears that the true agenda of those advocating paycheck protection is not to enhance freedom of association but to cripple the ability of organized workers to participate meaningfully in the political process.

Perhaps the clearest instance of silencing workers was in North Carolina, where in early 2012 the legislature voted to prohibit schoolteachers from paying voluntary union dues through the public payroll system. North Carolina is not merely a right-to-work state; its public employees also have no right to collective bargaining. Thus, teachers do not negotiate contracts with local school boards; rather, the North Carolina Association of Educators (NCAE) is strictly an advocacy organization. In 2011, after Republican legislators supported a plan to cut education funding by $1 billion, NCAE organized a demonstration by thousands of teachers; the dues prohibition was widely seen as retaliation for this protest.[34] Under North Carolina's preexisting law, employees had the option to "authorize in writing the periodic [payroll] deduction . . . [of] voluntary contributions for the employees' association."[35] The new statute eliminated that right for school district employees.[36]

Teachers argued against the bill on exactly the terms that paycheck protection advocates originally invoked. "We should have the right to choose what we decide is taken out of our paycheck," explained Kristy Moore, president of the Durham Association of Educators.[37] An unsuspecting reader might think this statement came from ALEC itself. In fact, however, ALEC, the Chamber of Commerce, and other antiunion advocates do not support employees' right to choose whether or not to support union political activities; they only support the right *not* to support such efforts.

Beyond arguments about workers' rights, prohibitions against public employee dues deductions have also been portrayed as efforts to conserve scarce taxpayer dollars. ALEC's Public Employer Payroll Deduction Policy Act, for instance, argues that "it is in the interest of this State's citizens that government resources . . . be used exclusively for activities that are essential to carrying out the necessary functions of government," which "do not include . . . the special convenience of deducting membership dues from . . . [employees'] paychecks."[38] So too, when Michigan legislators banned teachers from paying union dues through the payroll system, Governor Snyder suggested that the law would ensure that "state public school resources be devoted to the education of our children."[39] Unsurprisingly, the Michigan Chamber of Commerce "strongly" supported this bill, arguing that "in these challenging economic times, those responsible for expending government resources must be ever more vigilant that monies are being directed for the public good. . . . Since the monitoring and collection of union dues requires financial resources, it should be the obligation of the union to undertake this activity and not look to taxpayers to ensure the collection of dues."[40]

But electronic payroll deductions are essentially costless. Michigan's own Senate Fiscal Agency concluded that this bill "would have no fiscal impact on the state."[41] The Michigan House of Representatives' legislative analysis of the bill reports that even in small school districts, "the bill would have no significant fiscal impact" because "payroll deduction for union dues . . . is largely automated, so there is very little work districts must go through on a regular basis."[42] Indeed, in every state where the issue has been addressed by fiscal authorities, the conclusion has been the same: there is no identifiable cost to electronic payroll deductions.[43] The ultimate hollowness of cost-saving arguments was driven home in Kansas, where the legislature debated a 2015 proposal to ban all union dues deductions— for political or any other purpose—through the public payroll system. At the time, the Kansas Organization of State Employees was paying the state 6.5 cents per employee per month to cover the cost of processing dues. Nevertheless, the Chamber of Commerce and NFIB argued that, at a time of budget constraints, the government couldn't continue providing this service.[44]

Finally, in at least two states, union opponents have gone so far as to seek to block unions from collecting dues even outside the payroll system. Traditionally, where there is no agreement for dues to be contributed by payroll deduction, unions ask members to provide voluntary authorization for regular monthly dues to be paid from their individual bank accounts or credit cards; this avoids wasting inordinate staff time collecting monthly checks from each member. But even these actions have come under attack. When Alabama adopted a ban on payroll deduction of dues for political activities, the National Right to Work Committee celebrated the law for finally ensuring that "teacher unions must collect their own dues."[45] But Alabama officials apparently intended something even more sweeping. Two months after the bill passed, the state announced that union representatives were prohibited from visiting community college campuses in order to sign members up for bank drafts so that they could make their dues contributions in the easiest manner. The state's Department of Postsecondary Education issued a memo to all community college presidents instructing them to prohibit union representatives from coming to campus "for the purpose of signing up its members for bank drafts to pay Alabama Education Association dues."[46] Since Alabama is a right-to-work state, all dues are strictly voluntary. The state was thus engaged in extensive efforts to block employees from *voluntarily* contributing to a union political fund out of their own bank accounts. This has nothing to do with safeguarding employee rights or saving the state money; the only purpose is to silence the voice of organized workers.

Muzzling the Political Opponents of a Corporate Economic Agenda

If paycheck protection laws do not grant employees new rights to control whether money taken out of their paychecks is used for political purposes, what are such proposals truly aimed at?

In part, the bills represent a political agenda—particularly for those who may view unions as, in the words of the columnist George Will, "transmission belts conveying money to the Democratic Party."[47] The conservative strategist Grover Norquist has promoted restrictions on union dues payments as a strategy to "crush labor unions as a political entity."[48] The Missouri house speaker Tim Jones echoed this sentiment in promoting his state's paycheck protection bill, noting that "money is extremely important to the labor unions" and stressing that "Democrats in this state rely on that money."[49]

But if Republican operatives see paycheck protection as an opportunity to defund Democrats, what motivates the corporate lobbies to devote so much time, money, and effort to promoting these laws? In 1998, when California debated Proposition 226, the Restaurant Association contributed $250,000 to support that effort. In a confidential memorandum to its members, the state association explained its rationale. The organization's director did not mention anything about workers' rights, state budgets, or tax increases caused by overpaid public employees. Instead, he explained that

> the Association took this action because restaurant owners and opera-tors in California have been under attack for years by labor union officials, most notably when unions sponsored Proposition 210 that added $1.50 to the minimum wage. These hikes have cost restaurants hundreds of millions of dollars since 1995. . . . Union leaders have . . . maintained this offensive by proposing this year further minimum wage hikes of 75-cents to a dollar. . . . Union officials are also sponsoring numerous other policies that would increase costs for and reduce jobs in restaurants: increased unemployment compensation, increased work-ers' comp. benefits, mandatory benefits for part-time employees, and imposition of the eight-hour overtime rule, among others. . . . Sup-port for Proposition 226 by the California Restaurant Association is an appropriate, focused response to these attacks by labor unions.[50]

Similarly, the California chapter of NFIB rallied its members to support Proposi-tion 226 by insisting, "Your business is under siege. The union bosses demand? Minimum-wage increase, mandated health insurance, opposition to legal reform."[51]

As detailed throughout this book, the most important advocates of paycheck protection—ALEC, the Chamber of Commerce, NFIB, Americans for Prosperity, and allied corporate lobbies—are seeking to enact a sweeping economic agenda, including opposition to minimum wage, sick leave, unemployment insurance and the right to sue over job description, privatizing Social Security, expanding the use of guest workers and youth labor, cutting taxes for the rich, and adopting more NAFTA-style treaties making it easier to ship jobs abroad.

None of these is a union issue per se. None of them have to do with labor law, union governance, union dues, or the terms of collective bargaining agreements. Yet on all these issues, unions serve as the primary obstacle that stands in opposition to the corporate vision of economic reform.

It is a staple of both Republican and corporate rhetoric to depict attacks on unions as efforts to protect hard-working nonunion taxpayers in the private sec-tor against the abuses of public employees. It appears, however, that the central goal of attacks on unions is not to help nonunion workers but just the opposite: to prevent labor unions from helping them—either by assisting them in organiz-ing their own unions or by advocating for minimum wage and similar policies that would raise their standard of living.[52]

The most sweeping of all assaults on union dues came in the form of a lawsuit brought to the U.S. Supreme Court by a conservative legal institute supported by the Kochs and allied far-right foundations.[53] The Mackinac Center, Cato Institute, and National Right to Work Foundation all filed briefs in the case, and both the Chamber of Commerce and NFIB issued declarations of support.[54] The death of Justice Antonin Scalia left the Court in a four-to-four deadlock, which led it to drop the case; however, the antiunion claims articulated in this case are likely to be revisited in future litigation. The lawsuit urged by far the broadest possible definition of "political activities," arguing that *all* activities of public-sector unions—including negotiating wages and benefits—are inherently political. On this basis, the plaintiffs argued that all public employee union dues payments—in every state—must be subject to the same restrictions as dues earmarked for political purposes. The result would be to abolish fair-share dues for all public employees in the country. Yet again, the corporate lobbies' primary concern appeared to be not anything that might occur in the unionized public sector but the potential impact in the nonunion private sector. The national NFIB's blog post on the case noted that "this case is significant for small business owners . . . because . . . if unions are dealt a blow in the public sector, private sector businesses might see decreased pressure from pro-labor forces on issues ranging from the minimum wage to paid sick leave and other employee benefits."[55]

This, then, finally points to the end goal driving paycheck protection legislation and clarifies how much is at stake if labor's voice is effectively excluded from political debates. The result of unchecked corporate political power would be further dismantling of the legal and institutional protections that workers still rely on. If the corporate lobbies succeed in eliminating the labor movement as a meaningful political force, the political inequality described by Gillens may appear tame by comparison with what comes next. And those who suffer the harshest penalty under such a system would not be union members, but the vast nonunion workforce whose rights and livelihoods are dependent on state law.

POPULIST PUSHBACK AND THE SHRINKING OF DEMOCRACY

The task of deciphering the legislative agenda of the nation's largest corporate lobbies poses a daunting challenge. Every year, these organizations promote hundreds of bills, covering all fifty states and a wide range of issues. Furthermore, the cast of characters is constantly in flux; different issues attract shifting coalitions of allies, and the corporate lobbies themselves do not always agree with one another. Despite these challenges, it is possible, in surveying the field as a whole, to identify the broad outlines of a coherent program.

First, it is important to emphasize what the corporate agenda is *not*. For starters, it is not about standing up to protect hard-working taxpayers in the nonunion private sector. The same lobbies that are leading the charge against public employee unions are also hard at work trying to roll back minimum-wage, prevailing-wage, and living-wage laws; to eliminate entitlements to overtime or sick leave; to scale back regulation of occupational safety; to make it harder for employees to sue over race or sex discrimination or even to recover back wages they are legally owed; and to replace adult employees with teenagers and guest workers. All these initiatives affect primarily nonunion, private-sector employees, on whose behalf corporate lobbyists' claim to be acting. Indeed, it's difficult to identify a single piece of corporate-backed legislation that would strengthen, rather than undermine, the wages, working conditions, legal protections, or bargaining power of either organized or unorganized employees.[1]

The corporate agenda is also not about responding to budget crises. The lobbies' response to fiscal shortfalls has not been to plug budget holes urgently, in whatever manner possible, and restore services as revenues allow. Rather, it has been to cut public services beyond the level required by revenue shortfalls; to exacerbate such shortfalls by enacting new tax cuts for the privileged; and to lock in drastic cuts as the new high-water mark of public services, forswearing the restoration of essential services even after economic performance and tax revenues improve.

Nor is the corporate agenda simply a reasoned platform for economic growth. This book has examined many specific policies and found them unsupported by economic evidence; the same is true for the agenda as a whole. ALEC publishes an annual report ranking the fifty states on what it claims are the most essential policies for producing rapid growth. Five years into its rankings, however, an independent analysis found that the states that most fully embraced ALEC policies actually enjoyed significantly lower growth rates—in both employment and income—than those ALEC deems politically incorrect.[2] Minnesota—a state that ALEC deems the third-worst policy regime in the country—was crowned by CNBC as the best state for business in 2015.[3] Any one of these policies may of course be subject to debate, but it is clear that the broad platform put forth by ALEC, AFP, and the Chamber is not the result of disinterested economic analysis; more often than not, it ignores or contradicts the bulk of economic evidence.

Finally, the corporate agenda is not a response to a cycle of corruption in which public employee unions donate generously to elect favored politicians, are rewarded with sweetheart contracts, and then use the dues money from those contracts to keep favored politicians in office. There is no correlation between the existence of public employee unions and the size of state budget deficits. Furthermore, the corporate attack on the public sector—both employee compensation and the level of services provided—has been vigorously pursued even in states where public employees are unorganized. Thus, the logic of this agenda cannot be explained as an effort to liberate taxpayers from the budget-busting power of government unions.

The arguments most commonly used as justifications for corporate political activism, it turns out, are entirely misleading. None of them can explain the pattern of business-backed legislation.

What Pattern?

When one brings all its components together, it is apparent that the corporate agenda is rife with contradictions. For example, ALEC's model legislation opposing minimum-wage increases argues that "increasing starting wages lures high school students into the full-time work force, resulting in an increase in high school drop-out rates," and therefore that the minimum wage should be kept low in order to prevent students from working more and studying less.[4] Yet in Michigan, Wisconsin, and Maine, ALEC and other business lobbies worked to lift restrictions on the number of hours high school students are permitted to work during the school week. The ALEC-affiliated Restaurant Association argued that student work hours should be expanded because "employment teaches teenagers [valuable] skills such as . . . responsibility, problem-solving, and customer service."[5]

Even some of the principles that seem closest to genuine conservative ideology turn out to be mere conveniences. This is particularly true regarding the doctrine of local control. ALEC's Founding Philosophy and Principles Act demands that all high school students be taught the importance of "federalism, government as close to the people as possible."[6] Indeed, ALEC's State Sovereignty through Local Coordination Act requires local governments to do everything possible—including taking state or federal authorities to court—in order to guarantee that local ordinances cannot be overridden by state or federal statute. But there's a catch: the law applies only when "a city, town, [or] county . . . has laws . . . that are *less restrictive* than a federal or state regulation."[7] If a city has lower environmental or labor standards, these must be upheld at all costs; if a city has higher standards, however, these must be voided. Indeed, ALEC has been at the forefront of efforts to prohibit local governments from establishing labor, environmental, or consumer-protection standards higher than the state's.

Corporate contortions around the principle of local rule can sometimes be dizzying. In Kentucky, the Chamber of Commerce has suggested that local governments have the legal right to adopt their own right-to-work laws but not to raise the minimum wage.[8] Similarly, ALEC has promoted legislation in multiple states that bans localities from using project labor agreements for public construction; but when California mandated that cities seeking state construction funds retain the option of PLAs—not requiring that they be used but simply that the possibility remain on the table—the ALEC-affiliated Associated Builders and Contractors denounced the measure as a potentially unconstitutional "interfer[ence] with local control."[9]

Such contradictions are so glaring and numerous that they seem to indicate rampant hypocrisy or the absence of any deeply held belief. In fact, they throw into sharp relief the unity of interests and goals underlying the corporate lobbies' agenda—the coherence and logic that reconcile seemingly contradictory positions. All of them aim, most fundamentally, at shifting the balance of power between the economic elite and the rest of the country toward even greater inequality. This means weakening or eliminating whatever legal or institutional mechanisms enable working people to exercise control over their terms of employment. At the same time, it means efforts to maximize American companies' ability to transfer jobs to the world's lowest-wage and most politically repressive countries, while permitting immobile service industries to import "guest workers" from those same countries. Combined, the catalog of corporate-backed bills amounts to a formula not only for decreasing American workers' wage standards but also for structurally undermining nonprofessional workers' ability to ever improve their lot.

Economic Decline, Combustible Politics, and Luxury Survival

The success of the corporate lobbies has helped bring the United States to a troubling point. In the bottom two-thirds of the labor market—where jobs do not require a college degree—things have been slowly but steadily worsening for forty years. In the four years following the official start of the post-2008 recovery, real incomes fell for 80 percent of Americans.[10] And few see a path to improvement—only 14 percent of the public believes the current generation of children will be better off than their parents.[11]

The problem has become too big to ignore. In recent years, an increasing number of mainstream voices have warned that America's current economic trajectory is unsustainable. In 2014, Standard & Poor's issued a report warning that the country's "extreme income inequality" has created "a drag on long-run economic growth."[12] Most ominously, scientists using a NASA-funded model projected that unsustainable demands on natural resources, combined with "the economic stratification of society into Elites and Masses" could lead to a widespread collapse of civilization. The study modeled the history of advanced societies that have collapsed over the past five thousand years and concluded that in each case, dissolution followed the onset of extreme inequality "closely reflecting the reality of the world today."[13]

A sense of foreboding has entered America's political culture as well, manifesting itself in some unexpected places. In 2012, Wyoming Republicans introduced—and nearly passed—a bill creating a task force charged with developing a plan for how the state might cope with a complete collapse of federal government authority. One of the bill's sponsors explained that with wealthy Americans leaving the country and global confidence in the dollar waning, there is a real possibility that the currency could suddenly become useless.[14]

Even among investors, there are growing signs of concern that inequality has become so extreme that it threatens not merely recession but a broader social unraveling. The New York Times published a column by the longtime CEO of

Young & Rubicam declaring that "we are creating a caste system from which it's almost impossible to escape."[15] Likewise, private-equity billionaire John Paul Tudor warns that the gap between the wealthy and the rest of the country "cannot and will not persist," and a former Wall Street executive worries that "the real danger" of unchecked inequality is "this little thing called the French Revolution."[16]

These warnings are particularly striking, as they come from those who presumably have the most sophisticated understanding of the market. Predictably, the rich have plans for dealing with this crisis that do not involve making the economy more equal. During a packed session at the World Economic Forum's annual gathering in Davos, Switzerland, in January 2015, a former financial executive reported that "I know hedge fund managers all over the world who are buying airstrips and farms in places like New Zealand because they think they need a getaway."[17]

For those who can't afford their own island, several companies now offer high-end underground condominiums—located in former missile silos. Luxury Survival Condo offers units ranging from $1.5 to $4.5 million in a silo designed to serve as a community of royal refugees, complete with swimming pool, dog park, and a five-year supply of food. In addition to providing protection from natural disasters or terrorist attacks, the company explains that its clientele includes "people who are worried about a global economic collapse."[18] One of its competitors likewise lists "riots," "economic collapse," and "widespread anarchy" among the threats facing potential buyers; in response, it offers luxury bunkers as "the ultimate life assurance solution for high net worth families."[19]

But we are not doomed. The policies that helped create our current situation can be democratically reversed.

Populist Pushback

While corporate power may be more impressive than ever, there is one key battle that the country's business elites have failed to win: they have not been able to convince the voting public that their platform makes sense. On the contrary, polling shows that the public is deeply suspicious of the corporate project and, on specific issues, is often in sharp disagreement. Eighty percent of Americans— including 72 percent of Republicans—believe that the Supreme Court's *Citizens United* decision was a mistake.[20] In the summer of 2015, likely voters ranked the disproportionate political influence of corporations and the wealthy as their single most urgent concern.[21] More than 60 percent of Americans believe that "the economic system in this country unfairly favors powerful interests." Even during the years of recovery following the Great Recession, two-thirds of the public believed the government was helping the major banks, big corporations, and the wealthy while doing little or nothing for the middle class.[22]

The public's view of what should be done to address these problems presents a dramatic challenge for the corporate lobbies. A majority of the country in 2015 favored capping the incomes of corporate executives, and two-thirds called for raising taxes on the very rich.[23] More than two-thirds support eliminating the carried-interest loophole in order to tax hedge-fund managers at the same rates as everyone else.[24]

Nearly 70 percent of the country says the government should do more to reduce the gap between rich and poor.[25] And the list of what people think the government should do must read like a nightmare script for the corporate lobbies. Nearly three-quarters of the country—including a majority of Republicans—supports immediately raising the minimum wage to $10.10.[26] A strong majority wants to expand unemployment insurance for the long-term jobless.[27] Eighty percent of voters believe employers should be required to provide a minimum number of paid sick days to all workers.[28]

There is also strong support for public services and social insurance. Eighty-four percent of the public supports making universal prekindergarten available to all children.[29] Not only do nearly 90 percent of Americans want to protect Social Security and Medicare from any budget cuts, but three-quarters think we should consider *increasing* Social Security benefits.[30] Nearly 80 percent believe that the federal government should ensure that everyone who wants to go to college can, and nearly 90 percent believe "the federal government should spend whatever is necessary to ensure that all children have really good public schools."[31]

When asked about principles rather than specific programs, public opinion is diametrically opposed to that of economic elites. Policy prescriptions long since written off by elected officials are common sense to the American public. Just over half the country, for example, supports the view that "our government should redistribute wealth by heavy taxes on the rich," and six in ten favor "national health insurance, which would be financed by tax money."[32] More than half believe "the federal government should provide jobs for everyone willing to work who cannot find a job in private employment," and nearly 80 percent say the "minimum wage should be high enough so that no family with a full-time worker falls below the official poverty line." More than two-thirds of the country supports the principle that the "government must see that no one is without food, clothing, or shelter," and a majority believe the government should guarantee a "decent standard of living" for those unemployed.[33]

With the Tea Party's failure to produce a strictly pro-corporate mass movement, and the revival of conservative populism in the Trump campaign, the corporate lobbies have effectively lost control of the conservative base. Voters choose candidates for a wide variety of reasons, including their positions on issues unrelated to economic policy. Partly for this reason, corporate-backed candidates have continued to win state legislative elections in impressive numbers. When given a chance to vote on specific policies, however—most commonly through ballot initiatives—even conservative voters have often broken with the corporate agenda.

In Florida, for example, the legislature asked voters in 2010 to lift a constitutional cap on the size of public school classes. While 65 percent of legislators supported the proposal, voters strongly rejected it.[34] This vote took place during the Tea Party "wave" election of 2010, when Florida elected a very conservative governor and a Tea Party legislature. The public did not waiver in support of extremely conservative candidates, but on this issue they chose to undo the will of their chosen representatives. By rough estimate, at least two hundred thousand voters must have gone to the polls thinking something like, "I hate government, Democrats, taxes, and unions, but I want my kid in small classes."

Similarly, nearly 65 percent of Idaho voters supported Mitt Romney for president in 2012, but by nearly the same margin they overturned a series of laws their legislators had adopted eliminating teacher tenure, instituting "merit" pay for teachers based on standardized test scores, and requiring online courses for high school students. Similar results were seen in deep-red South Dakota, where two-thirds of voters—including 45 percent of self-described conservatives—chose to overturn a 2012 law that eliminated tenure and instituted merit pay. Likewise, the Florida legislature in 2012 adopted a "taxpayer bill of rights"—strictly limiting future budget authority—by a two-to-one margin, but voters overwhelmingly rejected it. The same year, voters in Michigan rejected a constitutional amendment that would have required a supermajority for future tax increases, and they repealed the "emergency manager" law that let state appointees slash local government budgets and void union contracts.

The public's progressive economic views have been manifested most clearly in the growing prevalence of ballot initiative campaigns aiming to increase wages and improve working conditions. From 2012 to2015, four states and thirty cities or counties voted to raise their minimum wage.[35] A minimum of $15 per hour—until recently unthinkable—was adopted in 2015 first by the city of SeaTac, surrounding Seattle's airport, then by Los Angeles, then for New York's fast-food industry, and quickly gained momentum as a new standard of what low-wage workers deserve. Furthermore, while the highest wages were set in traditionally Democratic states, support for wage increases is strongly bipartisan. Thus, in 2014, voters in Arkansas, Nebraska, and South Dakota—all states where Republicans control all three branches of government—approved ballot initiatives to raise their states' minimum wage.[36] Following on the success of minimum-wage campaigns, community and labor groups began organizing to establish a right to paid sick leave. In 2006, San Francisco became the first city in the country to require employers to provide a minimum number of paid sick days. Gradually over the next five years, Washington, D.C., Seattle, and the state of Connecticut adopted similar statutes. Then, from 2013 to 2015, three more states and sixteen cities created a right to paid sick leave. In 2016, Arizonans voted both to raise their state's minimum wage and to establish a right to paid sick leave.

These successes have emboldened labor and community groups to aim higher still—most immediately at creating a right to reasonable work schedules for the millions of Americans whose jobs require them to be "on call," subject to just-in-time scheduling that makes it impossible to ensure child care, pursue education, or get a second job.[37] In 2014, San Francisco created the country's first scheduling ordinance; by the fall of 2015, efforts to promote similar laws were under way in Minneapolis and Massachusetts, where the Retail Association described the proposal as "one of the worst pieces of legislation ever written."[38]

Repealing Democratic Rights

Having so far failed to win the public's hearts and minds, the corporate lobbies have sought to protect their privilege by enacting laws that make it harder for populist sentiment to be translated into action. At the individual level, they have sought to limit the ability of aggrieved workers or consumers to challenge corporate actions through the means normally available to a democracy's citizens. One of the distinguishing features of democratic societies is the right of ordinary citizens to seek judicial redress of illegal acts by the rich and powerful. Corporate-backed legislation, however, has served to create a system of increasingly unequal access to the courts.

In debates over wage-theft ordinances or other attempts to police corporate behavior, the business lobbies routinely oppose citizens' legal rights of action on the grounds that their exercise would encourage an overly litigious society. The U.S. Chamber of Commerce complains, for instance, that since passage of the 1964 Civil Rights Act, "litigation in employment discrimination has exploded . . . resulting in increased costs associated with attorneys' fees and employment investigations as employers must respond to each charge filed."[39] The Chamber's ranking of state employment policies warns against allowing court enforcement of employee rights, noting that a state's "litigation and enforcement environment relating to employment and labor issues" can negatively impact its economy. "There is a substantial body of economic evidence," the Chamber insists, showing that "the propensity of employees . . . to engage in litigation . . . raises the costs to employers of conducting necessary worker separations," and it cautions that "even the most well-intended regulations can have unintended consequences when they lead to . . . excessive enforcement."[40]

It has become increasingly common for employees to be forced—as a condition of employment—to waive their constitutional right to sue over unlawful termination in favor of addressing all complaints to an internal, employer-dominated arbitration process.[41] So too, employers increasingly demand that new hires sign noncompete agreements, barring them from working in similar jobs upon leaving their current firm. Such restrictive covenants have been demanded for an increasingly wide range of jobs, including gardeners, barbers, fast-food workers, and camp counselors.[42] When a Massachusetts hairstylist fell out with his boss and left to work at a nearby salon, he was taken to court and ultimately forced to spend a year living on unemployment benefits, in constant danger of eviction, before being permitted to take another job in his field. "It was pretty lousy that you would take away someone's livelihood like that," he complained.[43] In arguing against occupational license requirements, ALEC's Economic Civil Rights Act insists that Americans have a fundamental "right to earn an honest living" and calls for a private right of legal action for any individual whose career is stymied by unnecessary licensing requirements.[44] It appears, however, that this right does not apply when it conflicts with employers' interests. Thus, in 2015, a trio of ALEC-affiliated Wisconsin state legislators introduced a bill—supported by the state Chamber of Commerce—to repeal the requirement that noncompete covenants be "reasonably necessary for the protection of the employer," granting firms wider power to restrict their employees' market freedom and legal rights.[45]

The corporate lobbies' opposition to a private right of action in policing wage theft and other workplace rights is particularly striking, given their avid promotion of such a right in multiple policy arenas aimed at undermining workers' bargaining leverage in the labor market. Under ALEC's Economic Civil Rights Act, any individual has the right to sue—and recover attorneys' fees—if a state or local government provides services that could be provided more cheaply by a private contractor, or if a state maintains licensing requirements that the individual believes are unnecessary.[46] Similarly, the organization's Right to Work Act creates a private right of action for employees who believe they have been unfairly required to share in the costs of negotiating their union contract; they are entitled to injunctive relief, damages, and attorneys' fees.[47] ALEC further urges that any taxpayer have the right to sue, including recovering costs and attorneys' fees, if a government agency uses a Project Labor Agreement.[48] If public employees' union dues are paid through electronic payroll deductions, and any portion of these is used for political communication, ALEC demands that employees have a private right to sue for recovery of double damages (along with attorneys' fees).[49] Thus the corporate political agenda includes one-sided access to the courts, in which citizens are free to file suit to undermine labor standards but not to enforce them.

Most important, corporate lobbies have sought to create a system of selective democracy in the very process of lawmaking itself. From 2011 to 2015, twenty-two states established new laws making it more difficult for citizens to vote.[50] Typically, these laws target lower-income residents; in 2016 a primary election analysis found that Democratic turnout was significantly hampered in the states that adopted such laws.[51] Even further, states are explicitly restricting citizens' ability to vote for policies opposed by corporate interests. In several policy areas, corporate legislation creates one-way doors that allow citizens to vote only for one type of policy outcome. So-called parent trigger laws, for example, typically allow families to vote to convert a public school into a charter school but not the reverse. If, after several years, parents conclude the decision was a mistake, they have no right to vote to convert the charter back into a traditional public school. More commonly, corporate advocates promote state laws that prohibit towns or counties from voting to adopt progressive statutes.

At the simplest level, corporate advocates have sought to restrict citizens' ability to set tax policy. ALEC's Super-Majority Act argues that "the ability to raise taxes . . . should be made as politically difficult as possible."[52] On the basis of this model, seven states now require a supermajority in both chambers of the legislature in order to raise taxes or establish new taxes.[53] The NFIB has issued a call for states not only to adopt such restrictions but also to prohibit localities within the state from raising their own taxes.[54] So too, corporate-backed legislators have moved to suspend democratic rule in cities deemed fiscally irresponsible. In Michigan, such a process was imposed over the explicit objection of voters. Legislators approved a 2011 law empowering the governor to appoint "emergency financial managers" for cities in fiscal crisis, with the appointees' authority superseding that of all elected officials. In November 2012, this law was overturned by a popular referendum. The next month, however, legislators dismissed the voters' will and adopted a slightly revised version of the bill, reinstating the power of emergency managers; this time, they added a modest appropriation so that, under Michigan law, the act could not be invalidated by referendum.[55]

Above all, the corporate lobbies have sought to shrink the scope of democracy by denying citizens in urban areas the right to vote on establishing local economic standards. Corporate power is greatest at the level of state legislatures. As noted earlier, few people know the names of their legislative candidates, much less what they do. Thus, modest sums of money go a long way in swaying elections. Because every state has cities within it that are more progressive than the state as a whole, local government has become a prime location of pushback against the corporate agenda. As an ALEC representative explained in 2014, "The biggest threat comes from the local level. So . . . one solution that ALEC has passed is state legislation that preempts the polities within the state from raising the minimum wage higher than the state level."[56] At ALEC's 2014 legislative conference, one avid member explained that local school boards and city councils may take away liberties even faster than the federal government. "We need to stomp out local control," Utah senator Howard Stephenson declared.[57] In this spirit, ALEC, the Chamber, and allied groups have worked everywhere to block the authority of city councils or municipal referenda to improve workers' rights.

In 2011, Indiana prohibited any of its cities or counties from voting for a minimum wage higher than the state's own—which is itself no higher than the federal minimum—and Wisconsin made it illegal for localities to establish a right to paid sick leave. By the end of 2015, eight more states had prohibited minimum-wage increases, and twelve had abolished the local right to vote for paid sick leave (figure C.1). These laws have attracted some of the most vociferous corporate lobbying. In Florida, for instance, the Chamber of Commerce was joined by the Manufacturers Association, the Restaurant Association, Darden Restaurants, and the Disney Corporation in helping pass a bill that bans both minimum-wage laws and any right to paid or unpaid sick leave.[58]

Preemption has become a favorite tool for blocking a wide range of local ordinances. In Fayetteville, Arkansas, the city council in 2014 adopted an

FIGURE C.1. State laws adopted 2011–15 preempting local minimum wage or sick leave ordinances. (Dark preempts minimum wage only; light preempts sick leave only; striped preempts both.)

ordinance—opposed by the local Chamber of Commerce—that banned employment discrimination on the basis of sexual identity or orientation. The following spring, Little Rock followed suit. In response, Arkansas's legislature in 2015
adopted a statute prohibiting any locality from establishing antidiscrimination
standards stricter than the state's own and retroactively invalidating those set
by Fayetteville and Little Rock.[59] In Dearborn, Michigan, the city council rec-
ommended budget cuts that included a significant reduction in the number
of police and firefighters. Because a previous city ordinance had mandated
minimum staffing levels for protective services, the budget cuts required voter
approval—which was not forthcoming.[60] To ensure other cities would not face
similar constraints, state legislators adopted a statute making it illegal for cities
to establish minimum staffing levels for police or fire service.[61]

Over time, states have enacted increasingly broad preemption statutes, con-
stricting local democracy even further. The Michigan Chamber of Commerce
declared in 2015 that "mandatory paid leave initiatives are sweeping the country," and warned that "we need to get ahead of this issue."[62] That year, the legislature adopted a bill labeled the "Death Star" by its opponents—prohibiting
cities or counties from adopting any regulation governing wages, benefits, paid
or unpaid leave, scheduling and work hours, or remedies for wage theft. Virtually the entire state business community—including the Chamber, Manufacturers Association, NFIB, Retailers Association, Restaurant Association, Bankers
Association, Institute of Laundering and Dry Cleaning, Homebuilders Association, Grocers Association, and Associated Builders and Contractors—united in
a successful effort to enact the bill.[63] So too, Arizona's 2013 omnibus preemption bill even prohibits establishing a right to meal breaks or rest periods for
employees.[64]

In some places, there is literally a race between local activists seeking to institute wage increases and corporate lobbyists working to outlaw them. In 2015,
Missouri legislators voted to preempt local wage or benefit standards, prohibiting any ordinance not already in place by August 28 of that year. City councillors
in St. Louis and Kansas City raced to implement minimum-wage increases before
the deadline. St. Louis made it; Kansas City did not.[65]

The corporate lobbies are thus engaged in an effort not only to reshape the
economy but also to reshape democracy. Were a state to adopt the entire package
of corporate-backed legislation, it would create a polity in which citizens can vote
to prohibit the use of PLAs but not to require that they remain an option. Local
residents could vote to turn a public school into a charter school or to undermine
unions through local right-to-work ordinances but not to raise the minimum
wage or establish a process to recover stolen wages. Individuals could sue for being
made to pay union dues but not for being unjustly terminated. And legislators

could vote to establish new tax breaks with a simple majority but would need a two-thirds vote to fund universal preschool. With each such bill that is adopted, corporate advocates are constructing a system in which the ability to address economic inequality through democratic means is increasingly restricted.

This, then, is the legislative agenda of the one percent—a concerted, coordinated, well-funded attack by some of the richest individuals and most powerful corporations in the country. Its aims are to concentrate an ever-larger share of income and wealth in the hands of the most privileged, eliminate institutions that give working people leverage in the labor market, defund public services, lower expectations of what workers should be able to demand from their employers and citizens from their government, and shrink the reach of our democracy in order to lock in place unpopular policies and forestall a populist backlash.

The recent success of the corporate lobbies is both impressive and daunting. Yet the issue is far from decided. Public opinion remains sharply opposed to much of the corporate agenda, and the country remains a democracy. Furthermore, labor and community activists continue to build on the momentum of fast-food strikes and campaigns for a higher minimum wage and sick leave. Each victory not only encourages voters in other jurisdictions to demand similar rights but also spurs organizers to continue testing the limits of what is politically possible.

When the Massachusetts fair-scheduling proposal was introduced, the president of the state's Retail Association accused labor and community activists of "piling on." After the state had voted in 2014 to raise its minimum wage and establish a right to paid sick leave, and now facing potential restrictions on on-call scheduling, he demanded to know "what the hell is next?"[66] Unfortunately for him, activists have a long list of proposals that are striking both for the scope of their ambition and for how deeply they resonate with the public's view of economic justice. In April 2016, San Francisco became the first city in the nation to establish a right to six weeks' paid leave for new parents.[67] At the state level, the Service Employees International Union in California is working on an initiative that would establish a right to retirement security—requiring private employers to contribute to a public-option pension plan.[68] Others are advocating a proposal to undo at-will employment—ensuring that employees can be fired only for just cause, whether poor job performance or a firm's financial need.[69] While Montana is currently the only state in the country with such a law, the principle seems so commonsense that many Americans mistakenly believe that it's already on the books nationwide. When a just-cause initiative was proposed in Colorado in 2008, it sufficiently scared the Chamber of Commerce and other business organizations that they contributed $3 million to other labor-backed initiative campaigns in exchange for having this measure withdrawn.[70] Finally, a coalition of environmental and community organizations in Colorado began organizing for a "community rights amendment" to that state's constitution, which would invalidate the full complement of preemption measures, guaranteeing the right of localities to establish their own environmental and labor standards.[71]

The most dramatic feature of the 2016 election cycle was the unexpected upsurge of populist anger, captured by Donald Trump on the right and Bernie Sanders on the left. Although supporters insisted that their candidacies represented a new political model, it is important to recognize the degree to which both Trump and Sanders were *sui generis*. Trump's wealth and media personality make him virtually unique. It is similarly difficult to imagine many others following Sanders's path. Here was a candidate who, having defended the same positions for forty years, emanated personal integrity, and whose political career was built on representing a state with a population of fewer than one million, where personal relationships count for much more—and campaign contributions for much less—than in most places.

It is telling that so few senators endorsed either candidate. The obstacle was not simply the candidates' politics; more important, it was virtually impossible for even progressive Democrats to risk alienating the entire donor class, as Sanders did. As a result, Sanders, like Trump, seemed to have very limited coattails. Even though Sanders had enviable polling numbers for his campaign, few candidates lined up to adopt his platform. One of the most important challenges to the Democratic Party posed by Sanders was his ability to match the Clinton campaign's fund-raising, which relied heavily on big-money donors, throughout the primary season. Yet here, too, it is unclear whether candidates for Congress— much less state legislatures—could generate sufficient excitement to replicate Sanders's small-donation campaign-finance model rather than relying on elite backers.

Both political parties are defined centrally by a contradiction between their donors and their base. For the Democrats, this has historically meant a tension between big-money backers in the financial, technology, and entertainment industries, and the party's grassroots, particularly the labor movement. In some ways, the demographic dynamics described by Dylan Loewe might have given hope to neoliberal Democrats that they could resolve this tension by reducing their dependence on labor. As unions shrink, the party might reinvent itself as a coalition of demographic groups, bringing together women, Latinos, African Americans, the LGBT community, young people, and urban liberals devoted to an ethos of multicultural inclusion. By mobilizing voters around identity politics rather than class, the Democrats might create an activist base that is less at odds with donors than the labor movement is.

The Sanders campaign, however, demonstrated the impossibility of transcending the party's internal class conflict. Sanders repeatedly pushed Clinton to the left on taxes, trade, health care, and wages. Furthermore, the Black Lives Matter movement made poverty and inequality an inseparable part of the agenda of the country's most dynamic identity-based civil rights movement. Finally, although both parties' elites may have hoped that Latino voters' loyalty could be won simply through humane immigration policies, polling data show that education, health care, jobs, and the economy are all more important than immigration for Latino voters.[72] All of these forces make it difficult to imagine a successful Democratic Party that does not place economic inequality at the center of its agenda. But what form that shift may take, in the aftermath of the Sanders campaign, remains unclear.

For the GOP no less than for the Democrats, 2016 signaled the limits of neoliberal politics; the Trump campaign was as much a rejection of traditional corporate Republicans—from Jeb Bush to Paul Ryan—as of Hillary Clinton. This is not to say that traditional corporate-backed candidates can no longer win elections—the house and senate are full of them, and it is certainly possible that Republicans will again choose a traditional corporate candidate as their presidential nominee. But this cannot be the GOP's long-term strategy; it is no longer possible for either party to ignore the clamoring anger produced by economic decline.

At the start of 2017, the GOP enjoys an almost unprecedented degree of political dominance. Republicans control all three branches of the federal government and most of the states, having benefited from a net increase of over nine hundred state legislative seats since 2010. Indeed, corporate success in the states has helped produce increased influence at the federal level. The corporate-funded RedMap project enabled the GOP to redraw the boundaries of congressional districts to such great effect that in 2012 the party won a 33-seat majority in the U.S. House of Representatives even though more Americans voted for Democratic than for Republican candidates.[73] Likewise, corporate advocates are working to harness their influence in state legislatures to amend the U.S. Constitution in order to permanently restrict federal spending.

In Washington, both Senate Majority Leader Mitch McConnell and House Speaker Paul Ryan are longtime corporate advocates and repeat attendees at the Koch brothers' donor summit. At the 2014 event, McConnell complained aloud about Democrats' efforts to raise the minimum wage and extend unemployment insurance, and he promised to dismantle corporate regulations.[74] On the other side of the Capitol, Ryan, in 2016, embodied the corporate GOP's alternative to Trump, promoting free trade despite the opposition of his party's nominee. Addressing the Koch network that summer, Ryan vowed that house Republicans remained dedicated to the corporate agenda, regardless of who occupied the White House.[75] Even setting aside differences on trade and immigration, the Trump administration and congressional Republican leaders are in accord on the vast majority of the agenda described in this book, creating a unique opportunity for corporate lobbyists to advance in Washington the same vision they have pursued in the states.

If the country's economic decline continues, however, the populist sentiments that Sanders and Trump channeled are sure to return in even more urgent form. The corporate lobbies have proved adept at adapting to changing circumstances and new challenges, working by trial and error to hone successful strategies. But if the Sanders campaign proved anything, it is that a type of economic progressivism long thought passé can reemerge under new conditions. Among many unanticipated developments, in January 2016, 54 percent of registered voters agreed that "a political revolution might be necessary to redistribute money from the wealthiest Americans to the middle class."[76]

There is no way to know how this story will end. Politics remains forever contingent, never settled. The struggle between public interest and private power will continue to play out in cities and states across the country; even with the heightened influence of money in the era of *Citizens United*, the power of popular conviction should not be underestimated. Economic decline for the many has fueled widespread discontent. In 2015, the Republican pollster Frank Luntz warned of an electorate characterized by widespread anger: "There's something happening out there that is profound.... We are in a dangerous political environment."[77] The direction this anger takes—toward progressive change, reactionary nationalism, or depressed resignation—will likely determine the country's future for many years to come. It is my hope that this book can shed some light on the political terrain we must navigate to chart a path from helplessness and despair to mobilization and hope.

Notes

INTRODUCTION

1. Perry Bacon, "In Rebuke of Tennessee Governor, Koch Group Shows Its Power," NBC News, February 6, 2015, http://www.nbcnews.com/politics/elections/rebuke-tennessee-governor-koch-group-shows-its-power-n301031.

2. Filippo Occhino and Timothy Stehulak, "Behind the Slow Pace of Wage Growth," U.S. Federal Reserve Bank, Cleveland, April 8, 2015, https://www.clevelandfed.org/news room-and-events/publications/economic-trends/2015-economic-trends/et-20150409-behind-the-slow-pace-of-wage-growth.aspx. Data date back to 1947. The Federal Reserve Bank reports that from 1960 through 2000, employees' share of total national income fell by an average of one percentage point per decade. Since the year 2000, the rate of incline has increased dramatically—to five percentage points per decade.

3. Prior to this ruling, corporations could spend unlimited sums on "issue advocacy" but not on advertisements that urged support for specific candidates. The *Citizens United* ruling abolished this distinction, allowing unlimited corporate spending advocating the election or defeat of particular candidates.

4. While not technically outlawing unions, the bill is likely to lead to the same end. For a description of the bill's components, see Roger Bybee, "After Proposing Draconian Anti-Union Laws, Wisconsin Governor Walker Invokes National Guard," *In These Times*, February 15, 2011.

5. These states are Idaho, Illinois, Indiana, Louisiana, Maine, Michigan, Minnesota, Nebraska, New Hampshire, New Jersey, Ohio, Oklahoma, Pennsylvania, Tennessee, and Wisconsin.

6. A detailed account of this legislation appears in chapter 3 and, on preemption of local minimum wage standards, in the book's conclusion.

7. Colin Gordon, "Growing Together, Growing Apart," *Working Economics Blog*, Economic Policy Institute, October 4, 2013, http://www.epi.org/blog/growing-growing.

8. Lawrence Mishel, Elise Gould, and Josh Bivens, "Wage Stagnation in Nine Charts," Economic Policy Institute, January 6, 2015, http://s1.epi.org/files/2013/wage-stagnation-in-nine-charts.pdf.

9. U.S. Bureau of Labor Statistics, "Occupations with the Most Job Growth, 2012 and Projected 2022," Occupational Employment Statistics, January 2014, http://www.bls.gov/emp/ep_table_104.htm. The top ten growing occupations in 2012–22 are personal care aides, registered nurses, retail sales, home health aides, food preparation including fast food, nursing assistants, secretaries, customer service representatives, janitors, and construction laborers. Average annual wages for all these occupations except RNs were $23,500 in 2012, when the poverty threshold for a family of four was $23,492.

10. Will Kimball, "Hourly Wages of All Workers, by Wage Percentile, 1973–2014," Economic Policy Institute calculations based on U.S. Bureau of Labor Statistics, provided to the author, September 2015. Women did better than men; women still earn less than men, but most women's wages increased over this period. Yet even women's wage growth is concentrated in one period of extended economic expansion (combined with a minimum wage increase, renewed labor organizing and the dotcom bubble) in the late 1990s. Since 2000, real wages have been flat or falling for the bottom 70 percent of women workers.

11. Mishel, Gould, and Bivens, "Wage Stagnation." Median household income grew by 6.5 percent from 1979 to 2014.

12. Elise Gould, "Longer Hours, Not Higher Wages, Have Driven Modest Earnings Growth for Most American Households," Economic Policy Institute, July 23, 2015, http://www.epi.org/publication/longer-hours-not-higher-wages-have-driven-modest-earnings-growth-for-most-american-households.

13. The likelihood of falling into poverty in one's prime working years has increased dramatically over the past forty years. In the twenty years between 1969 and 1989, for example, 17 percent of 35–45-year-olds fell into poverty for at least one year; over the twenty years from 1989 to 2009, 23 percent of that age group fell into poverty. For those aged 45–55, the share of those experiencing at least one year of poverty rose by more than half, from 11.8 percent to 17.7 percent. Hope Yen, "4 in 5 US Adults Face Near-Poverty, No Work for at Least Part of Their Lives," Associated Press, July 28, 2013, http://www.businessinsider.com/ap-poll-4-in-5-us-adults-face-near-poverty-no-work-for-at-least-parts-of-their-lives-2013-7.

14. "A New Majority: Low Income Students Now a Majority in the Nation's Public Schools," Research Bulletin, Southern Education Foundation, January 2015, http://www.southerneducation.org/getattachment/4ac62e27-5260-47a5-9d02-14896ec3a531/A-New-Majority-2015-Update-Low-Income-Students-Now.aspx. Low-income here is defined as families eligible for free or reduced-price meals in school. In 2013, a student living with a single parent was eligible for free meals if the parent made less than 135 percent of the poverty line ($19,669) and for reduced-price meals if the parent made less than 185 percent of poverty ($27,991). When low-income students come into school, one teacher explains, "The first thing I do is an inventory of immediate needs: Did you eat? Are you clean? A big part of my job is making them feel safe." Lindsay Layton, "Majority of U.S. Public School Students Are in Poverty," *Washington Post*, January 16, 2015, https://www.washingtonpost.com/local/education/majority-of-us-public-school-students-are-in-poverty/2015/01/15/df7171d0-9ce9-11e4-a7ee-526210d665b4_story.html.

15. Sabrina Tavernise, "Life Spans Shrink for Least-Educated Whites in the U.S.," *New York Times*, September 20, 2012, http://www.nytimes.com/2012/09/21/us/life-expectancy-for-less-educated-whites-in-us-is-shrinking.html.

16. "2014 Employer Health Benefits Survey," Kaiser Family Foundation, September 10, 2014, http://kff.org/health-costs/report/2014-employer-health-benefits-survey. Total health care costs increased by 70 percent, but employers forced employees to pay an increasing share of this, so average employee premium payments increased by 81 percent. Furthermore, at the same time that insurance costs more, it covers less. Thus in addition to steeper premiums, employees are paying increased out-of-pocket costs, primarily through higher deductibles and copays.

17. Emmanuel Saez, "Striking It Richer: The Evolution of Top Incomes in the United States," University of California at Berkeley, September 3, 2013, 3, 8, http://eml.berkeley.edu//~saez/saez-UStopincomes-2012.pdf.

18. Paul Bucchheit, "5 Facts about How America Is Rigged for a Massive Wealth Transfer to the Rich," Alternet, November 4, 2014, http://www.alternet.org/economy/5-facts-about-how-america-rigged-massive-wealth-transfer-rich.

19. Jeffrey Winters, *Oligarchy* (Cambridge: Cambridge University Press, 2011), 216.

20. Modern campaign finance rules were first adopted in 1974. Since then, the real cost of congressional campaigns has increased fourfold, fueled by the rise first of television and later of consultants, polling, digital media, and ever more sophisticated data analysis. The cost of presidential election campaigns doubled between 2000 and 2008 and then doubled again in 2012. Center on Responsive Politics, https://www.opensecrets.org/pres12. The dominant role of money is further visible in how candidates spend their time: during the course of his reelection campaign, President Obama's schedule included twice

as many fund-raising as public-speaking events. Nicholas Confessore, "Result Won't Limit Campaign Money Any More Than Ruling Did," *New York Times*, November 11, 2012, www.nytimes.com/2012/11/12/us/politics/a-vote-for-unilmited-campaign-financing. html?_r=o. Once elected, congresspeople commonly report that they spend one-third of their hours fund-raising for their next campaign.

21. Data are from the Federal Election Commission (FEC), compiled by the Center for Responsive Politics, https://www.opensecrets.org/bigpicture/donordemographics. php?cycle=2012&filter=A.

22. Winters, *Oligarchy*, 216. Indeed, in the early months of the 2016 presidential primary campaign nearly half the money raised for all candidates combined came from just 158 families, roughly one ten-thousandth of 1 percent of the country. Together, these families spent over $175 million shaping which candidates would survive into the election season, largely through channels that were illegal before 2010. Nicholas Confessore, Sarah Cohen, and Karen Yourish, "The Families Funding the 2016 Presidential Election," *New York Times*, October 10, 2015.

23. Federal elections from 2000 to 2014. Center for Responsive Politics, "Business-Labor-Ideology Split in PAC and Individual Donations to Candidates, Parties, Super PACs and Outside Spending Groups," 2015, https://www.opensecrets.org/overview/blio.php.

24. Liz Kennedy and Sean McElwee, "Do Corporations & Unions Face the Same Rules on Political Spending?," Demos, 2014, http://www.demos.org/sites/default/files/publications/CorpExplainer.pdf.

25. Peter Francia, "Onward Union Soldiers? Organized Labor's Future in American Elections," in *Interest Groups Unleashed*, ed. Paul Herrnson, Christopher Deering, and Clyde Wilcox (Washington, DC: CQ Press, 2013), 141–43.

26. "Advocacy organizations" here denotes groups other than candidate campaigns or political parties who make independent expenditures.

27. Data are from the FEC, compiled by the Center for Responsive Politics, https://www.opensecrets.org/outsidespending/index.php?type=Y.

28. Marty Cohen, David Karol, Hans Noel, and John Zaller, *The Party Decides: Presidential Nominations before and after Reform* (Chicago: University of Chicago Press, 2008).

29. Peter Overby and Andrea Seabrook, "'Independent' Groups behind Ads Not So Independent," National Public Radio, October 27, 2010, http://www.npr.org/templates/story/story.php?storyId=130836771.

30. John Pitney, "Iron Law of Emulation: American Crossroads and Crossroads GPS," in Herrnson, Deering, and Wilcox, *Interest Groups Unleashed*, 177.

31. Fang, *The Machine: A Field Guide to the Resurgent Right* (New York: New Press, 2013), 118.

32. Ibid., 227.

33. On the launch of the Kochs' candidate selection firm, see Andy Kroll, "New Koch-Linked Political Firm Aims to Handpick 'Electable' Candidates," *Mother Jones*, January 17, 2014, http://www.motherjones.com/politics/2014/01/koch-brothers-candidate-training-recruiting-aegis-strategic.

34. Theda Skocpol and Alexander Hertel-Fernandez, "The Koch Effect: The Impact of a Cadre-Led Network on American Politics" (paper presented to the Southern Political Science Association conference, January 8, 2016), 4, http://www.scholarsstrategynetwork.org/sites/default/files/the_koch_effect_for_spsa_w_apps_skocpol_and_hertel-fernandez-corrected_1-4-16.pdf.

35. Jeff Zeleny, "Top Donors to Republicans Seek More Say in Senate Races," *New York Times*, February 2, 2013, http://www.nytimes.com/2013/02/03/us/politics/top-gop-donors-seek-greater-say-in-senate-races.html?partner=rss&emc=rss&_r=1&.

36. *Washington Post* Editorial Board, "Don't Believe Mr. Boehner's Phony Excuse on Immigration," *Washington Post*, July 10, 2015, https://www.washingtonpost.com/opinions/a-decade-of-paralysis/2015/07/10/432b5adc-24f4-11e5-b72c-2b7d516e1e0e_story.html.

37. Tara Setmayer, "Welcome to the Tea Party Revolution," CNN, October 8, 2015, http://www.cnn.com/2015/10/08/opinions/setmayer-tea-party-revolution.

38. Theda Skocpol and Vanessa Williamson, *The Tea Party and the Remaking of Republican Conservatism* (Oxford: Oxford University Press, 2013).

39. As far back as 1993, the then House majority leader Dick Armey—who would later head FreedomWorks—took out ads calling for "a second Boston Tea Party" and urging antitax activists to mail teabags to congresspeople. In 2007, the Michigan branch of Koch-funded Americans for Prosperity joined the Michigan Realtors Association to stage a Tea Party rally calling for corporate tax cuts. Fang makes brilliantly clear that, while the emotions of activists may have been heartfelt, the tactics, themes, costumes, theater, and media outreach that made up the 2009–10 Tea Party were the product of many years of experimentation and slow building of organizational capacity—all made possible by the persistent and generous funding of a few wealthy businessmen. Fang, *The Machine*, 16–27.

40. Jane Mayer, Dark Money: The Hidden History of the Billionaires behind the Rise of the Radical Right (New York: Doubleday, 2016), 183.

41. Fang, *The Machine*, 40, 129–30.

42. Skocpol and Williamson, *The Tea Party*.

43. Teddy Davis, "Tea Party Activists Craft 'Contract from America,'" ABC News, February 9, 2010, http://abcnews.go.com/Politics/tea-party-activists-unveil-contract-america/story?id=10376437&page=2.

44. Kate Zernike, "Tea Party Avoids Divisive Social Issues," *New York Times*, March 12, 2010, http://www.nytimes.com/2010/03/13/us/politics/13tea.html.

45. Grover Norquist, "The Coming Bush Dynasty: It Will Flourish If It Knocks Down Key Clinton Pillars," *American Spectator*, February 2001.

46. Ibid.; Lee Fang, "WI Senate GOP Leader Admits On-Air That His Goal Is to Defund Labor Unions, Hurt Obama's Reelection Chances," ThinkProgress, March 9, 2011, http://thinkprogress.org/politics/2011/03/09/ 149655/scott-fitzgerald-obama.

47. The U.S. Chamber of Commerce is the largest business organization in the world, with over three million member firms. It is also by far the single largest lobbying force in Washington, D.C., having spent $132 million on lobbying in 2010–15, nearly three times more than the country's next-biggest lobbying client. "Influence and Lobbying: Top Spenders," Center for Responsive Politics, 2015, https://www.opensecrets.org/lobby/top.php?showYear=2010&indexType=s. The NFIB is the country's largest organization of small businesses.

48. More than one hundred corporations and nearly twenty nonprofit groups have resigned their membership in ALEC since 2011. After the murder of Trayvon Martin—broadly perceived as, in part, the result of ALEC-promoted "Stand Your Ground" laws—public outcry led to a rash of corporate resignations, including both Wal-Mart and Coca-Cola. See Center for Media and Democracy, "Corporations That Have Cut Ties to ALEC," http://www.sourcewatch.org/index.php/Corporations_that_Have_Cut_Ties_to_ALEC. These corporations are noted as ALEC supporters in this book for several reasons. First, they were active ALEC supporters during the period in which most of the bills discussed in this report were formulated and initially promoted. Second, although these companies distanced themselves from ALEC as a result of the controversy surrounding the Martin killing or ALEC's position on immigration or climate change, they in no way distanced themselves from ALEC's economic or labor agenda, and it is possible that these companies will either renew ties with ALEC in the future or find parallel channels through

which to promote the same policy goals. In some cases, these interests may already be supporting ALEC's activities through other channels. For instance, while Wal-Mart resigned from ALEC, the Walton Family Foundation remains an active member. So too, many of the companies that ended their ALEC membership are members of the U.S. Chamber of Commerce, which in turn is an active supporter of ALEC. It is possible that some corporations may shield themselves from public criticism by resigning from direct ALEC membership but continue to support the organization's activities with funds channeled through the Chamber of Commerce or the many other trade associations that remain active ALEC members.

49. American Legislative Exchange Council, "ALEC 101," ALEC Exposed, http://alecex posed.org/w/images/5/5b/ALEC_101_Exposed_1.pdf.

50. For a 2011 database of ALEC-affiliated corporations that have donated to the campaigns of ALEC-affiliated legislators, see "ALEC-Related Contributions," ProPublica, August 2011, http://projects.propublica.org/alec-contributions.

51. Fang, *The Machine*, 202.

52. Common Cause, "Legislating under the Influence: Money, Power and the American Legislative Exchange Council," Civil Liberties Defense Center, June 24, 2011, http://cldc.org/wp-content/uploads/2011/12/MONEYPOWERANDALEC.pdf. The discrepancy between this number and ALEC's claim of 20 percent success may reflect the difficulty that outsiders face in tracing ALEC's full impact, as ALEC-affiliated lawmakers may put forth bills that accomplish the organization's aims without mirroring its exact model language.

53. Tax records show that in 2012, more than half the Chamber's total revenue came from just sixty-four corporations. Sam Jewler, "The Gilded Chamber," Public Citizen, February 6, 2014, http://www.citizen.org/documents/us-chamber-of-commerce-funders-dominated-by-large-corporations-report.pdf.

54. Chris Frates, "Exclusive: AHIP Gave More Than $100 Million to Chamber's Efforts to Derail Health Care Reform," *National Journal*, June 13, 2012, http://www.modern healthcare.com/article/20120613/INFO/306139980.

55. "The U.S. Chamber of Commerce: Backing Corporate Greed at the Expense of Working Families & Small Businesses," Bridge Project, 2015, http://bridgeproject.com/app/uploads/US-Chamber-Of-Commerce-Report.pdf; Public Citizen, "The U.S. Chamber and BP," ChamberWatch, http://www.fixtheuschamber.org/news/news/us-chamber-and-bp.

56. Danny Hakim, "U.S. Chamber Fights Smoking Laws While Hospitals and Insurers Sit on Its Board," *New York Times*, July 1, 2015, http://www.nytimes.com/2015/07/02/busi ness/international/many-board-members-fight-smoking-even-as-chamber-opposes-tobacco-laws.html?_r=0.

57. Timothy Kuhner, *Capitalism v. Democracy: Money in Politics and the Free Market Constitution* (Stanford: Stanford University Press, 2014), 2.

58. Corrections Corporation of America (CCA), which was long active in ALEC before resigning in 2010, at one point offered to purchase publicly owned prisons on condition that they be guaranteed "a minimum 90 percent occupancy rate." Greg Bluestein, "Corrections Firm Offers States Cash for Prisons," Associated Press, March 9, 2012.

Arizona's strict anti-immigrant law was modeled on ALEC legislation largely crafted by a CCA executive. As SB1070 was being debated, thirty Arizona lawmakers affiliated with ALEC received campaign contributions from CCA and other private prison companies. Fang, *The Machine*, 213–15.

59. Arthur Laffer, Stephen Moore, and Jonathan Williams, *Rich States, Poor States: ALEC-Laffer State Economic Competitiveness Index*, 4th ed. (Arlington, VA: American Legislative Exchange Council, 2011), http://washingtonpolicywatch.files.wordpress.com/2012/08/rsps_4thedition.pdf; "ALEC: The Voice of Corporate Special Interests in State Legislatures," People for the American Way, 2011, http://www.pfaw.org/ rww-in-focus/alec-the-voice-of-

corporate-special-interests-state-legislatures; Laura Sullivan "Prison Economics Help Drive Ariz. Immigration Law," *NPR Morning Edition*, October 28, 2010, http://www.npr.org/2010/10/28/130833741/prison-economics-help-drive-ariz- immigration-law.

60. Laffer, Moore, and Williams, *Rich States, Poor States*.

61. For instance, while voicing support for marriage equality, the Kochs have funded both pro- and anti-gay rights organizations, on condition that both support free-market principles Fang, *The Machine*, 91. What they have never done, however, is advocate an ideological position that undermines their financial self-interest.

62. Fang, *The Machine*, 89; Mayer, *Dark Money*, 9, 151; Skocpol and Hertel-Fernandez, "The Koch Effect," 26.

63. The Kochs have created their own network of constituent outreach organizations, including separate organizations for Latino voters, veterans, and millennials. Contacts from each of these organizations are also fed back into the brothers' i360 database, which has become a direct competitor with the mainstream GOP voter file. In 2015, one GOP operative described "all-out war" over what the GOP saw as Koch attempts to take control of the party through development of this independent voter file—viewed by many as superior to the GOP's own database—and recruitment of candidates to use the Kochs', rather than the GOP's, voter-contact system. Eliana Johnson, "The Koch Brothers: Selling Freedom, Collecting Data," *National Review*, October 21, 2015, http://www.nationalreview.com/article/425872/koch-brothers-data-i360.

64. Matea Gold, "Americans for Prosperity Plowing Millions into Building Conservative Ground Force," *Washington Post*, October 6, 2014, http://www.washingtonpost.com/politics/americans-for-prosperity-plows-millions-into-building-conservative-ground-force/2014/10/06/692469b6-4b35-11e4-b72e-d60a9229cc10_story.html; Carl Hulse and Ashley Parker, "Koch Group Spending Freely, Hones Attack on Government," *New York Times*, March 201, 2014, http://www.nytimes.com/2014/03/21/us/politics/koch-group-seeks-lasting-voice-for-small-government.html. AFP's contact list grew dramatically, from less than three hundred thousand in 2008 to five times that size three years later. Over the same period, its budget increased from $7 million to $40 million. Eric Lipton, "Billionaire Brothers' Money Plays Role in Wisconsin Budget Dispute," *New York Times*, February 22, 2011.

65. Each of the major political parties raised slightly over $800 million in 2011–12. FEC data reported by Center for Responsive Politics, http://www.opensecrets.org/bigpicture/ptytots.php?cycle=2012. On the breadth and depth of the Koch network's 2016 activities, see Bolton 2015.

66. When the Washington State Senate proposed to mandate an eight-hour workday for women in 1911, the Spokane Chamber of Commerce predicted the law would lead businesses to leave the state, resulting in widespread economic hardship. Margaret Riddle, "Washington State Senate Approves Eight-hour Workday for Women on March 2, 1911," History Link, October 8, 2007, http://www.historylink.org/_content/printer_friendly/pf_output.cfm?file_id=8315. In 1917, voters in the city of Cleveland approved a referendum to create an eight-hour day for police and firefighters; the city's Chamber of Commerce bitterly opposed the measure, with full-page ads insisting it posed an unaffordable burden on public resources.

67. At the time they were proposed, the Chamber of Commerce vice president Philip Fay denounced Social Security and related New Deal policies as reflecting "philosophies of government control and foreign ideas of repression of the individual that have no place in this land of freedom." Fay, quoted in "Denounces Spread of Federal Power," *New York Times*, April 28, 1936.

68. National Employment Law Project, "Consider the Source: 100 Years of Broken-Record Opposition to Minimum Wage," March 2013, http://www.nelp.org/content/uploads/2015/03/Consider-The-Source-Minimum-Wage.pdf.

69. Among others, see Margaret Weir, *Politics and Jobs: The Boundaries of Employment Policy in the United States* (Princeton: Princeton University Press, 1993); Kim Phillips-Fein, *Invisible Hands: The Businessmen's Crusade against the New Deal* (New York: Norton, 2009); William Domhoff, *The Myth of Liberal Ascendancy: Corporate Dominance from the Great Depression to the Great Recession* (Boulder: Paradigm, 2013); and Benjamin Waterhouse, *Lobbying America: The Politics of Business from Nixon to NAFTA* (Princeton: Princeton University Press, 2014).

70. Waterhouse, *Lobbying America*; Mark Mizruchi, *The Fracturing of the American Corporate Elite* (Cambridge, MA: Harvard University Press, 2013).

71. In 2009 Apple, Nike, Pacific Gas and Electric, and Exelon quit the U.S. Chamber of Commerce in response to its position on climate change. Robert Boatright, "The Voice of American Business: The U.S. Chamber of Commerce and the 2010 Elections," in Herrnson, Deering, and Wilcox, *Interest Groups Unleashed*, 50.

72. William Domhoff, *Who Rules America? The Triumph of the Corporate Rich*, 7th ed. (New York: McGraw-Hill, 2014), 17.

73. Boatright, "The Voice of American Business."

74. The actual quote of GM president Charlie Wilson, in Senate confirmation hearings as president Eisenhower's nominee to become secretary of defense, when asked what he would do if he had to make a decision in which the interests of the country conflicted with those of GM, was that "I cannot conceive of one, because for years I thought what was good for our country was good for General Motors and vice versa." Justin Hyde, "GM's 'Engine Charlie' Wilson Learned to Live with a Misquote," *Detroit Free Press*, September 14, 2008.

75. "2014 Annual Report," General Motors Company, 2014, http://www.gm.com/content/dam/gmcom/COMPANY/Investors/Stockholder_Information/PDFs/2014_GM_Annual_Report.pdf.

76. In 2014 GM spent over $1 million on direct, reportable contributions to congressional candidates and $8.5 million in lobbying the federal government. "Influence and Lobbying: Top Spenders," Center for Responsive Politics, 2015.

77. Timothy Pollard, "S&P 500 Foreign Sales Up in 2014," *Pensions and Investments*, July 14, 2015, http://www.pionline.com/article/20150714/INTERACTIVE/150719950/sampp-500-foreign-sales-up-in-2014. The average foreign share of revenue for the S&P 500 as a whole was 47.8 percent in 2014, up from 41.8 percent in 2003.

78. Howard Silverblatt, *S&P 500 2014: Global Sales*, S&P Dow Jones Indices LLC, July 2015, http://us.spindices.com/documents/research/research-sp-500-2014-global-sales.pdf.

79. Over the course of the 1980s, almost half of publicly traded corporations experienced a takeover attempt, and one-quarter of the Fortune 500 were seized in hostile takeovers by investors who believed the company could be managed so as to produce a higher return for investors. As a defense, the remaining firms restructured operations in order to show higher market values relative to the company's assets.

80. As CEOs were incentivized to meet these goals, stock options as a share of total CEO compensation skyrocketed from 20 percent in 1980 to 50 percent by the end of the decade. Eileen Appelbaum and Rosemary Batt, *Private Equity at Work: When Wall Street Manages Main Street* (New York: Russell Sage Foundation, 2014), 27–29. At the same time, the average tenure of CEOs was getting shorter. Thus, corporate decision makers became increasingly focused on financial returns rather than long-term development of the enterprise.

81. Appelbaum and Batt, *Private Equity at Work*, 27.

82. Erdogan Bakir and Al Campbell, "Neoliberalism, The Rate of Profit, and the Rate of Accumulation," *Science and Society* 74 (2010): 323–42, http://guilfordjournals.com/doi/abs/10.1521/siso.2010.74.3.323.

83. William Lazonick, "Profits without Prosperity," *Harvard Business Review*, September 2014, https://hbr.org/2014/09/profits-without-prosperity/ar/1.

84. In 2013–14, 40 percent of survey respondents held the title of CEO or equivalent officer.

85. Jim Tankersley, "America's Execs Seem Ready to Give Up on U.S. Workers," *Washington Post*, September 11, 2014, http://www.washingtonpost.com/news/storyline/wp/2014/09/11/americas-top-execs-seem-ready-to-give-up-on-u-s-workers; Michael Porter and Jan Rivkin, "Prosperity at Risk: Findings of Harvard Business School's 2011–12 Survey on U.S. Competitiveness," Harvard Business School, January 2012, http://www.hbs.edu/competitiveness/Documents/hbscompsurvey.pdf; Michael Porter and Jan Rivkin, "An Economy Doing Half Its Job: Findings of Harvard Business School's 2013–14 Survey on U.S. Competitiveness," Harvard Business School, September 2014, http://www.hbs.edu/competitiveness/Documents/an-economy-doing-half-its-job.pdf.

86. Tankersely, "America's Execs."

87. Mizruchi, *The Fracturing*, 6, 8.

88. Skocpol and Williamson, *The Tea Party*, 83.

89. Jane Mayer's history of the Kochs documents that the same is true of each of the primary family foundations that have been largely responsible for funding the modern right, including those of the Bradley, Olin, and Mellon-Scaife families. Mayer, *Dark Money*.

90. Likewise, radical conservative Grover Norquist sits on the board of the gay organization GOProud and has been periodically attacked by social conservatives for both his outreach to gay voters and his support for George W. Bush's immigration reform proposal. Fang, *The Machine*, 55.

91. Skocpol and Hertel-Fernandez, "The Koch Effect," 21, 4.

92. Mayer, *Dark Money*, 212–13.

93. Ibid., 140.

94. Ibid., 136–37.

95. Ibid., 21.

96. Skocpol and Hertel-Fernandez, "The Koch Effect," 5.

97. Ibid., 52–53.

98. Veronique de Rugy and Diane Katz, "The Export-Import Bank's Top Foreign Buyers," Mercatus Center, George Mason University, April 2015, http://mercatus.org/sites/default/files/DeRugy-Ex-Im-Foreign-Buyers.pdf. See also Steve Lohr, "Ex-Im Bank Dispute Threatens GE Factory That Obama Praised," *New York Times*, October 25, 2015, http://www.nytimes.com/2015/10/26/business/ex-im-bank-dispute-threatens-ge-factory-that-obama-praised.html.

99. Koch and Enron together pioneered energy-based derivatives, which grew into a substantial segment of the business.

100. For a detailed account of Koch Industries' record as a polluter, see Tim Dickinson, "Inside the Koch Brothers' Toxic Empire," *Rolling Stone*, September 24, 2014, http://www.rollingstone.com/politics/news/inside-the-koch-brothers-toxic-empire-20140924.

101. The Kochs also funded a "Regulation Reality Tour" with paid staffers dressed as "Carbon Cops" who circulated throughout Tea Party events claiming the EPA was planning to hire "cops" who would require every church to get a government permit for its refrigerators. Fang, *The Machine*, 115–17.

102. Ibid., 115–17, 136.

103. Ibid., 113–14.

104. Skocpol and Williamson, *The Tea Party*, 103.

105. "Paul Ryan's Koch Problem," Wisconsin Jobs Now, September 7, 2012, http://wisconsinjobsnow.org/2012/09/paul-ryans-koch-problem.

106. Kyle Cheney, "Polls: Ryan Plan Unpopular," *Politico*, August 11, 2012, http://www.politico.com/story/2012/08/polls-ryan-plan-unpopular-079607.

107. Skocpol and Williamson, *The Tea Party*, 116–17.

108. The Kochs' first choice for the 2012 presidential nominee was Chris Christie—a relative moderate on social issues and hard-liner on economic issues, who appeared able to win a general election. Andy Kroll, "Mitt Romney Has a Koch Problem," *Mother Jones*, January 22, 2015, http://www.motherjones.com/politics/2015/01/mitt-romney-koch-brothers-donor-network.

109. Senators Pat Toomey (PA), Rand Paul (KY), Marco Rubio (FL), Ron Johnson (WI), and Mike Lee (UT) all won election with Tea Party support in 2010, having triumphed over more mainstream Republican primary candidates.

110. Matt Friedman, "Poll: NJ Voters Overwhelmingly Support Minimum Wage Hike," NJ.com, September 23, 2013, http://www.nj.com/politics/index.ssf/2013/09/poll_nj_voters_overwhelmingly_support_minimum_wage_hike.html.

111. Elizabeth Mendes, "In U.S., Fear of Big Government at Near-Record Level," Gallup Politics, December 12, 2011, http://www.gallup.com/poll/151490/fear-big-government-near-record-level.aspx; Steve Inskeep, "Americans Underestimate U.S. Wealth Inequality," National Public Radio, October 7, 2010, http://www.npr.org/templates/story/story.php?storyId=130395070.

112. Pew Research Center, "Public Divided over Occupy Wall Street Movement," October 24, 2011, http://www.people-press.org/2011/10/24/public-divided-over-occupy-wall-street-movement.

113. Thomas Edsall, "The Trump-Sanders Fantasy," *New York Times*, February 24, 2016, http://www.nytimes.com/2016/02/24/opinion/campaign-stops/the-trump-sanders-fantasy.html; Cassie Spodak, "Trump or Sanders? Some Voters Can't Decide," CNN, February 8, 2016, http://www.cnn.com/2016/02/08/politics/new-hampshire-primary-independent-voters.

114. Doyle McManus, "Americans Reluctant to Bail Out Wall Street," *Los Angeles Times*, September 24, 2008, http://articles.latimes.com/2008/sep/24/nation/na-econpoll24.

115. Karlyn Bowman, "The Public View of Regulation, Revisited," American Enterprise Institute, January 19, 2011, 9, https://www.aei.org/publication/the-public-view-of-regulation-revisited; "Banning Big Wall Street Bonuses Favored by 70% of Americans," Bloomberg Business News, December 12, 2010, http://www.bloomberg.com/news/articles/2010-12-13/banning-big-wall-street-bonus-favored-by-70-of-americans-in-national-poll.

116. Jeffrey Jones, "Most Americans Favor Gov't Action to Limit Executive Pay," Gallup, June 16, 2009, Gallup. www.gallup.com/poll/120872/american5-favor-gov-action-limit-executive-pa-.a5px.

117. Robin Toner and Janet Elder, "Most Support U.S. Guarantee of Health Care," *New York Times*, March 2, 2007; Knowledge Networks, The Associated Press-Yahoo Poll, Wave 2, conducted by Knowledge Works, December 2007, http://surveys.ap.org/data/KnowledgeNetworks/AP-Yahoo_2007-08_panel02.pdf; Seth Brohinsky and Mark Schulman, "Time/Abt SRBI Poll: Most Americans Eager for Healthcare Reform," Abt/SRBI, July 29, 2009, http://www.srbi.com/Research-Impacts/Polls/Time-Abt-SRBI-Poll-Most-Americans-Eager-for-Health.aspx; *New York Times*/CBS News, Poll, June 12–16, 2009.

118. Taxes: Historical Trends," Gallup, http://www.gallup.com/poll/1714/taxes.aspx?version=print. From 2008 to 2010, much of the debate around taxation concerned the question of whether the Bush-era tax cuts should be extended for families making over $250,000 per year. Throughout this period, a solid majority of the country consistently supported raising taxes on this population; in several polls this included a majority of Republicans. Brian Montopoli, "CBS News Poll: Most Oppose GOP Tax Plan," CBS, December 2, 2010, http://www.cbsnews.com/8301-503544_162-20024494-503544.html; Jennifer Pinto, "Polls Show

Most Americans Support Raising Taxes on Wealthy," CBS News, September 23, 2011, http://www.cbsnews.com/news/polls-show-most-americans-support-raising-taxes-on-wealthy.

119. Kevin Gardner, "If This Proposal Passes, Michigan Would Have the Second Highest Sales Tax in the Nation," Generation Opportunity, April 15, 2015, https://generation opportunity.org/articles/2015/04/15/if-this-proposal-passes-michigan-would-have-the-second-highest-sales-tax-in-the-nation.

120. Adam Brandon, fund-raising appeal from FreedomWorks e-mailed to the author, August 31, 2015.

121. As part of the research for this book, the author sought interviews with a number of prominent ALEC-affiliated companies, including Exxon Mobil, Verizon, Sprint Nextel, Dow Chemical, Pfizer, UPS, Altria, Anheuser-Busch, AT&T, Bayer, Crown Industries, Eli Lilly, FedEx, Kraft Food, Peabody Energy, and U.S. Steel. After being told the topic of the book, all refused to speak.

122. Oliver Burkeman, "Memo Exposes Bush's New Green Strategy," *Guardian*, March 3, 2003, http://www.theguardian.com/environment/2003/mar/04/usnews.climatechange. The environmental section of Luntz's original memo can be found at https://nigguraths. files.wordpress.com/2013/03/luntzresearch_environment.pdf.

123. Fang, *The Machine*, 77.

124. This follows the strategy outlined by the whistleblower Wendell Potter, former vice president of Cigna insurance, explaining that the health insurance industry had determined to respond to the Obama legislation by publicly embracing reform while privately seeking to kill all aspects of the bill except those that would enrich profits. The BCBS lobbyist Joan Gardner was one of three individuals charged with drafting the ALEC model legislation. Fang, *The Machine*, 137–50.

125. Mizruchi, *The Fracturing*, 261.

126. William Kristol, "Defeating President Clinton's Health Care Proposal," Project for a Republican Future, December 2, 1993, http://delong.typepad.com/egregious_moderation/2009/03/william-kristol-defeating-president-clintons-health-care-proposal.html.

127. Dylan Loewe, *Permanently Blue: How Democrats Can End the Republican Party and Rule the Next Generation* (New York: Three Rivers Press, 2010), 8, 48.

128. Josh Israel, "No, The Koch Brothers Aren't Socially Liberal," ThinkProgress, February 10, 2015, http://thinkprogress.org/politics/2015/02/10/3617677/koch-brothers-moderate-message. Despite this professed belief, not only have the Kochs backed numerous candidates who campaigned against marriage equality, but the Koch-backed Freedom Partners donated over $8 million to an antigay religious organization that staged protests outside the Supreme Court. The Kochs' belief in marriage equality is apparently not important enough to trump the imperatives of political alliances aimed at electing those who carry forward their economic agenda. The Freedom Partners funding further suggests the possibility of agreements for Christian-right organizations to receive financial support in return for supporting the economic principles of the corporate right.

129. Kevin Sack and Sarah Wheaton, "Republicans' First Challenge: Find Common Ground among Themselves," *New York Times*, November 11, 2012, http://www.nytimes. com/2012/11/12/us/politics/first-republicans-must-find-common-ground-among-themselves.html.

130. Maggie Haberman, "Karen Hughes: I'll 'Cut Out' the Tongue of GOPers Talking Rape," *Politico*, November 9, 2012, http://www.politico.com/blogs/burns-haberman/2012/11/karen-hughes-ill-cut-out-the-tongue-of-gopers-talking-rape-149146.

131. Janet Hook, "Initiatives to Ban Gay Marriage Could Help Bush in Key States," *Los Angeles Times*, July 12, 2004, http://articles.latimes.com/2004/jul/12/nation/na-gaymarry12; Associated Press, "Voters Pass All 11 Bans on Gay Marriage," November 3, 2004, http://www.nbcnews. com/id/6383353/ns/politics/t/voters-pass-all-bans-gay-marriage/#.VgrSubRVhBd. In 2010,

Bush 2004 campaign manager Ken Melman publicly announced that he is gay. In discussing his personal path toward this announcement, Melman described Karl Rove's effort to place anti-gay initiatives on the ballot in 2004 and 2006 as a strategy for boosting Republican electoral chances. Marc Ambinder, "Bush Campaign Chief and Former RNC Chair Ken Mehlman: I'm Gay," *Atlantic*, August 25, 2010, http://www.theatlantic.com/politics/archive/2010/08/bush-campaign-chief-and-former-rnc-chair-ken-mehlman-im-gay/62065.

132. Pew Research Center, "Changing Attitudes on Gay Marriage," July 29, 2015, http://www.pewforum.org/2015/07/29/graphics-slideshow-changing-attitudes-on-gay-marriage.

133. Henry Barbour et al., Growth and Opportunity Project, Republican National Committee, 2013, 6, http://goproject.gop.com.

134. Zernike, "Tea Party."

135. *New York Times*/CBS News, National Survey of Tea Party Supporters, April 5–12, 2010, http://s3.amazonaws.com/nytdocs/docs/312/312.pdf.

136. Fang, *The Machine*, 2–4.

137. Skocpol and Hertel-Fernandez, "The Koch Effect," 32–35.

138. Renae Merle, "Why the Rise of Donald Trump Has Even Wall Street Worried," *Washington Post*, March 23, 2016, https://www.washingtonpost.com/business/economy/why-the-rise-of-donald-trump-has-even-wall-street-worried/2016/03/23/dd0a710e-df31-11e5-8d98-4b3d9215ade1_story.html.

139. Alan Abramowitz, Ronald Rapoport, and Walter Stone, "Why Donald Trump Is Winning and Why His Nomination Could Shatter the Republican Party," University of Virginia Center for Politics, March 10, 2016, http://www.centerforpolitics.org/crystalball/articles/why-donald-trump-is-winning-and-why-his-nomination-could-shatter-the-republican-party.

140. Lee Fang, "Donald Trump Says He Can Buy Politicians, None of His Rivals Disagree," The Intercept, August 7, 2015, https://theintercept.com/2015/08/07/donald-trump-buy.

141. Byron York, "As Vote Nears, a More Radical Trump Emerges," *Washington Examiner*, February 8, 2016, http://www.washingtonexaminer.com/byron-york-as-vote-nears-a-more-radical-trump-emerges/article/2582703#.VriJa5SYN7c.twitter.

142. A majority of Republicans in the spring of 2016 opposed cuts to Social Security or Medicare and supported higher taxes on the rich. Abramowitz, Rapoport, and Stone, "Why Donald Trump Is Winning."

143. CNN exit polls, last accessed November 9, 2016, http://edition.cnn.com/election/results/exit-polls.

144. "Stephen Moore, Author Profile," American Legislative Exchange Council, last accessed November 9, 2016, https://www.alec.org/person/stephen-moore.

145. Michael Corkery, "Trump Expected to Seek Deep Cuts in Business Regulations," *New York Times*, November 9, 2016, http://www.nytimes.com/2016/11/10/business/dealbook/trump-expected-to-seek-deep-cuts-in-business-regulations.html.

146. It is still the case that most state legislators have very thin staff support. Alexander Hertel-Fernandez shows that one of the reasons legislators turn to ALEC for model legislation is that they lack the staff capacity to draft their own bills. Hertel-Fernandez, "Who Passes Business's 'Model Bills'? Policy Capacity and Corporate Influence in U.S. State Politics," *Perspectives on Politics* 12, no. 3 (September 2014): 582–602, http://scholar.harvard.edu/files/ahertel/files/bizbills_-_draft.pdf.

147. Meghan Reilly, "States Limiting Legislative Debate," State of Connecticut, Office of Legislative Research, July 8, 2009, https://www.cga.ct.gov/2009/rpt/2009-R-0249.htm.

148. Martin Gilens, *Affluence and Influence: Economic Inequality and Political Power in America* (Princeton: Princeton University Press, 2010), 173.

149. Vanderbilt Poll, Center for the Study of Democratic Institutions, May 2012, http://www.vanderbilt.edu/csdi/tl2012.pdf; "Evaluations of Government and Society Study," American National Election Studies, 2010, http://www.electionstudies.org/studypages/2010_2012EGSS/2010_2012EGSScriteria.htm.

150. Steven Rogers, "Accountability in State Legislatures: How Parties Perform in Office and State Legislative Elections," Center for the Study of Democratic Institutions, Vanderbilt University, October 17, 2013, http://www.stevenmrogers.com/Dissertation/ChapterDrafts/CollectiveAccountability/Rogers-CollectiveAccountability.pdf (chapter from PhD diss., Princeton University, 2013).

151. Tilman Klumpp, Hugo Mialon, and Michael Williams, "The Business of American Democracy: Citizens United, Spending, and Elections," University of Alberta, October 2015, https://www.ualberta.ca/~klumpp/docs/cu.pdf.

The authors culled data from more than thirty-eight thousand state legislative races over seven election cycles—five preceding *Citizens United* and two following the decision. The analysis compared the impact of the Supreme Court decision in states that had previously allowed corporate independent expenditures with those that had banned them before 2010. This differences-in-differences analysis provides the first rigorous statistical measure of the law's impact on state legislative elections. The data show that independent expenditures increased the likelihood of Republican incumbents' seeking reelection, decreased the number of Democrats choosing to stand as candidates, and increased the odds of the Republican candidate's winning.

152. Chris Kromm, "How Much Did Art Pope's Network Really Spend on North Carolina's 2010 Legislative Election?" October 7, 2011, http://www.artpopeexposed.com/explainer_how_much_did_art_pope_really_spend. For a detailed account of Pope's political activities, see Jean Mayer, "State for Sale: A Conservative Multimillionaire Has Taken Control in North Carolina, One of 2012's Top Battlegrounds," *New Yorker*, October 10, 2011, http://www.newyorker.com/magazine/2011/10/10/state-for-sale.

153. Author's calculations based on Kromm, "How Much Did Art Pope's Network Really Spend?" and National Institute on Money in State Politics, overview of North Carolina 2008 election, FollowTheMoney, https://www.followthemoney.org/election-overview?s=NC&y=2008.

154. Author's calculations based on National Institute on Money in State Politics, overview of North Carolina 2008 election. .

155. Competitiveness in state legislative races—measured by the share of all races decided by 5 percent or less—has been declining since the 1970s. Two thousand fourteen saw the fewest closely contested races of any state election on record. Reid Wilson, "Study: Elections Becoming Less Competitive," *Washington Post*, May 7, 2015, https://www.washingtonpost.com/blogs/govbeat/wp/2015/05/07/study-state-elections-becoming-less-competitive.

156. Peter Hancock, "Pro-Business Groups Wielding Big Influence in Legislature, Democrats Say," *Lawrence Journal-World*, April 5, 2015, http://www2.ljworld.com/news/2015/apr/05/pro-business-lobby-groups-wielding-big-influence-l.

157. Chief Justice Louis Brandeis, *New State Ice Co. v. Liebmann*, 285 U.S. 262 (1932).

158. Andrew Karch, *Democratic Laboratories: Policy Diffusion among the American States* (Ann Arbor: University of Michigan Press, 2007), 1.

159. Thomas Volscho and Nathan Kelly, "The Rise of the Super-Rich: Power Resources, Taxes, Financial Markets, and the Dynamics of the Top 1 Percent, 1949 to 2008," *American Sociological Review* 77, no. 5 (2012): 679–99.

160. Adam Bonica et al., "Why Hasn't Democracy Slowed Rising Inequality?" *Journal of Economic Perspectives* 27, no. 3 (Summer 2013): 112.

161. Quoted in Mayer, *Dark Money*, 193.

162. Ibid., 7.

163. Kenneth Vogel, "A Koch Love-Fest in California," *Politico*, August 3, 2015, http://www.politico.com/story/2015/08/koch-love-fest-in-california-120928; Nicholas Confessore, "Koch Brothers' Budget of $889 Million Is on Par with Both Parties' Spending," *New York Times*, January 26, 2015, http://www.nytimes.com/2015/01/27/us/politics/kochs-plan-to-spend-900-million-on-2016-campaign.html.

164. Quoted in Mayer, *Dark Money*, 378.

165. In 2006, just 2 percent of outside political spending came from undisclosed donors; by 2010 this figure had jumped to 40 percent, representing hundreds of millions of dollars in secret spending. Ibid., 248.

166. The RedMap project targeted state house races in Colorado, Michigan, North Carolina, Ohio, Pennsylvania, Texas, and Wisconsin—all states where Republicans constituted between 40 and 50 percent of the legislature in 2008 and where corporate independent expenditures were banned prior to 2010. ALEC member companies contributing to Redmap included Altria/Philip Morris, Reynolds America, Blue Cross Blue Shield, WellPoint, AstraZeneca, Verizon, AT&T, Wal-Mart, Comcast, Eli Lilly, Citigroup, Exxon Mobil, Home Depot, Anheuser-Busch, and Monsanto. Klumpp, Mialon, and Williams, "The Business of American Democracy."

167. "Project Labor Revolt," *Wall Street Journal*, July 19, 2011, http://www.wsj.com/articles/SB10001424052702303365804576434071389103838?cb=logged0.9715004123281687. The four early states are Montana, Utah, Arkansas, and Missouri. In 2011–15 they were joined by Idaho, Arizona, North and South Dakota, Kansas, Oklahoma, Iowa, Michigan, Ohio, Louisiana, Mississippi, Alabama, Georgia, North and South Carolina, Virginia, West Virginia, and Maine.

168. Alexander Hertel-Fernandez, "Who Passes Business's 'Model Bills'?"

169. "Chamber Releases 2012 Top 10 Legislative Priorities," Indiana Chamber of Commerce, December 14, 2011, http://www.indianachamber.com/index.php/media-center/press-releases/2011-press-releases/1544-chamber-releases-2012-top-10-legislative-priorities; "Top 5 Reforms for a Stronger Wisconsin," Wisconsin Manufacturers and Commerce, https://www.wmc.org/wp-content/uploads/Legislative-Agenda-2015-16-Top-5.pdf; "Policy Agenda," New Mexico Association of Commerce and Industry, http://www.nmaci.org/policy-agenda.aspx.

170. For several recent examples, see Jane McAlevey, *Raising Expectations and Raising Hell*, (London: Verso, 2012); Steve Early, *Save Our Unions: Dispatches from a Movement in Distress* (New York: Monthly Review Press, 2013); and Alexandra Bradbury et al., *How to Jump-Start Your Union: Lessons from the Chicago Teachers* (Detroit: Labor Notes, 2015).

171. Alia Beard Rau, "Prop 206: Arizona Voters Approve $12 Minimum Wage," *Arizona Republic*, November 8, 2016, http://www.azcentral.com/story/news/politics/elections/2016/11/08/arizona-minimum-wage-proposition-206-election-results/92970650.

172. Michael Wines, "Inside the Conservative Push for States to Amend the Constitution," *New York Times*, August 22, 2016, http://www.nytimes.com/2016/08/23/us/inside-the-conservative-push-for-states-to-amend-the-constitution.html.

1. WISCONSIN AND BEYOND

1. Bob Williams, "Differences between Private Sector Unions and Government Unions," policy brief, State Budget Solutions, March 23, 2011, http://www.statebudgetsolutions.org/publications/detail/differences-between-private-sector-unions-and-government-unions.

2. Megan Thee-Brenan, "Poll Finds Disapproval of Bush Unwavering," *New York Times*, January 16, 2009, http://www.nytimes.com/2009/01/17/us/politics/17poll.html; "Bush's Final Approval Rating: 22 Percent," CBS News, January 16, 2009, http://www.cbsnews.com/news/bushs-final-approval-rating-22-percent.

3. Maura Reynolds, "More Say Oval Office Is to Blame: We're Worse Off Because of Bush Policies, Americans Say," *Los Angeles Times*, June 26, 2008, http://articles.latimes.com/2008/jun/26/business/fi-poll26.

4. Doyle McManus, "Americans Reluctant to Bail Out Wall Street," *Los Angeles Times*, September 24, 2008, http://articles.latimes.com/2008/sep/24/nation/na-econpoll24; Karlyn Bowman, "The Public View of Regulation, Revisited," American Enterprise Institute, January 19, 2011, https://www.aei.org/publication/the-public-view-of-regulation-revisited; "Banning Big Wall Street Bonuses Favored by 70% of Americans," Bloomberg Business News, December 12, 2010, http://www.bloomberg.com/news/articles/2010-12-13/banning-big-wall-street-bonus-favored-by-70-of-americans-in-national-poll.

5. At the height of the financial crisis, the longtime conservative strategists Karl Rove and Ed Gillespie conducted a series of polls designed to identify a messaging road map for attacking public employee unions. On the basis of their results, the pair wrote a memo arguing that it was possible to "galvanize citizens" against "the new federal bureaucrat elite—paid for by struggling private sector families." Fang, *The Machine*, 219.

6. Quoted in Charles J. Skyes, "The Empire Strikes Back," *WI Magazine* 21, no. 1 (March 2012), Wisconsin Policy Research Institute, http://www.wpri.org/WPRI/WI-Magazine/Volume21No1/The-Empire-Strikes-Back.htm.

7. 2011 Wisconsin Act 10, http://docs.legis.wisconsin.gov/2011/related/acts/10.

8. Idaho, Illinois, Indiana, Maine, Michigan, Minnesota, Nebraska, New Hampshire, New Jersey, Nevada, Ohio, Oklahoma, Pennsylvania, Tennessee, and Wisconsin. This list does not include states that cut wages and benefits without otherwise restricting bargaining rights.

9. As described in Danielle Carne and Martin Kehoe, "Subcommittee Report: States without Bargaining Legislation," American Bar Association, January 28, 2012, http://www.americanbar.org/content/dam/aba/events/labor_law/2012/01/state_local_government_bargaining_employment_law_committee_midwinter_meeting/statelocal2012_carne_kehoe.authcheckdam.pdf. Maine's repeal of farm-worker collective bargaining works was contained in LD 1207, http://www.mainelegislature.org/legis/bills/bills_125th/chapters/PUBLIC565.asp. On the repeal of bargaining rights for child-care workers, see Susan Cover, "Maine House Backs End to Careers' Union Rights," *Portland Press Herald*, April 10, 2012, http://www.pressherald.com/news/house-backs-end-to-care-providers-union-rights_2012-04-10.html. The removal of bargaining rights for graduate research assistants was contained in Michigan's HB 4246, http://www.legislature.mi.gov/documents/2011-2012/billenrolled/House/pdf/2011-HNB-4246.pdf. On this point see also Jack Spencer, "Snyder Signs Bill Clarifying That Graduate Students Are Students, Not Employees," *Capitol Confidential*, Mackinac Center for Public Policy, March 14, 2012, https://www.mackinac.org/16596. Michigan's emergency management law was initially included in HB 2414, and by May 2013 six cities had been taken over under the law's provisions. http://www.huffingtonpost.com/2013/03/15/michigan-emergency-manager-law-cities_n_2876777.html.

10. Minnesota's SF 247 was vetoed by the governor. Both the bill text and the governor's veto statement are available at http://votesmart.org/bill/15204/39944/20301/mark-dayton-vetoed-sf-247-relating-to-the-public-employee-insurance-program#39944.

11. Legislation outlined in this paragraph is described in Carne and Kehoe, "Subcommittee Report." Indiana's 2011 budget bill, HB 1001, made collective bargaining by state agencies and strikes by state employees illegal. The bill summary provided by the house speaker can be found at http://indianalawblog.com/documents/Summary%20of%20HB%201001%20-%20CCR1.pdf.

12. Walker did campaign on asking for cuts in employee health care and pension benefits but not by eliminating the right to bargain. Dave Umhoefer, "A Look at Scott Walker's Campaign Promises," *Milwaukee Journal Sentinel*, January 1, 2011, http://www.politifact.com/wisconsin/article/2011/jan/01/look-scott-walkers-campaign-promises. Walker later claimed that he had campaigned on the same principles embodied in his

2011 Budget Repair Bill, but after extensive fact-checking, the state's largest newspaper rated this claim "false." Dave Umhoefer, "PolitiFact: Scott Walker Says He Campaigned on His Budget Repair Bill, including Curtailing Collective Bargaining," *Milwaukee Journal Sentinel*, February 22, 2011, http://www.politifact.com/wisconsin/statements/2011/feb/22/scott-walker/wisconsin-gov-scott-walker-says-he-campaigned-his-/.

13. Transcript of prank Koch-Walker conversation, *Wisconsin State Journal*, February 23, 2011, http://host.madison.com/transcript-of-prank-koch-walker-conversatio... icle_531276b6-3f6a-11e0-b288-001cc4c002e0.html?print=true&cid=print.

14. Tip O'Neill, *All Politics Is Local and Other Rules of the Game* (Holbrook, MA: Adams Media Corp., 1995).

15. Eric Lipton, "Billionaire Brothers' Money Plays Role in Wisconsin Budget Dispute," *New York Times*, February 22, 2011.

16. Together, these legislators received a total of $276,000 in contributions from ALEC member corporations over the previous two election cycles. Brendan Fischer, "ALEC Exposed in Wisconsin: The Hijacking of a State," Center for Media and Democracy, 2012, http://alecexposed.org/w/images/c/cd/ALEC_Exposed_in_Wisconsin.pdf.

17. Rich Cooper, "Walker Leading Wisconsin—You Can't Always Get What You Want," U.S. Chamber of Commerce Foundation, January 17, 2012, http://www.uschamberfoundation. org/blog/post/walker-leading-wisconsin-you-can-t-alwayThe s-get-what-you-want/34238. Cooper is the U.S. Chamber of Commerce Foundation's vice president of research.

18. Kurt Bauer, "WMC Statement on Wisconsin Supreme Court Act 10 Ruling," Wisconsin Manufacturers and Commerce, July 31, 2014, https://www.wmc.org/news/press-releases/ wmc-statement-on-wisconsin-supreme-court-act-10-ruling; "Wisconsin Business Climate Improves in 2011," press release, Wisconsin Manufacturers and Commerce, December 20, 2011, https://www.wmc.org/news/press-releases/wisconsin-business-climate-improves-in-2011.

19. Don Walker, "Americans for Prosperity in Budget Fight to Win," *Milwaukee Journal Sentinel*, February 28, 2011, http://www.jsonline.com/blogs/news/117082778.html.

20. Jim Ragsdale, "The Right Finds Its Champion: Wisconsin Gov. Walker," *St. Paul Star Tribune*, June 1, 2012, http://www.startribune.com/the-right-finds-its-champion-wisconsin-gov-walker/156110145.

21. On this point, see John Schmitt, "The Wage Penalty for State and Local Government Employees," Center for Economic and Policy Research, May 2010, http://www.cepr.net/ documents/publications/wage-penalty-2010-05.pdf; and a series of state-by-state reports authored by Jeffrey Keefe, including "Are Wisconsin Public Employees Over-Compensated?" (Economic Policy Institute Briefing Paper No. 290, February 10, 2011), http://www.epi.org/ publication/are_wisconsin_public_employees_over-compensated. Data are based on a comparison of public and private employees with similar levels of education and training.

22. Corina Eckl, "State Budget Actions: FY 2007 and FY 2008," National Conference of State Legislatures, April 2008, 36.

23. Henry J. Kaiser Family Foundation, http://kff.org/other/state-indicator/state-budget-shortfalls-sfy10/.

24. Sylvia Allegretto, Ken Jacobs, and Laurel Lucia, "The Wrong Target: Public Sector Unions and State Budget Deficits," University of California at Berkeley, Institute for Research on Labor and Employment, October 2011, http://www.irle.berkeley.edu/research/ state_budget_deficits_oct2011.pdf; David Madland and Nick Bunker, "State Budget Deficits Are Not an Employee Compensation Problem," Center for American Progress, March 10, 2011, http://www.americanprogressaction.org/issues/labor/report/2011/03/10/9206/ state-budget-deficits-are-not-an-employee-compensation-problem.

25. Erica Williams et al., "New Fiscal Year Brings More Grief for State Budgets, Putting Economic Recovery at Risk," Center on Budget and Policy Priorities, June 29, 2010, http:// www.cbpp.org/files/6-29-10sfp.pdf.

26. Statistical analysis shows no correlation whatsoever between the presence of public employee unions and the size of state budget deficits. Allegretto, Jacobs, and Lucia, "The Wrong Target."

27. Erica Williams, Michael Leachman, and Nicholas Johnson, "State Budget Cuts in the New Fiscal Year Are Unnecessarily Harmful," Center on Budget and Policy Priorities, July 28, 2011, http://www.cbpp.org/cms/?fa=view&id=3550.

28. Brian Beutler, "Wisconsin Gov. Walker Ginned Up Budget Shortfall to Undercut Workers Rights," Talking Points Memo, February 17, 2011.

29. Zaid Jilani, "Scott Walker Admits Union-Busting Provision 'Doesn't Save Any' Money for the State of Wisconsin," ThinkProgress, April 14, 2011, http://thinkprogress.org/politics/2011/04/14/158690/walker-admits-union-money.

30. Joe Vardon, "Kasich Moves on from Loss on Issue 2," *Columbus Dispatch*, November 16, 2011, http://www.dispatch.com/content/stories/local/2011/11/16/kasich-moves-on-from-loss-on-issue-2.html.

31. Grover Norquist, "The Coming Bush Dynasty," *American Spectator*, February 2001, http://crywolfproject.org/sites/default/files/docs/briefs/the_coming_bush_dynasty_-_norquist_on_strategy.pdf.

32. "Union Members in 2009," news release, U.S. Bureau of Labor Statistics, February 22, 2010, http://www.bls.gov/news.release/archives/union2_01222010.pdf.

33. Grover Norquist, "The Democratic Party Is Toast," *Washington Monthly*, September 2004, http://www.washingtonmonthly.com/features/2004/0409.norquist.html.

34. Henry Olsen, vice president, American Enterprise Institute, quoted in "What the Recall Means," *National Review Online* Symposium, June 6, 2012, http://www.nationalreview.com/blogs/print/301946.

35. Robert Samuels, "Walker's Anti-union Law Has Labor Reeling in Wisconsin," *Washington Post*, February 22, 2015, http://www.washingtonpost.com/politics/in-wisconsin-walkers-anti-union-law-has-crippled-labor-movement/2015/02/22/1eb3ef82-b6f1-11e4-aa05-1ce812b3fdd2_story.html.

36. Steven Greenhouse, "Wisconsin's Legacy for Unions," *New York Times*, February 22, 2014, http://www.nytimes.com/2014/02/23/business/wisconsins-legacy-for-unions.html?_r=0; Matt Batzel, "Act 10 Bonus: Crushing Big Labor's War Chest," Right Wisconsin, July 12, 2013,http://www.rightwisconsin.com/perspectives/215183051.html. Batzel is the Wisconsin director of American Majority Action, an organization with links to the Club for Growth and Tea Party groups, which spent $140,000 to elect Republicans in 2010. For background on AMA and its primary donor, the Sam Adams Alliance, see http://www.sourcewatch.org/index.php/American_Majority_Action and http://www.sourcewatch.org/index.php/Sam_Adams_Alliance.

37. Melissa McQuay, quoted in Greenhouse, "Wisconsin's Legacy for Unions."

38. Greenhouse, "Wisconsin's Legacy for Unions."

39. For one statistical analysis of how private-sector wage discrimination may have driven black workers to seek government jobs, see Jared Llorens, Jeffrey Wenger, and J. Edward Kellough, "Pushed into the Public Sector? Private Sector Discrimination and the Employment of Women and Minorities in State Government" (paper presented at conference "Third Transatlantic Dialogue—Leading the Future of the Public Sector," University of Delaware, 2007), http://www.ipa.udel.edu/3tad/papers/workshop2/Kellough.pdf. The public sector has been more open to black workers at least since 1941, when President Roosevelt created the Fair Employment Practices Committee and opened the civil service to African Americans. Public-sector nondiscrimination and affirmative action practices were further strengthened in a series of laws and executive actions in the 1960s and 1970s, including the Equal Employment Opportunity Act of 1972. Nina Martin, "Who Are Those

'Greedy' Public Workers? Blacks and Women," New America Media, March 1, 2011, http://newamericamedia.org/2011/03/who-are-those-evil-public-workers-blacks-and-women.php; David Cooper, Mary Gable, and Algernon Austin, "The Public-Sector Jobs Crisis: Women and African Americans Hit Hardest by Job Losses in State and Local Governments" (Economic Policy Institute Briefing Paper No. 339, May 2, 2012), http://s3.epi.org/files/2012/bp339-public-sector-jobs-crisis.pdf.

40. Steven Pitts, "Research Brief: Black Workers and the Public Sector," Labor Center, University of California, Berkeley, April 4, 2011, http://laborcenter.berkeley.edu/pdf/2011/blacks_public_sector11.pdf.

41. Ibid.

42. Lawrence Mishel and Algernon Austin, "Race, the Jobs Crisis and Recovery" (PowerPoint presentation, Economic Policy Institute, 2011).

43. Quoted in Martin, "Who Are Those 'Greedy' Public Workers?"

44. Scott Walker, quoted in Jason Stein, "Gov. Scott Walker and Mary Burke on Public Unions," *Milwaukee Journal Sentinel*, July 21, 2014, http://www.jsonline.com/blogs/news/267949681.html?ipad=y.

45. Associated Press, "Wis. Governor: Ax $900 Million from Education," NBC News, March 1, 2011, http://www.nbcnews.com/id/41840204/ns/us_news-life/t/wis-governor-ax-million-education.

46. "Tax Law Changes since January 2011," State of Wisconsin, Legislative Fiscal Bureau, April 30, 2014, http://legis.wisconsin.gov/lfb/publications/miscellaneous/documents/2014_04_30_tax%20law%20changes.pdf.

47. "Missing Out: Recent Tax Cuts Deliver Little to People Who Earn the Least," Wisconsin Budget Project, June 3, 2014.

48. Tamarine Cornelius and Jon Peacock, "Breaking with Tradition: How Wisconsin Lawmakers Have Shortchanged a Legacy of Investment in the State's Future," Wisconsin Budget Project, August 6, 2014, http://www.wisconsinbudgetproject.org/breaking-with-tradition-how-wisconsin-lawmakers-have-shortchanged-a-legacy-of-investment-in-the-states-future.

49. The wages of public employees whose compensation was cut by Act 10 put them between the twentieth and sixtieth percentile of Wisconsin income earners. "Wisconsin's Public Employees," Center on Wisconsin Strategy, May 2011, http://www.cows.org/_data/documents/1092.pdf; Tamarine Cornelius, "Wisconsin's Public Sector Leaner Than in Most Other States," Wisconsin Budget Project, March 12, 2014, http://www.wisconsinbudgetproject.org/wisconsins-public-sector-leaner-than-in-most-other-states; Wisconsin Budget Project, "Missing Out."

50. Author's calculation based on Deirdre Baker, "Annual Summary of Public Employment and Payroll Summary Report: 2011," U.S. Census Bureau, August 22, 2013, https://www.census.gov/prod/2013pubs/g11-aspep.pdf. In some cases, such actions were carried out in the same states that also limited employees' bargaining rights; in others, legislators ignored bargaining rights by directly mandating wages and benefits that were supposed to be decided through negotiations. Minnesota froze employees' wages for a year, and Maine for three years. Six different states passed laws mandating that employees pay an increased share of health care premiums.

51. "ALEC's Statement of Principles on Fixing State and Local Government Defined-Benefit Plans," American Legislative Exchange Council, 2011, http://www.alec.org/model-legislation/alecs-statement-of-principles-on-fixing-state-and-local-government-defined-benefit-plans. Defined benefit pensions guarantee retirees a given monthly payment, with employers responsible for providing that amount. Defined contribution plans simply require employers to contribute a set sum to a retirement fund but not to ensure that this results in any specific level of monthly support for retirees. Employers generally

prefer defined contribution plans because their contributions tend to be lower, and they avoid responsibility for retirees' welfare, shifting risk to retirees themselves.

52. "Behind The Cuts: Gwendolyn Beasley, Librarian from Detroit," National Public Pension Coalition, 2013, http://www.truthaboutpensions.org/behind-the-cuts/stories/gwendolyn-beasley.

53. "Behind The Cuts: Shawn Connors, Teacher from Pennsylvania," National Public Pension Coalition, 2013, http://www.truthaboutpensions.org/behind-the-cuts/stories/shawn-connors-teacher.

54. Eli Lehrer and Steve Stanek, "The State Public Pension Crisis: A 50-State Report Card," Heartland Institute, April 2010, https://www.heartland.org/policy-documents/no-126-state-public-pension-crisis-50-state-report-card.

55. "Full Text of Gov. Christi's State-of-the-State Address," nj.com, January 11, 2011, http://www.nj.com/politics/index.ssf/2011/01/full_text_of_gov_christies_sta.html.

56. Elizabeth McNichol and Iris Lav, "A Common-Sense Strategy for Fixing State Pension Problems in Tough Economic Times," Center on Budget and Policy Priorities, May 12, 2011, http://www.cbpp.org/cms/?fa=view&id=3492.

57. South Carolina's public employee pension fund was funded at 69.3 percent of liabilities. Keith Brainard, "Public Fund Survey Summary of Findings for FY 2009," National Association of State Retirement Administrators, November 2010, http://www.publicfundsurvey.org/publicfundsurvey/pdfs/Summary%20of%20Findings%20FY09.pdf.

58. On the absence of collective bargaining rights, see Milla Sanes and John Schmitt, "Regulation of Public Sector Collective Bargaining in the States," Center for Economic and Policy Research, March 2014, http://www.cepr.net/documents/state-public-cb-2014-03.pdf. South Carolina's history of gubernatorial elections is at http://en.wikipedia.org/wiki/South_Carolina_gubernatorial_elections, and history of legislative control is at http://en.wikipedia.org/wiki/Political_party_strength_in_South_Carolina.

59. Dean Baker, "The Origins and Severity of the Public Pension Crisis," Center for Economic and Policy Research, February 2011, http://www.cepr.net/publications/reports/the-origins-and-severity-of-the-public-pension-crisis.

60. Numerous conservative sources have argued that public employee pensions should invest only in risk-free, low-earning government bonds, cutting expected earnings by nearly half—and then calculate the current value of pension funds according to this much-reduced projected growth rate. By assuming a significantly lower rate of return, a pension deficit that conventional accounting measured at about $1 trillion in 2009 was instead described as three or four times that size. This argument was articulated in Robert Novy-Marx and Joshua Rauh, "The Liabilities and Risks of State Sponsored Pensions," *Journal of Economic Perspectives* 23, no. 4 (2009): 191–210.

61. "Putting State Pension Costs in Context," Good Jobs First, January 2014, http://www.goodjobsfirst.org/statepensions.

62. ALEC, "ALEC's Statement of Principles on Fixing State and Local Government Pension and Other Post Employment Benefit (OPEB) Plans," ALEC Exposed, 2009, http://www.alecexposed.org/w/images/5/56/8D1-ALEC_on_State_and_Local_Govt_Pension_and_OPEB_Plans_exposed.pdf.

63. ALEC, "Public Employees Portable Retirement Option Act," 2001, ALEC Exposed, http://www.alecexposed.org/w/images/d/df/1I0-Public_Employees_Portable_Retirement_Option_PRO_Act_Exposed.pdf.

64. Barry Poulson and Arthur Hall, "State Pension Funds Fall Off a Cliff," American Legislative Exchange Council, 2010, http://www.alec.org/wp-content/uploads/ALEC_FINAL_pension_funds_split.pdf.

65. Zach Carter, "Wisconsin's Pension Fund among Nation's Healthiest," *Huffington Post*, February 22, 2011, http://www.huffingtonpost.com/2011/02/22/wisconsin-pension-fund-among-healthiest-us_n_826709.html?

66. Defined-benefit plans are run by professional managers who make better investment choices, on average, than individual employees, and they maintain an investment portfolio based on long-term horizons, meaning they can achieve a higher rate of return by remaining invested in volatile but higher-earning equity markets, whereas individuals must look to lower-risk, lower-return investments as they approach retirement. Beth Almeida and William Fornia, "A Better Bang for the Buck: The Economic Efficiencies of Defined Benefit Pension Plans," National Institute on Retirement Security, August 2008, http://www.nirsonline.org/storage/nirs/documents/Bang%20for%20the%20Buck%20 Report.pdf; William Fornia and Nari Rhee, "Still a Better Bang for the Buck: An Update on the Economic Efficiencies of Defined Benefit Pension Plans," National Institute on Retirement Security, December 2014, http://www.rsa-al.gov/uploads/files/DB_plans_better_ bang_for_buck_2014.pdf; Stephen Herzenberg, "How to Dig an Even Deeper Pension Hole," New Jersey Policy Perspective, October, 2014, Appendix B. HYP.

67. See, for example, David Sirota, "The Plot against Pensions," Institute for America's Future, 2013, http://ourfuture.org/plotagainstpensions; and Matt Taibbi, "Looting the Pension Funds: How Wall Street Robs Public Workers," *Rolling Stone*, September 26, 2013, http://www.rollingstone.com/politics/news/looting-the-pension-funds-20130926.

68. ALEC, "Public Employees Portable Retirement Option Act," 2001.

69. William Wiatrowski, "The Last Private Industry Pension Plans: A Visual Essay," *Monthly Labor Review*, U.S. Bureau of Labor Statistics, December 2012, http://www.bls.gov/ opub/mlr/2012/12/art1full.pdf.

70. Ibid.

71. Ibid.

72. A 2013 survey by a leading human resources consulting firm reported that approximately one-third of employees named health care and retirement benefits as important reasons for choosing a given job. Employees are particularly driven to take—and stay in—jobs with defined benefit plans. Forty-five percent of employees whose employers offered a DB plan pointed to it as an important reason for taking the job, and 68 percent of those with DB plans said it was "an important reason I will stay with my current employer"; the corresponding numbers for DC plans were just over half, at 25 percent and 39 percent. Jonathan Gardner and Steve Nyce, "Attracting and Keeping Employees: The Strategic Value of Employee Benefits," *Insider*, Towers Watson, May 2014, http://www.towerswatson.com/en-US/Insights/Newsletters/Americas/insider/2014/ attracting-and-keeping-employees-strategic-value-of-employee-benefits.

73. Christina DiSomma, "Illinois' Pension Crisis: The Future of American Entitlements," FreedomWorks, April 3, 2013, http://www.freedomworks.org/content/illinois-pension-crisis-future-american-entitlements.

74. Stephane Fitch, "Gilt-Edged Pensions," *Forbes*, January 29, 2009, http://www.forbes. com/forbes/2009/0216/078.html.

75. For a review of such proposals see Teresa Ghilarducci, Robert Hiltonsmith, and Lauren Schmitz, "Guaranteed Retirement Accounts: A Low-Cost, Secure Solution to America's Retirement Crisis," Demos, November 2012, http://www.demos.org/sites/ default/files/publications/StateGRAReport-1.pdf.

76. "Secure Choice Savings Not Needed," press release, Illinois Chamber of Commerce, January 6, 2015, http://ilchamber.org/uncategorized/14865/secure-choice-savings-not-needed.

77. "Resolution to Align Pay and Benefits of Public Sector Workers with Private Sector Workers," American Legislative Exchange Council, 2011, http://www.alec.org/model-legislation/a-resolution-to-align-pay-and-benefits-of-public-sector-workers-with-private-sector-workers.

78. "Where We Stand: A Guide to the Florida Chamber's 2012 Business Agenda," Florida Chamber of Commerce, 2011, http://www.flchamber.com/wp-content/uploads/

WhereWeStand_20121.pdf. The chamber has promoted such bills in repeated sessions, but as of this book's writing none has yet become law.

79. John Schmitt, "The Unions of the States," Center for Economic and Policy Research, February 2010.

80. Larry Mishel and Matthew Walters, "How Unions Help All Workers (Economic Policy Institute Briefing Paper No. 143, August 26, 2003), http://www.epi.org/publication/briefingpapers_bp143.

81. Floyd Norris, "Under Obama, a Record Decline in Government Jobs," *New York Times*, January 6, 2012, http://economix.blogs.nytimes.com/2012/01/06/under-obama-a-record-decline-in-government-jobs/. Total state employment was reduced by 1.2 percent in 2011.

82. Bryce Covert and Mike Konczal, "The GOP's State Project of Slashing the Public Workforce," Roosevelt Institute, March 27, 2012, http://www.rooseveltinstitute.org/sites/all/files/GOPProjectSlashingPublicWorkforce.pdf.

83. Ibid.

84. Author's analysis of data presented in Elizabeth McNichol, Phil Oliff, and Nicholas Johnson, "States Continue to Feel Recession's Impact," Center on Budget and Policy Priorities, January 9, 2012, http://www.cbpp.org/cms/index.cfm?fa=view&id=711.

85. U.S. Bureau of Labor Statistics, "The Recession of 2007–09," BLS Spotlight on Statistics, February 2012, http://www.census.gov/history/pdf/greatrecession-bls.pdf.

86. David Cooper, "Public-Sector Cuts Drag Down Local Economies," *Economic Snapshot*, Economic Policy Institute, August 21, 2014, http://www.epi.org/publication/public-sector-cuts-drag-state-local-economies.

87. Since such data were first collected in 1955, local government employment continued to grow throughout the months of recession in all but one case. Ben Polak and Peter Schott, "America's Hidden Austerity Program," *New York Times*, June 11, 2012, http://economix.blogs.nytimes.com/2012/06/11/americas-hidden-austerity-program.

88. Polak and Schott, "America's Hidden Austerity Program."

89. Cooper, "Public-Sector Cuts."

90. Moody's chief economist, Mark Zandi, quoted in Zachary Goldfarb, "Threat from Mounting Public Job Losses Tested Obama's Economic Strategy," *Washington Post*, April 29, 2012, http://www.washingtonpost.com/business/economy/threat-from-mounti...-tested-obamas-economic-strategy/2012/04/29/gIQAhJpMqT_story.html.

91. Justin Lahart, "Lowering Unemployment Rate Is A Tough Job," *Wall Street Journal*, July 1, 2015, http://www.wsj.com/articles/lowering-unemployment-rate-is-a-tough-job-1435766148.

92. Orcam Financial Group CEO, Cullen Roche, quoted in Patrice Hill, "Government Job Cuts Create a Historically Slow Recession Recovery," *Washington Times*, September 17, 2013, http://www.washingtontimes.com/news/2013/sep/17/government-job-cuts-create-a-historically-slow-rec/?page=all.

93. Quoted in Jeanna Smialek, "Stiglitz Says More Fiscal Stimulus Needed in U.S.," *Bloomberg Business*, April 9, 2013, http://www.bloomberg.com/news/articles/2013-04-09/stiglitz-says-more-fiscal-stimulus-needed-in-u-s-tom-keene.

94. Shaila Dewan and Motoko Rich, "Public Workers Face New Rash of Layoffs, Hurting Recovery," *New York Times*, June 19, 2012, http://www.nytimes.com/2012/06/20/business/public-workers-face-continued-layoffs-and-recovery-is-hurt.html.

95. Doug Bandow, "Federal Spending: Killing the Economy with Government Stimulus," *Forbes*, August 6, 2012, http://www.forbes.com/sites/dougbandow/2012/08/06/federal-spending-killing-the-economy-with-government-stimulus.

96. "Fact Sheet: Big Cuts in State Income Taxes Not Yielding Promised Benefits," Center on Budget and Policy Priorities, March 25, 2015, http://www.cbpp.org/cms/index.cfm?fa=view&id=5295.

97. Luige del Puerto and Jeremy Duda, "Gov. Brewer Budget Hits Arizona Health Care Cost Containment System Universities," *Arizona Capitol Times*, January 14, 2011; "AHCCCS Cuts Compromise Patient Care and Chill Arizona's Economy," Arizona Hospital and Healthcare Association, http://www.azhha.org/member_and_media_resources/documents/FY2012 BudgetFactSheet.pdf. In early 2013, Governor Brewer changed course, proposing to expand the state's Medicaid program in order to access federal funds available under the Affordable Care Act. See Rebekah L. Sanders and Yvonne Wingett Sanchez, "Brewer Opts to Expand Medicaid to More Arizonans," *Arizona Republic*, January 14, 2013, http://www.azcentral.com/news/politics/articles/20130114arizona-brewer-state-of-state-medicaid-more-arizonans.html.

98. Morgan Smith, "Texas Schools Face Bigger Classes and Smaller Staff," *New York Times*, March 16, 2012, http://www.nytimes.com/2012/03/16/education/texas-schools-face-bigger-classes-and-smaller-staff.html; Meghan Ashford-Grooms, "Perry OK'd Cut in Grants, but Pre-K Goes On," *Austin American-Statesman*, August 5, 2011; Tami Luhby, "States Kick Grandma to the Curb," *CNN Money*, March 14, 2011, http://money.cnn.com/2011/03/14/news/economy/senior_citizens_elderly_state_budget_cuts/index.htm. Texas continued to fund half-day prekindergarten for at-risk children but eliminated funding that allowed school districts to expand from half-day to full-day programs for one hundred thousand preschoolers.

99. Joseph Goldstein, "Police Force Nearly Halved, Camden Feels Impact," *New York Times*, March 6, 2011, http://www.nytimes.com/2011/03/07/nyregion/07camden.html?pagewanted=all&_r=0.

100. Dewan and Rich, "Public Workers."

101. Ibid.

102. Lisa Lambert, "Despite Recovery, U.S. Public Employees Face More Layoffs," Reuters, April 8, 2012, http://www.reuters.com/article/2012/04/08/us-usa-states-employees-idUSBRE83706720120408.

103. Laffer, Moore, and Williams, *Rich States, Poor States*, 4th ed., xi.

104. Laffer, Moore, and Williams, *Rich States, Poor States*, 4th ed.

105. ALEC, "The Capital Gains Tax Elimination Act," *1995 Sourcebook of American State Legislation*, ALEC Exposed, http://www.alecexposed.org/w/images/5/58/8H18-The_Capital_Gains_Tax_Elimination_Act_Exposed.pdf.

106. ALEC, "Resolution Urging Congress to Permanently Extend the Bush Tax Cuts," ALEC Exposed, http://www.alecexposed.org/w/images/5/52/8H14-Resolution_Urging_Congress_to_Permanently_Extend_the_Bush_Tax_Cuts_Exposed.pdf.

107. "ALEC 2013: Jobs, Innovation, and Opportunity in the States: Twenty-Five Proposals to Put the States Back to Work," ALEC, 2013, http://www.alec.org/publications/alec-2013-jobs-innovation-and-opportunity-in-the-states.

108. "Libraries Connect Communities: Public Library Funding and Technology Access Study 2009–10," American Library Association, 2011, http://www.ala.org/research/sites/ala.org.research/files/content/initiatives/plftas/pressmaterials/2009_10PLFTAS_keyfindings.pdf.

109. Ibid.

110. "Public Library Funding and Technology Access Study 2011–12," American Library Association, 2013, http://www.ala.org/research/sites/ala.org.research/files/content/initiatives/plftas/2011_2012/plftas12_execsummary.pdf.

111. "The 2012 State of America's Libraries Report," American Library Association, 2013, http://www.ala.org/news/mediapresscenter/americaslibraries/soal2012/public-libraries; Miranda Green, "Can Libraries Survive in an Era of Budget Cutbacks?" *Daily Beast*, February 16, 2013, http://www.thedailybeast.com/articles/2013/02/16/can-libraries-survive-in-an-era-of-budget-cutbacks.html.

112. Geoff Mulvhill, "Camden, New Jersey, Preparing to Close All Its Libraries," Associated Press, August 6, 2010, http://www.huffingtonpost.com/2010/08/06/camden-new-jersey-libraries-closing_n_674175.html.

113. David A. Graham, "Libraries Face Increasing Budget Cutbacks," *Newsweek*, August 23, 2010, http://www.newsweek.com/libraries-face-increasing-budget-cutbacks-71597.

114. "Local Health Department Job Losses and Program Cuts," research brief, National Association of County and City Health Officials, May 2010, http://www.naccho.org/topics/infrastructure/lhdbudget/upload/Job-Losses-and-Program-Cuts-5-10.pdf.

115. Ibid.

116. Donna Brown, Government Affairs Counsel, National Association of County and City Health Officials, communication with the author, March 15, 2010.

117.Tazra Mitchell, "Connecting Workers to Jobs through Reliable and Accessible Public Transit," *Policy and Progress*, North Carolina Justice Center, November 2012, http://www.ncjustice.org/?q=budget-and-tax/connecting-workers-jobs-through-reliable-and-accessible-public-transit.

118. American Public Transportation Association, "Impacts of the Recession on Public Transportation Agencies, 2011 Update," August 2011.

119. "Funding Challenges in Highway and Transit: A Federal-State-Local Analysis," Pew Charitable Trusts, February 24, 2015, http://www.pewtrusts.org/en/research-and-analysis/analysis/2015/02/24/...ding-challenges-in-highway-and-transit-a-federal-state-local-analysis.

120. Larry Sandler, "State Budget Cuts Transit Funding, but It Could Have Been Worse," *Milwaukee Journal Sentinel*, July 6, 2011, http://www.jsonline.com/news/statepolitics/125060014.html.

121. Public News Service, "Broad Support for a Hoosier Mass Transit Bill," January 23, 2013, http://www.publicnewsservice.org/2013-01-23/senior-issues/broad-support-for-a-hoosier-mass-transit-bill/a30398-1.

122. Angie Schmitt, "The Koch Brothers' War on Transit," *Streetsblog USA*, September 25, 2014, http://usa.streetsblog.org/2014/09/25/the-koch-brothers-war-on-transit.

123. Emily Goff, "Reject Bloated Transportation Budget," Heritage Foundation, February 18, 2015, http://www.heritage.org/research/commentary/2015/2/reject-bloated-transportation-budget.

124. Center on Education Policy, "Strained Schools Face Bleak Future: Districts Foresee Budget Cuts, Teacher Layoffs, and a Slowing of Education Reform Efforts," June 2011, http://www.eric.ed.gov/PDFS/ED521335.pdf.

125. Phil Oliff, Chris Mai, and Michael Leachman, "New School Year Brings More Cuts in State Funding for Schools," Center on Budget and Policy Priorities, September 4, 2012, http://www.cbpp.org/cms/?fa=view&id=3825; W. Steven Barnett et al., "The State of Preschool 2011," National Institute for Early Education Research, 6, 9, http://nieer.org/sites/nieer/files/2011yearbook.pdf. Cited in Oliff, Mai, and Leachman, "New School Year Brings More Cuts."

126. Ida Lieszkovszky, "Ohio's Public Education Is Far from Free," National Public Radio, August 18, 2011, http://stateimpact.npr.org/ohio/2011/08/18/the-rising-cost-of-public-education; W. Steven Barnett et al., "The State of Preschool 2010," National Institute for Early Education Research, http://www.nieer.org/publications/state-preschool-2010.

127. Reported in Jeff Bryant, "Starving America's Public Schools: How Budget Cuts and Policy Mandates Are Hurting Our Nation's Students," Campaign for America's Future, 2012, http://www.ourfuture.org/files/documents/starving-schools-report.pdf.

128. Noelle Ellerson, "Weathering the Storm: How the Economic Recession Continues to Impact School Districts," American Association of School Administrators, March 2012, http://www.aasa.org/uploadedFiles/Policy_and_Advocacy/files/Weathering_the_Storm_Mar_2012_FINAL.pdf. ASA's survey included 528 school administrators in forty-eight states. While the respondents cannot be assumed to be statistically representative of all superintendents in the country, the distribution of respondents does mirror the distribution of both schools and students in the respective states.

129. John O'Connor and Sarah Gonzalez, "How Florida Schools Are Coping with Budget Cuts," National Public Radio, September 6, 2011, http://stateimpact.npr.org/florida/2011/09/06/schools-run-out-of-easy-budget-choices.

130. Bryant, "Starving America's Public Schools."

131. Ibid.

132. Recent research on the impact of librarians is summarized in Debra E. Kachel and Keith Curry Lance, "Latest Study: A Full-Time School Librarian Makes a Critical Difference in Boosting Student Achievement," *School Library Journal*, March 7, 2013, http://www.slj.com/2013/03/research/librarian-required-a-new-study-shows-that-a-full-time-school-librarian-makes-a-critical-difference-in-boosting-student-achievement/#. See also Alison DeNisco, "School Librarian Cutbacks Widen Digital Divide," District Administration, August 2014. http://www.districtadministration.com/article/school-librarian-cutbacks-widen-digital-divide.

133. See, for instance, "Corporate Tax Dodging in the 50 States, 2008–10," Institute on Taxation and Economic Policy, 2011, http://www.itep.org/pdf/CorporateTaxDodgers50StatesReport.pdf; and "The ITEP Guide to Fair State and Local Taxes," Institute on Taxation and Economic Policy, 2012, http://www.itep.org/state_reports/guide2011.php.

134. Aggregate budget deficits for all fifty states in 2011 were estimated at $130 billion. McNichol, Oliff, and Johnson, "States Continue to Feel Recession's Impact." Taxing capital gains and dividends as regular income would generate an estimated $88.1 billion per year. "A Budget Blueprint for Economic Recovery and Fiscal Responsibility," Economic Policy Institute, November 29, 2010, http://epi.3cdn.net/9bd5101bda57040a94_djm6byfuu.pdf.

135. Williams, Leachman, and Johnson, "State Budget Cuts in the New Fiscal Year."

136. Ibid. Michigan's HB 4361, establishing the corporate tax reform, is at http://www.legislature.mi.gov/documents/2011-2012/publicact/htm/2011-PA-0038.htm. The bill was introduced by Representative Judson Gilbert, an ALEC member. The cuts to education funding were mandated in HB 4325, http://www.legislature.mi.gov/documents/2011-2012/publicact/htm/2011-PA-0062.htm.

137. "Testimony of the Michigan Chamber of Commerce before the House Tax Committee," March 9, 2011, http://www.michamber.com/files/michamber.com/Testimony%20on%206%20percent%20CIT%20HB%204361%20and%202.pdf; "Read NFIB's Letter to the Michigan Senate on Historic Tax Vote," National Federation of Independent Business, May 12, 2011, http://www.nfib.com/nfib-in-my-state/nfib-in-my-state-content?cmsid=47403; "MRA Applauds Michigan Senate for Vote to Reform Taxes," press release, Michigan Restaurant Association, April 27, 2011, http://www.michiganrestaurant.org/displaycommon.cfm?an=1&subarticlenbr=1344.

138. Williams, Leachman, and Johnson, "State Budget Cuts in the New Fiscal Year." HB 153 is at http://www.legislature.state.oh.us/bills.cfm?ID=129_HB_153.

139. "Victories: January—June 2011," Ohio Chamber of Commerce, http://www.ohiochamber.com/dococc/Policypolitics/-pdf/Victories11.pdf; "Ohio's Budget," National Federation of Independent Business, http://www.nfib.com/nfib-in-my-state/nfib-in-my-state-content?cmsid=56224; "Ohio Senate Budget Keeps Estate Tax Repeal," press release, Americans for Prosperity and American Family Business Institute, June 8, 2011, http://americansforprosperity.org/ohio/legislativealerts/060911-senate-version-budget-retains-estate-tax-repeal/#ixzz2OfglV2l0.

140. Michael Leachman and Chris Mai, "Most States Still Funding Schools Less Than before the Recession," Center on Budget and Policy Priorities, October 16, 2014, http://www.cbpp.org/cms/index.cfm?fa=view&id=4213.

141. ALEC, Model Legislation: "Tax and Expenditure Limitation Act," 2008; "TABOR and Colorado: A Model of Liberty for Virginia," Americans for Prosperity, November 2005, www.americansforprosperity.org/node/6828.

142. For a summary of the Colorado experience, see Iris Lav and Erica Williams, "A Formula for Decline: Lessons from Colorado for States Considering TABOR," Center on Budget and Policy Priorities, 2010, http://www.cbpp.org/cms/?fa=view&id=753.

143. Charles Owens, NFIB state director, quoted in Lester Graham, "Proposal 5 Pros and Cons," Michigan Radio, October 30, 2012, http://www.michiganradio.org/post/proposal-5-pros-and-cons.

144. Toluse Olorunnipa, "Protesters: Florida Amendment Will Slice Spending on Social Services," *Miami Herald*, October 2, 2012, http://www.miamiherald.com/2012/10/01/3029575/protesters-florida-amendment-will.html#storylink=cpy. Florida voters, however, were unconvinced, rejecting the proposal by a 58 percent to 42 percent margin. "Florida State Revenue Limitation, Amendment 3 (2012)," Ballotpedia, December 12, 2012, http://ballotpedia.org/wiki/index.php/Florida_State_Revenue_Limitation,_Amendment_3_(2012).

145. Williams, Leachman, and Johnson, "State Budget Cuts in the New Fiscal Year." A summary of HB 2001 is at http://www.azleg.gov//FormatDocument.asp?inDoc=/legtext/50leg/2s/summary/h.hb2001_02-16-11_astransmittedtogovernor.doc.htm&Session_ID=105.

146. "Business Coalition in Support of HB 2001 and SB 1001," February 16, 2011, Arizona Chamber of Commerce and Industry, http://www.azchamber.com/uploads/Support%20Letter,%20HB%202001_SB%201001.pdf; "Huge Tax-Reduction Bill Passes Legislature, Signed by Governor," National Federation of Independent Business, http://www.nfib.com/nfib-in-my-state/nfib-in-my-state-content?cmsid=56064.

147. Barnett et al., "The State of Preschool 2011."

148. "2011 Arizona Legislative Policy Plan," Americans for Prosperity, February 9, 2011, http://americansforprosperity.org/files/afp2011lpp02-09-11.pdf. The TABOR statute proved too much for Governor Brewer, who vetoed the legislation in favor of retaining more discretionary control over state fiscal policy.

149. "Fiscal Survey of the States, Fall 2013," National Association of State Budget Officers, http://www.nasbo.org/publications-data/fiscal-survey-states/fiscal-survey-states-fall-2013; "Fiscal Survey of the States, Fall 2014," National Association of State Budget Officers, http://www.nasbo.org/publications-data/fiscal-survey-states/fiscal-survey-states-fall-2014.

150. Quoted in Gregory Korte, "State of the States: What to Do with Their Surpluses," *USA Today*, January 29, 2014, http://www.usatoday.com/story/news/politics/2014/01/29/state-of-the-state-addresses-2014/4944317.

151. Tim Jones, "Wisconsin to Skip Debt Payments to Make Up for Scott Walker's Tax Cuts," Bloomberg, February 18, 2015, http://www.bloomberg.com/politics/articles/2015-02-18/wisconsin-to-skip-debt-payments-to-make-up-for-walker-s-tax-cuts.

152. Ibid.

153. Leachman and Mai, "Most States Still Funding Schools Less."

154. Michael Mitchell, Vincent Palacios, and Michael Leachman, "States Are Still Funding Higher Education below Pre-Recession Levels," Center on Budget and Policy Priorities, May 1, 2014, http://www.cbpp.org/cms/index.cfm?fa=view&id=4135; Patrick Marley and Karen Herzog, "UW Predicts Layoffs, No Campus Closings under Budget," *Milwaukee Journal Sentinel*, January 27, 2015, http://www.jsonline.com/news/statepolitics/289929831.html.

155. "Fitch Rates Wisconsin's $279MM GO Bonds 'AA,' Outlook Stable," Business Wire, February 2, 2015, http://www.businesswire.com/news/home/20150202006227/en/Fitch-Rates-Wisconsins-279MM-Bonds-AA-Outlook#.VS3tuBaXRUR.

156. "Legislative Update 2013," North Carolina Association of Educators, www.ncae.org/wp-content/uploads/LegislativeUpdate2013.pdf.

157. "State Tax Cut Roundup: 2013 Legislative Session," American Legislative Exchange Council, November 2013, http://www.alec.org/publications/taxcutroundup/.

158. Meg Wiehe, "North Carolina Facing Disastrous New Tax Laws," *Tax Justice Blog*, Citizens for Tax Justice and Institute on Taxation and Economic Policy, July 16, 2013, http://www.ctj.org/taxjusticedigest/archive/2013/07/north_carolina_facing_disastro. php.

159. Leachman and Mai, "Most States Still Funding Schools Less"; Mitchell, Palacios, and Leachman, "States Are Still Funding Higher Education Below."

160. Tazra Mitchell, "Budget Deal Released: Tax Cuts and Tight Revenues Are Making It Hard to Meet Tar Heel Priorities," *Progressive Pulse Blog*, North Carolina Justice Center, July 31, 2014, http://pulse.ncpolicywatch.org/2014/07/31/budget-deal-released-tax-cuts-and-tight-revenues-are-making-it-hard-to-meet-tarheel-priorities.

161. "AFP Praises Tax Relief and Reform Compromise, Urges Lawmakers to Support," press release, Americans for Prosperity, July 15, 2013, http://americans forprosperity.org/north-carolina/newsroom/afp-praises-tax-relief-and-reform-compromise-urges-lawmakers-to-support; "2013 North Carolina Chamber Annual Report," North Carolina Chamber of Commerce, http://ncchamber.net/wp-content/ uploads/2013/12/NC-Chamber-13-02-Annual-Report-2013-Single-Page-HR. pdf.

162. Reuters, "Texas Gov. Rick Perry: Give Excess Tax Money Back to the People," *Washington Post*, January 29, 2013, http://www.washingtonpost.com/politics/ texas-gov-rick-perry-give-excess-tax-money-back-to-people/2013/01/29/3f0cc442-6a6e-11e2-95b3-272d604a10a3_print.html; Mark Whittington, "Texas Gov. Rick Perry Proposes Tax Rebate Constitutional Amendment," Yahoo.com Contributor Network, January 29, 2013, http://news.yahoo.com/texas-gov-rick-perry-proposes-tax-rebate-constitutional-180900241.html; Awr Hawkins, "Gov. Rick Perry: Change State Constitution, Return Money to the People," Breitbart.com, January 30, 2013, http://www.breitbart.com/Big-Government/2013/01/30/Gov-Rick-Perry-Change-State-Constitution-And-Send-Money-Back-To-The-People; Peggy Fikac, "Perry Has a Surprise in His State of the State Address," *Houston Chronicle*, January 29, 2012, http://www.chron.com/news/politics/article/Perry-has-a-surprise-in-his-State-of-the-State-4231648.php.

163. ALEC, "State Tax Cut Roundup."

164. Texas Association of Business and Chambers of Commerce, "The Results: The 2013 Report of the Texas Legislature," 83rd Regular and Special Sessions, Texas Association of Business, http://www.txbiz.org/External/WCPages/WCWebContent/ WebContentPage.aspx?ContentID=351.

165. Dick Lavine, "2013 Lege Wrap-Up: Tax Giveaways," *Better Texas Blog*, Center for Public Policy Priorities, June 3, 2013, http://bettertexasblog.org/2013/06/2013-lege-wrap-up-tax-giveaways.

166. Terrence Stutz, "Class Size Waivers Still Rampant in Texas Elementary Schools," *Dallas Morning News*, July 2, 2014, http://www.dallasnews.com/news/ education/headlines/20140702-class-size-waivers-still-rampant-in-texas-elementary-schools.ece.

167. Chuck Lindell, "Judge: Texas School Finance System Unconstitutional," *Statesman*, August 28, 2014, http://www.statesman.com/news/news/judge-texas-school-finance-system-unconstitutional/nhBWz.

168. Texas Association of Business and Chambers of Commerce, "The Results."

169. Benjamin Waterhouse, *Lobbying America: The Politics of Business from Nixon to NAFTA* (Princeton: Princeton University Press, 2014), 130.

170. Jin Siegel, "Ohio House Passes Senate Bill 5," *Columbus Dispatch*, March 30, 2011, http://www.dispatch.com/content/stories/local/2011/03/30/ohio-house-expected-to-approve-sb5-this-afternoon.html.

2. DEUNIONIZING THE PRIVATE SECTOR

1. Amanda Terkel, "Mitch Daniels' Evolution on Right to Work in Indiana," *Huffington Post*, January 19, 2012, http://www.huffingtonpost.com/2012/01/19/mitch-daniels-indiana-right-to-work_n_1216949.html.

2. Walker quote is from May 2012, reported in Patrick Marley and Jason Stein, "Behind Scott Walker's Claim of Doing What He Says, a Record of Dropping Bombshells," *Milwaukee Sentinel Journal*, March 2, 2015, http://www.jsonline.com/news/statepolitics/behind-scott-walkers-cla…-he-says-a-record-of-dropping-bombshells-b99452872z1-294600171.html.

3. David Weigel, "Rick Snyder Didn't Want to Sign Right-to-Work Legislation Until He Signed It," Slate.com, December 11, 2012, http://www.slate.com/blogs/weigel/2012/12/11/rick_snyder_didn_t_want_to_sign_right_to_work_legislation_until_he_signed.html.

4. Don Walker, Bill Glauber, and Jason Stein, "Walker 'Conquer' Video Becomes Campaign Fodder," *Milwaukee Journal Sentinel*, May 12, 2012, http://www.jsonline.com/news/statepolitics/barrett-walker-at-odds-over-divide-and-conquer-union-remark-oi5coda-151148935.html. The donor was Diane Hedricks, CEO of the roofing and siding wholesaler ABC Corp.; she later contributed $500,000 to Walker's campaign.

5. Michigan Legislature, Senate Bill 116, Public Act 348 of 2012, http://www.legislature.mi.gov/(S(f3f4bvb51seh5ye0upscbtwy))/mileg.aspx?page=GetObject&objectname=2011-SB-0116; Paul Egan, Kathleen Gray, and Lori Higgins, "Michigan Lawmakers Fast-Track Right-to-Work Legislation during Chaotic Day at the Capitol," *Detroit Free Press*, December 6, 2012, http://www.freep.com/article/20121206/NEWS06/121206088.

6. Jason Stein and Patrick Marley, "Wisconsin Senate to Quickly Take Up Right-to-Work Legislation," *Milwaukee Journal Sentinel*, December 4, 2014, http://www.jsonline.com/news/statepolitics/state-senate-to-quickly-take-up-right-to-work-legislation-b99402895z1-284760711.html.

7. Michigan governor Snyder remained opposed to repeal of that state's prevailing wage law. In response, the Michigan Freedom Fund (linked to the DeVos family) and Michigan Associated Builders and Contractors helped fund a $1.5 million petition drive to put repeal on the ballot in a form that was not subject to gubernatorial veto. A fall 2015 drive foundered as a result of forged petition signatures, but the backers launched a second drive in early 2016. Jonathan Oosting, "Michigan Prevailing Wage Repeal Group Preparing to Launch Second Petition Drive," Michigan Live, December 9, 2015, http://www.mlive.com/lansing-news/index.ssf/2015/12/michigan_prevailing_wage_repea_2.html.

8. "Ball State Poll: Half of Hoosiers Undecided on Right-to-Work," *Indianapolis Business Journal*, December 15, 2011, http://www.indianaeconomicdigest.net/print.asp?SectionID=31&SubsectionID=171&ArticleID=63070. A January 2012 poll found 33 percent supporting RTW, 36 percent opposed, and 30 percent with no opinion. Hart Research Associates, "Survey of Indiana Voters on Right to Work," memorandum to interested parties, January 16, 2012.

9. "Statehouse Capacity of 3,000 Would Limit Protests," *Indianapolis Star*, December 30, 2011, http://www.indystar.com/fdcp/?unique=1327946705434. Mary Beth Schneider, "Daniels Throws Rules Out the Door, Rescinding Crowd Limits," *Indianapolis Star*, January 5, 2012, http://www.indystar.com/article/20120105/NEWS05/201050363/Daniels-throws-rules-out-door-rescinding-crowd-limits.

10. Egan, Gray, and Higgins, "Michigan Lawmakers."

11. Marquette Law School poll, April 7–10, 2015, https://law.marquette.edu/poll/wp-content/uploads/2015/04/MLSP28Toplines.pdf.

12. Dan Shaw, "Right-to-Work Ad Wars," *Daily Reporter*, February 27, 2015, http://dailyreporter.com/2015/02/27/right-to-work-ad-wars.

13. Egan, Gray, and Higgins, "Michigan Lawmakers"; Steven Verburg and Dee Hall, "Clash over Right-to-Work Bill Continues in Wisconsin Assembly Hearing," *Wisconsin State Journal*, March 3, 2015, http://host.madison.com/wsj/news/local/govt-and-politics/clash-over-right-to-work-bill-continues-in-wisconsin-assembly/article_f044ed38-106d-5e7e-a0c2-84b2fb9279ef.html.; Dan Kaufman, "Scott Walker and the Fate of the Union," *New York Times*, June 12, 2015, http://www.nytimes.com/2015/06/14/magazine/scott-walker-and-the-fate-of-the-union.html.

14. Hart Research Associates, "Survey of Indiana Voters."

15. Michael O'Brien, "Michigan House Passes Right-to-Work Legislation," NBC News, December 11, 2012, http://nbcpolitics.nbcnews.com/_news/2012/12/11/15843991-michigan-house-passes-right-to-work-legislation?lite.

16. Tom Fahey, "State House Dome: Mileage Feud Erupts in Emails," *New Hampshire Union Leader*, August 21, 2011, http://www.unionleader.com/article/20110821/NEWS0604/708219970

17. Joel Siegel, "New Hampshire Anti-Bullying Proposal Takes Aim at Lawmaker," ABC News, January 27, 2012, http://abcnews.go.com/US/hampshire-anti-bullying-proposal-takes-aim-lawmaker/story?id=15453168.

18. Amanda Loeder, "Leading Republicans Lose Positions for Opposing Right-to-Work," State Impact, National Public Radio, December 1, 2011. http://stateimpact.npr.org/new-hampshire/2011/12/01/leading-republi…to-work/?utm_source=bit.ly&utm_medium=twitter&utm_campaign=twitter.

19. Siegel, "New Hampshire."

20. Skocpol and Hertel-Fernandez, "The Koch Effect," 44–47, note that 61 percent of Republican House members signed AFP's "no climate tax" pledge despite the fact that a majority of voters in their own districts supported climate change legislation.

21. Mayer, *Dark Money*, 276–77, describes how the threat of a primary challenge led the House Energy and Commerce Committee chair, Representative Fred Upton, to reverse his position on climate change, declaring his newfound opposition to carbon regulation in an opinion column coauthored with AFP president Tim Phillips.

22. Andy Kroll, "Meet the New Kochs: The DeVos Clan's Plan to Defund the Left," *Mother Jones*, January/February 2014, http://www.motherjones.com/politics/2014/01/devos-michigan-labor-politics-gop.

23. Ibid.

24. Ibid.

25. Chad Livengood, "Snyder: Right-to-Work on the Agenda, but No Decision Yet on Bill," *Detroit News*, December 4, 2012, http://www.detroitnews.com/article/20121204/POLITICS02/212040399/…nda-no-decision-yet-bill?odyssey=tab%7Ctopnews%7Ctext%7CFRONTPAGE.

26. Ben Freed, "Right-to-Work Efforts Announced Thursday by Republican Leaders," *Ann Arbor News*, December 6, 2012, http://www.annarbor.com/news/right-to-work-efforts-set-to-be-announced-thursday-by-republican-leaders.

27. Dave Eggert, "Right-to-Work Bills Win Approval from Michigan Senate, House," Michigan Live, December 6, 2012, http://www.mlive.com/politics/index.ssf/2012/12/right-to-work_bill_wins_approv.html; Brendan Fischer, "Michigan Passes 'Right to Work' Containing Verbatim Language from ALEC Model Bill," Center for Media and Democracy, December 11, 2102, http://www.prwatch.org/news/2012/12/11903/michigan-passes-right-work-containing-verbatim-language-alec-model-bill.

28. Felicia Sonmez, "Rick Snyder Signs 'Right to Work' Legislation," *Washington Post*, December 11, 2012, http://www.washingtonpost.com/blogs/post-politics/wp/2012/12/11/rick-snyder-signs-right-to-work-legislation.

29. Tom Jensen, "Snyder's Popularity Plummets," Public Policy Polling, December 18, 2012, http://www.publicpolicypolling.com/main/2012/12/snyders-popularity-plummets.html.

30. Tim Phillips, "The First Thanksgiving," e-mail message to members, Americans for Prosperity, November 21, 2012.

31. Jody Knauss, "Cookie-Cutter ALEC Right-to-Work Bills Pop in Multiple States," PR Watch, March 11, 2015, http://www.prwatch.org/news/2015/03/12766/alec-right-work-bills-move-through-states. New Hampshire's bill was championed by house speaker (and ALEC member) Bill O'Brien; Indiana's by house speaker (and ALEC member) Brian Bosma; in Missouri by house speaker (and former ALEC state chair) Tim Jones; and in Wisconsin by former ALEC state chair Senator Scott Fitzgerald.

32. Dan Carden, "Right-to-Work Tops Indiana Chamber of Commerce's Agenda," *Northwest Indiana Times,* November 21, 2011, http://www.nwitimes.com/business/local/right-to-work-tops-chamber-s-agenda/article_67471464-7b54-5715-9cf8-71008abff3fb.html; "Top 5 Reforms for a Stronger Wisconsin," Wisconsin Manufacturers and Commerce, 2015, https://www.wmc.org/wp-content/uploads/Legislative-Agenda-2015-16-Top-5.pdf; "2015 Policy Agenda," 5, New Mexico Association of Commerce and Industry, http://www.nmaci.org/uploads/files/2015%20ACI%20Legislative%20Policy%20Agenda.pdf.

33. Mike Blakely, chairman, Indiana Chamber of Commerce, quoted in chamber press release accompanying publication of the 2011 RTW report. The $12,000 income gain was projected for a family of four.

34. "Michigan Freedom to Work" flyer, 2011, Michigan Freedom to Work Coalition, www.mifreedomtowork.com/materials/trifoldoutside.pdf.

35. "Right to Work Can Save Illinois' Middle Class," flyer, Illinois Policy Institute, April 2015.

36. Unions may receive a variety of funds designated to carry out particular services, such as operating health insurance plans or federal job training programs. The everyday work of union organizing and contract negotiations and enforcement, however, is overwhelmingly dependent on employee dues.

37. Ozkan Eren and Serkan Ozbeklik, "What Do Right-to-Work Laws Do? Evidence from a Synthetic Control Method Analysis," *Journal of Policy Analysis and Management,* July 2015, http://onlinelibrary.wiley.com/doi/10.1002/pam.21861/full.

38. Elise Gould and Heidi Shierholz, "The Compensation Penalty of 'Right to Work' Laws" (Economic Policy Institute Briefing Paper No. 299, February 17, 2011), http://s4.epi.org/files/page/-/old/briefingpapers/BriefingPaper299.pdf.

39. In 2015, Gould reran her analysis with updated data, subjecting it both to new robustness tests and to a series of criticisms voiced by the Heritage Foundation. The results strongly confirm the initial research—this time finding that RTW lowers wages by 3 percent, nearly identical to the original findings. Elise Gould and Will Kimball, "'Right-to-Work' States Still Have Lower Wages," Economic Policy Institute, April 22, 2015, http://www.epi.org/publication/right-to-work-states-have-lower-wages. In testimony before the Wisconsin Senate, James Sherk, a senior policy analyst for Heritage, stated that he had "rerun" the 2011 Gould and Shierholz analysis and found it unreliable. When its errors were corrected, Sherk stated, the data revealed that RTW results in higher—not lower—wages. James Sherk, "How Unions and Right-to-Work Laws Affect the Economy," testimony before the Committee on Labor and Government Reform, Heritage Foundation, February 24, 2015, http://www.heritage.org/research/testimony/2015/how-unions-and-right-to-work-laws-affect-the-economy. There are at least two problems with Sherk's methodology that make his results unreliable. First, while he also controls for forty-two factors, his choice of factors is eccentric, such as breaking the population without a high school diploma into seven subgroups based on highest year of school attended. Similarly, he uses separate categories for those never married, separated, divorced, and widowed. Second, Sherk fails to control for any of the industries or occupations that make up a state's economy. Sherk argues that RTW attracts manufacturers to a state, so controlling

for manufacturing masks RTW's impact. But this is circular reasoning: there is no evidence that RTW draws manufacturers to a state. The tautology of simply asserting by fiat that RTW improves manufacturing and then constructing a statistical formula designed to confirm that does not constitute rigorous or impartial analysis. For a detailed review of Sherk's analysis, see Gould and Kimball, "'Right-to-Work' States."

40. Lawrence Mishel and Matt Walters, "How Unions Help All Workers" (Economic Policy Institute Briefing Paper No. 143, August 26, 2003), http://www.epi.org/publication/briefingpapers_bp143.

41. Richard Vedder, Matthew Denhart, and Jonathan Robe, "Right-to-Work and Indiana's Economic Future," Indiana Chamber of Commerce Foundation, January 2011, http://www.indianachamber.com/images/media/studies/IndianaRightToWork-1-27-11.pdf.

42. So too, the U.S. Chamber of Commerce explains that "higher rates of unionization lead to higher labor costs . . . [and are] associated with higher unemployment rates and slower rates of new business formation." "The Impact of State Employment Policies on Job Growth: A 50-State Review," 20, 2011, U.S. Chamber of Commerce, https://www.uschamber.com/sites/default/files/legacy/reports/201103WFI_StateBook.pdf.

43. States without RTW laws are deemed "fair share" because all employees benefiting from union contracts in these states must pay their fair share of contract negotiation and enforcement costs.

44. Quoted in Bill May, "Proponents Foretell Benefits of Right to Work," *Journal Record*, September 19, 2001, http://www.highbeam.com.

45. Kurt Bauer, "Continuing Wisconsin's Era of Reform," Wisconsin Manufacturers and Commerce, December 8, 2014, https://www.wmc.org/issues/continuing-wisconsins-era-of-reform.

46. Quoted in Dan Mayfield, "New Mexico Partnership Head Joins Push for Right-to-Work," *Albuquerque Business Journal*, January 9, 2015, http://www.bizjournals.com/albuquerque/news/2015/01/09/new-mexico-partnership-head-joins-push-for-right.html?page=all.

47. "Right to Work Is about Judging Unions: Interview with Sen. Jim Buck," *Kokomo Perspective*, December 13, 2011, http://kokomoperspective.com/news/right-to-work-is-about-judging-unions/article_0a1d5312-25ac-11e1-b110-0019bb2963f4.html?mode=print.

48. Testimony of Representative Will Smith before the New Hampshire House Labor, Industrial and Rehabilitative Services Committee, February 3, 2011.

49. Dan Mehan, president of the Missouri Chamber of Commerce, quoted in "Right to Work Supporters Prepare for Possible Veto," KMOX CBS News, May 14, 2015, http://stlouis.cbslocal.com/2015/05/14/gov-nixon-right-to-work-would-take-missouri-backwards.

50. "Right to Work Is about Judging Unions."

51. Indiana Economic Development Commission, "Legislative Update," PowerPoint presentation, August 2012.

52. Grover Norquist and Patrick Gleason, "Right to Work's Magnetic Appeal," *Politico*, January 25, 2012, http://www.politico.com/story/2012/01/right-to-works-magnetic-appeal-071960.

53. On RTW lowering unionization, see Eren and Ozbeklik, "What Do Right-to-Work Laws Do?"

54. Holmes uses the manufacturing share of overall employment to define the success of RTW, but this is an unreliable measure; manufacturing share may rise as a result of falloffs in service, agricultural, or government employment, unrelated to RTW. Further, Holmes's study is based on data from 1947 through the mid-1990s and thus does not capture the regime of global trade initiated with the 1994 NAFTA treaty.

55. Thomas J. Holmes, "The Location of Industry: Do States' Policies Matter?" *Regulation* 23 (2000): 47, 50.

56. See Charlene M. Kalenkoski, and Donald J. Lacombe, "Right-to-Work Laws and Manufacturing Employment: The Importance of Spatial Dependence," *Southern Economic Journal* 73, no. 2 (October 2006): 402–18; Dale Belman, Richard Block, and Karen Roberts, "Economic Impact of State Differences in Labor Standards in the United States, 1998–2000," www.employmentpolicy.org/topic/15/blogeconomic-impact-state-differences-labor-standards-united-states-1998–2000; Lonnie Stevans, "The Effect of Endogenous Right-to-Work Laws on Business and Economic Conditions in the United States: A Multivariate Approach," *Review of Law and Economics* 5, no. 1 (2009): 595–612; Michael Hicks, "Right-to-Work Legislation and the Manufacturing Center," Ball State University, Center for Business and Economic Research, January 2012. https://cms.bsu.edu/-/media/WWW/DepartmentalContent/MillerCollegeofBusiness/BBR/Publications/RightToWork/RightToWork.pdf; Eren and Ozbeklik, "What Do Right-to-Work Laws Do?"

57. Paula Voos and Richard Freeman, "Standards for Evaluating the Impact of 'Right to Work' Laws," policy brief provided to West Virginia legislators, April 2015.

58. Indiana and Michigan adopted RTW laws in 2012, but this is too recent to have sufficient data for serious analysis.

59. Marie Price, "GOP Platform Missing Right-to-Work Plank," *Journal Record*, January 4, 2001, http://www.high- beam.com.

60. Manufacturing employment has recovered since the 2009–10 recession and in 2015 was at 138,000, an improvement over 2010 but still nearly 40,000 jobs below the pre-RTW level of 2000. Oklahoma manufacturing employment, seasonally adjusted, U.S. Bureau of Labor Statistics, http://data.bls.gov/pdq/SurveyOutputServlet.

61. Allegretto's analysis was published in Gordon Lafer and Sylvia Allegretto, "Does 'Right to Work' Create Jobs? Answers from Oklahoma," (Economic Policy Institute Briefing Paper No. 300, March 2011), http://www.epi.org/files/page/-/BriefingPaper300.pdf.

62. The data show Oklahoma improving relative to its neighbors in the years leading up to adoption of right to work—strongly suggesting that factors other than right to work are driving the state's employment trends. By contrast, most robust data suggest that Oklahoma's employment declined by 1–3 percent, relative to its neighbors, in the five years following adoption of RTW. Allegretto's primary conclusion is reaffirmed by Eren and Ozbeklik, "What Do Right-to-Work Laws Do?"

63. Oklahoma Department of Commerce, "Announced New and Expanded Manufacturers and Services, 2010 Annual Report," Oklahoma Department of Commerce, January 2011, www.okcommerce.gov/Libraries/ Documents/2010-Annual-Report-Announced-N_3224.pdf.

64. "28th Annual Survey of Corporate Executives: Availability of Skilled Labor New Top Priority," *Area Development*, 2014, http://www.areadevelopment.com/Corporate-Consultants-Survey-Results/Q1-2014/28th-Corporate-Executive-RE-survey-results-6574981.stml?Page-2.

65. Stan Greer, quoted in Matthew DeFour, "Right-to-Work Would Trim Union Clout, but Broader Economic Impact Unclear," *Wisconsin State Journal*, December 14, 2014, http://host.madison.com/349156d2-33b1-563e-9183-b09b3315e40e.html.

66. Quoted in Marie French, "Missouri GOP Lawmakers Send 'Right-to-Work' Bill to Governor," Associated Press, May 13, 2015, http://abcnews.go.com/Politics/wireStory/missouri-gop-lawmakers-send-work-bill-governor-31020024.

67. Mark Ames and Mike Elk, "Big Brothers: Thought Control at Koch," *Nation*, April 20, 2011, http://www.thenation.com/article/160062/big-brothers-thought-control-koch.

68. "Gov. Snyder on Signing Right-to-Work into Law," WOOD TV8 (Grand Rapids, Michigan), December 12, 2011, https://www.youtube.com/watch?v=KJNHI1zMaoo.

69. Letter from Jody Wassmer, executive vice president, Owensboro, Kentucky Chamber of Commerce, September 8, 2005.

70. William Domhoff, *Who Rules America? The Triumph of the Corporate Rich*, 7th ed. (New York: McGraw-Hill Education, 2014), 190.

71. One senior executive articulated a common view at a 1970s conference on the need for increased corporate political activity, lamenting that "letting the Wagner Act pass was the biggest mistake we ever made—it is at the root of all our troubles." Leonard Silk and David Vogel, *Ethics and Profits: The Crisis of Confidence in American Business* (New York: Simon & Schuster, 1976). In 1974–75, the journalist Leonard Silk and academic David Vogel were invited to sit in on a series of extended discussions by corporate executives regarding businesses' political challenges. While the quotes are anonymous, they all come from top executives of some of the nation's largest corporations, listed in the book.

72. Elise Gould, "2014 Continues a 35-Year Trend of Broad-Based Wage Stagnation" (Economic Policy Institute Brief No. 393, February 19, 2015), http://www.epi.org/publication/stagnant-wages-in-2014.

73. Tali Kristal, "The Capitalist Machine: Computerization, Workers' Power, and the Decline in Labor's Share within U.S. Industries," *American Sociological Review* 78, no. 3 (2013): 361–389; American Sociological Association, "Labor Union Decline, Not Computerization, Main Cause of Rising Corporate Profits," Phys.org, May 30, 2013, http://phys.org/news/2013-05-labor-union-decline-computerization-main.html.

74. Steven Greenhouse, "The Mystery of the Vanishing Pay Raise," *New York Times*, October 31, 2015, http://www.nytimes.com/2015/11/01/sunday-review/the-mystery-of-the-vanishing-pay-raise.html.

75. This calculation defines "worker" as someone who had been employed for at least ten hours per week, at least twenty-seven weeks per year. Ken Jacobs, Ian Perry, and Jenifer MacGillvary, "The High Public Cost of Low Wages," 3, U.C. Berkeley Center for Labor Research and Education, April 2015, http://laborcenter.berkeley.edu/the-high-public-cost-of-low-wages.

76.Lynne Shallcross, "Survey: Half of Food Workers Go to Work Sick Because They Have To," National Public Radio, October 19, 2015, http://www.npr.org/sections/thesalt/2015/10/19/449213511/survey-half-of-food-workers-go-to-work-sick-because-they-have-to.

77. Mishel, Gould, and Bivens, "Wage Stagnation in Nine Charts."

78. "Kissing Employee Raises Goodbye," National Federation of Independent Business, July 31, 2015, http://www.nfib.com/article/kissing-employee-raises-goodbye-70293.

79. Patricia Cohen, "One-Time Bonuses and Perks Muscle Out Pay Raises for Workers," *New York Times*, May 25, 2015, http://www.nytimes.com/2015/05/26/business/one-time-bonuses-and-perks-muscle-out-pay-raises-for-workers.html?hp&action=click&pgtype=Homepage&module=second-column-region&region=top-news&WT.nav=top-news&_r=1.

80. Alana Semuels, "As Employers Push Efficiency, the Daily Grind Wears Down Workers," *Los Angeles Times*, April 7, 2013, http://articles.latimes.com/2013/apr/07/business/la-fi-harsh-work-20130407.

81. Many years of polling find that approximately one-third of nonunion employees wish they had a union in their workplace. Dunlop Commission on the Future of Worker-Management Relations, *Fact Finding Report* (Washington, DC: Bureau of National Affairs, 1994); David Cingranelli, "International Elections Standards and NLRB Representation Elections," in *Justice on the Job: Perspectives on the Erosion of Collective Bargaining in the United States*, ed. Richard N. Block et al. (Kalamazoo, MI: Upjohn Press, 2006). In 2014 there were approximately 115 million nonunion employees in the United States. "Union Members Summary," U.S. Bureau of Labor Statistics, January 23, 2015, http://www.bls.gov/news.release/union2.nr0.htm.

82. John Logan, "The Union Avoidance Industry in the United States," *British Journal of Industrial Relations*, December 2006, 651–75, http://www.jwj.org/wp-content/uploads/2014/03/JohnLogan12_2006UnionAvoidance.pdf.

83. For example, see Steven Greenhouse, "How Walmart Persuades Its Workers Not to Unionize," *Atlantic*, June 8, 2015, http://portside.org/2015-06-09/how-walmart-persuades-its-workers-not-unionize; Verne Kopytoff, "How Amazon Crushed the Union Movement," *Time*, January 16, 2014, http://time.com/956/how-amazon-crushed-the-union-movement; "Leaked Verizon Wireless Anti-Union Video Tells Workers to 'Do Your Research,'" Occupy Wall Street, June 24, 2015, http://www.occupywallst.nyc/news/2015/6/24/verizon-fights-unions; Hamilton Nolan, "Lowe's Anti-Union Training Video Walks a Fine Line," Gawker, March 13, 2015, http://gawker.com/lowes-anti-union-training-video-walks-a-fine-line-1691295289; Michael Arria, "T-Mobile Workers Say the Company Has Repeatedly Engaged in Union-Busting," *In These Times*, October 1, 2015, http://inthesetimes.com/working/entry/18468/t-mobile-union-busting.

84. Menards employee, interviewed by the author on condition of anonymity, November 2015. In April 2016 the National Labor Relations Board charged Menards with violation of federal labor law. "NLRB: Menard Inc. Violates Federal Labor Law in Employee Treatment," Associated Press, April 2, 2016, http://www.stltoday.com/business/local/nlrb-menard-inc-violates-labor-law-in-employee-treatment/article_b3505da6-8f2e-510c-8b20-82d46081e05a.html.

85. Richard Henderson, "Industry Employment and Output Projections to 2020," *Monthly Labor Review*, U.S. Bureau of Labor Statistics, January 2012, http://www.bls.gov/opub/mlr/2012/01.

86. For a history of antiunion efforts by the Business Roundtable and Associated Builders and Contractors, see Thomas Kriger, "An Analysis of Associated Builders and Contractors (ABC)" (labor research paper, National Labor College, May 2012), http://www.knowyourabc.com/ULWSiteResources/abc/Resources/file/TJK_Reports/ABCResearchReport-FINAL5-31-12.pdf; Marc Linder, *Wars of Attrition: Vietnam, the Business Roundtable, and the Decline of Construction Unions* (Iowa City: Fanpihua Press, 2000), http://ir.uiowa.edu/books/11/; and David Moberg, "Union-Busting Is As Easy as ABC," *In These Times*, June 5, 2012, http://inthesetimes.com/working/entry/13321/union-busting_is_as_easy_as_abc_the_associated_builders_and_contractors.

87. Maria Figueroa, Jeff Grabelsky, and Ryan Lamare, "Community Workforce Provisions in Project Labor Agreements: A Tool for Building Middle-Class Careers" (Cornell University, School of Industrial and Labor Relations, October 2011). A PLA for the construction of Nationals Park in Washington, D.C., for instance, led to the employment of six hundred D.C. residents on the project.

88. Idaho's S1006 bans localities from requiring any particular wage in public construction contracts. http://legislature.idaho.gov/legislation/2011/S1006.htm. Nearly identical language is used in Louisiana's SB76 (http://www.legis.state.la.us/billdata/streamdocument.asp?did=756174) and in Arizona's SB1403, prohibiting localities from requiring either prevailing wages or PLAs. The bill was strongly supported by the state's chapter of Associated General Contractors. http://www.azagc.org/azagc-news/senator-shooter's-bill-sb1403-mandatory-project-labor-agreements-prohibition-advances-to-house. Iowa's prohibition on local prevailing wages was included in an executive order banning PLAs, issued by Governor Brandstadt in 2011. https://governor.iowa.gov/wp-content/uploads/2011/01/Exec_Order_69.pdf.

89. David Denholm, "Virginia Prevailing Wage," *Jefferson Policy Journal*, May 27, 2011, http://www.jeffersonpolicyjournal.com/?p=1461#printpreview.

90. American Legislative Exchange Council, Professional Licensure and Certification Reform Act, approved by the ALEC board of directors, June 2008, ALEC Exposed, http://www.alecexposed.org/wiki/Professional_Licensure_and_Certification_Reform_Act_Exposed.

91. American Legislative Exchange Council, Economic Civil Rights Act, *1995 Sourcebook of American State Legislation*, http://www.alecexposed.org/w/images/c/c2/1C4-Economic_Civil_Rights_Act_Exposed.pdf.

92. Elizabeth Dickson, "Guest Worker Programs: Impact on the American Workforce and Immigration Policy," Statement of the U.S. Chamber of Commerce before the U.S. House of Representatives' Committee on Education and the Workforce, July 19, 2006.

3. REMAKING THE NONUNION ECONOMY

1. Scott Walker, text of Governor Walker's budget address, State of Wisconsin, March 1, 2011, http://walker.wi.gov/journal_media_detail.asp?locid=177&prid+5668.

2. This argument is made, among other sources, in James Sherk, "How Unions and Right-to-Work Laws Affect the Economy," testimony before the Wisconsin Senate Committee on Labor and Government Reform, Heritage Foundation, February 24, 2015, http://www.heritage.org/research/testimony/2015/how-unions-and-right-to-work-laws-affect-the-economy.

3. Value is for 2015, using Bureau of Labor Statistics' inflation calculator, http://data.bls.gov/cgi-bin/cpicalc.pl?cost1=1.60&year1=1968&year2=2015.

4. National Employment Law Project, "Data Brief: Big Business, Corporate Profits, and the Minimum Wage," July 2012, http://www.nelp.org/publication/big-business-corporate-profits-and-the-minimum-wage.

5. David Cooper, "It's Time to Raise the Minimum Wage," Economic Policy Institute, April 30, 2015, http://www.epi.org/publication/its-time-to-raise-the-minimum-wage/#data-tables-characteristics-by-state6.

6. John Schmitt and Marie-Eve Augier, "Issue Brief: Affording Health Care and Education on the Minimum Wage," Center for Economic and Policy Research, March 2012, http://cepr.net/blogs/cepr-blog/blog-post-health-and-education-on-the-minimum-wage.

7. John Schmitt, "Issue Brief: The Minimum Wage Is Too Damn Low," Center for Economic and Policy Research, March 2012, http://cepr.net/documents/publications/min-wage1-2012-03.pdf.

8. The best research on this question is a series of studies comparing employment in counties whose states increased their minimum wage with neighboring counties across state lines in a state that did not increase its minimum wage; all found no impact on job growth. David Card and Alan Krueger, "Minimum Wages and Employment: A Case Study of the Fast Food Industry in New Jersey and Pennsylvania," *American Economic Review* 84, no. 5 (1994): 772–93; Arindrajit Dube, William Lester, and Michael Reich, "Minimum Wage Effects across State Borders: Estimating Using Contiguous Counties" (Institute for Research on Labor and Employment Working Paper No. 157-07, University of California at Berkeley, 2010), www.irle.berkeley.edu/workingpapers/157-07.pdf. A 2009 metastudy compiled data from sixty-four separate minimum wage studies conducted from 1972 to 2007, finding minimum wage increases had no significant impact on employment. Hristos Doucouliagos and T. D. Stanley, "Selection Bias in Minimum-Wage Research? A Meta-Regression Analysis," *British Journal of Industrial Relations* 47, no. 2 (2009): 406–28, http://www.deakin.edu.au/buslaw/aef/workingpapers/papers/2008_14eco.pdf. A 2014 meta-analysis reran calculations from twenty-seven minimum wage studies conducted since the year 2000, concluding that the impact on employment was minimal. Dale Belman and Paul Wolfson, *What Does the Minimum Wage Do?* (Kalamazoo, MI: W.E. Upjohn Institute for Employment Research, 2014). In 2014, the Congressional Budget Office calculated that increasing the minimum wage to $10.10 would provide immediate wage increases for 16.5 million workers but would also decrease overall employment by 500,000. Congressional Budget Office, "The Effects of a Minimum Wage Increase on Employment and Family Income," February 2014, http://www.cbo.gov/sites/default/files/44995-MinimumWage.

pdf. Even if this number is correct, it's not very large compared with the benefit gained. But this CBO projection is contradicted by a 2014 statement signed by over six hundred economists, including seven Nobel Prize winners and eight past presidents of the American Economic Association, supporting a $10.10 minimum wage. http://www.epi.org/minimum-wage-statement. Methodological critiques of the CBO report are explained by one of those economists in Michael Reich, "The Troubling Fine Print in the Claim That Raising the Minimum Wage Will Cost Jobs," ThinkProgress, February 19, 2014, http://thinkprogress.org/economy/2014/02/19/3307661/cbo-minimum-wage-methodology.

9. National Employment Law Project, "Data Brief: Big Business."

10. Ibid. Wal-Mart had been active in ALEC at least since the 1990s and was a chairman-level sponsor of the group's 2011 annual meeting. In 2012, Wal-Mart quit ALEC after protests following the murder of Trayvon Martin. The Walton Family Foundation, however, continued its affiliation with ALEC throughout this time. Tiffany Hsu, "Wal-Mart Latest to Leave Conservative Advocacy Group ALEC," *Los Angeles Times*, May 31, 2012, http://articles.latimes.com/2012/may/31/business/la-fi-mo-walmart-alec-20120531.

11. "Americans' Views on Income Inequality and Workers' Rights," *New York Times*/CBS Poll, June 3, 2015, http://www.nytimes.com/interactive/2015/06/03/business/income-inequality-workers-rights-international-trade-poll.html?_r=0. Another 2015 poll found 75 percent of Americans and 53 percent of Republicans supported raising the minimum wage to $12.50 by the year 2020. Guy Molyneux, "Support for a Federal Minimum Wage of $12.50 or Above," Hart Research Associates, January 14, 2015, http://www.nelp.org/content/uploads/2015/03/Minimum-Wage-Poll-Memo-Jan-2015.pdf.

12. ALEC, "Starting (Minimum) Wage Repeal Act," *1996 Sourcebook of American State Legislation*, ALEC Exposed, http://www.alecexposed.org.

13. ALEC, "Resolution in Opposition to any Increase in the Starting (Minimum) Wage," *1996 Sourcebook of American State Legislation*, ALEC Exposed, http://www.alecexposed.org.; ALEC, "Resolution Opposing Increases in Minimum Wage Linked to the CPI," approved by the ALEC Board of Directors, September 11, 2008, ALEC Exposed, http://www.alecexposed.org.

14. ALEC, "Resolution Opposing Increases in the Minimum Wage," 2008.

15. National Employment Law Project, "Delivering Economic Opportunity: Local Living Wage Ordinances and Coverage," December 2010.

16. ALEC, "Starting (Minimum) Wage Repeal Act."

17. U.S. Chamber of Commerce spokesman Randy Johnson, quoted in Dave Boyer, "Democrats Debate Timing of Wage Bill," *Washington Times*, May 6, 2002, http://www.highbeam.com/doc/1G1-85928951.html.

18. U.S. Chamber of Commerce, http://www.uschamber.com/issues/labor/minimum-wage.

19. U.S. Chamber of Commerce, "The Impact of State Employment Policies on Job Growth."

20. Ibid.

21. Bill text is at http://votesmart.org/static/billtext/35424.pdf. Governor's veto: http://www.governor.nh.gov/media/news/2011/060911-hb133.htm. Override: http://legiscan.com/gaits/view/225846.

22. Quoted in Michael McCord, "N.H. Fights over Minimum Wage," *Seacoast Online*, June 20, 2011, http://www.seacoastonline.com/articles/20110620-BIZ-106200329.

23. http://legis.state.sd.us/sessions/2011/Bills/HB1148ENR.pdf. The bill's primary sponsors were Representative Mike Verchio (R) and Senator Shantel Krebs (R). Krebs is former house majority whip and an ALEC member. "Minimum Wage Exemption for Seasonal Amusement Businesses," *Legislative Bulletin*, no. 3, South Dakota Restaurant Association, February 9, 2011.

24. Bob Mercer, "If Youth Minimum Wage Becomes Law, State Could Save Only $27,000," *Rapid City Journal*, March 2, 2015, http://rapidcityjournal.com/news/legislature/

if-youth-minimum-wage-becomes-law-state-could-save-only/article_7ded82a8-f4a9-5db8-a440-f92b53c744dc.html.

25. "South Dakota's Youth Minimum Wage Law," South Dakota Retailers Association, April 2015, https://www.sdra.org/userfiles/files/News/2015TeenMinimumWageSheetRE VISED.pdf.

26. LD1729, http://www.mainelegislature.org/legis/bills/bills_125th/chapdocs/PUB LIC483.rtf. In a move hailed by the state retailers association as a "success story," the Maine legislature also repealed the requirement that the state Department of Labor calculate an annual "livable wage" for localities within the state. http://www.mainelegislature.org/legis/bills/getPDF.asp?paper=HP1311&item=3&snum=125. Statement of the Maine Merchants Association (MMA): http://www.mainemerchants.org/legislative-affairs/position.php?llD=705. MMA is the association of retailers in the state.

27. SJR 2 was introduced by Senator Joseph Hardy, a member of ALEC's Health and Human Services Task Force. Statements supporting the bill by the Reno and Las Vegas chambers, as well as the retail association, can be found in "Minutes of the Senate Committee on Commerce, Labor and Energy," 76th sess., February 16, 2011.

28. See Dave Jamieson, "Minimum Wage, Labor Investigations Target of Missouri Republicans," Huffington Post, April 28, 2011, http://www.huffingtonpost.com/2011/04/28/missouri-republicans-minimum-wage_n_855117.html.

29. HCR2056, http://www.azleg.gov/legtext/50leg/2r/bills/hcr2056s.htm. On the political failure of this effort see Howard Fischer, "Proposal to Kill Arizona Minimum Wage Pulled," East Valley Tribune, March 23, 2012, http://www.eastvalleytribune.com/money/article_c097d6f8-72e6-11e1-a22c-001871e3ce6c.html.

30. Quoted in Bill Glauber, "Mary Burke Backs Minimum Wage Hike Scott Walker Calls 'Job-Killing,'" Milwaukee Journal Sentinel, February 2, 2014, http://www.jsonline.com/news/statepolitics/mary-burke-backs-minimum-wage-hike-scott-walker-calls-job-killing-b99196818z1-243221541.html.

31. Wisconsin Statute chap. 104.01, http://docs.legis.wisconsin.gov/statutes/statutes/104.

32. Josh Eidelson, "What's a 'Living Wage' in Wisconsin?" Bloomberg Business, October 27, 2014, http://www.bloomberg.com/bw/articles/2014-10-27/whats-a-living-wage-in-wisconsin.

33. Bryce Covert, "Low-Wage Workers Confront Scott Walker, Accuse Wisconsin of Breaking the Law," ThinkProgress, September 24, 2014, http://thinkprogress.org/economy/2014/09/24/3571547/wisconsin-minimum-wage.

34. Jonathan Stempel, "Labor Group Suing Wisconsin Governor Walker to Raise Minimum Wage," Reuters, October 27, 2014, http://www.reuters.com/article/2014/10/27/us-wisconsin-minimumwage-lawsuit-idUSKBN0IG23A20141027.

35. Wisconsin State Legislature, Omnibus Budget Amendment, Joint Finance Committee, July 3, 2015, http://host.madison.com/omnibus-budget-motion/pdf_64f03373-a6ac-5061-999b-d983fb21b985.html; Janet Velencia, "Scott Walker Strips Wisconsin Workers of 'Living Wage' in New State Budget," Huffington Post, July 13, 2015, http://www.huffingtonpost.com/2015/07/13/scott-walker-eliminates-living-wage_n_7789472.html.

36. Indiana House Bill 1538, 2011, http://legiscan.com/gaits/view/232193. The Indiana Chamber of Commerce was also one of the largest donors to Rep. Mike Speedy, the bill's prime sponsor. Mike Speedy contribution profile, National Institute on Money in State Politics, http://www.followthemoney.org/database/uniquecandidate.phtml?uc=140295.

37. Sylvia Allegretto and David Cooper, "Twenty-Three Years and Still Waiting for Change: Why It's Time to Give Tipped Workers the Regular Minimum Wage" (Economic Policy Institute Briefing Paper No. 379, July 10, 2014), http://s2.epi.org/files/2014/EPI-CWED-BP379.pdf.

38. Ibid., 14.

39. Molyneux, "Support for a Federal Minimum."

40. National Employment Law Project, "Florida Senate Bill 2106: Slashing Minimum Wage for Florida's Tipped Workers Is Bad Policy and Unconstitutional; Suggestions That Florida's Tipped Wage Is Hurting Businesses Are Unfounded," Fact Sheet, NELP, February 2012, http://www.nelp.org/content/uploads/2015/03/FactSheet_FL_TippedMinWageBill_Feb2012.pdf.

41. Ibid.; Florida Senate, Commerce and Tourism Committee, "Committee Meeting Expanded Agenda," February 7, 2012, http://www.flsenate.gov/PublishedContent/Committees/2010-2012/CM/MeetingRecords/MeetingPacket_1778.pdf.

42. Quoted in Sandra Pedicini, "Senate Bill Could Cut Hourly Wages of Servers, Bartenders," *Orlando Sentinel*, February 7, 2012, http://articles.orlandosentinel.com/2012-02-07/business/os-minimum-wage-servers-20120207_1_minimum-wage-senate-bill-florida-senate-committee.

43. Florida Senate, Commerce and Tourism Committee, "Committee Meeting Expanded Agenda."

44. HB 131 did not become law. On supporters, see Wyoming Lodging and Restaurant Association, "Wyoming Lodging & Restaurant Association (WLRA) Positions," http://www.wlra.org/displaycommon.cfm?an=1&subarticlenbr=87. Cosponsors, Representatives Tim Stubson and Dan Zwonitzer and Senator Henry Coe, are all ALEC task force members.

45. For the legal definition of bussers as tipped employees, see U.S. Department of Labor, Wage and Hour Division, "Fact Sheet #15: Tipped Employees under the Fair Labor Standards Act (FLSA)," March 2011, http://www.dol.gov/whd/regs/compliance/whdfs15.htm.

46. Senate Bill 57, http://www.mainelegislature.org/legis/bills/bills_125th/chapters/PUBLIC118.asp.

47. The law stipulates that an "employer in a banquet or private club setting may use some or all of any service charge to meet its obligation to compensate all employees." Bill language is at http://www.mainelegislature.org/legis/bills/bills_125th/chapters/PUBLIC118.asp. SB57 was sponsored by ALEC Education Task Force member Brian Langley, who stated it came with the support of the Maine Restaurant Association; Steve Mistler, "Who Should Control the Tips?" *Bangor Daily News*, February 5, 2011, http://bangordailynews.com/2011/02/05/business/who-should-control-the-tips/

48. Montana Restaurant Association, "Legislative Reports," April 14, 2011, http://www.mtrestaurant.com/displaycommon.cfm?an=1&subarticlenbr=37; Montana Chamber of Commerce, "2011 Voting Review: 62nd Montana Legislature and Governor, 2012," http://www.montanachamber.com/files/2011_Voting_Review.pdf.

49. Annette Bernhardt et al., "Broken Laws, Unprotected Workers: Violation of Employment and Labor Laws in America's Cities," National Employment Law Project, 2009, http://www.nelp.org/page/-/brokenlaws/BrokenLawsReport2009.pdf?nocdn=1. Low-wage workers are defined as nonmanagerial employees in industries where the median nonmanagerial wage is 85 percent or less of the median nonmanagerial wage for all employees in the city of employment.

50. Brad Meixell and Ross Eisenbrey, "An Epidemic of Wage Theft Is Costing Workers Hundreds of Millions of Dollars A Year" (Economic Policy Institute Issue Brief No. 385, September 11, 2014). The total value of all robberies in 2012 was $340.8 million. Federal Bureau of Investigation, "Crime in the United States 2012: Table 23, Offense Analysis," http://www.fbi.gov/about-us/cjis/ucr/crime-in-the-u.s/2012/crime-in-the-u.s.-2012/tables/23tabledatadecoverviewpdfs/table_23_offense_analysis_number_and_percent_change_2011-2012.xls. EPI surveyed federal and state departments of labor and state attorneys general and consulted research on private litigation for wage recovery; it found a total of $933 million in unpaid wages that was recovered in 2012. Data were unavailable for

six state departments of labor and five state attorneys general; thus this estimate is low. Furthermore, this figure represents only that fraction of wage theft for which victims successfully won restitution. For both these reasons, the real relationship between wage theft and robberies is even more extreme than that pictured here.

51. Kim Bobo, "Is the Department of Labor Effectively Enforcing Our Wage and Hour Laws?," testimony before the Committee on Education and Labor, U.S. House of Representatives, July 15, 2008, http://web.archive.org/web/20091022041853/http://www.iwj.org/template/page.cfm?id=124.

52. National Employment Law Project, "Florida Senate Bill 2106."

53. Jacob Meyer and Robert Greenleaf, "Enforcement of State Wage and Hour Laws: A Survey of State Regulators," Columbia Law School, National State Attorneys General Program, April 2011, 22.

54. U.S. Chamber, "Impact of State Employment Policies," 30.

55. "Shrinking Employment Law Enforcement Funding Raises Risk of Wage Theft," May 26, 2011, Policy Matters Ohio, http://www.policymattersohio.org/wp-content/uploads/2011/10/ShrinkingEmploymentWageTheftPR2011_05.pdf.

56. See Jamieson, "Minimum Wage."

57. Ibid.

58. Rudi Keller and Janise Silver, "State Wage Inquiries at Risk," *Columbia Daily Tribune*, April 3, 2011, http://www.columbiatribune.com/news/2011/apr/03/state-wage-inquiries-at-risk.

59. Missouri General Assembly, "Fiscal Year 2012, Truly Agreed and Finally Passed (After Veto)," Department of Labor and Industrial Relations, House Bill 7, 96th General Assembly, 1st Reg. Sess.

60. U.S. Department of Labor, "Performance and Accountability Report," 2009, http://www.dol.gov/_sec/media/reports/annual2009/2009annualreport.pdf.

61. Tim Judson and Cristina Francisco-McGuire, "Where Theft Is Legal: Mapping Wage Theft Laws in the 50 States," Progressive States Network, June 2012.

62. Cynthia Hernandez and Carol Stepick, "Wage Theft: An Economic Drain on Florida," Florida International University, Research Institute on Social and Economic Policy and Center for Labor Research and Studies, 2012, http://www.risep-fiu.org/wp-content/uploads/2012/01/Wage-Theft_How-Millions-of-Dollars-are-Stolen-from-Floridas-Workforce_final.docx1.pdf.

63. Chapter 2002-194, L.O.F., http://www.flsenate.gov/Committees/InterimReports/2011/2011-107cm.pdf.

64. Reported in Andy Reid, "Religious Group: Palm Beach County's Wage Theft Fight Falls Short: Business Leaders Fighting Push for Local Wage-Theft Law," *Sun Sentinel*, November 10, 2011, http://articles.sun-sentinel.com/2011-11-10/news/fl-stealing-wages-palm-20111110_1_wage-theft-religious-group-legal-system.

65. Tim Judson and Cristina Francisco-McGuire, "Cracking Down on Wage Theft: State Strategies for Protecting Workers and Recovering Revenues," Progressive States Network, 2012.

66. Marc Restrepo, "Miami Judge Rules in Favor of County's Wage-Theft Program," *Florida Independent*, March 27, 2012, http://floridaindependent.com/73618/miami-dade-county-wage-theft.

67. Reported in Reid, "Religious Group."

68. Ibid.; Andrew Marra, "Editorial: Continue Palm Beach County's Policy on Wage Theft,"*Palm Beach Post*, December 3, 2012, http://www.palmbeachpost.com/news/news/opinion/editorial-continue-palm-beach-countys-policy-on-wa/nTKSH.

69. Andy Reid, "Palm Beach County Scraps Wage-Theft Ordinance," *Sun Sentinel*, December 4, 2012, http://articles.sun-sentinel.com/2012-12-04/news/fl-wage-theft-showdown-palm-20121204_1_wage-theft-law-wage-theft-hal-valeche.

70. Mitch Perry, "With Emotions Flaring, Hillsborough County Commission Advances Potential Wage Theft Ordinance," *Saint Peters Blog*, June 3, 2015, http://www.saintpeters blog.com/archives/232380.

71. Senate Bill 862, http://www.flsenate.gov/Session/Bill/2012/0862/BillText/Filed/ HTML. On support of business lobbies, see "Wage Theft Bill Passes House Judiciary despite Objections," *Sunshine Slate*, February 24, 2012, http://www.sunshineslate.com/ tag/hb-609.

72. Dave Jamieson, "Florida Wage-Theft Laws Could Be Blocked by GOP Bill," *Huffington Post*, March 6, 2012; masthead editorial, "Florida Dead Last in Protecting Workers," *Miami Herald*, June 13, 2012, http://www.miamiherald.com/2012/06/13/2848224/florida-dead-last-in-protecting.html.

73. Senate Bill 926, 2014, https://www.flsenate.gov/Session/Bill/2014/0926/BillText/c2/ PDF.

74. Statement of Shelby County Chamber of Commerce, quoted in "Wage Theft Ordinance Supporters Face Opposition," Fox News, January 5, 2013, http://www.myfoxmemphis. com/story/20512698/picketers-raise-awareness-for-wage-theft-ordinance.

75. Tennessee Legislature, House Bill 501, 2013, http://www.tn.gov/sos/acts/108/pub/ pc0091.pdf.

76. NFIB, "Tennessee Bills of Interest to Small Business (Updated 4/15/2013)," http:// www.nfib.com/article/tennessee-bills-of-interest-to-small-business-updated-4152013-61915.

77. The preemption of local wage theft ordinances was originally introduced as a stand-alone bill sponsored by Representative Mark White and Senator Brian Kelsey. Tennessee House Bill 208/ Senate Bill 231, http://tls.mleesmith.com/downloads/2013_2014/ bills/SB0231.pdf. It was later incorporated into HB 501 as an amendment.

78. Representative Mark White, Tennessee legislature, House Committee on Local Government, March 5, 2013, http://wapp.capitol.tn.gov/apps/Billinfo/default.aspx?BillNumber= HB0501&ga=108.

79. Emily Lawler, "'Death Star' Bill Stopping Local Wage, Benefit Ordinances Passes Senate," MLive.com, June 11, 2015, http://www.mlive.com/lansing-news/index.ssf/2015/06/ death_star_bill_stopping_local.html.

80. Brian De Los Santos, "5 biggest Wins for Iowa Small Businesses This Legislative Session," National Federation of Independent Business, July 14, 2015, http://www.nfib.com/ article/5-biggest-wins-for-iowa-small-businesses-this-legislative-session-70066.

81. "Floor Alert," California Chamber of Commerce, May 27, 2014, http://cbpa.com/ wp-content/uploads/2014/06/AB-2416-ASM-Floor-Alert.pdf.

82. Laura Rosenthal, "'Job Killer' Wage Recovery Bill Fails in California Senate," *Sacramento Bee*, August 28, 2014, http://www.sacbee.com/news/politics-government/capitol-alert/article2608083.html.

83. ALEC, "Economic Civil Rights Act," *1995 Sourcebook of American State Legislation*, ALEC Exposed, http://www.alecexposed.org.

84 Quoted in ABC News, "Full Transcript: ABC News Iowa Republican Debate," December 11, 2011, http://abcnews.go.com/Politics/full-transcript-abc-news-iowa-republican-debate/story?id=15134849&singlePage=true#.UNvPRrSmDwx.

85. Meridian school district spokesman Eric Exline, quoted in Ty Brennan, "Lunchroom Controversy Spurs Change in Idaho Law," KTVB.com, April 7, 2011, http://www. KTVB.com/news/local/lunchroom-controversy-spurs-change-in-Idaho-law-119366994. html.

86. These changes were made as part of the state's budget bill, Act 32. New child labor policies are described in Jessica Van Egeren, "GOP Set to Roll Back Child Labor Laws," *Capital Times*, June 15, 2011. On negative impacts of working during the school year, see Child Labor Coalition, "NCL: Eroding Child Labor Protections in 2012 Will Put Some Teens at Risk in US," http://stopchildlabor.org/?p=2746.

87. Wisconsin Grocers Association lobbyist Michelle Kussow, quoted in Holly Rosenkrantz, "Taking Aim at Child Labor Laws," *BloombergBusinessWeek*, January 5, 2012, http://www.businessweek.com/magazine/taking-aim-at-child-labor-laws-01052012.html.

88. Text of bill is at http://www.mainelegislature.org/legis/bills/getPDF.asp?paper=SP0149&item=9&snum=125. On support of the restaurant association, see Steve Mistler, "Bill to Loosen Child Labor Restrictions Heads to Maine Senate," *Bangor Daily News*, March 29, 2011, http://bangordailynews.com/2011/03/29/politics/bill-to-loosen-child-labor-restrictions-heads-to-maine-senate.

89. Representative Bruce Bickford, quoted in Amanda Terkel, "Maine GOP Legislators Looking to Loosen Child Labor Laws," *Huffington Post*, March 30, 2011, http://www.huffingtonpost.com/2011/03/30/maine-gop-legislators-loo_n_842563.html.

90. Terkel, "Maine GOP Legislators."

91. Under the old law, when school is in session, enrolled students were limited to "a combined school and work week of 48 hours." The new law deletes that limit and simply says students can't work for more than 24 hours per week while school is in session. The Michigan Department of Education mandates a minimum of 1,098 class hours per student per year and a minimum of 170 days. That averages 6.45 hours per day. If you have a 5-day school week, that's 32.2 hours, which under the old law would leave 15.7 hours of work. In other words, the new law lets students work 9 more hours per week. In 2014, Michigan went one step further, adopting a bill that removes all limits on work hours for sixteen- and seventeen-year-olds who have obtained a GED or high school equivalency degree.

92. Michigan legislature, "Minutes of the House Standing Committee on Commerce," June 21, 2011, http://www.house.mi.gov/SessionDocs/2011-2012/Minutes/COMM062111.pdf.

93. Andy Deloney, vice president for public affairs, "Statement of the Michigan Restaurant Association in support of House Bill 4732," House Commerce Committee, June 21, 2011, http://house.michigan.gov/SessionDocs/2011-2012/Testimony/Committee4-6-21-2011-4.pdf. At the time this statement was made (June 2011), Michigan's unemployment rate was 10.6 percent, with 495,000 people officially unemployed. Michigan Department of Technology, Management and Budget, News Release, "Michigan's June Unemployment Rate Increases Slightly," July 18, 2012, http://www.michigan.gov/documents/dtmb/LMI-JulyRelease_392680_7.pdf.

94. Child Labor Coalition, "NCL: Eroding Child Labor Protections." The official state legislative summary of Missouri's SB 222 explains,

> This act modifies the child labor laws. It eliminates the prohibition on employment of children under age fourteen. Restrictions on the number of hours and restrictions on when a child may work during the day are also removed. It also repeals the requirement that a child ages fourteen or fifteen obtain a work certificate or work permit in order to be employed. Children under sixteen will also be allowed to work in any capacity in a motel, resort or hotel where sleeping accommodations are furnished. It also removes the authority of the director of the Division of Labor Standards to inspect employers who employ children and to require them to keep certain records for children they employ. It also repeals the presumption that the presence of a child in a workplace is evidence of employment. (Missouri's SB 222 http://www.senate.mo.gov/11info/BTS_Web/Bill.aspx?SessionType=R&BillID=4124271)

Cunningham's ties to ALEC, are described in "ALEC in Missouri: Who's Writing Our Laws?," *Progress Missouri*, April 16, 2012, http://www.scribd.com/doc/89654442/ALEC-Exposed-in-Missouri-2012-04-16.

95. Immigration Works USA, "The Economic Impact of H-2B Workers," U.S. Chamber of Commerce, Labor, Immigration and Employee Benefits Division, October 28, 2010, http://www.uschamber.com/reports/economic-impact-h-2b-workers.

96. In addition to the cases described below, Montana ended overtime rights for computer professionals earning more than $27 per hour, and both Arkansas and Connecticut made it easier to classify truck drivers as independent contractors, thus exempting them from overtime rights.

97. Maine law had previously required that drivers and helpers paid on a nonhourly basis be paid the "reasonable equivalent" of overtime; this requirement was removed by the new statute. See "2012 Summary of New Maine Laws," final issue, Pierce Atwood LLP, June 1, 2012, 8, www.pierceatwood.com/webfiles/2012SummaryofNewMaineLaws_Final Issue.pdf. LD1685 was designated one of the year's "important bills" by the National Federation of Independent Business. "New Laws Affect Wide Range of Business Activity," National Federation of Independent Business, http://www.nfib.com/nfib-in-my-state/ nfib-in-my-state-content?cmsid=60000.

98. "Meet Rep. Beth O'Connor, Tea Partier and Friend of ALEC," Dirigo Blue, August 2011, http://dirigoblue.com.lb.soapblox.net/diary/3495/meet-rep-beth-oconnor-tea-partier-and-friend-of-alec.

99. Nevada Senate Bill 332, 2011, http://www.leg.state.nv.us/Session/76th2011/Bills/ SB/SB332.pdf.

100. SB 332 was introduced by Senator James Settelmeyer, an ALEC Commerce, Insurance and Economic Development Task Force member. ALEC, "Commerce, Insurance, and Economic Development Task Force," committee roster, June 29, 2011, 20, www.commoncause. org/atf/cf/%7BFB3C17E2-CDD1-4DF6-92BE-BD4429893665%7D/cied_35-day_mail- ing_2011_annual_meeting%20New%20Orleans.pdf. Cosponsors include Senator Barbara Cegavske, ALEC's Nevada state chairman and a member of ALEC's Education Task Force, "State Chairmen," ALEC, http://www.alec.org/about-alec/state-chairmen/; ALEC, "Education," committee roster, July 1, 2011, 3, www.commoncause.org/atf/cf/%7BFB3C17E2- CDD1-4DF6-92BE-BD4429893665%7D/education_35-day_mailing%20-%20new%20 orleans.pdf; Senator Joseph Hardy, a member of ALEC's Health and Human Services Task Force, ALEC, "HHS Task Force," committee roster, June 29, 2011, www.commoncause.org/ atf/cf/%7BFB3C17E2-CDD1-4DF6-92BE-BD4429893665%7D/35-day_mailing_hhs%20 New%20Orleans.pdf; and Senator Don Gustavson, a member of ALEC's Public Safety and Elections Task Force, ALEC, "Public Safety and Elections Task Force," committee roster, June 29, 2011, 5, www.commoncause.org/atf/cf/%7BFB3C17E2-CDD1-4DF6-92BE- BD4429893665%7D/pse_35-day_mailing_2011_annual_meeting%20new%20orleans. pdf.

101. Senate Committee on Commerce, Labor and Energy, "Minutes of the Senate Committee on Commerce, Labor and Energy," 76th sess., March 28, 2011.

102. Thomas Donohue, "Overtime Rule Would Hurt More Than Help," *In Your Corner*, U.S. Chamber of Commerce, July 13, 2015. https://www.uschamber.com/above-the-fold/overtime-rule-would-hurt-more-help. Donohue is president of the U.S. Chamber.

103. All data reported in Sarah Leberstein, "Independent Contractor Misclassification Imposes Huge Costs on Workers and Federal and State Treasuries," National Employment Law Project, October 2011.

104. All data reported ibid.

105. "Misclassification," pp. 17–20 of Judson and Francisco-McGuire, "Where Theft Is Legal."

106. Ibid.

107. ALEC, "Independent Contractor Definition Act," *1996 Sourcebook of American State Legislation*, http://www.alecexposed.org/w/images/a/a0/1Q0-Independent_Contractor_ Definition_Act_Exposed.pdf.

108. U.S. Chamber of Commerce, "Impact of State Employment Policies," 26. Colorado example is on page 40.

109. "2012 Summary of New Maine Laws," final issue, 6, provides a summary of the bill.

110. National Federation of Independent Business, "New Laws."

111. New Hampshire HB 420, http://www.gencourt.state.nh.us/legislation/2012/HB0420.html. For descriptions of the law's impact, see "NHDOL Issues New Poster with Revised Independent Contractor Criteria," *New Hampshire Employment Law Letter*, ed. Edward M. Kaplan, Jeanine L. Poole, and William D. Pandolph, November 1, 2012, http://benefits.hrlaws.com/node/1217314; and Karyl Roberts Martin, "New Test for Classifying Independent Contractors in New Hampshire," *Business Law Insights Blog*, August 24, 2012, http://blog.sheehan.com/index.php/business-litigation/classifying-independent-contractors; Bob Sanders, "Business Groups Give Lawmakers a B for Their Work in the Last Session," *New Hampshire Business Review*, July 13, 2012, http://www.nhbr.com/news/967654-395/business-groups-give-lawmakers-a-b-for.html.

112. Elise Gould, Kai Filion, and Andrew Green, "The Need for Paid Sick Days: The Lack of a Federal Policy Further Erodes Family Economic Security" (Economic Policy Institute Briefing Paper No. 319, June 29, 2011), http://www.epi.org/publication/the_need_for_paid_sick_days.

113. Ibid.

114. Results from a survey of San Francisco employers and employees are reported in Vicki Shiabo, "San Francisco Paid Sick Days Law Is a Proven Success," blog posting, National Partnership for Women and Families, February 16, 2011, http://blog.nationalparntership.org/index/php/2011/02/san-fancisco-success.

115. Mayor's Task Force on Paid Sick Leave, "Recommendations on Paid Sick Leave Policies in Philadelphia," Office of the Mayor, December 2014, http://www.phila.gov/mayor/pdfs/Paid%20Sick%20Leave%20Task%20Force%20Report.pdf; Jennifer Romich et al., "Implementation and Early Outcomes of the City of Seattle Paid Sick and Safe Time Ordinance," University of Washington, April 23, 2014, http://www.seattle.gov/Documents/Departments/CityAuditor/auditreports/PSSTOUWReportwAppendices.pdf; "Paid Sick Days: Low Cost, High Reward for Workers, Employers and Communities," National Partnership for Women and Families, November 2015, http://www.nationalpartnership.org/research-library/work-family/psd/paid-sick-days-low-cost-high-reward.pdf.

116. "Overview of Paid Sick Time Laws in the United States," A Better Balance, August 5, 2015, http://www.abetterbalance.org/web/images/stories/Documents/sickdays/factsheet/PSDchart.pdf.

117. U.S. Chamber of Commerce, *Labor and Immigration: Policies Positions and Activities 2008* (Washington, DC: U.S. Chamber of Commerce, 2008), https://www.uschamber.com/sites/default/files/legacy/issues/labor/files/14483laborimmigrationactv.pdf.

118. Campaign for a Healthy Denver and ROC United, "The National Restaurant Association: Behind the Fight against Working Families and an Economy that Works for All," 1, October 2011, http://familyvaluesatwork.org/wp-content/uploads/2011/10/NRA-CO-Report-and-Coversheet.pdf.

119. See Joel Dresang, "Researcher Sees Both Sides of Sick Pay Debate," *Journal Sentinel*, November 21, 2008, http://www.jsonline.com/business/34916009.html. The Milwaukee ordinance had guaranteed a minimum of one hour of paid sick leave for every thirty hours worked, up to a maximum of nine sick days per calendar year; firms with fewer than ten employees had a maximum of only five days per year. Pamela Ploor and Mike Fischer, "Milwaukee Paid Sick Leave Ordinance Revived by Court of Appeals," March 2011, http://www.quarles.com/milwaukee_paid_sick_leave_ordinance_2011/#_ftn2. "Wisconsin Business Climate Improves in 2011," Wisconsin Manufacturers and Commerce, December 20, 2011. http://www.wmc.org/news/press-releases/wisconsin-business-climate-improves-in-2011.

120. "Support HB 4052, Legislation to Preempt Local Employment Laws," Michigan Chamber of Commerce, 2015, http://www.michamber.com/sites/michamber.com/files/TalkingPts4052.mcc.pdf.

121. Georgia adopted such a law in 2010; following Wisconsin were Alabama, Arizona, Arkansas, Florida, Indiana, Kansas, Louisiana, Michigan, Mississippi, Missouri, North Carolina, and Oklahoma.

122. NFIB state director Farrell Quinlan, "More Small Business Bills Signed into Law," National Federation of Independent Business, May 23, 2013, http://www.nfib.com/article/more-small-business-bills-signed-into-law-62505.

123. The state's Construction Safety Standards Commission, the General Industry Safety Standards Commission, and the Occupational Health Standards Commission were all abolished by this legislation. All of these are appointed commissions that had been charged with recommending new workplace regulations. Instead, authority was transferred to the Department of Licensing and Regulatory Affairs, but that agency was permitted to issue regulations that exceeded federal standards only if it could demonstrate a clear and convincing need based on the showing that conditions in Michigan's industry were fundamentally different from those in industries nationwide. Legislative analysis of the bills is at https://www.legislature.mi.gov/documents/2011-2012/billanalysis/House/pdf/2011-HLA-5917-65880DB7.pdf. For corporate lobby support, see http://www.legislature.mi.gov/documents/2011-2012/billanalysis/House/pdf/2011-HLA-5917-01230FE5.pdf.

124. Enrolled Senate Bill No. 20, State of Michigan, 96th Leg., Reg. Sess., March 24, 2011, http://www.legislature.mi.gov/documents/2011-2012/publicact/htm/2011-PA-0010.htm. This bill was sponsored by Senator Rick Jones, a longtime ALEC member who resigned his membership in 2012. Center for Media and Democracy, "Michigan ALEC Politicians," http://www.sourcewatch.org/index.php/Michigan_ALEC_Politicians; "Corporate Sponsors Quit ALEC, Lansing Politicians Should Follow Suit," press release, Progress Michigan, April 10, 2012, http://www.progressmichigan.org/2012/04/corporate-sponsors-quit-alec-lansing-politicians-should-follow-suit. For corporate lobbies' support see Wendy Block, Director of Health Policy and Human Resources, Michigan Chamber of Commerce, "MI Chamber Supports Statutory End to Job-Killing Ergonomics Rule, SB 20," memorandum to the Michigan House of Representatives, February 23, 2011, http://www.michamber.com/files/michamber.com/documents/Memo-Hse-SB%2020-Supp.pdf; "Prohibition of Mandatory Workplace Ergonomics Rules Passes Senate, Teed Up in the House," Michigan Restaurant Association, press release, http://www.michiganrestaurant.org/display common.cfm?an=1&subarticlenbr=1237; and "Voting Record 2011–12 Michigan," National Federation of Independent Business, http://www.nfib.com/LinkClick.aspx?file ticket=MgmxJS8qzi4%3D&tabid=1018.

125. In 2011, the latest year on record, 27,690 people experienced repetitive motion injuries and were off the job for a median of twenty-four days. More than 53 percent of employees with repetitive motion injuries lost twenty-one days or more of work and more than 44 percent (about 12,000 workers) lost thirty-one days or more of work. "R. 70. Detailed Event or Exposure by Number of Days Away from Work," 2011, 21, Bureau of Labor Statistics, www.bls.gov/iif/oshwc/osh/case/ostb3272.pdf; http://www.bls.gov/iif/oshcdnew.htm.

126. ALEC, "Resolution Opposing Ergonomic Regulations Based on Unsound Science," 1996 Sourcebook of American State Legislation, ALEC Exposed, http://www.alecexposed.org/w/images/7/7c/1F10-Resolution_Opposing_Ergonomic_Regulations_Based_on_Unsound_Science_Exposed.pdf.

127. ALEC, "Proposed Resolution Opposing Proposed Ergonomics Work Restriction Protection Plan," 2000, ALEC Exposed, http://www.alecexposed.org/w/images/6/6a/1F4-Proposed_Resolution_Opposing_OSHAs_Proposed_Ergonomics_Work_Restriction_Protection_Plan_Exposed.pdf.

128. U.S. Chamber of Commerce, "Impact of State Employment Policies."

129. HB 574. As initially introduced, the bill completely eliminated the requirement for employers to provide a meal break. The bill passed in amended form, which retained the requirement for meal breaks but allowed employers to work people for six hours rather than five before granting them a meal break. http://legiscan.com/NH/text/HB1574/id/507508

130. Bob Allen, "Wal-Mart Employees Denied Lunch Breaks Awarded $172 Million," *Ethics Daily*, December 28, 2005, http://www.ethicsdaily.com/wal-mart-employees-denied-lunch-breaks-awarded-172-million-cms-6756-printer.

131. Berhnardt et al., "Broken Laws."

132. "This Week," *The Advocate*, Greater Nashua Chamber of Commerce, March 16, 2012, http://www.nashuachamber.com/the_advocate/2012/2012-03-16.htm.

133. Arizona Legislature, House Bill 2280, 2013, http://www.azleg.gov/legtext/51leg/1r/laws/0139.pdf.

134. Howard Fischer, "Arizona Senate Gives Early Approval to 'Living Wage' Ban," *Arizona Daily Star*, March 28, 2013, http://tucson.com/business/local/arizona-senate-gives-early-approval-to-living-wage-ban/article_68dc0dd4-0f15-56ff-a249-f573e85c8420.html.

135. The proposal was first introduced in 2014 by two senators, who reported Wisconsin Manufacturers and Commerce as the source of the proposal. Todd Richmond, "GOP Lawmakers Propose Allowing 7-Day Work Week in Wisconsin," *Milwaukee Journal Sentinel*, January 12, 2014, http://www.jsonline.com/news/statepolitics/gop-lawmakers-propose-allowing-7-day-work-week-in-wisconsin-b99182532z1-239830241.html. The original bill was also supported by the Metropolitan Milwaukee Association of Commerce. Kathleen Gallagher, "Budget Amendment Would Allow 7-day Workweeks," *Milwaukee Journal Sentinel*, July 7, 2015, http://www.jsonline.com/business/budget-amendment-would-allow-7-day-workweeks-b99533515z1-312310311.html. And by the Wisconsin Grocers Association, http://www.wisconsingrocers.com/images/GA%20-%20Legislative%20report%20card%202013-2014%20(2).pdf. The proposal was approved by legislators and was adopted as part of the 2015–17 state budget. https://dwd.wisconsin.gov/er/labor_standards_bureau/one_day_rest_in_seven_law.htm.

136. "Legislative Agenda: 2015-16 Session," Wisconsin Manufacturers and Commerce, https://www.wmc.org/issues/legislative-agenda.

137. Wisconsin AB118, https://docs.legis.wisconsin.gov/2015/proposals/ab118. Representatives Ballweg, Knodl, and Murphy and Senator LeMahieu, all sponsors of the bill, are listed as ALEC members at http://www.sourcewatch.org/index.php/Wisconsin_ALEC_Politicians.

138. Chris Reader, WMC Director of Health and Human Resources Policy, "Two Minute Drill: Wisconsin is NOT Repealing the Weekend," July 15, 2015, https://www.youtube.com/watch?v=wW8nWAC51ag&index=1&list=PLOA1uE6yekDmP-0qSGejflPtshj3OTNkZ.

139. U.S. Chamber, "Impact of State Employment Policies," 31.

140. Robert Pear, "House Passes Two Measures on Job Bias," *New York Times*, January 9, 2013, http://www.nytimes.com/2009/01/10/us/10rights.html.

141. ALEC, "Resolution Opposing Comparable Worth Legislation," adopted by the ALEC board of directors, September 1999, ALEC Exposed, http://www.alecexposed.org. ALEC's bill further suggests that when one controls for the proper variables, women are already being paid just about the same as men.

142. Key vote letter on S. 3220, the "Paycheck Fairness Act," June 4, 2012, U.S. Chamber of Commerce, http://www.uschamber.com/issues/letters/2012/key-vote-letter-s-3220-paycheck-fairness-act.

143. ALEC, "Resolution Opposing Comparable Worth."

144. A good explanation of the law is provided by Wisconsin Manufacturers and Commerce (WMC). Its statement explaining and endorsing SB 202 is at http://www.wmc.org/PDFfiles/gr/SB_202_testimony_10.19.11.pdf. The ALEC affiliation of bill sponsors can be found at http://www.sourcewatch.org/index.php/Wisconsin_ALEC_Politicians.

145. WMC statement endorsing SB 202, http://www.wmc.org/PDFfiles/gr/SB_202_testimony_10.19.11.pdf.

146. Wisconsin Government Accountability Board, "Senate Bill 2012: Organizations Lobbying," April 9, 2012, http://ethics.state.wi.us/scripts/currentSession/LegProps.asp?key-REGSB202.

147. See Jamieson, "Minimum Wage."

148. Text of bill is at http://www.house.mo.gov/billsummary.aspx?bill=HB1219&year=2012&code=R.

149. Missouri legislature, Senate Bill 36, 2015, http://www.senate.mo.gov/15info/BTS_Web/Bill.aspx?SessionType=R&BillID=150. "Legislature Tackles Employment Law with Several Bills in Committee this Week," Blog for Business, Missouri Chamber of Commerce and Industry, March 20, 2015, https://mochamber.wordpress.com/2015/03/20/legislature-tackles-employment-law-with-several-bills-in-committee-this-week.

150. New Hampshire's bill was adopted despite business opposition, in 2014. Amanda Loder, "'Paycheck Fairness Act' to Become Law," New Hampshire Public Radio, May 14, 2014, http://nhpr.org/post/nh-paycheck-fairness-act-become-law. In Texas, the Association of Business was successful in defeating HB187 in 2015. "The Record: The 2015 Report of the Texas Legislature," Texas Association of Business, 2015, http://www.txbiz.org.

151. Jessica Silver-Greenberg and Robert Gebeloff, "Arbitration Everywhere, Stacking the Deck of Justice," New York Times, October 31, 2015, http://www.nytimes.com/2015/11/01/business/dealbook/arbitration-everywhere-stacking-the-deck-of-justice.html.

152. Claire McKenna, "The Job Ahead: Advancing Opportunity for Unemployed Workers," National Employment Law Project, February 2015, http://www.nelp.org/content/uploads/2015/03/Report-The-Job-Ahead-Advancing-Opportunity-Unemployed-Workers.pdf.

153. Among other changes, eight states reduced the number of weeks of maximum benefit; five states reduced the value of weekly benefit one can receive; five states reduced employer UI tax rates; and two states broadened the exemption for "seasonal" employment (defined in one case as up to thirty-six weeks (eight months) per year.

154. HB 1450 and SB 86, passed in 2011.

155. This was part of the budget bill and was effective January 1, 2012.

156. The number of weeks of benefits is set on a sliding scale, from twenty-six weeks when unemployment is over 9 percent to twelve weeks when it is at or below 5.5 percent. Mitchell Hirsch, "N.C. Enacts Harshest Cuts to Unemployment Insurance, Shutting Off Federal Extension Benefits," UnemployedWorkers.org, February 13, 2013, http://unemployedworkers.org/sites/unemployedworkers/index.php/site/blog_entry/n.c._enacts_harshest_cuts_to_unemployment_insurance_shutting_off_federal_ui; "NC's UI Debt Falls $1.5 Billion," North Carolina Chamber of Commerce, May 13, 2014, https://ncchamber.net/ncs-ui-debt-falls-1-5-billion; Joshua Smith, Valerie Wilson, and Josh Bivens, "State Cuts to Jobless Benefits Did Not Help Workers or Taxpayers," July 28, 2014, Economic Policy Institute, http://www.epi.org/publication/state-unemployment-insurance-cuts.

157. U.S. Chamber, "Impact of State Employment Policies."

158. The forced work would be paid at 90 percent of the state minimum wage but not less than the federal minimum; Food Stamp recipients who are aged, blind, or disabled would be exempted from the forced-work requirement. ALEC, "Full Employment Act," 1995 Sourcebook of American State Legislation, ALEC Exposed, http://www.alecexposed.org.

159. LD1725, adopted in 2012.

160. Tennessee General Assembly, Bill Summary: SB 3658, the Unemployment Insurance Accountability Act of 2012, http://wapp.capitol.tn.gov/apps/billinfo/BillSummaryArchive.aspx?BillNumber=SB3658&ga=107. SB 3658 was sponsored by Senators Johnson,

Ramsey, Watson, Ketron, Bell, and Tracy; all but Watson are current or former ALEC members. http://www.sourcewatch.org/index.php/Tennessee_ALEC_Politicians.

161. U.S. Bureau of Labor Statistics, "Table 26. States: Unemployed Persons by Sex, Race, Hispanic or Latino Ethnicity, and Duration of Unemployment, 2011 Annual Average," September 17, 2012, http://www.bls.gov/opub/gp/gpsec2.htm. Pew Research Center reports that, in 2011, 24.1 percent of unemployed Tennessee residents had been out of work for at least one year. Reported in Rebecca D. Williams, "Long-Term Unemployment Takes Its Toll: 'You Get So Down and Out,'" *Knoxville News Sentinel*, February 17, 2013, http://www.knoxnews.com/news/2013/feb/17/long-term-unemployment-takes-its-toll-you-get-so/?print=1.

162. Such laws were passed in Arkansas, Florida, Kansas, Montana, Oklahoma, South Carolina, Tennessee, Wisconsin, and Wyoming.

163. Arkansas SHRM State Council, "Please Support HB 1728 and SB 593," 2011, http://www.arshrm.com/images/downloads/LegeslativeAlertHB170311110853.pdf.

164. Senate Bill 593, 2011, http://www.arkleg.state.ar.us/assembly/2011/2011R/Bills/SB593.pdf.

165. Brian Reisinger, "Businesses Push Efforts to Reform Tennessee Unemployment," *Nashville Business Journal*, March 16, 2012, http://www.bizjournals.com/nashville/print-edition/2012/03/16/tennessee-reform-unemployment.html?page=all.

166. Tennessee General Assembly, Bill Summary: SB 3658, the Unemployment Insurance Accountability Act of 2012, http://wapp.capitol.tn.gov/apps/billinfo/BillSummaryArchive.aspx?BillNumber=SB3658&ga=107.

167. Ibid.

168. http://www.nfib.com/tennessee/nfib-in-my-state-content?cmsid=60149.

169. http://www.flsenate.gov/Session/Bill/2011/7005/BillText/er/PDF.

170. Quoted in Ihosvani Rodriguez, "Hallandale Beach Lifeguard Fired after Participating in Beach Rescue," *South Florida Sun-Sentinel*, July 3, 2012, www.sun-sentinel.com/news/broward/hallandalr/fl-hallandale-beach-lifeguards-20120703,0,5326638.story.

171. The bill's prime sponsor was Representative Doug Holder. Holder's affiliation with ALEC is at http://media.progressflorida.org/files/alecinflorida.pdf. "Unemployment Compensation Bill Passes Florida House of Representatives," March 10, 2011, Florida Chamber of Commerce, http://www.flchamber.com/article/unemployment-compensation-bill-passes-florida-house-of-representatives.

172. On the very broad range of seemingly personal behaviors that employers are legally permitted to restrict, monitor, or prohibit, see Lewis Maltby, *Can They Do That? Retaking Our Fundamental Rights in the Workplace* (New York: Portfolio, 2009).

173. Scott Walker, Transcript: Scott Walker's presidential campaign announcement speech, July 13, 2015, https://caffeinatedthoughts.com/2015/07/transcript-scott-walkers-presidential-campaign-announcement-speech; "Gov. Scott Walker: It's One Thing to Fight, It's Another to Win," *On the Record with Greta Van Susteren*, Fox News, February 24, 2015, http://www.foxnews.com/on-air/on-the-record/2015/02/25/gov-scott-walker-its-one-thing-fight-its-another-win.

174. Scott Hagerstrom, executive director, AFP-Michigan, quoted in Andrea Billups, "Michigan Set to Pass Right-to-Work Law," *Washington Times*, December 10, 2012, http://www.studentnewsdaily.com/daily-news-article/michigan-set-to-pass-right-to-work-law.

4. THE DESTRUCTION OF PUBLIC SCHOOLING

1. Dexter Mullins, "New Orleans to Be Home to Nation's First All-Charter School District," Al Jazeera America, April 4, 2014, http://america.aljazeera.com/articles/2014/4/4/new-orleans-charterschoolseducationreformracesegregation.html.

2. Colleen Kimmett, "10 Years after Katrina, New Orleans' All-Charter School System Has Proven a Failure," *In These Times*, August 28, 2015, http://inthesetimes.com/article/18352/10-years-after-katrina-new-orleans-all-charter-district-has-proven-a-failur. Francesca Lopez and Amy Olson, analysis of National Assessment of Educational Progress data, reported in Julian Vasquez Heilig, "Policy Brief: Should Louisiana and the Recovery District Receive Accolades for Being Last and Nearly Last?," Network for Public Education, August 28, 2015, http://www.networkforpubliceducation.org/2015/08/policy_brief_louisiana.

3. Kimmett, "10 Years After."

4. Ibid.

5. For two recent academic overviews of research on New Orleans, see William Mathis, Huriya Jabbar, and Mark Gooden, "New Orleans Recovery School District Not Quite as Recovered as Advertised," National Education Policy Center, July 13, 2015, http://tinyurl.com/p5ecoc5; and Frank Adamson, Channa Cook-Harvey, and Linda Darling-Hammond, "Whose Choice? Student Experiences and Outcomes in the New Orleans School Marketplace," Stanford Center for Opportunity Policy in Education, September 2015, https://edpolicy.stanford.edu/sites/default/files/publications/scope-brief-student-experiencesneworleans.pdf.

6. Lopez and Olson, in Heilig, "Policy Brief."

7. Susan Saulny, "U.S. Gives Charter Schools a Big Push in New Orleans," *New York Times*, June 13, 2006, http://www.nytimes.com/2006/06/13/us/13charter.html?_r=0.

8. Quoted in Andrea Gabor, "The Myth of the New Orleans School Makeover," *New York Times*, August 22, 2015, http://nyti.ms/1JD7Qt5.

9. Reed Hastings, quoted at 2014 California Charter Schools Association conference, http://www.charterconference.org/2014/program/keynotes.php.

10. Diane Ravitch, "Broad Picks Pastorek to Lead Privatization Effort," *Diane Ravitch's Blog*, October 21, 2015, http://dianeravitch.net/category/new-orleans.

11. "Reading and Math Score Trends," in "The Condition of Education 2015," National Center for Educational Statistics, https://nces.ed.gov/programs/coe/pdf/coe_cnj.pdf.

12. See Joseph Bast, "2002: The Year of School Vouchers," *The Heartlander Monthly*, February 2002, http://news.heartland.org/policy-documents/february-2002-year-school-vouchers.

13. 2012 PDK/Gallup Poll, *Phi Delta Kappan*, September 2012. Indeed, between 1996 and 2000, vouchers were voted on twenty-five times in referenda and rejected all but once. Ziad Jilani, "Report: Meet the Billionaires Who Are Trying to Privatize Our Schools and Kill Public Education," ThinkProgress, May 21, 2011, https://thinkprogress.org/report-meet-the-billionaires-who-are-trying-to-privatize-our-schools-and-kill-public-education-1630dd67054c#.73jr37vft.

14. Phi Delta Kappa International, "The PDK/Gallup Poll of the Public's Attitudes toward the Public Schools," October 2014, http://pdkpoll.pdkintl.org/october/#3.

15. For instance, smaller class size was the number one request of the 450,000 parents surveyed by the New York City school system in 2014. New York City Department of Education, "NYC School Survey Citywide Results," August 2014, http://schools.nyc.gov/NR/rdonlyres/7D257715-FEB1-47D3-99C2-098CBB06A1FD/0/survey_2014_publicdeckforwebsite.pdf.

16. "PDK/Gallup Poll," 2014.

17. STAR was a multimillion-dollar study that tracked thousands of students over a four-year period in the late 1980s. It is the largest statistically rigorous study ever conducted and remains the premier evidence on this issue. Although the experiment ended with third grade, the benefits of small classes continued at least through eighth grade. Alex Molnar, "Smaller Classes, Not Vouchers, Increase Student Achievement," Keystone

Research Center, 1998, http://nepc.colorado.edu/files/smClasssizes.pdf. Indeed, later research showed that students enrolled in small class sizes in kindergarten through third grade under the STAR program were statistically more likely to graduate from high school, enroll in honors classes, graduate near the top of their senior class, and apply to college. In addition, the achievement gap between black and white students was cut in half for black students whose first four years of school took place in smaller classes. After California in 1996 undertook an effort to cut k–3 class sizes from thirty to twenty, researchers reached similar conclusions. Christopher Jensen and Steven Rivkin, "Class Size Reduction and Student Achievement: The Potential Tradeoff between Teacher Quality and Class Size," *Journal of Human Resources* 44 (2009): 223–50.

18. Center for Public Education, 2006, http://www.centerforpubliceducation.org/Main-Menu/Organizing-a-school/Class-size-and-student-achievement-At-a-glance/Class-size-and-student-achievement-Research-review.html. For a recent summary of research, see Diane Whitmore Schanzenbach, "Does Class Size Matter?," National Education Policy Center, February 2014, http://nepc.colorado.edu/publication/does-class-size-matter.

19. Molnar, "Smaller Classes."

20. John Zahorik, Alex Molnar, and Philip Smith, "SAGE Advice: Research on Teaching in Reduced-Size Classes," National Education Policy Center, January 2003, http://nepc.colorado.edu/publication/sage-advice-research-teaching-reduced-size-classes.

21. Sam Dillon, "Tight Budgets Mean Squeeze in Classroom," *New York Times*, March 6, 2011, http://www.nytimes.com/2011/03/07/education/07classrooms.html?_r=0.

22. Matthew Chingos, "Class Size Tradeoffs in the Court of Public Opinion," Brown Center Chalkboard, Brookings Institution, January 30, 2013, http://www.brookings.edu/research/papers/2013/01/30-class-size-chingos.

23. "Texas Legislators Rethink Class Size Rules amid Budget Shortfall," February 18, 2011, www.news.heartland.org/print/29343.

24. Ohio House Bill 30, https://legiscan.com/OH/text/HB30/id/221645.

25. Patricia Mazzei, "Lawmakers Seek Ways around Class-Size Rules," *Miami Herald*, April 1, 2011.

26. Laura Isenisee, "Fallout from the Florida Legislature Gutting the Class Size Amendment," *Miami Herald*, August 30, 2011.

27. Florida Chamber of Commerce, "Where We Stand: A Guide to Florida's 2007 Business Agenda, 2007," http://www.yumpu.com/en/document/view/21032751/2007-where-we-stand-florida-chamber-of-commerce/3.

28. HB 7185 was cosponsored by Representatives Jimmy Patronis, Jr., Stephen Precourt, Clay Ford, and Scott Plakon. All four are ALEC members, with Patronis serving as ALEC state chairman. See Center for Media and Democracy, "Florida ALEC Politicians," http://www.sourcewatch.org/index.php/Florida_ALEC_Politicians; "How They Voted: Where Legislators Stood on the Florida Chamber's 2011 Business Agenda," 13, Florida Chamber of Commerce, http://www.flchamber.com/wp-content/uploads/HowTheyVoted_2011.pdf.

29. "Keeping Informed about School Vouchers: A Review of Major Developments and Research," 14, Center on Education Policy, July 2011, http://cep-dc.org/displayDocument.cfm?DocumentID=369.

30. Corey Wilson, "Wis. Gov. Signs Budget Cutting Education $1.85B," June 3, 2011, CBS News, www.cbsnews.com/stories/2011/06/26/politics/main20074509.shtml#ixzz1QPws3PGA, and Patrick Marley and Jason Stein, "Senate OK'd Budget Goes to Walker," June 16, 2011, www.jsonline.mobi/more/news/124004679.htm.

31. "2013 Budget Resource Page," Wisconsin Education Association Council, www.weac.org/Issues_Advocacy/Legislative_Resources/School_Funding_Resource_Page.aspx.

32. Indiana's program was established in 2011, open to families with incomes below $61,000. Ohio's HB 59 (2013) caps eligibility at 200 percent of the poverty line, but once in the system students can continue to receive vouchers as long as their family income is less than 400 percent of poverty.

33. Arizona SB 1237, HB 2139, HB 2150.

34. Arizona SB 1236. For AFP's support of both the bills that passed and this stalled effort, see "Action Alert- Legislative Update—April 29, 2014," Americans for Prosperity—Arizona, http://americansforprosperity.org/arizona/legislativealerts/action-alert-legislative-update-april-29-2014/#ixzz38mRTOiNU.

35. Quoted in Susan Redden, "Right-to-Work Issue Prompts Push in Republican Party," *Joplin Globe*, September 25, 2015, http://m.joplinglobe.com/news/local_news/right-to-work-issue-prompts-push-in-republican-party/article_d85f6293-dfb2-5af6-908a-6901fb719543.html?mode=jqm.

36. Georgia HB 283. Virginia Galloway, "Americans for Prosperity GA: General Assembly Session Review," April 29, 2013, http://gapundit.com/2013/04/29/americans-for-prosperity-ga-ga-general-assembly-session-review-by-virginia-galloway.

37. "Voucher Veneer: The Deeper Agenda to Privatize Public Education," 24–25, People for the American Way, 2003, http://www.pfaw.org/media-center/publications/voucher-veneer-deeper-agenda-privatize-public-education.

38. Maitre, Michelle, "High School Grades Are a Better Predictor of College Success than SAT, ACT, Study Says," EdSource, February 21, 2014, http://edsource.org/2014/high-school-grades-are-a-better-predictor-of-college-success-than-sat-act-study-says/58033#.UziuKK1dVvY; William Hiss and Valerie Franks, "Defining Promise: Optional Standardized Testing Policies in American College and University Admissions," National Association for College Admissions Counseling, http://www.nacacnet.org/research/research-data/nacac- research/Documents/DefiningPromise.pdf.

39. Pasi Sahlberg, *Finnish Lessons: What Can the World Learn from Educational Change in Finland?* (New York: Teachers College Press, 2010), 67.

40. National Council on Teacher Quality (NCTQ), "State of the States 2012: Teacher Effectiveness Policies," October 2012, http://www.nctq.org/dmsView/State_of_the_States_2012_Teacher_Effectiveness_Policies_NCTQ_Report.

41. Kathy Williams and Barbara Miner, "Failing Our Kids: Why the Testing Craze Won't Fix Our Schools," in *Pencils Down: Rethinking High-Stakes Testing and Accountability in Public Schools*, ed. Wayne Au and Melissa Bollow Tempel (Milwaukee: Rethinking Schools Publications, 2012).

42. Bill Bigelow, "Standards and Tests Attack Multiculturalism," in Au and Bollow Tempel, *Pencils Down*, 56–57.

43. Gayle Gregory and Carolyn Chapman, *Differential Instructional Strategies: One Size Doesn't Fit All* (Thousand Oaks, CA: Corwin Press, 2013), 164.

44. "2012 Teacher of the Year on What Helps Teachers and Students Succeed," PBS NewsHour, September 26, 2012, http://www.pbs.org/newshour/bb/education-july-dec12-2012teacher_09-26.

45. National Alliance for Public Charter Schools, http://www.publiccharters.org/get-the-facts.

46. Gary Miron and Charisse Gulosino, "Profiles of For-Profit and Nonprofit Education Management Organizations, Fourteenth Edition—2011–2012," iv, National Education Policy Center, 2013, http://nepc.colorado.edu/publication/EMO-profiles-11-12.

47. Gary Miron and Jessica Urschel, "The Impact of School Choice Reforms on Student Achievement," in *Exploring the School Choice Universe: Evidence and Recommendations*, ed. Gary Miron et al. (Charlotte: Information Age Publishers, 2012), 228–30.

48. "Multiple Choice: Charter School Performance in 16 States," 3, 22, Center for Research on Education Outcomes, Stanford University, 2009, http://credo.stanford.edu/reports/MULTIPLE_CHOICE_CREDO.pdf.

49. "National Charter School Study 2013," 56–57, Center for Research on Education Outcomes, Stanford University, 2013, http://credo.stanford.edu/documents/NCSS%202013%20Final%20Draft.pdf.

50. Ibid., 44.

51. Ibid., 75.

52. "2012 A–F School Grade Results," Indiana Department of Education, 2012, http://www.doe.in.gov/improvement/accountability/f- accountability.

53. Bill Bush, "Charter Schools' Failed Promise," *Columbus Dispatch*, September 1, 2013, http://www.dispatch.com/content/stories/ local/2013/09/01/charter-schools-failed-promise.html.

54. Valerie Strauss, "Study on Online Charter Schools: 'It Is as If the Kid Did Not Go to School an Entire Year,'" *Washington Post*, October 31, 2015, https://www.washingtonpost.com/news/answer-sheet/wp/2015/10/31/study-on-online-charter-schools-it-is-literally-as-if-the-kid-did-not-go-to-school-for-an-entire-year.

55. Will S. Dobbie and Ronald G. Fryer, Jr., *Charter Schools and Labor Market Outcomes* (NBER Working Paper No. 22502), National Bureau of Economic Research, August 2016, http://www.nber.org/papers/w22502. The authors found that, compared with otherwise similar public school students, the average Texas charter school had no effect on test scores and a negative impact on earnings. The subset of charter schools that had a positive impact on test scores nevertheless had no discernible impact on earnings after graduation.

56. David Stuit and Thomas Smith, "Research Brief: Teacher Turnover in Charter Schools," National Center on School Choice, June 2010, http://www.vanderbilt.edu/schoolchoice/documents/briefs/brief_stuit_smith_ncspe.pdf.

57. Morgaen Donaldson and Susan Moore Johnson, "TFA Teachers: How Long Do They Teach? Why Do They Leave?" *Phi Delta Kappan*, October 4, 2011, http://www.edweek.org/ew/articles/2011/10/04/kappan_donaldson.html. In fact, part of Teach for America's (TFA) recruitment message is that the program will make participants competitive candidates for either graduate school or the corporate world after their two years in the classroom. A company that relies on TFA to supply its teachers can't be surprised by a high degree of turnover; that is part of how TFA is *supposed* to work. "Graduate School and Employer Partnerships," Teach for America, http://www.teachforamerica.org/why-teach-for-america/compensation-and-benefits/graduate-school-and-employer-partnerships.

58. Thomas Carroll and Elizabeth Foster, "Who Will Teach? Experience Matters," National Commission on Teaching and America's Future, http://nctaf.org/wp-content/uploads/2012/01/NCTAF-Who-Will-Teach-Experience-Matters-2010-report.pdf.

59. "Keeping Informed about School Vouchers," 9.

60. T. Ott, "Cleveland Students Hold Their Own with Voucher Students on State Tests," *Cleveland Plain Dealer*, February 22, 2011.

61. Erin Richards and Amy Hetzner, "Choice Schools Not Outperforming MPS: Latest Tests Show Voucher Scores about Same or Worse in Math and Reading," *Milwaukee Journal Sentinel*, March 29, 2011, www.jsonline.com/news/education/118820339.html.

62. "Education Empire: David Brennan's White Hat Management Inc. A Comprehensive Report on the Origins, Evolution and Business Model of Ohio's Largest Charter School Company," Food and Allied Service Trades Division, AFL-CIO, March 2006, http://oh.aft.org/files/article_assets/E0B509E4-04D7-1131-E6AC03D0698CD6DC.pdf.

63. "AYP Results for 2010–11," Center for Education Policy, December 15, 2011, http://www.cep-dc.org/displayDocument.cfm?DocumentID=386.

64. Gary Miron et al., "Profiles of For-Profit and Nonprofit Education Management Organizations, Thirteenth Annual Report, 2010–2011," National Education Policy Center, January 2012, http://nepc.colorado.edu/publication/EMO-profiles-10-11.

65. Richards and Hetzner, "Choice Schools."

66. Rick Hess, "Non-Effects of Milwaukee Vouchers: What's It Mean?" *Rick Hess Straight Up* (blog), April 9, 2010, http://blogs.edweek.org/edweek/rick_hess_straight_up/2010/04/non-effects_of_milwaukee_vouchers_whats_it_mean.html.

67. American Legislative Exchange Council, "Next Generation Charter Schools Act," https://www.alec.org/model-policy/the-next-generation-charter-schools-act.

68. "Multiple Choice"; Miron and Gulosino, "Profiles … 2011–2012."

69. ALEC's Virtual Public Schools Act, for instance, mandates that online schools be provided the same dollars per student as physical, in-person schools; legislation based on this model was adopted in five states in 2011–12.

70. Miron et al., "Profiles … 2010–11."

71. James Marshall Crotty, "Reed Hastings on How to Build a $20 Billion Education Juggernaut," *Forbes*, May 11, 2012, http://www.forbes.com/sites/jamesmarshallcrotty/2012/05/11/reed-hastings-on-what-it-takes-to-grow-a-20-billion-education-company/2.

72. Lee Fang, "Venture Capitalists Are Poised to 'Disrupt' Everything about the Education Market," *Nation*, September 25, 2014.

73. Derek Sarley, "Innovators Convene to Discuss Ways to Improve Education," news release, Arizona State University, December 2, 2010, https://asunews.asu.edu/20101129_educationinnovators.

74. Quoted in Lee Fang, "How Online Learning Companies Bought America's Schools," *Nation*, November 16, 2011, http://www.thenation.com/print/article/164651/how-online-learning-companies-bought-americas-schools.

75. Kelsey Sheey, "States, Districts Require Online Ed for High School Graduation," *U.S. News and World Report*, October 24, 2012, http://www.usnews.com/education/blogs/high-school-notes/2012/10/24/states-districts-require-online-ed-for-high-school-graduation.

76. Rob Lytle, partner with The Parthenon Group, quoted in Stephanie Simon, "Privatizing Public Schools: Big Firms Eyeing Profits from U.S. K-12 Market," Reuters, August 2, 2012, http://www.huffingtonpost.com/2012/08/02/private-firms-eyeing-prof_n_1732856.html?view=print&comm_ref=false.

77. Simon, "Privatizing Public Schools"; Fang, "Online Learning Companies."

78. Quoted in Simon, "Privatizing Public Schools."

79. Cambridge Associates LLC, "U.S. Venture Capital Index and Selected Benchmark Statistics," September 30, 2013, http://www.nvca.org/index.php?option=com_content&view=article&id=344&Itemid=103.

80. Mokoto Rich, "Intensive Small-Group Tutoring and Counseling Helps Struggling Students," *New York Times*, January 26, 2014, http://www.nytimes.com/2014/01/27/education/intensive-tutoring-and-counseling-found-to-help-struggling-teenagers.html.

81. Meredith Kolodner, "Baltimore Summer School Does the Seemingly Impossible— The kids actually want to be there," *Hechinger Report*, August 8, 2016. http://hechinger report.org/baltimore-summer-school-does-the-seemingly-impossible-the-kids-actually-want-to-be-there.

82. Quoted in Fang, "Online Learning Companies."

83. Fang, "Online Learning Companies."

84. Arkansas, Georgia, Idaho, Michigan, and Virginia have since adopted similar laws, though Idaho's was overturned by citizen referendum.

85. Baird Equity Research, note to investors, quoted in Fang, "Online Learning Companies."

86. Eric Hippeau of Lerrer Ventures (a major investor in BuzzFeed, among other ventures), quoted in Fang, "Online Learning Companies."

87. "School Reform Group Hails Jersey Victories," *New York Sun*, June 7, 2007.

88. Joanne Barkan, "Hired Guns on Astroturf: How to Buy and Sell School Reform," *Dissent*, Spring 2012, http://www.dissentmagazine.org/article/hired-guns-on-astroturfhow-to-buy-and-sell-school-reform.

89. Francis Huang, "Is Experience the Best Teacher? A Multilevel Analysis of Teacher Qualifications and Academic Achievement in Low Performing Schools," *Educational Assessment, Evaluation and Accountability* 21, no. 3 (2009): 209–34, http://link.springer.com/article/10.1007%2Fs11092-009-9074-2.

90. Sahlberg, *Finnish Lessons*, 78.

91. Liana Heitin, "U.S. Found to Recruit Fewer Teachers from Top Ranks," *Education Week*, October 20, 2010, http://www.edweek.org/ew/articles/2010/10/15/08teachers.h30.html.

92. Sahlberg *Finnish Lessons*, 52.

93. Ibid., 65, 76.

94. Jeffery Ware, "Privatizing Teacher Certification," Mackinac Center for Public Policy, September 12, 2001, www.educationreport.org.

95. Wisconsin's Act 20 largely reflects ALEC's Alternative Certification Act.

96. "Jobs for Texas: 2015 Legislative Priorities," Texas Association of Business, http://www.txbiz.org.

97. ALEC, "Public Charter Schools Act," draft, August 1, 2014.

98. Rocketship executives Kristoffer Haines (senior vice president of growth and development), Caryn Voskuil (manager of school model innovation), and Farah Dilbe (director of teachers and learning), in interview with the author, March 31, 2014.

99. Gerald Conti, quoted in Valerie Strauss, "Teacher's Resignation Letter: 'My Profession . . . No Longer Exists,'" *Washington Post*, April 6, 2013.

100. Jamie Duffy, "Schools Noticing Teacher Shortage," *Fort Wayne Journal Gazette*, November 8, 2015.

101. Rebecca Klein, "Kansas Underfunded Education. And Tenure. Now It Can't Find Enough Teachers to Fill Classrooms," *Huffington Post*, July 13, 2015, http://www.huffingtonpost.com/entry/kansas-teacher-shortage_us_55b913ebe4b0074ba5a729d5.

102. Celia Llopis-Jepsen, "Kansas State Board of Education Passes Controversial Teacher Licensure Waiver," *Topeka Capital-Journal*, July 14, 2015. The districts in question had previously been granted a waiver from state education regulation under an earlier piece of ALEC-modeled legislation.

103. Scott Bauer, "Walker's Teacher Licensing Plan Criticized," Associated Press, January 23, 2015, http://gbpg.net/1JmXnMs; Bob Kellogg, "Wisconsin Suggests Simple Way to Meet Need for Teachers," One News Now, February 3, 2015.

104. Julie Mead, chair of Educational Leadership and Policy Analysis at the University of Wisconsin-Madison, quoted in Brendan Fischer, "Scott Walker, GOP Slip ALEC Education Agenda into Wisconsin Budget," PR Watch, Center for Media and Democracy, May 23, 2013, http://www.prwatch.org/news/2013/05/12099/scott-walker-gop-slip-alec-education-agenda-wisconsin-budget.

105. The U.S. Chamber of Commerce supports "alternative certification programs," stating that "it is increasingly important to cast a wide net and allow the best candidates to enter the profession, whether or not they have conventional education-school credentials." "Report Card 2009: Recommendations," U.S. Chamber of Commerce, https://www.uschamber.com/report-card-2009-recommendations-0; in the Kochs' home state, AFP Kansas promoted the lowering of teacher certification criteria as an element of "economic freedom." Americans for Prosperity, Kansas Economic Freedom Index, 2012, statement on HB 2634.

106. Achievements School District, http://achievementschooldistrict.org; http://edexcellencemedia.net/publications/2013/20130423-Redefining-the-school-district-in-tennessee/20130423-Redefining-the-School-District-in-Tennessee-FINAL.pdf.

107. The most sweeping version of this legislation is described in Gordon Lafer, "Do Poor Kids Deserve Lower Quality Education Than Rich Kids? Evaluating School Privatization Proposals in Milwaukee, Wisconsin" (Economic Policy Institute Briefing Paper No. 375, April 24, 2014), http://www.epi.org/publication/school-privatization-milwaukee. A slightly more modest version—the "Opportunity Schools and Partnership Program" was adopted as part of the 2015–17 budget signed into law in July 2015.

108. Motoko Rich, "Crucible of Change in Memphis as State Takes on Failing Schools," *New York Times*, April 2, 2013, http://www.nytimes.com/2013/04/03/education/crucible-of-change-in-memphis-as-state-takes-on-failing-schools.html?_r=1&; Lafer, "Do Poor Kids."

109. Neerav Kingsland, "The Recovery School District Model," in *Pathway to Success for Milwaukee Schools*, ed. Warren Kozak, Wisconsin Policy Research Institute, 2013, 40–49, http://www.aei.org/files/2013/05/29/-pathway-to-success_170815996739.pdf.

110. Reed Hastings, quoted in Crotty, "Reed Hastings." Hastings is a venture capitalist and major charter school booster. He has been a major funder of the Rocketship chain of charter schools and is a strategic adviser to the company; he is also a major owner of DreamBox Learning, a math application that Rocketship uses for online classes.

111. Miron and Gulosino, "Profiles … 2011–2012."

112. In 2014 ALEC advertised a presentation titled "On the Rocketship: Expanding the High-Quality Charter School Movement," sponsored by the Thomas B. Fordham Institute, a member of ALEC's Education Task Force. ALEC digital exchange, June 12, 2014, http://www.alec.org/alec-exchange-06-12-2014.

113. Brad Bernatek et al., "Blended Learning in Practice: Case Studies from Leading Schools, Featuring Rocketship Education," 29, Dell Foundation, September 2012, http://5a03f68e230384a218e0-938ec019df699e606c950a5614b999bd.r33.cf2.rackcdn.com/msdf-rocketship_04.pdf; https://library.educause.edu/~/media/files/library/2012/9/csd6147e-pdf.pdf . The California Charter School Association named the Dell Foundation its Supporter of the Year in 2014, noting its investment in multiple charter school companies over the past decade. *Cal Charters* (blog), http://www.calcharters.org/blog/2014/03/michael-susan-dell-foundation-presented-with-hart-vision-award-for-supporter-of-the-year-at-the-21st.html.

114. Rocketship Education and the proposed 2014 Wisconsin legislation are described in detail in Lafer, "Do Poor Kids."

115. Ibid.

116. Quoted in Crotty, "Reed Hastings."

117. Chad Livengood, "Education Reform Group Forges Voucher-like Plan for Michigan," *Detroit News*, April 19, 2013, http://www.gceapride.org/education-reform-group-forges-voucher-like-plan-for-michigan.

118. This case, including the state's defense, is discussed in Jenny DeMonte and Akash Patel, "The Right to Read: Suing a State for Better Teaching," Center for American Progress, December 5, 2013, https://www.americanprogress.org/issues/education/news/2013/12/05/80350/the-right-to-read-suing-a-state-for-better-teaching.

119. Kate Wells, "Michigan Court Rules against ACLU in 'Right to Read' Case," Michigan Radio, November 7, 2014, http://michiganradio.org/post/michigan-court-rules-against-aclu-right-read-case#stream/0.

120. ALEC, The Founding Philosophy and Principles Act, 2013. http://www.alecexposed.org/w/images/4/4a/The_Founding_Philosophy_and_Principles_Act.pdf.

121. Florida Statutes, Section 1003.42, cited in "2010 Social Studies Specifications for the 2011–2012 Florida State Adoption of Instructional Materials," Florida Department of Education, http://www.fldoe.org/bii/instruct_mat/pdf/SocialStudies2011.pdf.

122. Quoted in in "Arizona Bans Ethnic Studies for K-12 Students," PBS NewsHour, December 28, 2010, http://www.pbs.org/newshour/extra/features/us/july-dec10/arizona_12-24.html.

123. Tom LoBianco, "Mitch Daniels: I Just Wanted to Keep Kids from Reading Howard Zinn," *Huffington Post*, July 19, 2013, http://www.huffingtonpost.com/2013/07/19/mitch-daniels-howard-zinn_n_3625599.html.

124. Roger Freeman, education adviser to then California Governor Reagan and later to President Nixon, quoted in Ron Moskowitz, "Professor Sees Peril in Education," *San Francisco Chronicle*, October 30, 1970.

125. Raquel Laneri, "Special Report: America's Best Prep Schools," *Forbes*, April 29, 2010, http://www.forbes.com/2010/04/29/best-prep-schools-2010-opinions-private-education_print.html.

126. Quoted in Mike Elk, "Director of Private School Where Rahm Sends His Kids Opposes Using Testing for Teacher Evaluations," *In These Times*, September 11, 2012.

127. Steve Baas, Statement on behalf of Metropolitan Milwaukee Association of Commerce before the Senate Committee on Public Education, Hearing on Senate Bill 76, October 3, 2013.

128. Interviews with both hometown schools conducted by Jennifer Smith of University of Oregon. The MMAC chair and president do not have kids in these schools—they are beyond the age of having elementary-school-aged kids—but these are the schools that would be their neighborhood schools according to where they live.

129. Christopher Tienken and Yon Zhao, "How Common Standards and Standardized Testing Widen the Opportunity Gap," in *Closing the Opportunity Gap: What America Must Do to Give Every Child an Even Chance*, ed. Prudence Carter and Kevin Welner (New York: Oxford University Press, 2013) 111–22.

130. "National Charter School Study 2013."

131. Richard Rothstein "Why Children from Lower Socioeconomic Classes, on Average, Have Lower Academic Achievement Than Middle-Class Children," in Carter and Welner, *Closing the Opportunity Gap*, 61–74.

132. Fang, "Online Learning Companies."

133. Dave Weston, "It's Time for State Government to Stop Collecting Union Dues," *Tulsa World*, March 21, 2015, http://www.tulsaworld.com/opinion/readersforum/dave-weston-it-s-time-for-state-government-to-stop/article_6deb6a2c-62c1-5359-9dc7-68d60be59528.html.

5. SILENCING LABOR'S VOICE

1. Martin Gillens, *Affluence and Influence: Economic Inequality and Political Power in America* (Princeton: Princeton University Press, 2012), 81–83, 1.

2. Ibid., 173.

3. Larry Bartels, *Unequal Democracy: The Political Economy of the New Gilded Age* (Princeton: Princeton University Press, 2008), 275.

4. Jasmine Kerrissey and Evan Schofer, "Union Membership and Political Participation in the United States," *Social Forces* 91, no. 3 (2013): 895–928.

5. Nate Silver, "The Effects of Union Membership on Democratic Voting," *New York Times*, February 26, 2011, http://fivethirtyeight.blogs.nytimes.com/2011/02/26/the-effects-of-union-membership-on-democratic-voting/?_r=0.

6. Richard Cobb and Jonathan Cobb, *The Hidden Injuries of Class* (New York: Norton, 1973).

7. William Domhoff, *Who Rules America? The Triumph of the Corporate Rich*, 7th ed. (New York: McGraw-Hill, 2014), 113.

8. Laws were passed in Alabama, Arizona, Georgia, Kansas, Michigan, Missouri, Ohio, Oklahoma, North Carolina, and Wisconsin. Seven of these have been enacted. Missouri's law was vetoed, Ohio's overturned by citizen referendum, and Arizona's permanently enjoined by federal court.

9. Larry Sabato, "The Real Story Behind 'Paycheck Protection': The Hidden Link between Anti-Worker and Anti-Public Education Initiatives," National Education Association, 1998; "Election Watch 2006: Education Alliance Back in Battle for OUSD," Orange

Net News, September 19, 2006, http://greaterorange.blogspot.com/2006/09/election-watch-2006_19.html. The organization is the Educational Alliance, whose chief financial backer was Howard F. Ahmanson, a member of the board of trustees of the Chalcedon think tank. Ahmanson was also the single largest financial supporter of Proposition 226. Chalcedon's mission included the conviction that "it is not only our duty as individuals, families and churches to be Christian, but it is also the duty of the state, the school, the arts and sciences, law, economics, and every other sphere to be under Christ the King."

10. David Broder, "California GOP's Bid to Curb Union Funds Is Faltering," *Washington Post*, May 26, 1998, www.washingtonpost.com/wp-srv/politics/campaigns/keyra ces98/stories/key052698.htm.

11. ALEC, "Paycheck Protection Act," 1998, ALEC Exposed, http://alecexposed.org/w/images/b/b8/Paycheck_Protection_Act_Exposed.pdf.

12. ALEC, "Public Employee Freedom Act," 1999, ALEC Exposed, http://alecexposed.org/w/images/1/15/1R8-Public_Employee_Freedom_Act_Exposed.pdf; ALEC, Public Employer Payroll Deduction Policy Act, 1999, ALEC Exposed, http://alecexposed.org/w/images/c/c9/1R9Public_Employer_Payroll_Deduction_Policy_Act_Exposed.pdf.

13. "Missouri Chamber Testifies to Protect Employee's Paychecks," Missouri Chamber of Commerce, 2013, http://www.mochamber.com/mx/hm.asp?id=020113paycheck.

14. ALEC, "Resolution in Support of the Citizens United Decision," ALEC Exposed, September 29, 2010, http://alecexposed.org/w/images/f/f2/7G4-Resolution_in_Support_of_the_Citizens_United_Decision_Exposed.pdf.

15. Mariah Blake, "ALEC Attacks Shareholders," *Salon*, April 23, 2012, www.salon.com/2012/04/23/alec_attacks_shareholders.

16. ALEC, "Resolution in Support of the Citizens United Decision," ALEC Exposed, 2010, http://alecexposed.org/w/images/f/f2/7G4-Resolution_in_Support_of_the_Citizens_United_Decision_Exposed.pdf.

17. ALEC, "Memorandum to New York ALEC Members from ALEC's Public Safety and Elections Task Force, February 15, 2011," Common Cause, www.commoncause.org/atf/cf/%7Bfb3c17e2-cdd1-4df6-92be-bd4429893665%7D/1-ALEC_IssueAlerts.pdf.

18. Tim W. Jones, "Missouri House Perfects Paycheck Protection and Prevailing Wage Reform Legislation," 2013, http://timwjones.com/?page_id=37. Jones is Missouri state chairman for ALEC and a member of ALEC's education task force. http://www.sourcewatch.org/index.php/Missouri_ALEC_Politicians.

19. "AFP-MO Applauds Sen. Brown for Protecting Workers' Paycheck," press release, Americans for Prosperity—Missouri, March 12, 2013, http://americansforprosperity.org/missouri/newsroom/afp-mo-applauds-sen-brown-for-protecting-workers-paycheck/#ixzz2O0NvJXFj.

20. "Missouri Chamber Testifies."

21. Detailed sources for information in the following list are found in Gordon Lafer, "The Paycheck Protection Racket," Economic Policy Institute, April 24, 2013, http://www.epi.org/files/2013/paycheck-protection-racket-tilting-political.pdf.

22. Missouri General Assembly, Senate Bill No. 29, 97th General Assembly, 2013, www.senate.mo.gov/13info/pdf-bill/tat/SB29.pdf.

23. ALEC, "Paycheck Protection Act."

24. Tennessee Chamber of Commerce and Industry, "2011–12 Tennessee Chamber Positions," *Business Insider*, Summer 2012, 18; "Supreme Court to Consider California Union Dues Case," July 1, 2015, National Federation of Independent Business, http://www.nfib.com/article/supreme-court-to-consider-california-union-dues-case-69976.

25. Arizona Senate Bill 1365, 2011, http://www.azleg.gov/legtext/50leg/1r/bills/sb1365h.pdf.

26. Alabama Secretary of State, Act 2010-761, December 20, 2010, http://www.alabamaschoolboards.org/PDFs/Act%202010-761.pdf.

27. Kansas Statutes Annotated 2013, Supp. 44-501, https://www.dol.ks.gov/Files/PDF/SSubHB2023.pdf.

28. John Celock, "Kansas Chamber of Commerce Lobbyist: Bill Is Needed to End Public Sector Unions," *Huffington Post*, January 23, 2013, www.huffingtonpost.com/2013/01/23/kansas-chamber-of-commerce_n_2536360.html.

29. In 2013, Paul Kersey was labor policy director for the Illinois Policy Institute, a member of the ALEC-affiliated State Policy Network. Kersey had previously served in a similar role for the Mackinac Center in Michigan and before that at the Heritage Foundation. He presented several pieces of model antiunion legislation at ALEC's spring 2012 task force summit.

30. Such laws were proposed in thirteen states, including the right-to-work states of Alabama, Arizona, Florida, Kansas, Mississippi, South Dakota, and Tennessee.

31. ALEC, "Paycheck Protection Act."

32. Alabama Secretary of State, Act 2010-761.

33. John Logan, "The Shadowy Dark Money Groups behind California's Proposition 32," Truthout.org, November 5, 2012, http://www.truth-out.org/speakout/item/12535-the-shadowy-dark-money-groups-behind-californias-proposition-32?tmpl=component&print=1.

34. Melody Guyton Butts, "Durham Teachers' Group Prepares to Fight Veto Override," *Herald Sun*, January 5, 2012.

35. N.C. Gen. Stat. § 1438-426.40A(g).

36. General Assembly of North Carolina, Session 2011, Senate Bill 727, "An Act to Eliminate the Dues Checkoff Option for Active and Retired Public School Employees," http://www.ncleg.net/Sessions/2011/Bills/Senate/PDF/S727v4.pdf.

37. Butts, "Durham Teachers' Group."

38. ALEC, "Public Employer Payroll Deduction Policy Act."

39. "Governor Signs Bill to Ensure Proper Use of Public Resources," Governor Rick Snyder, March 16, 2012, http://www.michigan.gov/snyder/0,4668,7-277-57577_57657-273521--,00.html.

40. "Memorandum to Members of Michigan State Senate," Michigan Chamber of Commerce, March 7, 2012, http://www.michamber.com/files/michamber.com/HB4929%20Senate.pdf.

41. Michigan Senate Fiscal Agency, "Complete Summary: House Bill 4929," 2012, http://www.legislature.mi.gov/documents/2011-2012/billanalysis/Senate/pdf/2011-SFA-4929-S.pdf.

42. Ibid.

43. "Fiscal Impact Statements for H.B. 1749," Oklahoma Legislature, 2015, http://www.oklegislature.gov/BillInfo.aspx?Bill=hb1749; State of Texas, Legislative Budget Board, "Fiscal Note in re SB1968," 84th legis. sess., May 18, 2015, http://www.legis.state.tx.us/tlodocs/84R/fiscalnotes/pdf/SB01968E.pdf#navpanes=0; State of Kansas, Division of the Budget, "Fiscal Note for SB 212 by Senate Committee on Assessment and Taxation," February 19, 2015, http://www.kslegislature.org/li/b2015_16/measures/documents/fisc_note_sb212_00_0000.pdf.

44. Jonathan Shorman, "Bill Would Prohibit Paycheck Deductions for Union Dues," *Topeka Capital-Journal*, March 12, 2015, http://cjonline.com/news/2015-03-12/bill-would-prohibit-paycheck-deductions-union-dues.

45. Don Loos, "Lame Duck Session: Teachers Union Boss Upset over 'Hijacked Legislative Process,'" National Right to Work Committee, December 29, 2010, http://www.nrtwc.org/lame-duck-session-teachers-union-boss-upset-over-hijacked-the-legislative-process.

46. Tim Lockette, "AEA Banned from Enrolling Members on 2-Year Campuses," *Anniston Star*, February 17, 2011, http://www.annistonstar.com/news/anniston/aea-banned-from-enrolling-members-on--year-campuses/article_8352bb72-a10b-5a05-8944-a4e91f288fce.html.

47. George Will, "Liberals' Wisconsin Waterloo," *Washington Post*, August 24, 2011, http://www.washingtonpost.com/opinions/liberals-wisconsin-waterloo/2011/08/23/gIQArm5GcJ_story.html.

48. Rick Henderson and Steven Hayward, "Happy Warrior: Republican Agitator Grover Norquist on Building a 'Leave-Us-Alone' Coalition," *Reason*, February 1, 1997, http://reason.com/archives/1997/02/01/happy-warrior/print.

49. Jason Hancock and Brad Cooper, "Union Dues Collecting Is Examined by Missouri, Kansas Lawmakers," *Kansas City Star*, January 31, 2013, http://www.miamiherald.com/2013/01/31/3209846/union-dues-collecting-is-examined.html#storylink=cpy.

50. John Jacobs, "Unmasking 226's 'Paycheck Protection' Masquerade," *Sacramento Bee*, May 28, 1998.

51. Broder, "California's GOP Bid," 132.

52. In Texas, the Right-to-Work Committee's newsletter editor authored a twenty-page report in 2015, urging Texas legislators to adopt a complete prohibition on union dues deductions in order in part to "lessen the ability of unions . . . to use funds collected from public sector employees in funding their private-section unionization drives." Stanley Greer, "State Labor-Management Policy and the Texas Model: Keeping Unionism Voluntary Is Beneficial but Additional Safeguards Are Now Needed," Texas Public Policy Foundation, February 2015, http://www.texaspolicy.com/library/doclib/2015-02-RR03-CEF-StateLaborMgmtPolicy-SGreer-jag02242015.pdf. The Texas NFIB issued a statement in support of this bill, stressing the danger that "dues collected can . . . be used to target local business for union organizing drives." National Federation of Independent Business, "Government Transparency and Dues Collection: Support SB 1968 by Huffman, et al.," 2015, https://s3.amazonaws.com/NFIB/AMS%20Content/Attachments/1/1-68741-1968onepager.pdf.

53. *Rebecca Friedrichs et al. v. California Teachers Association*, petition for a writ of certiorari, January 26, 2015, https://www.cir-usa.org/legal_docs/friedrichs_v_cta_cert_pet.pdf.

54. "New Amicus Briefs Urge Supreme Court to Review Friedrichs," Center for Individual Rights, March 2, 2015, https://www.cir-usa.org/2015/03/nine-amicus-briefs-urge-supreme-court-to-review-friedrich; Sean Redmond, "SCOTUS to Consider Public Sector Right-to-Work" (blog), Workforce Freedom Initiative, July 22, 2015, http://www.workforcefreedom.com/blog/scotus-consider-public-sector-right-work;

"Supreme Court to Consider California Union Dues Case," National Federation of Independent Business, July 1, 2015, http://www.nfib.com/article/supreme-court-to-consider-california-union-dues-case-69976/.

55. NFIB, "Supreme Court," 2015.

CONCLUSION

1. On this point, see Tim Judson, "The Politics of Wage Suppression: Inside ALEC's Legislative Campaign against Low-Wage Workers," National Employment Law Project, February 2013, http://nelp.3cdn.net/4fad2aaa1917c35b4b_iom6i63pq.pdf.

2. Peter Fisher, "Selling Snake Oil to the States: The American Legislative Exchange Council's Flawed Prescriptions for Prosperity," Good Jobs First and Iowa Policy Project, November 2012, http://www.goodjobsfirst.org/snakeoiltothestates. *Politico*'s annual ranking of the states by fourteen independent quality-of-life measures also produced rankings largely opposite to ALEC's. "The States of Our Union . . . Are Not All Strong," *Politico*, January 24, 2014, http://www.politico.com/magazine/story/2014/01/states-of-our-union-are-not-all-strong-102547#.UuXwCBatu8U.

3. Arthur Laffer, Stephen Moore, and Jonathan Williams, *Rich States, Poor States*, 8th ed. (Arlington, VA: American Legislative Exchange Council, 2015), http://alec.org/docs/

RSPS_8th_Edition.pdf ; "America's Top States for Business 2015," CNBC, June 24, 2015. http://www.cnbc.com/2015/06/24/americas-top-states-for-business.html.

4. ALEC, "Resolution in Opposition to Any Increase in the Starting (Minimum) Wage," *1996 Sourcebook of American State Legislation*, http://www.alec.org/model-legislation/resolution-in-opposition-to-any-increase-in-the- starting-minimum-wage.

5. Andy Deloney, vice president for public affairs, "Statement of the Michigan Restaurant Association in support of House Bill 4732," House Commerce Committee, June 21, 2011, http://house.michigan.gov/SessionDocs/2011-2012/Testimony/Committee 4-6-21-2011-4.pdf.

6. ALEC, "Founding Philosophy and Principles Act," 2012, http://www.alec.org/model-legislation/founding-philosophy-and-principles-act.

7. ALEC, "State Sovereignty through Local Coordination Act," 2010, ALEC Exposed, http://www.alecexposed.org/w/images/0/05/3H15-State_Sovereignty_through_Local_Coordination_Act_Exposed.pdf. Emphasis added.

8. Greg Kocher, "Several Kentucky Counties Passing or Considering 'Right to Work' Laws," *Lexington Herald Leader*, January 17, 2015, http://www.kentucky.com/news/local/counties/scott-county/article44547798.html; Carolyn Tribble Greer, "Business Groups Urge Metro Council to Reject Minimum Wage Increase," *Louisville Business First*, September 29, 2014.

9. "California Lawmakers Pay Back Their Big Labor Allies, Take Steps to Deprive Charter Cities of Local Control," Truth about PLAs, May 1, 2012, http://thetruthabout plas.com/2012/05/01/california-lawmakers-pay-back-their-big-labor-allies-take-steps-to-deprive-charter-cities-of-local-control.

10. "Changes in U.S. Family Finances from 2010 to 2013: Evidence from the Survey of Consumer Finances," *Federal Reserve Bulletin*, September 2014, http://www.federal reserve.gov/pubs/bulletin/2014/pdf/scf14.pdf.

11. "New Low: Just 14% Think Today's Children Will Be Better Off Than Their Parents," July 29, 2012, Rasmussen Reports, www.rasmussenreports.com/public_content/business/jobs_employment/july_2012/new_low_just_14_think_today_s_children_will_be_better_off_than_their_parents.

12. Beth Ann Bovino, Gabriel Petek, and John Chambers. "How Increasing Income Inequality Is Dampening U.S. Economic Growth and Possible Ways to Change the Tide," Standard and Poor's Rating Services, August 5, 2014, http://www.ncsl.org/Portals/1/Documents/forum/Forum_2014/Income_Inequality.pdf.

13. Safa Motesharrei, Jorge Rivas, and Eugenia Kalnay, "Human and Nature Dynamics (HANDY): Modeling Inequality and Use of Resources in the Collapse or Sustainability of Societies," *Ecological Economics* 101 (May 2014): 90–102, http://www.sciencedirect.com/science/article/pii/S0921800914000615.

14. The bill, 2012 HB 85, was passed out of committee before finally being defeated by a vote of thirty to twenty-seven. Half the bill's sponsors were affiliated with ALEC. Jeremy Pelzer, "Wyoming Lawmaker Introduces Doomsday Bill," *Casper Star Tribune*, February 23, 2012, http://trib.com/news/state-and-regional/govt-and-politics/wyoming-lawmaker-introduces-doomsday-bill/article_a569afbd-61df-504f-bb55-e37547364bad.html.

15. Peter Georgescu, "Capitalists, Arise: We Need to Deal with Income Inequality," *New York Times*, August 7, 2015, http://www.nytimes.com/2015/08/09/opinion/sunday/capitalists-arise-we-need-to-deal-with-income-inequality.html.

16. Alan Feuer, "Billionaires to the Barricades," *New York Times*, July 3, 2015, http://www.nytimes.com/2015/07/05/opinion/sunday/billionaires-to-the-barricades.html.

17. Alec Hogg, "As Inequality Soars, the Nervous Super-Rich Are Already Planning Their Escapes," *Guardian*, January 23, 2015, http://www.theguardian.com/public-leaders-network/2015/jan/23/nervous-super-rich-planning-escapes-davos-2015.

18. Luxury Survival Condo, http://survivalcondo.com.

19. "Life Assurance for a Dangerous World," Vivos, http://www.terravivos.com.

20. Stan Greenberg, James Carville, and Erica Seifert, "Broad Bi-Partisan Consensus Supports Reforms to Supreme Court," Memo to Interested Parties, Greenberg Quinlan Rosner Research, May 7, 2014.

21. Patrick O'Connor, "Influence of Money in Politics a Top Concern for Voters," *Wall Street Journal*, June 21, 2015.

22. "Most Say Government Policies since Recession Have Done Little to Help Middle Class, Poor," Pew Research Center, March 4, 2015, http://www.people-press.org/2015/03/04/most-say-government-policies-since-recession-have-done-little-to-help-middle-class-poor.

23. Naomi Scheiber and Dalia Sussman, "Inequality Troubles Americans across Party Lines, Times/CBS Poll Finds," *New York Times*, June 3, 2015, http://nyti.ms/1IiuMwi.

24. Jeffrey M. Jones, "Fewer Americans Now View Their Income Taxes as Fair," Gallup, April 15, 2013, http://www.gallup.com/poll/161780/fewer-americans-view-income-taxes-fair.aspx.

25. "Most See Inequality Growing, but Partisans Differ over Solutions," Pew Research Center, January 23, 2014, http://www.people-press.org/2014/01/23/most-see-inequality-growing-but-partisans-differ-over-solutions.

26. Ibid.

27. Ibid.

28. David Mermin and Britany Stalsburg, "Recent Survey Findings," Lake Research Partners, January 16, 2015, http://www.makeitworkcampaign.org/wp-content/uploads/2015/02/MIW-SOTU-Poll-Memo.pdf.

29. John Halpin and Karl Agne, "50 Years after LBJ's War on Poverty: A Study of American Attitudes about Work, Economic Opportunity, and the Social Safety Net," Center for American Progress, January 2014, https://www.americanprogress.org/wp-content/uploads/2014/01/WOP-PollReport2.pdf.

30. Derek Pugh, "The American Majority Is a Populist Majority," Campaign for America's Future, June 2014, https://www.scribd.com/fullscreen/225509828?access_key=key-16Fj3fcbzItt5bATtVMg&allow_share=true&escape=false&show_recommendations=false&view_mode=scroll.

31. Ibid.

32. Ibid.

33. Ibid.

34. "Legislators Look for Way to Loosen Class Size Limits," *St. Petersburg Times*, March 31, 2011.

35. "Inventory of City and County Minimum Wage Ordinances," UC Berkeley Labor Center, 2015, http://laborcenter.berkeley.edu/minimum-wage-living-wage-resources/inventory-of-us-city-and-county-minimum-wage-ordinances.

36. Marianne Levine and Timothy Noah, "Minimum Wage Hikes Win," *Politico*, November 5, 2014, http://www.politico.com/story/2014/11/minimum-wage-increase-wins-in-four-red-states-112565.

37. Lonnie Golden, "Irregular Work Scheduling and Its Consequences" (Economic Policy Institute Briefing Paper No. 394, April 9, 2015), http://www.epi.org/publication/irregular-work-scheduling-and-its-consequences.

38. Justin Miller, "In Minneapolis, a Strong 'Fair Scheduling' Law for Workers Runs Into a Corporate Roadblock," *In These Times*, October 27, 2015, http://inthesetimes.com/working/entry/18544/minneapolis-betsy-hodges-working-families-agenda-fair-scheduling; Colin Young, "Retail Industry Lobbyists Attack 'Fair Schedule' Ballot Petition,"

State House News, August 31, 2015, http://arlington.wickedlocal.com/article/20150831/NEWS/150839849.

39. "Key Vote letter on S. 3220, the 'Paycheck Fairness Act,'" U.S. Chamber of Commerce, June 4, 2012, http://www.uschamber.com/issues/letters/2012/key-vote-letter-s-3220-paycheck-fairness-act.

40. U.S. Chamber of Commerce, "Impact of State Employment Policies," 21.

41. This practice was pioneered, in part, by ALEC member companies Walgreens and Novartis, both found guilty in class-action suits for race and sex discrimination; the U.S. Chamber of Commerce is among those voicing the legal argument for barring such lawsuits. Jessica Silver-Greenberg,and Robert Gebeloff, "Arbitration Everywhere, Stacking the Deck of Justice," *New York Times*, October 31, 2015, http://www.nytimes.com/2015/11/01/business/dealbook/arbitration-everywhere-stacking-the-deck-of-justice.html.

42. Steven Greenhouse, "Noncompete Clauses Increasingly Pop Up in Array of Jobs," *New York Times*, June 8, 2014, http://nyti.ms/1qdOj4y.

43. Ibid.

44. ALEC, "Economic Civil Rights Act," *1995 Sourcebook of American State Legislation*, ALEC Exposed, http://www.alecexposed.org/w/images/c/c2/1C4-Economic_Civil_Rights_Act_Exposed.pdf.

45. Wisconsin 2015 Assembly Bill 91, https://legiscan.com/WI/bill/AB91/2015; "WMC Legislative Agenda: 2015–2016 Session," Wisconsin Manufacturers and Commerce, https://www.wmc.org/wp-content/uploads/Legislative-Agenda-2015-16.pdf.

46. ALEC, "Economic Civil Rights Act."

47. ALEC, "Right to Work Act," *1995 Sourcebook of American State Legislation*.

48. ALEC, "Open Contracting Act," *1995 Sourcebook of American State Legislation*.

49. ALEC, "Political Funding Reform Act," approved by ALEC board of directors, January 1999, ALEC Exposed, http://alecexposed.org/w/images/f/fa/1R4-Political_Funding_Reform_Act_Exposed.pdf.

50. "States with New Voting Restrictions since the 2010 Election," Brennan Center for Justice, http://www.brennancenter.org/new-voting-restrictions-since-2010.

51. Janie Velencia and Alissa Scheller, "Fewer Democrats Are Voting This Year in (Surprise!) States with Strict New Voter Laws," *Huffington Post*, March 4, 2016, http://www.huffingtonpost.com/entry/voter-id-laws-democratic-turnout_us_56d8c5bae4b0000de403f238.

52. ALEC, "Super-Majority Act," 2013, http://www.alec.org/model-legislation/super-majority-act-2.

53. Delaware, Mississippi, Oregon, Arizona, California, Nevada, and Louisiana. "Policy Basics: State Supermajority Rules to Raise Revenues," Center on Budget and Policy Priorities, February 11, 2015, http://www.cbpp.org/research/policy-basics-state-supermajority-rules-to-raise-revenues?fa=view&id=3953.

54. "NFIB Legal Center Leads Coalition in Defense of Taxpayer Protections Nationwide," NFIB, August 4, 2015, http://www.nfib.com/article/nfib-legal-center-leads-coalition-in-defense-of-taxpayer-protections-nationwide-70360.

55. Associated Press, "Michigan Senate OKs New Emergency Manager Bill," December 14, 2012, http://news.yahoo.com/michigan-senate-oks-emergency-manager-bill-232840300.html.

56. Cara Sullivan, quoted in Steve Arnold, "Undercover at ACCE: ALEC Offshoot Spins City and County Officials on Dirty Energy, Local Control," Center for Media and Democracy, February 23, 2015, http://www.prwatch.org/news/2015/02/12747/undercover-acce-alecs-offshoot-spins-city-and-county-officials-dirty-energy.

57. Quoted in Chris Taylor, "Corporate Agenda Is Clear at ALEC Conference," Madison.com, June 2, 2014, http://host.madison.com/news/opinion/column/corporate-agenda-is-clear-at-alec-conference/article_f9579dd7-6ed7-5a1b-b790-0824efed0cff.html#.U49Tl0ncmJo.email.

58. Ashley Lopez, "Florida Senate May Consider House's More Restrictive Anti-Sick Pay Bill," Florida Center for Investigative Reporting April 25, 2013, http://fcir.org/2013/04/25/florida-senate-may-consider-houses-more-restrictive-anti-sick-pay-bill; "Governor Rick Scott Signs Paid Sick Leave Preemption Measure," news release, Florida Restaurant and Lodging Association, https://www.frla.org/news-release/governor-rick-scott-signs-paid-leave-preemption-measure; "References for Florida Manufacturers," Manufacturers Association of Central Florida, January 16, 2014, http://macf.biz/2014/01/16/references-for-florida-manufacturers.

59. Sachin Pandya, "Little Rock Passes Anti-Discrimination Ordinance: Conflict with Arkansas Statute Prohibiting Local Anti-Discrimination Ordinances?" *Workplace Prof Blog*, April 22, 2015, http://grassrootschange.net/little-rock-passes-anti-discrimination-ordinance-conflict-with-arkansas-statute-prohibiting-local-anti-discrimination-ordinances; Todd Gill, "Chamber Holds Press Conference to Announce a Call for Repeal of Fayetteville's Civil Rights Ordinance," *Fayetteville Flyer*, November 7, 2014, http://www.fayettevilleflyer.com/2014/11/07/chamber-holds-press-conference-to-announce-a-call-for-repeal-of-fayettevilles-civil-rights-ordinance; Arkansas Senate Bill 202, 2015, http://www.arkleg.state.ar.us/assembly/2015/2015R/Acts/Act137.pdf. Though the bill prohibits "enforcement" of any existing antidiscrimination ordinance, the city of Fayetteville has contested whether its ordinance is invalidated by the state statute. In March 2016 a judge ruled in Fayetteville's favor, and the Arkansas attorney general vowed to appeal this ruling. Andrew DeMillo, "Arkansas Appealing Ruling on City's LGBT Projections," Associated Press, March 20, 2016, http://www.gayly.com/arkansas-appealing-ruling-citys-lgbt-protections.

60. "Decision to Keep or Cut Police Staffing Levels May Rest with Voters," *Dearborn Patch*, June 29, 2011, http://patch.com/michigan/dearborn/decision-to-keep-or-cut-police-staffing-levels-may-re2cf11d93ad.

61. SB 485, 2011, https://www.legislature.mi.gov/documents/2011-2012/publicact/pdf/2011-PA-0133.pdf.

62. "Talking Points: Support HB 4052, Legislation to Preempt Local Employment Laws," Michigan Chamber of Commerce, 2015, http://www.michamber.com/sites/michamber.com/files/TalkingPts4052.mcc.pdf.

63. Michigan State Senate, Competitiveness Committee, draft minutes, June 11, 2015, http://www.senate.michigan.gov/committees/files/2015-SCM-MICOM-06-11-1.pdf; Emily Lawler, "Gov. Rick Snyder Signs 'Death Star' Bill Prohibiting Local Wage, Benefits Ordinances," MLive, June 30, 2015, http://www.mlive.com/lansing-news/index.ssf/2015/06/gov_rick_snyder_signs_death_st.html.

64. Arizona HB 2280, 2013.

65. Minimum wage ordinance, October 22, 2015 update, city of Kansas City, Missouri, http://kcmo.gov/minimum-wage. The St. Louis ordinance has not yet entered into effect because it remains held up in court after a challenge by the Chamber of Commerce, Restaurant Association, and allied corporate groups. David Bailey, "Missouri Judge Strikes Down St. Louis Minimum Wage Increase," Reuters, October 14, 2015, http://www.reuters.com/article/2015/10/15/us-usa-missouri-wages-idUSKCN0S900A20151015#S8X5H1tO L2YC24Uf.97.

66. Jon Hurst, quoted in Katie Johnston, "Bills Seek More Stable Hours for Low-Paid Workers," *Boston Globe*, July 20, 2015, https://www.bostonglobe.com/business/2015/07/19/growing-movement-stabilize-work-schedules/VdXNFH3AQQlD40xaHuzaIN/story.html.

67. Thomas Fuller, "San Francisco Approves Fully Paid Parental Leave," *New York Times*, April 5, 2016, http://www.nytimes.com/2016/04/06/us/san-francisco-approves-fully-paid-parental-leave.html.

68. "Creating a New Vision for Retirement Security," SEIU Local 1000, October 22, 2015, http://www.seiu1000.org/post/creating-new-vision-retirement-security.

69. Rand Wilson, "Viewpoint: A Smart Strategy to Defeat 'Right to Work,'" *Labor Notes*, March 17, 2015, http://www.labornotes.org/blogs/2015/03/viewpoint-smart-strategy-defeat-right-work.

70. Colorado Initiative 76, 2008, Ballotpedia, http://ballotpedia.org/wiki/index.php/Colorado_Initiative_76_(2008).

71. Simon Davis-Cohen, "In Colorado, a Revolutionary New Coalition Stands for Community Rights," The Leap, August 19, 2015, http://theleap.thischangeseverything.org/in-colorado-a-revolutionary-new-coalition-stands-for-community-rights.

72. Jens Manuel Krogstad, "Top Issue for Hispanics? Hint: It's Not Immigration," Pew Research Center, June 2, 2014, http://www.pewresearch.org/fact-tank/2014/06/02/top-issue-for-hispanics-hint-its-not-immigration.

73. Ezra Klein, "House Democrats Got More Votes Than House Republicans. But Boehner Says He's Got a Mandate?" *Washington Post*, November 9, 2012, https://www.washingtonpost.com/news/wonk/wp/2012/11/09/house-democrats-got-more-votes-than-house-republicans-yet-boehner-says-hes-got-a-mandate.

74. Lauren Windsor, "Caught on Tape: What Mitch McConnell Complained About to a Roomful of Billionaires," *The Nation*, August 25, 2014, https://www.thenation.com/article/caught-tape-what-mitch-mcconnell-complained-about-roomful-billionaires-exclusive.

75. Melanie Mason, "At Koch Retreat, Paul Ryan Stays Mum on Trump, Touts Economic Agenda," *Los Angeles Times*, August 31, 2016, http://www.latimes.com/politics/la-na-trailguide-updates-at-koch-retreat-paul-ryan-stays-mum-on-1470085907-htmlstory.html.

76. Sara Goddard, "'Redistribution Is No Longer a Dirty Word,'" Wonk Wire, February 8, 2016, http://wonkwire.com/2016/02/08/redistribution-is-no-longer-a-dirty-word.

77. Hadas Gold and Kenneth Vogel, "Fox's Luntz Blasted Trump at Koch Seminar," *Politico*, August 18, 2015, http://www.politico.com/story/2015/08/fox-luntz-blasted-trump-donald-koch-seminar-121466.

Index

abortion, 11, 21, 28–30, 80
Act 10: *See* Budget Repair Bill
Adelson, Sheldon, 82
Aetna Insurance Company, 164
Affordable Care Act: *See* Obamacare
Aflac, 14, 164
AFL-CIO, 8
Alabama, 71, 166–67, 169
Allegretto, Sylvia, 89
Alternative Certification Act, 146
American Association for Retired Persons
(AARP), 69
American Civil Liberties Union, 151
American Crossroads, 9, 38
American Enterprise Institute, 52, 140
American Federation of State, County, and
Municipal Employees (AFSCME), 52
American Legislative Exchange Council
(ALEC): Alternative Certification Act,
146; Associated Builders and Contractors
affiliation, 97, 99, 111, 118, 174; bill
introductions, 13, 33–34, 39, 49, 180; Blue
Cross Blue Shield (BCBS) lobbying efforts,
26; campaign spending, 13, 38, 49, 162,
164; corporate tax cut support, 17, 66,
74–75, 132, 170; discrimination lawsuits
opposition, 120–21; Economic Civil Rights
Act, 99, 113, 180; economic vitality ranking,
66–67, 173; education reform involvement,
15, 130, 132–34, 140–43, 146, 148, 152;
employee misclassification support, 116;
environmental regulations opposition,
14, 17; food stamps opposition, 15, 122;
Founding Philosophy and Principles
Act, 152, 174; Full Employment Act,
122; government shrinking goals, 62;
Heartland Institute affiliation, 55, 127;
Independent Contractor Definition Act,
116; Koch brothers support, 14–15; labor
unions opposition, 15, 17, 43, 156–57, 160,
162–64, 166–68, 170; Mackinac Center
affiliation, 82, 96, 146; meal/rest breaks
opposition, 119–20; minimum wage
opposition, 15, 17, 103–7, 170, 173–74,
182; Next Generation Charter Schools

Act, 140; overtime pay opposition, 115;
Paycheck Protection Act, 160, 164, 166;
pension reforms, 55–57, 59; prevailing-wage
opposition, 15, 99; Professional Licensure
and Certification Reform Act promotion,
99; Public Charter Schools Act, 146; public
employee compensation reductions, 59;
Public Employee Freedom Act, 160; Public
Employer Payroll Deduction Policy Act, 160,
168; public sentiment challenges, 24; Right
to Work Act, 180; right-to-work (RTW)
support, 15, 83, 180; sick leave opposition,
15, 17, 117–18, 170; Social Security
opposition, 15, 170; "Stand Your Ground"
laws support, 17; state level advantages,
34–36, 39; State Policy Network, 13, 39; State
Sovereignty through Local Coordination
Act, 174; taxpayer bill of rights (TABOR)
support, 72; trade agreements support, 15,
170; unemployment benefits opposition,
15, 17, 122–25, 170; workplace safety
opposition, 15, 118–19
Americans for Prosperity (AFP): climate
change opposition, 23; Common Core
opposition, 17, 148; corporate tax cut
support, 69, 72, 170; education reform
involvement, 128–30, 133–34, 141, 148;
election influence, 9–10, 12, 16, 23; Export-
Import Bank opposition, 17; ideological
convictions, 21; labor unions opposition,
156, 163, 170; Obamacare opposition, 36;
organizational structure, 30; public transit
opposition, 69; right-to-work (RTW)
support, 83, 91, 125; sick leave opposition,
118, 170; state level advantages, 36; taxpayer
bill of rights (TABOR) support, 72; Tea
Party, role in, 11, 23, 30; Troubled Assets
Relief Program (TARP) support, 22; *See also*
Koch brothers
Americans for Tax Reform, 11, 160
Amway, 14, 82
Appelbaum, Eileen, 18–19
Arizona: corporate tax cut support, 72–73;
education spending, 69, 71–73; health
services spending, 66, 72; labor legislation,

251

CPSIA information can be obtained
at www.ICGtesting.com
Printed in the USA
LVHW091508050921
697039LV00007B/66/J

9 781501 703065